ISBN: 9781313162074

Published by:
HardPress Publishing
8345 NW 66TH ST #2561
MIAMI FL 33166-2626

Email: info@hardpress.net
Web: http://www.hardpress.net

SYSTEMS OF LAND TENURE IN VARIOUS COUNTRIES.

SYSTEMS OF LAND TENURE

IN

VARIOUS COUNTRIES.

A SERIES OF ESSAYS

PUBLISHED UNDER THE SANCTION OF

The Cobden Club.

SECOND EDITION.

London:

MACMILLAN AND CO.

1870.

LONDON: PRINTED BY WILLIAM CLOWES AND SONS,
STAMFORD STREET AND CHARING CROSS.

PREFACE.

THE present volume contains a series of independent Treatises on various national systems of land tenure.

It is published by the Cobden Club, in the belief that they cannot better promote the objects which Cobden had at heart than by collecting, from competent authorities, statements of the law and practice prevailing in different civilized communities, in relation to property in land, and in thus contributing towards the formation of a public opinion on this important subject, founded upon a wide and varied experience.

The view taken by Cobden of the injurious effects upon the national economy, of the present state of the law with respect to property in land in this country, is well known ; and the advice and warning which he gave to his fellow-countrymen on the last occasion upon which he addressed them in public, possess a peculiar interest at the present time.

Political events have already brought into prominence in Ireland questions which, however they may be allowed to sleep in ordinary times, lie at the root of all social progress, and are now engaging the anxious attention of all parties in the State.

The Committee of the Cobden Club have thought that a comparative study of the different systems of land tenure described in this volume, will not only serve a useful purpose in affording sound information with respect to general principles of legislation, and their practical application, in the countries to which reference has been made, but will at the same time throw light upon the Irish Land Question, which forms the subject of the First Essay.

Each Author is solely responsible for his own contribution, and the Committee of the Club have exercised no editorial control over the expression of individual opinions.

It is right to state that M. de Lavergne had undertaken to furnish a paper on the Land System of France, but was prevented by ill health from fulfilling his intention. Under these circumstances the Committee have been fortunate in obtaining the assistance of Mr. T. Cliffe Leslie, who is well known to have devoted much attention to the rural economy of Western Europe, and who consented, at very short notice, to supply M. de Lavergne's place.

CONTENTS.

SYSTEMS OF LAND TENURE

IN

VARIOUS COUNTRIES.

I.

THE TENURE OF LAND IN IRELAND,

BY THE RT. HON. M. LONGFIELD.

CHAPTER I.

THE laws which govern the relation between landlord and tenant are not very different in England and Ireland; but there are some differences in their pedigrees, and in some collateral circumstances, which have made them produce very different effects. I shall mention a few of those circumstances.

In both countries the law is based upon the feudal system, which gave the landlord a certain superiority over his tenants. But the feudal relation, with its reciprocal rights and duties, never existed in Ireland. Here the landlord never led his tenants to battle; if they fought in the same field, it was on different sides. They had no traditions of common victories or common defeats. The relations that existed between them were hostile. According to the old feudal law, the lordship could not be transferred without the consent of the tenant, lest an enemy might be made his feudal superior; but in a great part of Ireland a sudden and violent transfer of the lordship was made to persons whom the tenants only knew as their victorious enemies.

The feudal law of distress was increased in force, to make it a more powerful instrument for extracting rent

B

from a reluctant or impoverished tenantry. The old laws, which were unduly favourable to the landlord, were generally retained, as if they had been unalterable laws of nature ; but they were at once altered when they appeared to afford a temporary protection to the tenant.

Take the case of a disputed account between the landlord and tenant. The former maintains that a year's rent is due to him ; the latter insists that he owes nothing. Do they come before a court of justice on equal terms, to have this question tried ? On the contrary, the landlord, as the feudal superior, takes the law into his own hands, and without making any proof of his demand, he sends his bailiffs to seize the goods of the tenant. The landlord was not obliged to apply to any officer of the law, or to give any security to pay damages if his demand should prove to be unfounded. But it was otherwise with the tenant ; if he saw his goods distrained by this summary process, he could not get them back without a troublesome replevin, which he could only get by giving security to pay the sum demanded. To discourage him from contesting the landlord's rights, he was compelled by an Act of Parliament to pay double costs if he failed. Still, at common law the distress, or goods distrained, could not be sold ; and a tenant, ruined and driven to despair, might submit to the loss, and still refuse to pay ; but an Act of Parliament was passed to enable the landlord to sell the goods, and pay himself.

Still, he could not seize the tenant's crops while they were growing, as by the common law crops while they were growing were considered as a part of the soil and freehold, and could not be distrained. But here Parliament again intervened, and passed a law to enable the landlord to distrain the crops while they were still growing, so that as soon as the corn appeared above the ground he might send his keepers to take possession, and cut and carry it away when it was ripe.

If the tenant removed his goods to avoid a distress, an Act of Parliament intervened to visit him and the friends who assisted him with a penalty, although the landlord himself may have been at the same moment hiding his own goods to evade an execution.

In the same manner Acts of Parliament were passed to give the landlord the power of evicting his tenant for non-payment of rent, and of recovering possession of the land in cases in which he was not entitled to this remedy either by the terms of his contract or by the rules of the common law.

Those laws were injurious by leading the landlord to rely more on the extraordinary powers given to him by law, than on the character of the tenant or the liberal terms on which he set his land; but I refer to them now as co-operating with other circumstances to lead the poor Irish farmer to the opinion that the laws were framed entirely in the interests of the landlord class.

Here one important difference between English and Irish law must be noticed. In Ireland there were no poor laws. The poor man, reduced to destitution by sickness or want of employment, had no legal claim to a maintenance out of the property of the country. I allude elsewhere to other effects of the poor laws; but the point which I now notice is, that, notwithstanding all the abuses attending on the administration of the poor laws in England, they had this effect, that the poor man could not shut his eyes to the fact that the laws were in some part framed in his interests, and that for the relief of his class a large sum was levied every year from the wealth and successful industry of the community.

Another circumstance tended to diminish the respect of the people for the law of the land. Religion did not, and could not, lend its aid to the authority of the law. The great mass of the agricultural population was Roman Catholic; and the Roman Catholic priest, their minister and instructor, was in some respects under the ban of the law. He could scarcely be an effectual teacher of the doctrine that it is a moral duty to obey the law of the land, when he himself was obliged to violate it almost daily in the discharge of his most sacred functions.

Of all laws, those which are framed for the protection of property are the most likely to be disregarded by the poor man. The man who never possessed any property can scarcely feel the duty of respecting it. He must be taught that duty, either by arguments, which do not bring conviction to all men, or by some authority which he respects. But the Roman Catholic priest had no property of his own, and he generally belonged to a family which did not possess much property. He had therefore no sympathy with the landlords, who, in general, did not belong to his flock. Religion, which ought to be the great bond of union between men of every race and every class, was in Ireland an additional source of disunion.

Under such circumstances, it was not surprising that the Irish farmer was generally discontented with his position, although the landlords did not give him much cause of complaint. As a class, the Irish landlords were not greedy nor oppressive. They did not plunder their tenants, but they neglected them.

For some time after the Act of Settlement, leases were granted more readily and for longer terms in Ireland than in England. Fee-farm grants, leases for lives renewable for ever, and leases for terms exceeding one hundred years in duration, covered no small portion of the soil of Ireland. But those long leases, at moderate rents, did not produce a contented tenantry; they only created a race of middlemen. The descendants of the men who granted those long leases had the mortification of finding that they were deriving a very small income from their estates in proportion to the value of the land, and yet that the occupying tenants were as poor as if they had rigidly demanded the utmost penny that the land could yield. It was felt to be bad management to grant such leases; and leases for three lives, or twenty-one years, or thirty-one years, were more usually granted in the latter half of the eighteenth century. The leases for lives were in some measure caused by the law which existed up to the Reform Bill. Freeholders alone could vote at an election for Members of Parliament; and this state of the law was injurious to agriculture by leading to a very inconvenient tenure. It was almost absurd that the duration of a farmer's interest should be made to depend upon such an accident as the longer or shorter duration of a stranger's life.

Although leases for lives were very common, their duration appears not to have been understood. It was very common in settlements to insert powers of granting leases for three lives, or thirty-one years, as if those leases were of about equal average duration; although in reality the average duration of the freehold was about double that of the chattel interest. In computing the compensation due to a landlord for renewal fines, it was assumed that a life to be named by the tenant would expire in seven years; and this gave the landlord, as compensation, more than five times what he had lost by the tenant's neglect.

In the early part of this century a great rise took place in the value of land, as the French war and the depreciation of the currency raised the price of agricultural produce. The tenants who had previously obtained leases became rich. The landlords who had not granted leases obtained a great accession to their income. The landlords who had granted leases found themselves poorer, inasmuch as their nominal income remained the same, while its purchasing power was diminished. This increased the desire of the tenantry to obtain leases, while it made the landlords less disposed to grant long leases

In 1816, and the three following years, land fell again in value; and the tenants who had got leases or farms during the high times were unable to pay their rents. In many cases they ran away and abandoned their farms; in other cases they put their landlords to the delay and costs of an ejectment; in other cases they were permitted to remain in occupation at a reduced rent. The landlords then perceived that a lease was a one-sided agreement. It prevented the landlord from obtaining the benefit of a rise in prices; but it did not prevent him from suffering if they fell.

Still, leases were frequently granted from political motives. The tenants, as a matter of course, voted as their landlords directed them; and the landlord increased his political influence by granting freehold leases to a numerous tenantry.

This condition of affairs was changed by the agitation that preceded the Act for granting Catholic emancipation; and first in the county of Waterford, and afterwards in a still more remarkable instance in Clare, the tenants voted against their landlords' wishes; and the latter had no longer any political inducement to grant leases to their tenantry; indeed, political motives rather acted in the opposite direction.

Although it became less usual to grant leases, the tenant was generally left undisturbed in possession at the old rent. Nothing was more common than to find a yearly tenant holding land at a rent fixed by a lease which had long since expired. No general change in the value of land took place of sufficient magnitude to cause a readjustment of rents.

But in the year 1846 the potato crop throughout Ireland generally failed; a fall greater than had ever taken place on any former occasion took place in the value of land. The tenant found that the possession of a farm could not secure him against starvation. Landlords were compelled to submit to a considerable temporary abatement. In 1851 the reaction commenced; landlords added to the rent by degrees the sums that had been taken off during the famine; and in some cases they added a little more. Frequent small additions to the rent are very annoying to the tenant, who on each occasion has to calculate whether it is more prudent to submit to this increase, or to incur the inconvenience and expense of giving up his farm and looking out for another.

Another circumstance occurred about this time. The Encumbered Estates Court was established in 1849, and many estates were sold subject only to existing leases and legal rights. The new landlords were more active, and effected more improvements in the land than their encumbered predecessors ; but they were less indulgent to their tenants ; old traditions of liberality were disregarded, and the new landlords were more disposed to exact the full value of the land. They also sometimes introduced changes, which, although to the advantage of the country and of the tenantry, were looked upon with suspicion, on account of their evident advantage to the landlords. The tenants did not like any interference with their customs, even when it was obviously for their interests.

On the whole, however, the condition of the Irish farmers steadily improved. The value of land increased faster than the rents. Never were they more prosperous than at the present moment. The marketable value of the interests which the occupying tenants have in their farms is about fifty millions sterling, exclusive of their stock in cattle, machinery, and agricultural produce, which is worth as much more.

But at the same time they never were more discontented. The reason of this is partly that they fear that their present prosperity is insecure, and partly that they hope to seize upon something more. Their wealth is as safe as that of any other class, so far as it depends upon their capital, or their skill and industry ; but it depends upon the will of the landlords, so far as it is a consequence of their holding land at less than the competition value. They are too dependent upon their landlords. It is not convenient that the prosperity of one class of men should depend upon the liberality of another class.

Besides, in many cases the tenants hope by agitation and outrage to acquire more than they at present possess. They have great political power, and are able to reward the agitators who inflame their passions or their cupidity. They are taught to believe that it is in their power to acquire the absolute ownership of the land which they have hired for a limited period. Their well-founded complaints are mixed up with the most unreasonable demands ; and by skilful sophistry and metaphorical language they are almost led to believe that murder may be justified when it is committed from motives of avarice or revenge. Before we endeavour to draw a distinction between the just and unjust demands of those who call themselves the tenants' friends, a question may be asked, " Will outrages against life and property cease when everything that justice requires shall be conceded ?" I do not think the question very important, because the claims of justice should be allowed, even if no beneficial results were expected. But the question itself cannot be answered by a direct " Yes " or " No." Whenever any just measure is passed, all discontent is not at once allayed. All that ought to be expected is to reduce the number of the malcontents, and to diminish the vehemence of those who remain dissatisfied. The friends of law and order are strengthened by an increase of their numbers, and by the removal of many of the topics on which their adversaries are accustomed to rely. In this manner a succession of just measures may produce such an overwhelming majority in favour of the law as to reduce the discontented to silence.

I do not expect such a result in Ireland to follow immediately from any legislation, until the people are taught to look upon murder with horror. If all the land in Ireland was divided in fee simple among the peasantry, the number of murders would not be diminished. The difference would only be in the heading of the sensation paragraphs in newspapers. Instead of an "agrarian outrage," it would be called a " domestic tragedy." The same feeling that prompts a man to murder his landlord, to prevent or revenge some real or imaginary wrong, would lead him to resort to the same remedy against a sister who claimed her fortune at an inconvenient time, or a brother who did not agree with his views respecting the partition of the estate.

Good consequences may be confidently expected from just legislation, although those consequences may not appear so quickly as sanguine people often expect.

It is not certain that the discontented farmer thinks that all his demands are just and reasonable, or that he expects them to be conceded. A farmer is generally disposed to make a bargain, and to begin by asking for a good deal more than he expects to get.

CHAPTER II.

THE opinions of English and Irish economists generally are different on the subject of absenteeism. The Irish, who feel it, think it a great evil. The English, who do not feel it, think that it does no harm to the country. It does not, however, follow that the Irish are right, for they may perhaps have fallen into the mistake of attributing to absenteeism evils which coexist with it, but are not caused by it.

For a short time the defenders of absenteeism had the arguments of logic on their side. The complainants made a mistake in the form of their complaint. The mercantile system was in full vogue. Money was thought to be synonymous with wealth. Every transaction which brought money into the country was supposed to increase its wealth, and every cause that led to the exportation of money was held to impoverish it. With this belief, nothing was more natural than to complain of the rents remitted to England to absentee landlords, and to calculate how much it amounted to in the course of half a century. It was no matter to be surprised at that Ireland was poor, when so much money was annually sent away without any return. The kingdom was in the same condition as if it paid a tribute to England equal to the amount of rent paid to the absentees.

The answer made to such complaints was, that no money was sent out of Ireland to the absentees. Commodities, chiefly cattle and corn, were exported ; these were paid for by bills, and the produce of those bills applied to the payment of rent to the absentees. Even if money was sent here to pay for the cattle, and that money paid to the absentees, it would come to the same thing in the end. The rent is still substantially paid, not in money, but in that agricultural produce by means of which the money was procured. As to the wealth sent out without return, that is treated as a matter of no consequence. No one has any cause of complaint. A hundred pounds worth of corn is sent to England, the produce of that corn is paid to the landlord. He buys a hogshead of French wine, which is consumed by himself and his family. How are the Irish people worse off than if that hogshead of wine was consumed by the same persons in Ireland ?

It might perhaps be admitted that Ireland would not suffer much by the absence of any landlord who, if he was present, would do nothing with his income except buying French wine. But in fact a landlord does not in general spend so much as half his income in the purchase of foreign goods. The greater part of his income is employed either in paying for services, or in the purchase of goods produced in the immediate nighbourhood. It makes a great difference to the producer whether his market is close at hand, or whether he must send his goods to a distance to seek for a customer ; and this difference will be the greatest when the goods which he pro-duces are bulky in proportion to their value, and when the roads and other means of communication are bad.

It may perhaps be said, "Let him produce such goods as may be readily exported, as he ought to know that he must seek a distant market." But in a poor and ignorant agricultural community the producer has no choice. He can produce certain things, and nothing else ; and it would be a dull mockery to tell the family of a poor peasant, who can find no convenient market for his eggs, and butter, and poultry, and honey, and the services of his children, that he ought to employ himself in making clocks and watches, or brushes, or gloves, or cloth, or paper. He earns his bread from day to day by the only business that he understands, however imperfectly,

and he never saw any one employed in any other pursuit, and he has no means of getting into any other
industry.

Let us abandon the argument derived from the
balance of trade, and examine the effect of absenteeism
upon the small village of C. All the property in the
neighbourhood, to the amount of 20,000*l.* a year, belongs
to absentees. There is not a gentleman's house or
garden near it. There is very little traffic, and the
roads are bad. The post arrives and departs at inconvenient hours, as there is not sufficient correspondence
to induce the Post-Office authorities to incur any expense in improving the postal service. There are no
public conveyances, as there is not traffic enough to
support them. The shops are few and ill-supplied, goods
are sold at a high price, and yet for want of sufficient
custom the profit of the shopkeepers is very small. The
district cannot support a market, and the people are
obliged to travel a considerable distance for their
supplies. The peasant finds it impossible to obtain any
price for butter, eggs, poultry, and other small rural
produce. They cannot be sold in the neighbourhood,
and the expense of carriage to a distance consumes
nearly the entire value. There are no means of
education. One medical practitioner, with very little
skill, has the monopoly of an immense territory, from
which he obtains a scanty subsistence, as the gentry who
are able to give him fees are absentees. Agriculture is
in a very backward state. The implements are of the
worst kind. The cattle are of the most unprofitable
breeds. No improvements in either cattle or implements have been introduced within living memory.
There are no gentlemen of wealth and education to know
what is done in other countries, to make experiments,
to instruct the people, and to introduce improvements.
I am writing about the state of things in the beginning
of this century.

The following extracts are taken from a report on the
state of the King's County, presented by Sir C. Coote to
the Royal Dublin Society, in the year 1801.

"Barony of Geshill.

"Every acre of this barony, being the estate of Lord D., it is almost entirely inhabited by farmers. They use the old Irish plough and harrow, and none of the improved kind are yet amongst them." "In this barony there is not a single town, and only two villages, those of Killagh and Geshill, but no market held in either, though each has a patent for one." "The roads throughout this barony are shamefully bad, and at times almost impassable. Deprived of a resident gentry, this district is in a lamentable state of neglect." "Farms run from fifty to three hundred acres; farm-houses have only the appearance of warmth; and if we except Dean D.'s, Mr. V.'s, and Mr. W.'s, they have nothing of neatness to recommend them. The tenant is obliged to repair: the old leases were for thirty-one years, or three lives, few of which now exist; those of later date do not exceed twenty-one years, and non-alienation is insisted on." "There is no want of bidders to every farm out of lease; and the highest gets the preference." "Where such short leases only are granted, little real improvement can be expected; the tenant is discouraged from it, lest he should have his rent raised in his next tenure to the value of his improvements, which he is fairly apprized of, the highest bidder having always the preference. When the peasantry become more civilized, perhaps this rigorous mode will be abandoned, and real solvent tenants may be granted encouragement proportionate to their abilities and industry." I may add that the owner of this estate was not an encumbered proprietor. He died without issue, and worth nearly a million sterling, and some of the leases which he granted were impeached by his successor.

Sir C. Coote's account of the Barony of Geshill is the natural description of a large property owned by absentees. The object was to give an account of the agriculture of the county; and he did not refer to those inconveniences which a resident only can feel.

Let us suppose that some of the proprietors return to reside in the district which I have described; and consider the results which are likely to follow. A better description of agricultural implements is introduced. The common cart of the country, with its wheels of solid wood without spokes, which only turn with the axle, gradually disappears. It draws only two hundred-weight, and is replaced by a cart with spoke wheels, which will draw from ten to twenty hundred. The improvement is introduced by a resident gentleman who is acquainted with the superior vehicle. He employs carpenters to make them; and these men and their apprentices are again employed by the farmers in the neighbourhood, who quickly perceive the benefit of an improvement which they see in actual operation, at the same time that the means of making the improvement are placed within their reach. The same thing occurs with respect to ploughs and other agricultural implements. The farmer is generally unwilling to alter his practice in submission to any theory or to any arguments. He will not adopt an improvement unless he sees it in actual successful operation.

In the same manner the resident landlord is the means of introducing an improved breed of cattle, a better rotation of crops, and that improved cultivation which he has witnessed in other parts of the country. He is the living mode of communication between the ignorant backward district and the more improved and more civilized parts of the kingdom. The resident gentlemen attend to the state of the roads, and insist that they shall be well made and duly repaired. They support by their advice and subscriptions schools, dispensaries, and various institutions of utility or charity. They assist in the preservation of the peace and the local administration of justice. The increase of correspondence caused by a number of wealthy residents leads to improved postal communication. The traffic and travelling of themselves and their families, their friends and their tradesmen, lead to the establishment of public conveyances, which formerly could not have been run

without a loss.   All the residents enjoy the advantages
of these conveyances.   The custom of the resident landlords is a great assistance to the shopkeepers in the
neighbourhood, and enables them to keep a better selection of goods, and to sell them at a lower price, and yet
a greater profit to themselves.   The resident gentry
must have houses, offices, and gardens, which become
part of the wealth of the country, and require masons,
carpenters, and workmen of a superior description to
make them and keep them in repair.   I need not proceed further to enumerate the advantages which may be
confidently expected from the residence of the landed
gentry on their estates.   They are certainly not met by
the argument that the rents of absentees are not remitted
in gold and silver, but in bills purchased by the sale of
Irish commodities.

We are not to consider merely the effects of absenteeism in the abstract, but its effects upon a poor
ignorant country such as Ireland was.   It can hardly be
doubted that the whole social system must suffer from
the absence of one important class.   A great gap is
made by the want of men with knowledge, wealth, or
leisure for anything more than the supply of their
immediate pressing wants.   The cases I have supposed
of the utility of a resident gentry, and the inconvenience
of their absence, could readily be supported by reference
to facts.

The causes of absenteeism are partly the superior
advantages which England by nature possesses over
Ireland.   Its civilization is older and more advanced.
It is a larger country, with a finer climate, much richer
in its mineral productions, and is more conveniently
and centrally situated.   The most convenient way for
an Irishman to go to any part of Europe is to pass
through England.   Ireland will always bear to England
a relation like that of a provincial town to the metro-
polis.   But this does not entirely account for the extent
to which absenteeism existed.

The chief cause is to be found in the confiscations and
grants which took place in the time of Cromwell, and

confirmed by the settlement made in the reign of
Charles II. By those grants large estates fell into the
hands of Englishmen who would not, for ten times
their value, have left their native country to dwell in
such a barbarous and disturbed country as Ireland
was. Accordingly they remained in England, and set
their newly-acquired estates in large tracts to tenants
who undertook to manage the land and pay the
rent. The leases were generally made at moderate
rents, and sometimes for very long interests. The laws
relating to land made it easier for men to set than to sell
their estates; and from this cause the estates remained in
the same families, and absenteeism continued to prevail.

It is, however, diminishing. In his Political Anatomy
of Ireland, Sir William Petty computed the absenteeism
of Ireland to extend to one fourth of the real and
personal property of the kingdom. Lists of absentees,
with their names and the value of their estates, were
published in 1729, and again in 1769. Many of the
estates mentioned there have since been sold, and
purchased by men who reside in Ireland; and in many
other cases where the estates remained in the same
families, the present representatives reside in Ireland for
a considerable portion of the year. It may be answered
that, although those particular estates are no longer held
by absentees, there may be other estates now possessed
by absentees, which were then held by residents. I do
not, however, believe that this has occurred to any
considerable extent. Especially it rarely happens that
the purchaser of an Irish estate becomes an absentee. Of
the estates sold in the Encumbered Estates Court, a very
small proportion was bought by Englishmen or Scotchmen, and even in those cases the purchasers frequently
came to reside in Ireland.

But not only has absenteeism diminished, but even
when it exists it is less injurious now than it was
formerly. This is the result of several causes. The
roads are no longer dependent upon the great proprietors for their existence or repairs. The ratepayers
now are permitted to take an active share in this part of

the county business, and county surveyors are officially appointed to see that all contracts for the formation and repairs of roads and bridges are duly performed. The poor laws now compel the absentees to contribute their fair proportion to the support of the destitute poor. The dispensaries are supported by a compulsory rate, and no longer depend upon the casual subscriptions of the resident gentry. A large parliamentary grant gives equal independence to the education of the poor. The appointment of stipendiary magistrates gives assistance to the residents, and supplies the places of the absentees. The penny postage and the cheap newspaper press bring information to every part of Ireland. Steam has almost made a bridge across the channel, and railways are now made to places that were formerly inaccessible. Thus in the Barony of Geshill, in which there was such a want of good roads in the beginning of this century, there is now a railway station ; and it is easier now for a man to travel from Geshill to Dublin than it was then to go from one part of the barony to another.

Besides the changes just mentioned, another cause tends to mitigate the mischievous effects of absenteeism. The wealth of Ireland not derived from the rents of land has considerably increased. Taking round numbers, we may say that in the course of two centuries the population has increased five-fold, the rental has increased fifteen-fold, and the general wealth of the country has increased fifty-fold. It is probable that the marketable value of the interests which the occupying tenants have in their farms is about fifty millions sterling.

But absenteeism is still an evil, although not so great as it was ; and it may be asked, " Can anything be done to mitigate or prevent it ?" Legislation is slowly moving in this direction. One great truth is gradually dawning on the public mind, that every matter of public importance (not of private interest) should be undertaken by the state, and not be permitted to depend upon the casual contributions of benevolent individuals. Whatever ought to be given to the poor, beyond what they can obtain by their own exertions, ought not to

depend upon the accident of their living in a rich and
liberal neighbourhood. Several of the changes which I
have noticed in our legislation follow at once from this
principle.

Nothing would more tend to diminish absenteeism
than free trade in land, and the absence of all restrictions
that impede its transfer. There is a natural tendency in
property to move towards its owner, or in the owner to
move towards his property. Thus, in the case of a
great Irish railway, it was thought expedient, soon after
it was formed, to compare the interests of the English
and Irish proprietors. It was then found that, although
the two classes were equal in number, the English
proprietors held two thirds of the stock. Some years
afterwards the same comparison was made, and it was
found that the proportions in the meantime had been
reversed, and that the Irish proprietors held twice as
much stock as the English. The change has since
gradually gone on in the same direction.

But there is a much greater tendency in land than in
railway shares to belong to the residents of the country
in which the property is situated. A railway share is
merely a right to receive a certain proportion of the
profits made by the company. What those profits are
can only be known from the accounts, which are equally
accessible to the nearest and the most distant proprietors. But land is something different; it is more
than a mere income, and an intimate acquaintance with
it is necessary in order to know its value, present and
prospective. No person has any special desire for a
particular railway share; but when any land is to be sold,
it frequently happens that there are several persons who
know its value well, and to whom that land is more
desirable than any property of equal value in any part
of the kingdom. Such persons must be residents in the
neighbourhood, or at no very great distance, and they
are therefore the most likely to purchase it.

The principal laws that prevent that frequent transfer
of land which would put an end to absenteeism, are
the law of primogeniture, the heavy stamp duties on

C

conveyance, the law which permits property to be settled
on unborn persons, and the general complications
permitted in the titles to real property. Something has
been done to facilitate the transfer of land by the
creation of the Landed Estates Court; but it is an
inconvenient anomaly, and exhibits the imperfection
of the law, that a lawsuit should be thought the best
and the most expeditious mode of selling an estate.
The Record of Title Act has been passed to facilitate
further the transfer of land; but it has not been very
effective, and as long as settlements are permitted, the
transfer of land cannot be free from difficulty.

CHAPTER III.

A VERY injurious custom prevalent in Ireland, and encouraged by the law, was the permitting an accumulation of arrears of rent to remain due by the tenantry. In many districts in the south and west, every tenant was in the condition of an uncertificated bankrupt, whose debts amount to more than he can ever hope to pay.

It is difficult to conceive anything more calculated to destroy the energies of a tenant, than the consciousness that no amount of skill, industry, or economy can improve his position, while idleness and prodigality can hardly make it worse. This is the state of a tenant who holds his land at a rent rather higher than he can afford to pay, and who finds that each year adds to the amount of arrears due to his landlord. If any lucky accident should increase his fortune, or add to the value of his farm, it is a gain to his landlord, but no benefit to himself; while a bad crop, whatever be the cause of it, only makes an addition to the bad debts due to his landlord, but is no concern to himself. As long as he owes more than he can pay, he is equally in his landlord's power, whether the arrears amount to fifty or to five hundred pounds. The landlord, if he wishes it, may seize all his goods, and evict him from his farm. His only hope lies in the forbearance of his landlord, *from whatever motive that forbearance may proceed.*

A tenant in this position will never make any payment until he has made every effort in his power to evade it. When he pays a portion of his rent, he feels himself so much the poorer; his property is less by the amount he has paid; but he does not obtain in exchange that independence and freedom from debt which in ordinary cases are the results or the motives of the payment. It is a most unsatisfactory thing to pay money, and yet to remain hopelessly insolvent.

Why, then, does he pay anything? He does it in order to avoid a distress, or an action, or an ejectment. He knows that he cannot expect to retain possession of his farm without paying something; he must only feel his way, and try to pay as little as possible. Hence a perpetual effort to avoid payment, by pleas of distress and poverty, and a contest between the landlord and the tenant. The former is uncertain whether the latter's pleas of poverty are true; the tenant is uncertain whether the landlord is serious in his threats of taking legal proceedings. The contract is disregarded, and the parties have no guide to direct them how much they may demand and how much they ought to concede.

When a single tenant succeeds in reducing his rent by pleading inability, every tenant will endeavour to do the same. A man will almost think it a hardship to be compelled to observe his contract, when he sees that his neighbour is permitted to evade it. The feeling of independent honesty is gone. The insolvent tenant is not looked upon in the same light as an ordinary debtor who is unable or unwilling to pay his creditors, but is considered as a man who has made a skilful bargain; for the payment of each gale of rent is made the subject of a separate bargain. I could narrate many instances in which tenants succeeded in their plea of poverty, and were afterwards by accident discovered to have been in possession of money far more than sufficient to pay their rent twice over.

I have known many estates in which no account was ever settled between the landlord and the tenant. Payments were made from time to time, but the tenant cared very little whether they were placed to his credit or not.

This vicious custom often led to the offer of rents which the farmer knew he could not pay. The solvent farmer, who hoped to cultivate the land skilfully, and to derive a profit from his industry, and skill, and capital, and to pay his rent punctually, had no chance of getting a vacant farm against the competition of a man who did not intend to fulfil his engagements.

Thus the system tended to throw the lands into the hands of dishonest or insolvent tenants. Such men began by promising to pay more than the land was worth, and ended by paying less than its fair value. Those tenants were not only unable from want of capital to make the land productive, but it was also their interest to avoid high and efficient cultivation. Their apparent poverty was the staff on which they relied in lieu of payment of their rent; and to preserve this appearance it was necessary that they should carefully avoid such things as a sufficient stock, or a good breed of cattle, improved agricultural implements, or any outlay on their farm, either for ornament or utility. Their object was, with the least possible expense, to raise a scanty crop, which would prove that they were unable to pay the rent.

By this proceeding the landlord, the country, and even the tenant himself, were sufferers. The landlord had his land deteriorated by bad cultivation, and received less than its fair value, and far less than his nominal income. In many cases it did him a further injury, by enabling him to excuse to himself his own extravagance. He owes a good deal to his creditors, but his tenants owe a considerable sum to him; and in this manner, without going into details, he is able to present a rough balance of accounts to his conscience if it accuses him of exceeding his income.*

The country obviously suffers by anything that diminishes the produce of the soil. The tenant hides his money instead of employing it in reproductive works. The fund for the subsistence of the labourer disappears,

---

* This may appear fanciful and far-fetched ; but it is certain that many do deceive themselves by comparing their expenditure with their nominal incomes. The observation is not new. " So when they have raised their rents they spend their fortunes by living up to a nominal rent-roll, which is frequently the reason we see so many families ruined and often extinct," &c. " Landlords would have a certain and well-paid rent, and would know exactly what they could depend upon. This would make them less lavish and extravagant than they are."—ARTHUR DOBBS, 1729.

and there is no profitable employment for the peasant and the artisan. A number of ill-paid labourers are employed to do badly a work which a few well-paid men could perform efficiently with proper capital and under skilful direction. Every man who observes the agriculture of England and Ireland, even with a careless eye, is struck by the contrast between the produce of the land and the number of men employed on it. To the Irish traveller in England it seems as if the work was done without hands. He sees the work finished, but nobody doing it. The Englishman wonders at the multitude of men whom he sees with agricultural implements in their hands, and nothing done to account for their appearance. It was often found that the land was most wretchedly cultivated in districts where labour in abundance could be had for sixpence a day, or even less. There is no profit to be made by employing ill-paid labourers. And without skill, and capital, and freedom, and security, the employer cannot afford to pay fair wages.

It may be said that, even for a tenant owing more rent than he could pay, it would be on the whole more prudent to cultivate his land skilfully and carefully. This may be the case, but men are naturally disposed to indolence, and a slight argument will often turn the scale. A man is often not industrious even when he knows that the produce of his industry will be his own; how much less will his industry be when he has good reason to fear that another will seize the fruits?

This complaint of high rents has been made without ceasing for more than three hundred years. There was never less ground for it than at the present day, although in some instances the rent demanded is still too high; but this chiefly occurs where the landlords are middlemen, or where the property is very small.

Several circumstances concurred in former times to make the competition for land keener, and the demand for high rent more inconsiderate then than now. One great difference between English and Irish law, the importance of which it is difficult to estimate, was that in

Ireland there were no poor laws.   The poorer tenant, of the class that in England would look to the parish for support, saw no resource in Ireland but to obtain on any terms possession of a sufficient quantity of land to produce as much potatoes as his family could consume, with, if possible, after the potatoes, on the following year, as much corn as with his pig would be sufficient to pay the rent.   The general poverty and ignorance of the people increased the competition.   There was not much difference among the people who applied for a vacant farm.   No man had such capital or skill as to enable him to make a greater profit than his competitors, and the most obvious distinction was the willingness to offer the highest rent.   For such tenants the landlord could not erect suitable buildings for residences or farm offices.   The tenant, if he got them, would not keep them in repair.

The law gave some encouragement to this mode of dealing on the part of the landlord by the absence of poor laws, by the law of distress, which enabled the landlord to help himself without the expense of litigation with an insolvent tenant, and by the want practically of any law of limitations to affect the landlord's claims against his tenants.   The law has been altered in this respect, although scarcely to a sufficient extent.

The imprudence of setting land at high rents to insolvent tenants was becoming apparent to many, and the events connected with the famine of 1847 made it manifest to all.   It is comparatively a rare thing now for a landlord to set land at a rent which he does not believe the tenant ought to be able to pay; and rents are now generally paid with reasonable punctuality.   Notwithstanding the outrages that occur in some parts of the country, I believe there never was a time in which the occupying tenants owed so little rent.

It is still, however, not unusual to insert in leases many clauses and covenants which are inconvenient to the tenant and useless to the landlord.   They are not observed; but they have the mischievous effect of giving the landlord too much power over his tenant.

This is not peculiar to Ireland. I have seen copies of English leases which would make it very difficult for a tenant to manage his farm with profit, if he did everything which by the terms of his lease he was bound to do.

The allowance of half a year's rent in arrear, under the name of the running gale, is almost a settled institution in some parts of the country. This is so much the case, that a tenant who had not paid his landlord the rent that fell due on the 1st of November, would in the following month of March describe himself as owing no rent to his landlord, and in a year after he would describe himself as owing only a year's rent. He would not count the rent that fell due the preceding November.

This custom is mischievous, as leading to accumulation of arrears; it keeps the tenant in the landlord's power; it prevents the tenant from looking to his lease as the measure of his obligations. In this, as in other cases, the prospect of long credit induces him to offer too high a price.

The institution of a running gale often compels the landlord to plunge into debt, from which he never extricates himself. A man dies in December possessed of a good estate. The eldest son gets possession, subject to a jointure and portion. Thus he has a smaller income than his father had, while he is naturally disposed to live in the same style. He has also to be at some expense in buying furniture, and other matters, when he takes possession of the family mansion. But all his difficulties are crowned by the running gale, which adds nearly six months to the period that intervenes before he receives any rent from his tenants. He receives very little before he is ten months in the possession of his estate; and in the meantime he often contracts inveterate habits of running into debt.

Arthur Young, in the interests of the tenantry, strongly recommended the enforcement of punctual payment of rent in his advice to Irish landlords. "The first object is a settled determination, never to be departed from, to let his farms only to the immediate occupiers of the land, and to avoid deceit; not to let a cottar,

herdsman, or steward, have more than three or four
acres on any of his farms. By no means to reject the
little occupier of a few acres from being a tenant to
himself, rather than annex his land to a larger spot.
Having by this previous step eased these inferior
tenantry of the burden of the intermediate man, let him
give out, and steadily adhere to it, that he shall insist on
the regular and punctual payment of his rent, but shall
take no personal service whatever. The meanest occupier
to have a lease, and none shorter than twenty-one years,
which I am inclined also to think is long enough for his
advantage. There will arise, in spite of his tenderness,
a necessity of securing a regular payment of rent. I
would advise him to distrain without favour or affection
at a certain period of deficiency. This will appear harsh
only upon a superficial consideration. The object is to
establish the system ; but it will fall before it is on its
legs, if it is founded on a landlord forgiving arrears or
permitting them to increase." "Such a steady regular
conduct would infallibly have its effect in animating all
the tenantry on the estate to exert every nerve to be
punctual ; whereas favour shown now and then would
make every one, the least inclined to remissness, hope
for its exertion towards himself ; and every partial good
would be attended with a diffusive evil ; exceptions, however, to be made for very great and unavoidable misfortunes, clearly and undoubtedly proved."

CHAPTER IV.

The subletting and subdivision of farms are not necessarily connected with each other. A farm may be sublet without being divided. But they partly produce the same effects, and proceed from the same causes; and, in many cases, subletting leads to subdivision. The common cause is the poverty of the country. This, when there are long leases, leads to subletting; when the leases are short and unprofitable, it leads to a subdivision of farms.

When a man holds land at a rent less than the full value of the land, whether the lowness of the rent is caused by the liberality of the landlord, or by the improvements which the tenant has made on his farm, or by a general rise in the value of land through the country, he has a property which he may enjoy in person, or transfer to another. If his inclination or any other circumstance leads him to any pursuit except the occupation of that particular farm, he will endeavour to dispose of his lease to the best advantage. In the wealthy districts of the north of Ireland he will readily find a purchaser. There are many men anxious to get a farm, and possessed of money sufficient not only to cultivate the land, but also to pay a fair price for the interest of the selling tenant.

After this transaction, the new tenant now in occupation of the land has gained nothing by the liberality of the landlord, or the general rise in the value of land, or the improvements made by the tenant. Whatever the land (from any cause) is worth above the rent, he has paid for in the purchase money which he has given to

the preceding tenant. To him it is the same thing as if
he had paid a fine to the landlord on getting possession
of the farm. The sum thus paid depends more on the
means of the purchaser than on a nice calculation of the
value of the farm, or of the interest which the tenant has
in it, although of course the greater the interest the
greater will be the price paid for it.

There is nothing in a transaction of this kind injurious
to any person. On the contrary, like the ordinary
operations of free trade, it appears beneficial to all
parties concerned. This is obvious with respect to the
immediate parties to the bargain. It is a voluntary
transaction, into which neither party would enter if he
did not consider it to be for his benefit. The outgoing
tenant prefers the money to the land, the incoming
tenant prefers the land to the money. The country
gains by the change, as the incoming tenant is probably
a better farmer or possessed of more capital than his
predecessor. The landlord is secured of his rent, and of
the performance of the covenants in his leases. It is
not likely that any man would pay a large sum for a
farm, and then expose himself to ruin, or put himself in
the landlord's power by neglecting to pay his rent, or by
breaking the covenants in the lease.

In one case, however, the change is not always to the
landlord's taste. If he conferred an obligation on the
outgoing tenant by granting him a lease on liberal terms,
he may not be pleased by the change which puts the
farm into the hands of a person who is under no obligation to him. But this is a very slight matter. The
sense of obligation is seldom very durable unless it is
kept up by continual kindness, and such conduct on the
part of the landlord would excite the same feeling in the
new tenant.

But there are parts of Ireland, chiefly in the south and
west, which are so poor, that a tenant who wished to
dispose of a valuable interest in a farm might find it
difficult, if not impossible, to procure a purchaser.
Many people might wish to get his farm, but none have
the money to pay for it. The outgoing tenant therefore

sublets the land instead of selling it, and thus receives
an annual profit rent instead of a gross sum in hand.
The new tenant hopes to pay the profit rent out of the
proceeds of the farm. He is in the same position with
respect to annual payments as if he had borrowed money
to buy the tenant's farm, paying as interest a sum
equivalent to the profit rent. He could not, however,
borrow the money, because there are few who have any
sum to lend, and because he has no security to offer.
The middleman trusts him with the land, relying upon
the extraordinary powers which the law gives the landlord for the recovery of his rent. It is probable that the
under-tenant will engage to pay a very high rent, to
compensate for the indifferent security which he offers to
his immediate landlord.

In many cases this subletting was a profession or
calling. The chief landlords thought it impossible, or at
least very unpleasant, to collect rent from the very poor
persons who were the occupying tenants of the country.
They gave leases for their lives, or longer, and on
reasonable terms as to rent, to men whom they considered good marks for the rent, and who sometimes
promised that they would make some improvements in
order to enable them to sublet at a profit. Thus subletting became very general, and there were large
districts in which scarcely a single occupying tenant held
directly from the owner of the fee.

This system was useful to nobody but the middleman.
He had a good income with very little risk or trouble;
and in the earlier part of this century, during the French
revolutionary war, and the depreciation of the currency
caused by the suspension of cash payments by the Bank
of England, rent of land rose so much that in many cases
the middleman had as much profit from the land as the
head landlord himself. Sometimes land rose so much in
value, that the tenant of the middleman was able to
sublet his farm at a profit, and thus to become a middleman himself.

The peasantry under this system were reduced to a
wretched state. The traditions of liberality which be-

long to men who inherit large estates did not exist
among men who took farms for the purpose of subletting
them at the highest rent they could obtain. They were
not expected to deal like gentlemen with their tenantry.
They belonged nearly to the same class as the farmers,
and made as hard a bargain in setting a farm as they
would in selling a horse. They could scarcely afford to
be liberal. If a gentleman whose estate is set for fifteen
hundred a-year makes a reduction of his rent at any
time to the extent of twenty per cent., he loses one-fifth
of his income; but if he was a middleman, paying a rent
of twelve hundred a-year, he could not make such a
reduction without losing his entire income. The same
principle extends to every case. Every act of liberality
by the middleman would cost him a much larger proportion of his income. His trade was to extract as much as
possible from the wretched occupiers of the land. The
increase of population was so rapid, and the general
poverty of the country was such, that men were found
willing to engage to pay him anything that he demanded.
The wages of labour were so low, and the difficulty of
getting employment was so great, that it was better to
get possession of land on any terms than to trust to
casual employment for a subsistence.

The middleman, not having a permanent interest,
did not care for the improvement or deterioration of the
estate. A thought upon the subject never crossed his
mind.

Two circumstances were of material assistance to the
middlemen, and to those who acted like middlemen in
their treatment of the tenantry. First, there were no
poor laws. They were therefore enabled to cover the
land with a starving population, without the possibility of being called upon by law to contribute anything to their support. Secondly, the law of distress
was more severe than it is now, and enabled the landlord to distrain growing crops. At common law, the
crop, until it was severed from the soil, was part of the
soil, and could not be seized by distress or execution;
but this was altered by Act of Parliament, to enable the

landlord to seize the crops before they were ripe, to put keepers in possession to watch them, and to carry them away when they were ripe, leaving the starving tenant and his family in possession of the naked land. Thus the landlord frequently thought it for his interest to encourage the subdivision of farms. I remember, many years ago, hearing an extensive land agent laying down the principle in a very authoritative manner, that it was better for the landlord that there should be as many occupiers as possible on the land, since the more occupiers, the more tillage was necessary to support the tenants, and the landlord was able to help himself to the produce of the soil before they got anything.

But although some landlords may have thought that subdivision was for their benefit, they could not long have retained that opinion of subletting. They soon saw that the middleman was no use to them, but was merely intercepting a portion of their natural income; and when the great fall of land took place after the year 1815, many middlemen were broken, and left the chief landlords to deal with the land itself or with the immediate occupiers. Many landlords resolved to grant renewals of leases to none but the tenants in actual occupation. Acts of Parliament were passed to prevent or discourage subletting, and the system of middlemen gradually died away. They exist now chiefly where the land is held under bishops' leases, or under leases for lives renewable for ever.

Although I have referred to the subletting Acts, I do not believe that they had much influence in preventing subletting. The law was always sufficient, if the landlords inserted covenants against subletting in their leases, and took a little trouble to enforce them. What really caused the change was that the landlords became alive to their interests on this point.

However mischievous the old custom of subletting may have been, it is guiltless of one charge that has been sometimes made against it. The landlord had a right to distrain for his rent, even when the land was in the hands of an under tenant, who had paid his own rent to the middleman. It has been frequently stated as a grievance of no unusual occurrence, that owing to this state of the law, the tenant in occupation was obliged to pay his rent twice over, once to his own immediate landlord, and again to the head landlord. I have seen this stated in tales written to illustrate the state of Ireland, and even in evidence given before commissioners to inquire into the state of Ireland. But the statement is untrue. Such statements could not obtain credence among any men who knew what the real grievance was under which the peasantry laboured from the middleman system. The real grievance was that the rent was so high as to reduce the tenant to indolent apathetic despair. His habitual state was one of hopeless insolvency, and the middleman secured him against being obliged to pay two rents, by charging him with one rent so high as to exceed his means of paying it.

The foundation of the charge is this : a man gets a farm for a long term at the moderate rent of 1*l*. an acre ; he sublets it to a farmer at the higher rent of 2*l*. an acre, and, to save himself trouble, he accepts his profit rent of 1*l*. from the tenant, and lets the tenant settle the balance with the head landlord. The tenant does not dislike this arrangement, as the head landlord is usually more indulgent than the middleman. He is apt, however, to describe himself as paying two rents (although he is in reality only paying one rent, divided between two persons), and to complain of it as a grievance that after he has paid his own landlord, another landlord should demand more from him.

The system of subletting, at once the cause and the effect of Irish poverty, has nearly disappeared, and the middleman by profession no longer exists. In general, the immediate landlord of the occupying tenant is either the actual lord of the fee, or he has an interest in the land equivalent for all practical purposes to that of a fee-simple proprietor.

The subdivision of farms arises from different causes ; one cause is subletting. The middleman who sublets looks for the highest price which he can procure. The

highest offers will be generally made by the poorest
farmers or labourers. These generally would not have
the means to cultivate more than a small patch of land,
and they would not be a mark for the rent of even a
middle-sized farm. In many cases the middleman held
a farm in his own hands, and received a considerable
part of the rent of the small holdings under him in
labour, or in such agricultural produce as the cottier
tenant could produce, and as his position as a farmer
enabled him to consume or utilize. His account with
his tenant would be something of this kind : on the one
side would be the rent, the per contra would be two
shillings and fourpence cash, forty days' labour, seven
days' work of a horse and cart, a young pig, two geese,
five pair of chickens, six dozen of eggs, and two loads
of turf. The accounts, however, were never settled ;
receipts were neither given nor demanded ; the tenant
knew that he owed more than he could pay, and he had
very little curiosity to know the exact amount. But
the race of middlemen has now nearly died away, and
subdivision from this cause rarely takes place.

A more fertile cause of subdivision of land is the
custom which prevailed among farmers of dividing their
farms among their children. In this manner, a farm
belonging to a man with several children would be
divided into five or six smaller farms ; and these in their
turn might be further subdivided in the following generation. The landlord found it impossible to stop this
proceeding. There were no formal acts which he could
notice ; the children who were born on the land remained
on it, and by mere verbal agreement each enjoyed some
particular part instead of all enjoying the whole in common. Sometimes they remained for a time in the same
house, and then the labour of a few days would erect a
separate cabin, which might appear to be intended as a
dwelling for a labourer, or as a pigsty, or as a residence
for some offset of the family.

The chief causes of this custom were the absence of
proper buildings on the land, and the ignorance and
poverty of the farmers. The son who built a wretched

cabin was as well lodged as he had been in his father's house ; he had never known anything better. As there were no farm buildings nor any capital on the chief farm, he did not want any for the plot assigned to him for his support. In fact, the want of capital and farm-buildings made a small farm more convenient and more profitable than one of larger size. If the large farm had been supplied with a suitable dwelling-house and other buildings useful for the cultivation of the farm, it could not have been divided without inconvenience and probable loss.

Thus the condition of the country made this subdivision a matter of convenience ; but the poverty and ignorance of the people made it a matter of necessity and justice. The farmer possessed nothing but his farm, and, there-fore, could not provide for a child in any manner except by giving him a part of it. He and his children appeared not to know that any mode of livelihood was open to them except the cultivation of the particular farm on which they had hitherto lived. In many cases they could only speak Irish, which put successful emigration out of the question.

Those causes of subdivision of farms are gradually losing their force. Many farms are so well provided with suitable dwelling-houses and convenient offices, that they could not be subdivided without considerable loss. Tenants have more money, and are able to push for-wards their children in various occupations. There are more sources of employment open to them, and their better education enables them to emigrate with success. The spread of education has been a great cause of the increase of emigration. A very small proportion of that increase has been caused by insecurity of tenure.

I do not believe that at present there is much ten-dency to an inconvenient subdivision of land in the greater part of Ireland ; things may be safely left to find their own level, and under a system of freedom land will naturally fall into those parcels which will make it most productive and useful to the entire community. There are physical causes in the land itself which in some cases will produce small, and in others large farms.

D

CHAPTER V.

IT has been supposed by many that a beneficial change might be produced in the condition of Ireland by creating and keeping up a large body of peasant proprietors, that is to say, of men holding small farms in fee simple. I shall not enter into much discussion respecting the utility of such proprietors, because I believe it would be very difficult to create them, and impossible to keep them up in such a country as Ireland. Where they have long existed, they may continue for a little longer, and be sustained by habits and feelings traditionary in the families. But such habits and feelings cannot be created by any law, and they are inconsistent with the mental activity of Irishmen. They are inconsistent with railways, penny postage, a cheap newspaper press, and national education. Men will follow where their interests lead them, and in general *it is not for a man's interest to be a peasant proprietor!*

This may appear a paradox to some who would lay it down as incontrovertible truth that every peasant would desire to become a proprietor. I do not deny that, but I say that in general the proprietor would not wish to remain a peasant. Take, for example, the case of a man who is the owner in fee of thirty acres of land, worth thirty shillings an acre. The value of this, together with the capital necessary for its cultivation, and the furniture of his house, &c., cannot be less than fifteen hundred pounds, and it is not to be supposed that a man who has received a fair education, and has so much capital at his command, would consider his intellect and time and capital sufficiently employed in the cultivation of five small fields. A farmer with the same capital and holding a hundred and fifty acres at a full rent would be much better off. He could live in greater comfort, give his children a better education, and leave them a larger provision at his decease. The small proprietor might improve his position by selling his land, and engaging in trade; or he might set his land, and enter into a profession, or some industrious calling with a salary, or he might emigrate and become the owner of five hundred acres of land instead of thirty, and have boundless prospects for his family instead of giving them the paltry provision of five or six acres each. In short, he can scarcely make a more unprofitable use of his estate than by occupying it himself as a peasant proprietor.

Of course, if you take a peasant of forty years of age, and make him suddenly a proprietor, although he may emigrate, he cannot readily betake himself to any other pursuit. But his sons will not remain on that farm. The latest agrarian crime that I saw mentioned in the newspapers was the murder of a man with a Celtic name. He was stated to have been the owner in fee of forty acres of land, which he set to four or five tenants, and went away to earn his bread elsewhere. He returned, having become entitled on his discharge from some public employment to a pension of about 14*l.* a year. He took back some of the land from the tenants to reside on it himself, forgiving them a year and a half's rent in exchange. He was brutally murdered.

In the sales in the Landed Estates Court it may be observed as a matter of constant occurrence that a man with an estate that would be the size of a single small farm does not hold it all in his own hands, but sets the greater part of it to several small tenants, not keeping more in his own hands than is necessary for the supply of his house.

The possession of a small fee-simple estate can have little tendency to prevent emigration. The price would furnish the means of a prosperous emigration. The owner of an estate of forty acres in Ireland may become

D 2

the owner of several hundred acres in Australia or America.

In those countries where there are many very small hereditary estates, the inhabitants are ignorant, unambitious, selfish, frugal, and laborious. The whole concerns of the family are centered in one care—how to preserve the patrimonial field. With this view, only one son may marry, and the occupations of all are settled beforehand with this one object. The peasant proprietor has the virtues which the Irish farmer wants, and the vices from which the Irishman is free.

I should not expect much advantage from the sudden creation of peasant proprietors ; but the law ought not to do anything to prevent their existence, as it now does by the law of primogeniture, the law of settlement, and every law that makes the transfer of land tedious, difficult, uncertain, or expensive.

The question of large and small farms is sometimes discussed as if it was intimately connected with the prosperity of Ireland. Some think that the country would be more prosperous if it was divided into large farms, held by men of capital, cultivating the land by means of well-paid labourers assisted by the most approved machinery. They wish to assimilate the agriculture of Ireland to the manufactures of England. Others are for the division into small farms, where the farmer would be his own labourer and overseer.

A great deal may be said on both sides ; but the nature of the land itself generally determines whether the farms should be large or small. Rich plains, well fitted for pasture, will be held in large tracts. Uneven, rocky, rough, light, arable land, will generally be divided into small farms.

The grazier, who buys and sells and fattens cattle for the market, requires far more skill than the village farmer. He has far more opportunities of gaining money by skill, or of losing it by ignorance. Hence the unskilful grazier breaks, the skilful enlarges his territory. This he may safely do, as it is not necessary for him, as it is for the tillage farmer, to watch his labourers all day.

He may even have several farms not adjacent to each
other. The more extensive his operations are, the more
opportunities he has of using and even of improving his
skill in the selection, purchase, sale, and management of
cattle. For these reasons there is a tendency for fattening pastures to be held in large tracts.

The case is different with rough tillage farms. The
expense of locomotion and of carriage from one part of the
farm to another, and the impossibility of adequate inspection if the farm is large, naturally lead to the
creation of small farms.

The nature of the soil also determines to a great
extent whether the land should be employed in pasturage
or tillage. There is a rich stiff clay that is excellent
for pasture, and while under pasture improves every
year, but is not profitable for tillage, as it requires so
much labour as to consume the value of the crop. Old
pasture land, if broken up, takes a long time to recover
its fattening qualities, although it will yield hay or be
fit for dairy produce. On the other hand, there is a light
soil which yields a fair crop without much expense of
cultivation, and will not improve by being kept long in
pasture, but has a tendency to run into unprofitable
moss. This land is necessarily employed in tillage, and
divided into small farms. If a farmer makes money, he
cannot conveniently extend his operations, which are
limited by the size of his farm. His success depends
more upon thrift and industry than upon superior skill.
The chief difference is that the good farmer is able to
live in greater comfort than the bad one. Agricultural
skill has not made such progress as to decide the contest
between high and low farming. The one makes much,
but the other spends little, and runs no risk.

I have given instances of land which must be held in
large pasture farms, and of land which must be held in
small tillage farms; but these shade into each other by
imperceptible gradations, and there is much debateable
ground, in which sometimes the one and sometimes the
other system prevailed.

At present I think the system of pasture and large

farms has a tendency to extend itself, for the following reasons.

In the first place, the price of meat has risen, while the price of corn has not advanced. This is an addition to the grazier's profit.

In the second place, the wages of labour have risen in a greater degree than the efficiency of the labourer, and this, by increasing the expense, reduces the profits of tillage.

Thirdly, the invention of machines for threshing, reaping, and mowing enables the farmer on a large scale to perform those important operations with less expense and greater rapidity. It would be unprofitable to a small farmer to possess those machines, for which his farm could not furnish more than one or two days' work in the year. It is true that they may be hired, and, in fact, this is often done with threshing machines. But with mowing and reaping machines this is more difficult. The farmer cannot so readily make an appointment some time beforehand, irrespective of the weather; and when his crop is ready he cannot wait for the reaping machine without some loss. The land also must be properly prepared, or the machinery will suffer damage.

These circumstances throw some difficulty in the way of hiring reaping and mowing machines; but it is not impossible, and it is sometimes done.

Another circumstance, which tends to keep up large farms when once they have been consolidated, is the larger capital now expended in the erection of farm-buildings. It is obvious that when a farm of two hundred acres is supplied with a suitable dwelling, a barn, houses for cattle, and other offices, it cannot be divided into two farms without loss.

The best remedy against too great an extension of the large farm system, without an injurious interference with the free course of industry, is to be found in a good agricultural education for the poor. It is a sad sight to see a holding of four acres, of which only one is in a state of cultivation, and that often a cultivation of a

wretched kind.   The remaining three acres are taking a
long rest, after having been over-cropped, and the entire
is full of weeds.   Meantime, the peasant is looking idly
on, and between the time of planting his potatoes, and
digging them, spends only a few days' labour on his farm
in earthing them.

His short or long tenure has nothing to do with the
matter.   The work which he neglects is precisely that
work which would yield him an immediate return.

It is not always the sloth of the owner which is the
cause of the wretched state of his little farm.   He is
often ready to work for any employer at very small
wages.   It has not been an uncommon thing for a man
to look for work at sixpence a day when he might earn
more than double that amount by working for himself
on his own little farm.

Ignorance is the chief cause of his idleness and mismanagement.   The peasant farmer knows only how to
raise potatoes according to the routine of the slovenly
farmers around him.   While he imitates them, he is
inferior to them, for he works with less capital and worse
tools; but he is unaware of the advantages which he
might possess by deviating from their practice, and treating his little plot as a garden, not as a farm.   He thus
might find employment for himself and all his family, and
treble the produce of his land when they spent that time
in profitable work which they from ignorance often spend
in worse than unprofitable idleness.   To enable him to
act thus he must be taught, for at present he has no
opportunity of learning the cultivation of a garden farm
by experience or observation of what is going on around
him.

He has the advantages on his side that the personal
expenses are inconsiderable.   Being himself the labourer,
he requires no steward or overseer, and he saves many
of the expenses incident to a larger farm.   Those advantages are lost as soon as he possesses more land than he
can cultivate without a horse.   It then ceases to be a
garden farm.

The small farmer in Ireland has never sufficiently

considered the necessity of keeping up the fertility of
the land. Ireland has been mercilessly over-cropped.
Notwithstanding the increase of pasture since 1848, the
land has not yet recovered from the exhaustion caused
by the over-tillage of a century.

Formerly the course of husbandry was of this kind.
1st. Potatoes, with manure. 2nd. Wheat. 3rd and
successive years, oats and barley until the land was so
barren as to be incapable of yielding another corn crop.
It was then permitted to rest in dirt and weeds until it
got a green skin or sole, and then the same exhausting
process recommences.

This was the case in Arthur Young's time, 1777.
Thus he describes the courses of Newtown Stewart:—
1. Oats on lay. 2. Wheat. 3. Oats. 4. Barley. 5.
Oats. 6. Barley. 7. Oats. 8. Left for lay. A few sow
clover or rye-grass for two years.

His account of the courses of Courtown are, 1. Potatoes.
2. Barley. 3. Oats: then more crops of oats, or barley
and oats, till the soil is exhausted, when they leave it to
turf itself, which it will not do under ten or fifteen years.
This system continued until the middle of this century
on many estates in which the agents seemed to consider
that their only duty was to collect the rents.

Even with careful management, it would not have been
easy to preserve the fertility of the soil unimpaired when
the chief exports were provisions, and no artificial manures were imported.

CHAPTER VI.

ULSTER TENANT RIGHT.

THE phrase " tenant right " is not unknown in England, and is sometimes found in wills and other legal documents. It signifies not merely the actual estate and right of the tenant, but also the good-will, and the expectation which the tenant has that he will be permitted to remain in possession of the land on reasonable terms. The phrase is used in many parts of Ireland besides Ulster ; and in every part of Ireland, any tenant-at-will, under a liberal landlord, could obtain a good price for his interest in the land if he were permitted to sell it.

The peculiarity of the Ulster tenant right is, that it has been reduced into a kind of system, with the consent or acquiescence of the landlords.   It has several qualities which may be found separately elsewhere.

In the first place, when land is set for agricultural purposes, the rent demanded is not a competition rent : it is not the utmost rent which a good and solvent tenant would be willing to pay. If there is a permanent increase in the value of land, either from the general improvement of the country or from the increased price of agricultural produce, the landlord may raise the rent at his discretion in the same manner as any other landlord may raise the rent of his yearly tenants.   It is, however, expected that this discretion will be guided by the same generous feeling which the landlord showed in the original letting.

Secondly, it is expected that as long as the tenant pays his rent, the landlord will not use his legal power of putting an end to the tenancy.

Thirdly, if a tenant finds it necessary or convenient to leave his farm, he may sell his tenant right, with the approbation of his landlord. This approbation is not to be capriciously refused; but, on the other hand, the tenant is not at liberty to select any substitute that he thinks proper, irrespective of his character, and possession of sufficient means for the efficient cultivation of the land.

He is not always permitted even to accept the utmost that an eligible successor would be willing to pay for the tenant right. The landlord has an obvious interest in preventing this price from being too high. Too high a price might deprive the incoming tenant of the means of doing justice to the farm. Moreover, it might impose a moral obligation on the landlord not to raise the rent so high as he might otherwise do without prejudice to the customary tenant right allowed on his estate. Thus, suppose the customary value of the tenant right on an estate has been 7*l.* an acre, but since the last settlement fixing the rate of rent the country has improved, or the price of agricultural produce has risen, so that it would be reasonable in a short time to make a new agreement with the tenants respecting the rents. In this case, if an incoming tenant, with the consent of the landlord, paid for the tenant right a price based on the calculation that the present amount of rent would not be altered for a considerable period, he would have a just cause of complaint if the landlord, by raising his rent, should disturb the arrangements, on the faith of which he had paid his money. If the selling tenant should say, have not I a right to sell my interest for the highest price I can get? the landlord might reply, have not I the same right? The selling tenant has no right to complain, if, when he sells his farm, he gets back the price which he originally paid, together with the value of all the improvements which he may have made in the meantime.

Fourthly, all arrears of rent must be paid before the transfer is completed. In a large and well-managed estate, the transaction proceeds in this manner:—John M'Garry holds a farm at the yearly rent of 30*l.* He

owes a year and a half's rent, and he wishes to sell his
farm, in order to emigrate, or to set up a shop, or to pay
his debts, or for any other purpose. Charles O'Neil
agrees to give him 500*l.* for it. He asks the agent's
consent, which is granted. They call on the agent at
his office; all arrears of rent are paid, probably out of
the 500*l.* An entry is made in the books, and the name
of Charles O'Neil is entered as tenant in place of John
M'Garry. The transaction is then complete, without
any law expenses or any risk of bad title. It is true
that as against the landlord it rests upon his honour,
and upon public opinion; but as against the rest of the
world, the title is perfect. No creditor, purchaser,
mortgagee, or claimant under any former tenant can disturb the purchaser. A notice to quit by the landlord
will protect him against every other claimant. It is no
small advantage to be emancipated from all the complicated laws of landed property.

Thus in Ulster, free trade in land, as far as the right
of occupation is concerned, prevails in the most perfect manner. Thus important property, to the value
of several millions, may be bought and sold without risk,
or trouble, or expense in reference to the title or conveyance as readily as a horse or a cow. Find a person
in possession willing to sell, agree upon the value, and
pay the price, and the thing is done—the property is
yours. It is true that this free trade affects only the
permanent right of occupation, and does not extend to
the absolute property in the soil; but this is enough, for
it is the industry and capital of the occupier that makes
the land the source of wealth.

I have alluded to the entry in the agent's books where
the estate is large; but where the estate is small, and
managed with less regularity, the same transaction is
accomplished, without any formal entries in books, by a
conversation with the landlord or his agent on the road,
or at a fair or market, or any place where the parties
meet each other.

There are some advantages attending the Ulster tenant
right independent of the free trade in land which it

creates : under this system the tenantry cannot be very poor. However, it may be said that this result is attained, not by giving property to the tenant, but by preventing any poor man from becoming a tenant. You cannot become a farmer unless you have capital sufficient not only to cultivate the land, but also to buy at a high price the interest of the tenant who is already in occupation.

To the manager of an estate the system is very agreeable. The rents are moderate, and paid with punctuality, and the agent is not subjected to the harassing labour and danger which attend the enforcement of rent in many parts of Ireland. There are no evictions by process of law ; but if the tenant is not thriving, and finds it difficult to pay his rent, he is warned by the agent or by his own prudence, that he ought to sell his tenant right, and retire from his farm with a good sum in hand to emigrate or support him in some other pursuit, before he is totally ruined by remaining in a farm that he is unable to cultivate with profit. He is succeeded by a wealthier or more skilful tenant, and the landlord and the country at large gain by the change.

Under the Ulster system, the landlord appears to receive a smaller rent than he might reasonably demand, but I doubt if he is injured by it. He is less apt to live beyond his real income. His rent-roll does not present him with an extravagant view of his means. Owing to the quietness and industry of the people, the value of land improves rapidly. It is better to receive two-thirds of the value of an estate worth 6000*l.* a year than the entire value of an estate worth only 3000*l.*, and this is often the difference between an Ulster landlord and a landlord in those parts of Ireland where the system does not prevail. It is doubtful whether an Ulster landlord does not receive as much rent as a Connaught landlord would receive for an estate of the same natural productive powers.

But the system is not without its disadvantages. The tenant is too dependent on his landlord for the property for which he has paid the full value. Not only are his rights against the landlord not recognized by law, but even while dependent upon usage and honour, they are

incapable of being exactly defined. The important
question, what ought to be the proportion between the
value of the tenant's and the landlord's interest is not
ascertained. It varies on different estates according to
the wealth and liberality of the landlord, and even on
the same estate it is liable to fluctuation.

When the value of land remains stationary, the matter
is easily settled by letting the rent remain as it is; but
when an improvement takes place gradually, a difficulty
arises. It is not easy for some time to determine whether
the change is temporary or is likely to be permanent.
Every small increase in value, even if it is likely to be permanent, cannot be met by an immediate increase of rent.
To make frequent, although small additions to the rent,
would be a very unpopular course for the landlord to
take. It would lead to frequent disputes, while it would
alarm the tenantry, and diminish their confidence in the
tenant right.

Thus, while an increase in the value of land is always
gradual, and scarcely seen while it is going on, a rise in
rent is a sharp change, and is immediately and unplea-
santly felt. Take the case of a farmer who holds eighty
acres at a rent of 120*l.* a year. The fair marketable
value of the land is 1*l.* 17*s.* an acre, so that he has a
profit of seven shillings an acre in addition to the ordinary profits of his capital. For this tenant right he
could readily get a price of 7*l.* an acre, 560*l.* or more, if
the people in the neighbourhood are prospering either in
trade or agriculture. The country is improving, so that
each year on an average adds three pence an acre to the
value of the land. This goes on for twelve years, when
the landlord thinks it right to make a new settlement of
the rent, by adding three shillings an acre, leaving the
customary seven shillings an acre tenant right. The
tenant will certainly complain loudly. He will see that
this increase of rent makes him worse off than he has
been for several years past, and that nothing has occurred
during the last three or four years to justify such an
addition to his rent. He cannot remember accurately
what was the general value of land twelve years ago,

while he has a very precise recollection of any improvements which he himself may have made in the meantime, and to such improvements, whether real or imaginary, he will attribute the increase of rent that has been imposed on him. He will complain all the more loudly, and feel a deeper sense of injury, because the justice of his complaint cannot be legally investigated. The legal power of the landlord to increase the rent is altogether independent of the circumstances by which his conduct may be justified.

Thus, whether by a gradual process or by starts at long intervals, the landlord finds it equally unpopular and disagreeable to increase the rents in proportion to the improvements, and in this manner the tenant right on large and liberally-managed estates has a constant tendency to increase in value. I believe it never was more valuable than it is now.

The right which the landlord has on the sale of a tenant right, to object to the purchaser or the price, is very rarely exercised. The ability to pay the purchase money may be taken as a fair proof that the incoming tenant will be able to cultivate the land and meet his engagements. As to the price, when the rent is all paid up, the incoming and outgoing tenant may make what bargain they like without the knowledge of the landlord, so that there is seldom an opportunity of objecting on this score.

So far everything seems to be in favour of the tenant. But if the value of land falls, the loss falls entirely upon him ; and when the great depreciation of land took place in 1848, the state of parts of the counties of Armagh and Monahan was nearly as bad as in King's County or Tipperary. To those who wanted to part with their farms, the tenant right was valueless, as there were no purchasers. The tenants were unable to sell what they had bought at a very high price. They expected that good times would return if they could hold out for a short time, and were inclined, in defiance of the law, to resist every attempt to deprive them of their holdings, or to make them pay their rents.

The value of the tenant right on an estate is not subject to any fixed principle. It does not depend on any improvements made by the tenant. If the landlord is a just man, he will, in all his dealings with the tenant, value the land as if those improvements had never been made. But beyond those improvements, and even in cases where it cannot be pretended that any improvement was made, the tenant right exists, and is often bought and sold for large sums of money. The price is often so high that the interest of the purchase money, together with the rent, is much more than the fair value of the land.

It seems essential to the existence of tenant right, that land should be owned in large masses by the landlords. The owner of an estate of 20,000*l.* a year may act with great liberality, and set the land for less than it is really worth. But if the same estate was divided among forty men, each with 500*l.* a year, it is not likely that they would all act so liberally without any regard to the ordinary commercial principle of getting as much as they reasonably could. There would be a chance that some at least among the number would take every opportunity of making small but frequent additions to the rent, so small that the tenant would not on any one occasion feel it worth his while to make a desperate resistance, but so frequent that the value of the tenant right would gradually dwindle away.

It is sometimes asked, would the tenant prefer leases to their present position as yearly tenants? This, of course, must depend upon the length of the lease. A very long lease would undoubtedly improve their position. A short lease might have a contrary effect by leading to an earlier readjustment of the terms of their tenures. They would sometimes hope that the present system might operate as an adjournment sine die of this readjustment. Time passes away, and it appears as far off as ever, as there is no reason why it should be required in one year rather than another. But if a lease was made, the time would be growing shorter every day. On the whole, however, I believe that most of the tenants would gladly accept a lease for thirty-one years at some increase of rent, rather than remain in their present somewhat dependent and precarious position.

It is not to be supposed that this system prevails universally through Ulster, or that any man could make a map to include only the parts in which it prevails. It is more usual to grant leases in towns, and in the neighbourhood of towns. There are also many scattered estates on which leases are granted, and there the leases are often sold, or the land sublet as in other parts of the country.

But although there would be no difficulty in the way to prevent the introduction of leases into Ulster, it would not be found so easy to introduce the Ulster system of tenant right into other parts of Ireland. It is too vague to be capable of exact definition, or of being enforced by law. It depends upon confidence on one side, and honour on the other—upon a mutual understanding and public opinion—and these feelings cannot be created by law or agreement; they can only grow up gradually and slowly.

No one would wish to break up a system as long as it is supposed to work well, and when no complaints are made by the persons affected by it. But even if it were possible, I should not wish to see it extended to the whole of Ireland. The tenant is dependent on the liberality of his landlord to a degree inconsistent with a democratic constitution. A landlord who would not venture altogether to destroy the tenant right, has still the power to make a very great reduction in its value. The tenant holds a valuable property at the mercy of another, who has an interest in taking it from him.

Another evil of the system is, that no man can take a farm unless he has double the capital that would otherwise have been necessary. The purchase of the tenant right takes as much capital as the stocking of the farm. Thus a barrier is placed against the acquisition of a farm by a poor man. The advantage of the landlord and tenant system, as distinguished from the proprietary system, is that it enables the farmer to apply his capital more efficiently to the cultivation of the soil, when the land itself is only paid for while he is using it. For the use of the land, the tenant pays a rent that would only be a moderate interest on the sum necessary to buy it. In Ulster, the saving in the amount of rent gives the tenant a very low interest on the sum that he is required to pay for the tenant right. A man with skill and energy and a moderate capital would scarcely think it prudent to set up as a farmer in Ulster.

The wealth obtained by the cultivation and manufacture of flax in Ulster, is the cause that when a farm is to be sold there is always at hand some person able and willing to pay for the tenant right. In the other provinces the case would be different. None of the neighbours would have money to buy the tenant right, and the purchaser would be obliged to borrow the purchase money at a high rate of interest, as the security for payment would be of an inferior character. We should therefore look for some source of improvement in Munster and Connaught, other than the introduction of Ulster tenant right.

Something, however, like the Ulster tenant right in all its useful characters, but without its vagueness and uncertainty, might be created by an agreement or a law to the following effect. Landlord demises land to tenant on the following terms:—Tenant shall hold as yearly tenant at the rent of 40*l.*, payable on the 1st of May and 1st of November, and subject to the covenants in the lease contained for the proper cultivation of the land. Landlord shall not be at liberty to evict the tenant for any cause except breach of covenant or non-payment of rent. On the first eviction for any breach, the tenant shall be entitled to redeem within three months on payment of damages, to be settled by the court. The tenant rights shall be considered as of the value of seven years' purchase. The landlord shall be at liberty to raise the rent by giving notice one year at least before the 1st of November. If the tenant is not satisfied to pay such increase of rent, he may at any time before the 1st of March give notice to the landlord that he will surrender

E

his holding on the 1st of November next, upon which
the landlord must pay him seven years of such increased
rent as compensation for his tenant right.   If the tenant
considers his rent to be too high, he may, one year before
the 1st of November, serve notice on his landlord to have
it reduced to such rent as he may choose to name.   In
this case the landlord, at any time before the 1st of
March, may serve notice on the tenant that he will not
consent to the reduction, and will take up the land and
pay him seven years' value of such reduced rent, and
upon tender of this sum on the 1st of November, the
tenancy shall be at an end.   The money is not to be
paid until the land is given up.   In all cases of eviction
the tenant shall be entitled to seven years' rent from
the landlord, deducting therefrom all money due for
arrears of rent or breach of covenant.   The tenant shall
not be permitted to divide or sublet his farm, but he
may sell his tenant right, with the consent of the landlord,
on giving two months' notice.   If the landlord refuses to
give his consent, he must purchase the tenant right himself, paying seven years' purchase, but deducting all
money due for arrears of rent or breaches of covenant.
The tenant shall not be permitted to charge or incumber
his holding.   Every contract or engagement that he
makes shall be considered as a merely personal contract,
binding himself, but not affecting the land until the
landlord shall have given his consent.

If the tenant finds it necessary to make any improvement on his farm, he shall serve notice on the landlord,
specifying the improvement and the estimated expense.
If the landlord objects, the tenant may refer it to the
Land Tribunal to determine whether the objection is
reasonable.   If the landlord does not object, or if the
Land Tribunal decides that the objection is not reasonable, the tenant may proceed with the improvement, and
when it is completed the tenant shall be entitled to compensation in the following manner :—He shall receive for
the term of forty years an annuity at the rate of 7*l.* 10*s.*
per cent., payable half-yearly.   As long as he remains
in possession, his enjoyment of the land shall be deemed

a payment of the annuity. If he sells his tenant right, the purchaser shall be entitled to the residue of the annuity on the same terms. If the landlord shall increase his rent with the consent of the tenant, the latter shall be entitled to deduct the annuity, during his term, from the increased rent. If the tenant objects to the increase of rent, the landlord shall pay, as compensation for the tenant right, seven years of the increased rent, plus the estimated value of the residue of the annuity, minus seven years of the annuity, or, at the option of the tenant, shall pay seven years of the increased rent.

To prevent frequent alterations of the rent, it might be provided that no increase shall be less than ten per cent. on the rent, and that no increase shall be made at a shorter interval than seven years from the last increase. The above may be called the parliamentary tenant right, which every landlord should have power to grant, notwithstanding any incumbrance or settlement affecting his estate.

CHAPTER VII.

A FEELING almost universal prevails in Ireland, that the relation between landlord and tenant is not in a satisfactory condition, and that some concessions are required from landlords, and it is thought by many that such concessions might be made without detriment to their real interests.

I shall mention some of the chief complaints, and shall endeavour to draw a distinction between those complaints which appear to have some foundation in real grievances, and those claims which arise from a greedy desire to obtain by political changes that wealth which ought to be the reward of thrift and industry.

The first complaint is, that landlords are frequently prevented by settlements from granting beneficial leases, or entering into reasonable agreements with their tenants. If a farmer obtains a beneficial lease or a fair agreement, and expends money upon the faith of such lease or agreement, he is liable to utter ruin. The landlord's successor, often his eldest son, may evict him without compensation, relying upon some settlement of which the tenant never could have suspected the existence.

The second grievance is, that the tenant gets possession of a farm in such a condition that he cannot cultivate it efficiently, or dwell on it with decency, without making a large outlay on buildings or other permanent improvements. But when he has made those necessary improvements, he is liable to be dispossessed before he has enjoyed the farm long enough to obtain a fair remuneration for his risk and outlay. He loses the money, which he expended in the reasonable belief that the landlord who permitted the expenditure, would also permit him to reap the benefit of it.

The third grievance is, that a tenant often purchases the interest of a tenant from year to year with the express or implied sanction of the landlord. Sometimes part of the purchase money is paid to the landlord in discharge of arrears of rent due by the outgoing tenant. Notwithstanding this, the tenant who paid the money is liable to be dispossessed by the landlord who received it. The landlord must have known that the tenant paid the money in the belief that he would be permitted to enjoy the land for a reasonable period.

In those three cases the tenant has expended money, or money's worth, on the faith of a contract expressed or implied, that he should be permitted to enjoy the fruits of his expenditure. These three grievances could be completely remedied without any revolutionary changes. The first grievance would cease to exist if every limited owner was empowered to grant a lease for a term of forty-one years, at a rent not less than three-fourths of the value. This would completely protect the tenant farmer; and if any man seeks to obtain a greater interest in land, there is nothing unreasonable in requiring him to investigate the title like any other prudent purchaser. A line must be drawn somewhere to distinguish the tenant from the purchaser.

The two latter grievances might be remedied by an enactment that any tenant from year to year who has purchased the interest of an outgoing tenant, or any tenant who has improved his farm with the consent of the landlord expressed or implied, may apply for a recognition of his legal tenant right. If the landlord refuses this recognition, an arbitrator appointed by Government should have authority to investigate the case, and determine whether the tenant has made out his claim for tenant right. If the claim is established, the arbitrator should in his award set forth what improvements, if any, the tenant has made, and the date and value of those improvements. Until those improvements are exhausted, the tenant should be entitled to enjoy them without paying any increased rent on their account; and if he is obliged to leave the farm in the meantime, he should receive a fair compensation, in addition to the value of his tenant right, for his improvements.

But the claims made by many on behalf of the tenants go far beyond the cases that I have mentioned. They claim rents determined by arbitration, not by contract; and fixity of tenure, irrespective of any custom of tenant right, or money paid to an outgoing tenant, or any improvement made upon the land. They claim in effect that a man who has taken a lease of a farm for twenty-one years, at a rent of 50*l.* a year, shall have it changed to a lease for ever at a rent of 25*l.*, although every farmer in the neighbourhood may be willing to pay 50*l.* rent for the farm.

It is scarcely necessary to use argument to prove the injustice of a claim which is made in contradiction to an express contract. If the contract is unequal or unjust, the utmost that can be demanded by the complaining party is, that it should be rescinded. But except in the claims made on behalf of Irish tenants, it was never known that a man who had made a contract beneficial to himself, the benefit of which he could sell at a considerable profit, and which he would be exceedingly unwilling to rescind, should set up a public cry to have that contract altered. What would be thought of such a case as this:—A man sells for 100*l.* a horse, for which, if he set it up to auction, he could probably get 130*l.* The following conversation takes place the next day between the buyer and the seller. Buyer: "You have charged me too much for that horse." Seller: "I am sorry you think so. However, I am ready to take it off your hands, and to return the price, or I can find a person who will pay you twenty pounds to stand in your shoes." Buyer: "I thank you; but that will not suit me. I am determined to keep the horse, and the price must be left to arbitration; and if I am satisfied with the price which the arbitrators award, I shall pay it, otherwise not." But such a conversation would not give an adequate idea of the claims of the Irish tenant. He demands not only to pay less, but to get more than he contracted for. His bargain is to get the land for twenty-one years, and his claim is to hold it for ever, although he has not a shadow of right to the land, except under that contract. I am confining myself to the case where the tenant has no claim, except that he is a tenant ; for if he has any other ground for his demand, it ought to be fairly and liberally considered.

It is not difficult to prove that a law establishing fixity of tenure would be as impolitic as it would be unjust. It would utterly fail in its professed object. It would be a mere violent and wrongful transfer of property from a certain number of individuals, who are now called landlords, to another set of individuals who are now called tenants, and who would then become landlords. The men now in possession would be enabled to violate their engagements, but no future tenants would gain anything by the change. It may be taken as an undoubted axiom in political economy, that if a man is permitted to sell or retain his own property, and to select the purchaser, he cannot be prevented from getting the utmost price that another person will be ready to pay for it. The only test of value is the price which the public is willing to pay.

Apply this axiom to the case of land. Suppose fixity of tenure, and the settlement of rents by a Government arbitrator to be the established law of the land. I am in possession as owner in fee simple of a farm of one hundred acres, worth two pounds an acre. A farmer would be willing to pay that rent, hoping to get a fair return for his capital and labour according to the ordinary rate of agricultural profit. If I set it to a tenant, he will have the rent settled by an arbitrator, who will probably award a rent of 100*l.* a year as the fair value. But I may set it to a trustee, who then becomes entitled to the land for ever at the fee-farm rent of 100*l.* a year. He sets up the tenant right for sale, which will sell for between two or three thousand pounds. The purchaser will probably be obliged to raise the greatest part of this by mortgage. In the end it will be found that between rent and interest the new tenant will have to pay more than 200*l.* a year, the rent at which he could have obtained it if the law had permitted me to set it to him at that rent. Moreover, he will have paid away a large portion of his capital, which would have been more profitably employed in the cultivation of the land.

The tenant will lie under another disadvantage, in being obliged to deal with two persons, from neither of whom can he expect any forbearance, instead of a single landlord, from whom he might get some assistance or abatement in a bad season. He cannot ask an abatement from the landlord to whom he is paying only half the value of the land as rent. He need not expect any reduction of interest from the mortgagee, for a money-lender is more apt to increase than to reduce the rate of interest in a season of hardship and scarcity.

The only mode in which any person could get a farm would be by paying a high price for the interest of some farmer who might be willing to sell his tenant right. The price would generally be as much as three times the capital that would be sufficient to till the land. A great obstacle would be opposed to agricultural improvement by this impediment to free trade in land. No man could become a farmer unless he had much more capital than would otherwise be found necessary; for he would not be able to borrow the entire sum necessary to purchase the tenant right; and without purchasing a tenant right, he could not obtain a farm. It is not to be supposed that the present tenants, when they had obtained a permanent title to the land, would part with their farms on the basis of the valuation on which they had obtained them. They would certainly require the highest price that could be obtained by free competition.

Thus, after the first confiscation of the landlord's estates, the law of valuation would become a dead letter. It would not be used to regulate future contracts, as men would find a way of settling the terms of their own contracts by mutual agreement.

As to fixity of tenure, it would soon be found intolerable, and would be repealed as soon as it had done its work of depriving the present owners of their estates. The public would not long bear a law which prevented two men from making a bargain just in itself, useful to the public, and profitable to both parties. I hold some land in fee. I am too old and infirm to cultivate it. In a few years my son will be old enough to undertake the management of it. I wish to set it for a term of seven years; and, on account of the shortness of the lease, to accept a lower rent than if I were granting a longer term. This exactly suits my neighbour, to whom a moderate rent is a greater object than a long lease; but the law of fixity of tenure would step in, and say that I must either hold on my land at a loss, or part with the possession for ever, and that he must either do without a farm, or pay a sum for a fee-farm tenure beyond what he could afford. The result would probably be, that he would be obliged to remain idle for want of a farm, and that my farm would remain nearly unprofitable for want of a tenant, and the wealth of the country would be proportionally diminished.

In general there is no mode of getting land so convenient to a good farmer with a competent capital as getting his land for a moderate term at a rent settled by mutual agreement. The term should not be too long, as the landlord would naturally and reasonably require a higher rent. A belief prevails very generally that land has a tendency to rise in value, irrespective of any improvements made upon it, or that money will fall in value, so that in the next century land will be worth a higher rent. The advantage of that rise will belong to the person who will then have the disposition of the land. This at present belongs to the owner in fee simple in possession, and if he is asked to part with it, he will require an increase of rent, or some present payment as an equivalent. This would be inconvenient to the tenant, who expects to make ten per cent. compound interest on his capital. To him it would be a loss to expend any of this profitable capital in the purchase of an expectation to be realised at the end of a century.

It is not material whether this belief in the probability

of a rise in the value of land be well founded or not, it
is sufficient that it exists and must have its influence
upon all contracts.   It certainly cannot be disproved,
and it has the experience of several centuries to support it.

I have assumed that fixity of tenure is to be founded
on a valuation, because I see no other mode in which
it can be established.   If the landlord and tenant can
fix the rent by agreement, there would be danger that
the land would be set in many instances at far more
than its real value, with an understanding (not supported
by any promise, and not capable of being enforced by
law) that the entire rent would never be demanded.
This, as far as the public is concerned, is the worst tenure
by which a tenant can hold his land.   If the fixity of
tenure is to be on the existing rents, it in many cases
would be unjust to liberal landlords who often set their
lands at less than the fair value; and also in the case of
land held by leases still unexpired and made in the last
century or earlier; while to the harsh landlord, who sets
his land for the highest rent that is offered, it would be
no injury, but it would be no boon to his tenantry.

But the settlement of rent by valuation appears just
only to persons who do not know what a valuation of
land is, and always must be.   The value certainly is,
that rent which a solvent tenant will be ready to offer
for the farm on a lease of moderate duration.   When a
landlord wishes to set his land, the proposals made by
persons willing to become tenants settle the value of
the land beyond the possibility of dispute.   The solvent
tenant will take care not to offer a rent which the profits
of the land will not enable him to pay.   He is under
the strongest inducements to discover the real value of
the land.   He may consult an experienced valuator if he
thinks proper; but he rarely takes this step, as he
generally knows the value of the land better than any one
whom he could consult.   He often talks the matter over
with his friends, to know their opinions, and then to form
his own judgment.   The professional valuator forms a
more rapid judgment; and unless he is living in the

immediate neighbourhood of the land, his judgment is not worth much.   A serious difference of value between two fields is often caused by circumstances which the most careful examination would fail to detect.

The tenant does not merely look to the soil, and to the condition of the roads, the fences, and the buildings : he knows what treatment the land has received for several years—the nature and quality of the crops—whether cattle appeared to thrive well on the land—what rent was usually paid for that and other similar land in the neighbourhood—and whether the tenants who paid such rents were prosperous or the reverse.   Many other inquiries, which I need not enumerate, he makes before he determines what rent he will bind himself to pay.

When men are competent to make their own bargain, it is unjust to compel them to submit to the opinion of a third person.

In the year 1865, I made the following observations, and I have seen no reason to alter my opinion since I made them :—" Many other things are to be considered, but I have said enough to show how utterly inadequate to the occasion is the cursory inspection that is made by a professional valuator.   All that he often does is to find out what is the rent actually paid for the adjacent farms, and whether the farm he is valuing is better or worse than those ; and then to make an abatement or increase on the result so obtained, according to the purpose for which the valuation was made.   If the valuation is made for the purpose of taxation, it is generally made low, for then there is less likelihood of an appeal. If the owner gets it valued for the purpose of a sale, the valuation is apt to be high—as more likely to suit the interests or wishes or feelings of the employer.

" The following cases are fair specimens of the discrepancies which are to be found in different valuations made of the same property."

" Since I wrote the above, the estate of John Campbell Jones was offered for sale ; and the following are the differences between the valuations made by a civil engineer and by the Ordnance valuation of the same lots :

Killiewingan.

	£	s.	d.
Engineer	120	0	0
Tenement valuation . . .	57	0	0

No. 5.

Valuator	8	10	0
Tenement valuation . . .	2	5	0

Ratheline.

Valuator	29	17	7
Tenement valuation . . .	8	0	0

Fox and Calf Island.

Valuator	40	0	0
Tenement valuation . . .	3	0	0

Lot 9.

Valuator	10	0	0
Tenement valuation . . .	1	6	0

Lot 10.

Valuator	8	4	3
Tenement valuation . . .	1	4	0

In the estate of Rutledge the following are two of the valuations :—

Cregganrae.

	£	s.	d.
Valuator	53	1	7
Tenement valuation . . .	17	10	0

Ballykit.

Valuator	226	13	7
Tenement valuation . . .	131	12	0"

I have given those examples, not as the most remarkable that could be found, but because they were the most striking cases that came before me within a few days after I had made the above remarks. I believe that, in those cases, both the valuations which I have contrasted were intended to be fair, and were made by skilful valuators.

It may be asked, " Is there no mode of valuing a farm ; must the tenant make a mere guess at what he is to offer ?" No ; the landlord and the intending tenant have means of knowing the value of the land which no other person is likely to possess and to employ. They both know the past history of the farm, and of all the farms in the neighbourhood ; what rent was paid for them ; in what manner they were cultivated ; and whether the tenants appeared to thrive on them, or the contrary. No man has such an interest in discovering the exact value as the person who proposes to become a tenant, and as his object is to make a profit by his occupation as farmer, it is not to be supposed that he will give more for the land than he can pay, reserving a reasonable profit to himself.

The injustice of setting aside a voluntary contract, and substituting a valuation, is not manifest at first sight, for the words appear fair. Why, it is said, should any tenant be required to pay more than the fair value for his farm ? But every one who has any experience knows that nothing can be more uncertain and undetermined than the valuation of land. It is not uncommon to see two valuators differing enormously in their estimates, and yet neither suffering in reputation as if he had made a discreditable mistake. It is probable the value as fixed by any tenant-right measure would be less than half the rent which a solvent tenant would be willing to pay.

All future valuations would be still more uncertain ; for as soon as the possession of land ceased to be a subject of contract by mutual agreement, the valuators would have no average market-value to refer to, and would form their estimates on the wildest principles.* This, however, would not be a matter of much

* It is highly probable that, in the excited state of feeling that would be raised by an alteration of the law, no valuator would venture to express an opinion of the value of the land that was not in accordance with the tenant's wishes.

importance, as I have shown that between rent and purchase of tenant right every new tenant will be obliged to pay the full value of the land, no matter what changes may be made in the law.

In the form of tenant right, which I have ventured to suggest as possible to be introduced and maintained in Ireland, I have therefore taken care that it should be self-working, and not depend upon any valuation of the land to be made by any third person.

Some reason should be given for making land an exception to the ordinary rules of commerce, and fixing the price by law, instead of letting it be arranged by mutual agreement between the buyer and the seller, the landlord and the tenant. The reason formerly assigned was, that the possession of land was a question of life or death to the tenant ; that he had no other resource to preserve himself and his family from starvation, and that therefore he was obliged to submit to any terms which an avaricious landlord might impose. That the parties to the contract stood on such unequal ground as to make it necessary for the law to interfere to protect the weaker party. It could not be pretended that this argument was ever applicable except to the case of small pauper tenants, and now the introduction of poor laws, and the increased demand for labour, put it out of any man's power to say that he is obliged to offer an exorbitant rent for a farm in order to save himself from destitution.

The argument never had any bearing on the case of those tenants who hold the greatest part of Ireland, who have capitals of two or three hundred pounds and upwards, and who are farmers, not from necessity, but from choice, because they find the occupation of a farmer more profitable or more suitable to their taste or education than any other employment. On the profits to be expected from their industry and capital it may necessary to make this remark. It is often said that agriculture is the most honourable, the most healthy, and the most delightful of all occupations. If this be the case, it follows from an elementary law of political economy that it must also be the least profitable. It will require greater profits to induce men to enter into any business that is less wholesome, less creditable, or less agreeable.

It should ever be remembered that it is a dishonest act for a man to make a contract which he does not believe that he can fulfil. The man who has obtained possession of a farm by promising a rent which he cannot afford to pay has committed a dishonest act. He has done wrong to the landlord, from whom he has obtained possession of the land on false pretences, and he has done wrong to the competitors for the farm whom he has outbid, and he has no just claim to have a law made to reduce his rent, and give him an advantage over his more honest competitors.

I should not have thought it necessary to point out the unreasonable injustice of the claim made for fixity of tenure on a rent to be settled by valuators, were it not for the mischief that is caused by the expectation of the measure. It not only diverts attention from more practicable means of improving the condition of the people, but it increases the desire (already too strong) to obtain, and to retain, possession of land, no matter how incapable the possessor may be of cultivating the property. There is a hope that the interest, which is now worth little or nothing, will be converted by law into a valuable estate. This hope vanishes if possession is transferred to another. The eviction from a farm is felt not as a loss of the interest which the tenant had, but as a loss of the interest which he hopes to acquire by a change in the law. In many cases a failing farmer, who could dispose of his farm for a sum that would enable him to emigrate or to set up himself or his family in some more profitable business, is tempted to hold on to his farm, by the belief that the approaching law of tenant right will give him an interest that he can dispose of for a much larger sum.

In some districts the agitation on the subject has fixed it like an axiom not to be controverted in the peasant's mind, that the possession of land, on whatever terms it is acquired, is a property which it is unjust to take

from him without paying him large compensation. The
relation between landlord and tenant is made the constant
subject of violent declamation. His imaginary rights are
assumed as if they were too clear for argument; and
indeed this is necessary, for they will not bear argument.

A landlord has twenty acres of land in his possession.
A peasant offers him twenty pounds a year for the land.
His offer is accepted. He is put into possession of the
land, but neglects to pay the rent, and finally he is
evicted, owing perhaps three years' arrears of rent, which
he never pays. He is considered an injured man, the
victim of landlord oppression. No questions are asked
about the merits of the case. The mere fact that he
has been deprived of his farm is sufficient to excite the
sympathies of the population, who will assist him to take
revenge, or to escape, after he has gratified his revenge
by murdering the tenant who succeeds, or his landlord,
or his agent, or any member of any of their families.
Others will take the part of justifying the murderer, or
blackening the character of the deceased. They will go
through the form of saying that it is not right to commit
murder, but they will exaggerate the provocation which
the murderer received; they will rake up charges true
or false against the deceased, and will at the same time
classify as murders of greater enormity many acts of
oppression never perpetrated, but which the populace
will readily credit.

In many cases the landlord is deterred from enforcing
his rights; and it is sometimes argued that it is therefore
no injustice to deprive him of them by law. The landlord, it is said, will suffer no substantial injury by being
deprived of a right which he can never venture to
enforce.

This is like putting a price upon the landlord's head.
It is to announce that everything will be conceded to the
tenants, provided they will shoot so many landlords as
may keep them for some time in subjection to the White-
boy code.

Success acquired by such means would not produce

the expected fruits. Riches acquired by fraud and
outrage are not long enjoyed, for the qualities by which
they are acquired are inconsistent with the qualities
which are necessary to retain them.

Anything that would retard the advance of the
country in civilization, and still more, anything that
would make it go back, would do an injury to the tenant
far beyond the value of anything that he could gain by
an alteration in the conditions of his tenure. The fee-
simple proprietor of a hundred acres of land two
centuries ago was not so well clothed, so well lodged, so
well taught, or so well fed, as the tenant of the same
lands who at the present time pays a fair rent for his farm.

This change is chiefly caused by the greater civilization
of Ireland. A very small part is caused by any improvements placed upon the land by the tenants. Not more
than ten per cent. of the present value of the land is
owing to such improvements.

The general question, how much of the improvements
made in the country is due to tenants, and how much to
landlords, or to possessors, whose tenure is substantially
equivalent to a fee, appears to be immaterial. When
once the tenant has received possession, his equitable
rights depend upon the contract which he has made, and
upon the condition of the land when he obtained possession. It is no concern of his how that condition was
caused. It may have been improved by the landlord, or
by a previous tenant, who may have received compensation from the landlord; or the previous tenant may have
wasted the land, or have run away owing large arrears
of rent, or have had his lease unjustly broken without
compensation for his improvements. With all this the
new tenant has nothing to do; he does not inherit the
claims or the liabilities of his predecessors.

On the whole, it would appear that the tenants would
have no just cause of complaint if, 1st, Such leasing
powers should be given to all landlords that no fair lease
should be broken; 2ndly, That when a tenant by lease
has improved his farm, he should be entitled to a fair
compensation; 3rdly, That when a yearly tenant has

improved his farm, or purchased the interest of an out
going tenant, he should be entitled to the seven years'
purchase tenant right on terms to be settled by an
<u>arbitrator</u>; 4th, That when there is no written contract,
the tenancy should be deemed to terminate on the 1st of
November, and the tenant be entitled to a year's notice
to quit.

As to evictions, the tenant can protect himself by
refusing to take a farm without security that he shall
enjoy it for a reasonable time.

I have made no allusion to a difference in race, as
creating any reason for a difference in legislation between
England and Ireland. When the Celt becomes the
absolute owner of land, he is just as willing as the Saxon
to become a landlord, and to insist upon all a landlord's
rights, which he then seems to think very reasonable.
It is only when he becomes a tenant that his peculiarity
is said to appear in a dislike to fulfil his engagements,
and in a wish to hold his land at a lower rent and for a
longer term than he is entitled to by his contract. I
suppose the Saxon farmer would have the same desire.
It is impossible to frame laws to suit the feelings of
people who dislike to pay their debts, or to fulfil their
engagements and to respect the rights of property, and
in general to act as men are required to do in every
civilized community. There is no valid foundation for
this charge against the Irish Celt. England had the
power of making laws for Ireland at a time when
selfishness reigned supreme in the councils of every
state; and Ireland, as the weaker country, suffered some
injustice from her stronger sister. But times are altered.
No man now would think of doing an injustice to
Ireland for the sake of any supposed benefit to England.
The two countries are now parts of one united kingdom.
All grievances have been swept away, although the
memory of them still remains, and will be kept alive by
the exertions of those who have an interest in fomenting
discontent. But a just policy will eventually bear its
fruits; and if the laws are framed for the good of all
without reference to party interests, and are impartially

and firmly administered, it will probably be found that
the Celt is as quiet and amenable to law, and as willing
to be honest and true to his engagements, as if he belonged
to any other race.

But even the best laws will be of little service unless
the people are disposed to act justly and reasonably.
The landlord should not strive to be the master of his
tenant.   He should set the land at a reasonable rent
and on fair conditions, and not hope to keep the tenant
in subjection, by exacting a rent which he cannot pay,
or inserting covenants which he cannot fulfil.   Even
when leases are granted they are often stuffed with
covenants which would ruin the tenant if he obeyed
them strictly.

But some change is also required in the tenant.   He
should not enter into any contract which he is unwilling
to fulfil.   It is no excuse for him to say that he cannot
get land on any other terms, and that he must be a
farmer as every other business is overcrowded with
competitors.   Such an excuse is contradictory to itself,
for if he cannot get a farm except by offering more than
it is worth, it shows that farming is subject to as keen a
competition as other trades.   If he cannot get a farm on
reasonable terms he should take to some other business,
or emigrate.   He may think that this is a great hardship,
but it is a hardship that is not caused either by the law
or by the landlord.   If two men desire to get the same
farm, one of them must do without it; and if the competitors are honest, and will not offer too much, the one
who succeeds will be better off, and the one who fails
will not be worse off than at present.   The same rule
that I suggest as to his rent should apply to all the
conditions of his tenure.

Instead of first taking a farm and then complaining of
the conditions, he should refuse to take any farm except
on such terms as he considers just and reasonable.

A man who is to have a voice in the government
of the country should not make any contract which
would make him dependent on the liberality or forbearance of any other man.

F 2

CHAPTER VIII.

IT is frequently said that in Ireland the landlord erects no buildings, and makes no improvements on the land; that everything is left to the tenant, who builds and improves at the risk of having the improvements made by his labour and capital seized by the landlord, or made an occasion of raising the rent; and that this was not a very unusual course for the landlord to take.

At no time was it a matter of every-day occurrence for a landlord to seize his tenant's improvements before he had enjoyed them for a remunerative period. Improving tenants without leases would not be so foolish as thus to lay out their capital without a confident expectation, founded on the prevailing customs, that the landlord would not take advantage of their confidence in his honour. Cases of inconsiderate and unjust harshness could never have been very frequent, and they are now exceedingly rare.

The real grievance was, not that the tenant frequently lost the value of his improvements, but that his liability to this loss generally prevented him from making those improvements which would have been profitable to himself and useful to the country.

It is true that if any man searches for cases of grievances suffered by tenants, he will have plenty of stories told to him: many of them will be utterly false, and many of them will have a slight foundation of truth, distorted by the most monstrous exaggerations. When names, dates, and facts, are not stated, it is impossible to expose and detect the falsehood. " One story is good until another is told."

I am told that a tenant held a farm at a rent of 40*l*., that he built a house at an expense of 100*l*., and then was ejected without any compensation as soon as he owed one year's rent. Such a story may lead to the murder of half-a-dozen landlords, or to the robbery of the entire class, when the propagator describes the look of inextinguishable hatred with which the narrator mentioned it to him. I do not believe in the possibility of such a case pure and simple. An ejectment is not a sudden irreversible process. The proceedings take some time to bring them to a termination; and, even after they are concluded, the law allows the tenant six calendar months to pay his rent and redeem the land. This period is reckoned not from the judgment in eject-ment, but from the actual dispossession of the tenant by the execution of the *habere*. The story, therefore, is that the tenant was rich enough to build a house and to cultivate his farm, which generally requires a capital equal to five years' rent, but that he could not get money to pay half a year's rent, and had not friends or credit to enable him to borrow money to pay his rent. A tenant is not evicted for non-payment of rent until after he has become hopelessly insolvent.

I should expect that on investigation it would be found, either that the story was totally false, or that it was subject to one or more of the following qualifications. The tenant did not build the house at his own expense; the landlord supplied the roof and timber-work, and gave other aid. The tenant was in the enjoyment of the house a sufficient length of time to recompense him for the portion of the outlay that he had incurred. The landlord at various times forgave him large arrears of rent in consideration of his outlay on the house. The tenant ran out and wasted the land, and owed consider-ably more than a year's rent at the time of the eviction. I suggest those qualifications to show with what reserve such a story should be received until it is fully investi-gated, especially when it is told by a person evidently anxious to make a case against Irish landlords.

I do not deny that, among the infinite number of cases

occurring between landlord and tenant, many may be found in which the landlord acted harshly and oppressively to an honest tenant, as well as cases in which the kindness of a generous landlord has met with a very ill-requital. But I believe that such cases are exceptions to the general rule, which is, that an honest and industrious tenant will meet with kind and generous treatment, and that a good and liberal landlord will find or make good tenants. But to state all the exceptions to this rule of which one hears on one side, without qualification or investigation, is not a good way of forming a correct opinion of the true state of the Irish land question. The cases in which landlords seized upon real improvements made by their tenants, without giving them compensation, are very few, and the landlords would suffer nothing by a law which would make such injustice impossible.

As to evictions of solvent tenants, I believe them to be more rare in Ireland than in England. To a superficial observer, the contrary might at first appear to be the case, for the following reason. In England, if the interest of a tenant is determined by a notice to quit, or by the expiration of his lease, and the refusal of the landlord to permit him to remain in possession, he gives up the farm, and nothing more is said about it. He merely complies with the conditions on which he obtained possession. But in Ireland he generally resists, and puts his landlord to the expense and delay of an ejectment, and has the newspapers filled with abuse of the landlord and articles on landlordism and evictions. Thus in Ireland nearly every case of removal of a tenant makes a noise, and is brought before the public, and therefore they appear to be more numerous than in England, where they pass without notice.

While I was writing this, I read in the newspaper a report of an action for a libel brought by a farmer. His complaint was that he was falsely accused of shooting foxes; and, on account of this false and unproved charge, he was deprived by a noble duke, his landlord, of two farms, one of which he had held for sixteen, and the other for twenty-one years. The eviction by the landlord was not made a matter of comment, and would have passed unnoticed, only that it was the special damage for which the action was brought. If a tenant was evicted on such grounds in Ireland, the circumstance would certainly be brought before the public, and probably before Parliament.

If there are a hundred men wishing for farms, and there are only fifty farms to be let, then fifty men must do without farms, and take to some other occupation. Whatever adds to the difficulty of evicting a tenant, adds to the difficulty of obtaining a farm, and thus makes the eviction a greater calamity when it occurs.

It is very much against the interests of a landlord to eject a good solvent tenant who is willing to pay him a fair rent. He will find it difficult to procure a tenant with skill and capital to take the vacant farm, and to put himself in the power of an oppressive and unreasonable landlord.

If a careful inquiry was made into the nature of the provocations which are supposed to have led to the late crop of agrarian outrages, a judgment might be formed of the frequency of landlord oppression. It would not be unreasonable to assume that all the worst instances would be included among those cases which have led to such extremity of revenge.

It may be generally said that four circumstances should combine to make a tenant an effectual improver. He must have, first, a sufficient motive; secondly, skill; thirdly, energy; fourthly, capital. And it is not an uncommon mistake, when some obvious improvement is neglected, to attribute the neglect solely to the want of some one of those circumstances, without taking the rest into consideration.

The landlord frequently is without the capital that is necessary for important improvements on his estate; for he must pay money for everything (in addition to his family and personal expenses), and the return for his expenditure comes in very slowly. But it is different with the tenant, who seldom wants capital to make some

small improvements yielding a quick return. In some
cases it might be thought that no capital was necessary,
as when a small farmer reclaims land by removing the
stones, all the work being done by himself and his family.
Some would say that his labour was equivalent to capital,
but this would not be strictly correct. The produce of
his labour did not support him during the progress of the
work. The store of food which he possessed, or the
money with which he purchased it, was the capital which
he expended in the prosecution of the work. Without
such capital, or credit to supply its place, he must have
abandoned the improvement, and supported himself by
working for daily wages.

Thus the tenant is seldom prevented from making improvements by want of capital. He may be prevented
from undertaking something grand, but if his land is in a
very wild, unimproved state, there must be some reason
other than want of capital for his permitting it to remain so.

For this neglected state of the land a different reason.
is given by the landlords and the tenants' friends. One
says that the cause is, that the tenant has not a sufficient
estate in the land, and Arthur Young's exaggerated assertion is quoted as if it was strictly true. But excuses
for not doing a thing are always to be viewed with great
suspicion, especially when they take the form of requiring some great boon as a preliminary to exertion.

I have known many cases in which the occupier held
in perpetuity or for very long terms, in which the agriculture was as defective and the land as much neglected
as if it had been held by tenants at will. A good
interest given to the tenant is a good thing, but it
removes only one impediment to improvement, namely,
want of motive ; but two impediments may yet remain—
sloth and ignorance.

Bishop Berkeley, indignant at the neglected appearance of the country, the houses full of dirt, and the land
covered with weeds, rejected this excuse of want of a
sufficiently long estate in the tenant, and remarked that
things were left undone which would be remunerative if

done by tenants even with the shortest leases, and that the Irish proprietors who occupied land which they held in fee were as slovenly and negligent as any tenants at will. He thus arrived unfairly at the conclusion that the cause of the neglected state of the land was Irish sloth. He did not see that there was a third cause which might be the operative one, namely, ignorance.

The Irish tenant acted according to his limited knowledge. He had no example to guide him to a better agriculture. Even if a resident gentleman improved his demesne, and made it more productive, the farmer saw clearly that he could not follow the example. The improvement seldom yielded a fair return for the outlay. Works were undertaken with a mixed view to ornament and utility. This was better for the country than if the same money had been spent in idle dissipation; but they conveyed no useful instruction to the farmer. It may be fairly doubted whether any improvement of land yields the average return that may be expected from invested capital. Thus I do not say that no drainage pays; but if all the drainage in Ireland was taken with the mistakes made by inadequate or superfluous drains, or drains badly made, or too deep, or too shallow, or too expensively, or works otherwise unskilfully executed, it is probable that half the works do not yield a return of five per cent. on the outlay. But a farmer will not undertake an expensive improvement, unless he is reasonably certain, not only that his landlord will not seize upon the fruits, but that there will be some fruits for himself to enjoy. Thus the want of agricultural knowledge is a serious obstacle to improvements.

There are some improvements which give a return in comfort and enjoyment, rather than in profit. A dwelling-house is of this class. In general a man does not willingly live in a worse house than that to which he has been accustomed; but he seldom desires one much better. It is very much a matter of habit. The starving occupier of a fetid, squalid hovel would wish for strong drink and tobacco, better and more abundant food, good clothes and less work; but the last of his desires would be a larger and cleaner house. He would scarcely accept it willingly on the terms of his keeping it clean and in good repair.

This has tended to discourage the landlords from building good houses for their tenants. They found that the tenants did not value them, and were often unwilling to keep them in repair, although it was generally found that after some experience they felt and appreciated the advantage of the decency and cleanliness which at first they disliked as cold and troublesome. Partly by the landlords, and partly by the tenants, comfortable farmhouses have been built, and improvement in this respect is still making progress. In a few instances, houses have been built by tenants relying on the honour of their landlords ; and very few would object to a law that would entitle a tenant to compensation who built a house suitable to his farm.

In many arguments on the compensation that a tenant should receive for his improvements, a calculation is made of the compensation or enjoyment that would be sufficient if the improvement was made in the most successful manner, and with the greatest skill and economy. This is hardly fair. Every improvement is to a certain extent tentative, and the enjoyment or compensation should be such as to remunerate a tenant of average skill and good fortune.

It is frequently said that drainage will repay the first outlay with interest in seven years. I do not assert that such a thing never happens, but I am sure that it could not be truly said of one-tenth of the drains that have been made in the United Kingdom.

It requires less skill to reclaim than to improve. The former is done either by carrying off surface water or by removing stones. These works are done by the cottier and his family. They yield a very moderate return, but the results are obvious to the most unskilful, and hence it happens that they are often executed by tenants with very precarious interests, while more profitable works, requiring more skill and foresight, are left undone by tenants with much longer leases. If sloth was very prevalent, the sterile land would not have been reclaimed ;

if want of tenure was the only cause, the good land would have been more generally improved. It was want of skill that confined the efforts of the most energetic to those works which required no skill to accomplish or to appreciate them.

Arthur Young describes the effects of letting land on profitable leases to persons without skill or energy : " They are, however, sometimes resident on a part of the land they hire, where it is natural to suppose they would work some improvements ; it is, however, very rarely the case. I have in different parts of the kingdom seen farms fallen in after leases of three lives of the duration of fifty, sixty, and even seventy years, in which the residence of the principal tenant was not to be distinguished from the cottared fields surrounding it." He attributes this to the idle, drunken habits of the small country gentlemen : " Living upon the spot, surrounded by their little under-tenants, they prove the most oppressive species of tyrant that ever lent assistance to the destruction of a country. Not satisfied with screwing up the rent to the uttermost farthing, they are rapacious and relentless in the collection of it." " If long leases at low rents, and profit incomes given would have improved it, Ireland had long ago been a garden." Such were the results of long leases given to persons ignorant of agriculture, and without efficient covenants to prevent them from subletting. If they had been possessed of sufficient skill, they would have found it more profitable to cultivate than to sublet.

CHAPTER IX.

Many think that the wealth of Ireland may be increased by the cultivation of new crops, or the employment of new instruments, which they accordingly recommend with great zeal. They are not aware of the difficulty of introducing improvements in agriculture, nor how little profit the persons who adopt them should expect. Nevertheless, several improvements in both crops and instruments have made their way in Ireland in the present century. Improved carts and ploughs have almost superseded the old-fashioned car and plough which were in general use seventy years ago. Through a great part of Ireland the threshing machine is used instead of the flails, and the scythe instead of the sickle. The American rake and the tedding machine are used in making hay, and even reaping and mowing machines may sometimes be seen in use.

But the use of new machines proceeds more slowly in agriculture than in manufactures. It is less necessary to the individual, as it does not diminish the price of agricultural produce, and therefore the farmer may, without loss, continue to cultivate his land in the manner to which he has been accustomed.

But the chief impediment is, that the operations of agriculture are periodic, and not continuous, and the division of labour does not produce a division of trades. The same loom may be employed every day in the year; and if one loom did its work at half the cost of another, no weaver could hold his ground who used the inferior loom. But a machine of great efficiency in sowing turnip seed may make its way very slowly.

The farmer would have occasion to use it only two or three days in the year, and the advantage of its use during those few days is all that is obtained to pay the interest of the first cost of the machine, and the expense of finding a place to hold it during the long time that it is unemployed. This latter item is not unimportant in the case of a small farm. Besides, sowing turnip seed is only a small part of the business of a farmer, and he may till with profit, although he does not perform this particular operation in the cheapest and most efficient manner. The same observations apply, with greater or less force, to all the operations of the farm.

Similar causes impede the introduction of new crops, or new modes of cultivation. The work that is done only at intervals of a year is not easily learned. When once it has taken root this difficulty is diminished, for the difference between the earliest and latest period of performing any operation extends the time during which the business may be learned by observation or by actual work.

Thus, if you introduce the cultivation of flax into a district into which it was not known before : it is necessary to steep it ; you superintend this operation, and give the most precise instructions to your workmen. The work is done, they are employed during the rest of the year on other business, and when the season for the same operation comes round again they will be found as ignorant as they were the preceding year.

Still some new crops have been introduced with advantage during the present century. Seventy years ago, turnips and mangolds were unknown to the working farmer, and even clover and artificial grasses were seldom sown except by a gentleman farmer.

The manner in which the cultivation of flax has been almost confined to one province of Ireland shows very strongly the difficulty of introducing the general cultivation of a new crop. It is not unknown in the other provinces, but it is generally profitable only in Ulster. This is not caused by any peculiarity of soil or climate.

The crop is equally good in other parts; but it is
not equally profitable, and missionaries go about in vain
recommending its cultivation. Some say that a large
profit may be expected; others say that they have tried
it, and found it unprofitable. A short sketch of flax
culture may show the cause of this disagreement, and
how the true state of the case may be discovered.

I give an account of the culture as it existed at the
beginning of this century, and of some of the changes
that have since been made :—

1. Having prepared the land as if for oats, but with a
finer tilth, the seed is sown rather thickly in order that
the flax may be drawn up without sending out side
branches.

2. When the flax is fit, which is generally before the
seeds are ripe, it is pulled up instead of being cut like
corn. This is not an operation of much difficulty.

3. It is then carried to a dub, or flax pond, to be steeped.
This is necessary to detach the outside fibre, which is the
valuable product of the flax, from the inside woody part,
which is worthless. This is an operation of some nicety.
If it is overdone, the quality of the flax may be injured.
If it is underdone, the fibre will be wasted in the subsequent operations. The duration of the steeping must
depend upon the temperature. The experienced flax
cultivator forms his judgment by the sight, and smell,
and taste.

4. It is then taken out of the dub, and carted to a
field, where it is spread and dried. The spreading may
be done by men, women, or children. The taking out
of the dub and spreading are not operations of much
difficulty; but a practised hand will do the work better
and more cheaply than a novice.

5. When the flax is sufficiently dried, it is gathered,
and bound in sheaves, and put into stocks, and sometimes
into stacks or ricks, like corn.

6. The next operation is scutching, or beating the
flax with a heavy wooden mallet. The steeping dissolved
and destroyed the glutinous matter which fastened the
wood to the fibre; but it is still enclosed by the fibre,

and the scutching is necessary to break into small parts
the wood, which has been made very brittle by the steeping and drying, in order that it may more readily escape
between the threads of the fibre.   The scutching should
break the wood as much as it can be done without injury
to the fibre.

7. The next operation is cloving.   The cloves are
made of two small boards, or a board and piece of iron ;
they move on a hinge or pivot, and meet each other
edgeways.   The operator takes a handful of flax, and
places the part near his right hand between the cloves ;
he then presses the upper clove on the flax with his left
hand, and with his right pulls the flax through.   This
operation, repeated several times, forces the broken wood
between the fibres, and rubs it away from the flax, which
remains in the clover's hands.   Some of the fibre is
necessarily broken in this operation, and is detached
along with the broken wood.   This is called tow, which
is an inferior product.   The quantity of waste depends
upon the skill of the clover, and the efficiency of the
preceding operations, as well as upon the quality of the
flax.   Cloving is often performed with great skill by women.

8. The next operation is hackling.   This requires
more skill and more expensive instruments than any of
the preceding operations.   It is frequently performed by
women.   The hackle is a board about six inches by four
inches.   On one of the longer sides there is a handle.
One face of the board is covered with a number of sharp
steel spikes from three to five inches long, according to
the fineness of the hackle.   The hackler takes a bunch
of the fibre in hand and swings it gently on the spikes of
the hackle and draws it through the spikes.   This is
repeated several times to disentangle the fibres, and to
reduce them to parallel threads, and to remove the small
particles of wood which, after the cloving, still remain
adhering to the fibre.   An awkward person may seriously injure his hand on the spikes, or by injudicious
force may break the fibre, and tear some of it away,
producing worthless tow instead of valuable thread.
Sometimes it is passed through several hackles in-

creasing successively in fineness. It is then made up
into suitable hanks or parcels.

9. The next operation is spinning, which I need not
describe. After being spun on the spinning-wheel (in
the last century the distaff and spindle were often used),
it is reeled off, and made into hanks of thread or yarn.

10. The next operation is weaving, which I need not
describe.

11. The next operation is bleaching, which formerly
consisted in washing the linen well, and spreading it on
the grass, frequently watering it until it became white
under the influence of the sun and air.

The Ulster small farmer performed all these operations with the aid of his family. This domestic manufacture was carried on during the spare hours for which
the farm found no employment. As generally happens
in such cases, the produce was sold at a price which
gave the workers a very small remuneration. The work
cost them nothing; I may say, less than nothing, as it
saved the family from those evil habits which idleness
seldom fails to engender.

The above short sketch may give an idea of the
difficulties which prevented the introduction of the
culture and manufacture into the other provinces. It
could only be extended from neighbour to neighbour,
and when the continuity was broken by mountains, and
by the fertile plains of Leinster, in which flax could not
be profitably cultivated, the rest of the island was deprived of the best means of acquiring the necessary skill.

Some changes have been made in the manufacture
which may facilitate the extension of flax culture. The
manufacture and the agriculture are becoming more distinct. In the first place the process of bleaching is no
longer carried on by the farmer. Mere grass bleaching
has disappeared, and the chemical processes can be more
cheaply conducted in large establishments. Still, on
this point, Ulster has some advantages in the possession
of bleach greens, in which, in consequence of the scale in
which their business is done, linen can be bleached more
cheaply than in the other provinces.

Flax is now almost always sent to scutch-mills instead of being scutched at home by the farmers. The spinning has also become a separate manufacture, and only a small portion is spun in the cottage of the grower. The power-loom has reduced the profits of the hand-loom weaver ; and even when the hand-loom is used, the trade is carried on under a new system. Intermediate men, called drapers, purchase yarn and give it out to weavers, who work for wages. The draper by his capital and skill in buying yarn and selling linen can undersell the weaver who works on his own account. The customer gets his goods cheaper, although an additional profit is received. The manufacture has outrun the agriculture. There is not enough of flax grown in Ulster to supply the manufacturers.

It will not be easy to introduce the hand-loom to extensive use in the other provinces. The wages of the weaver are low ; in some parts of the year they are less than those of the ordinary agricultural labourer. In Ulster, where the business is learned in the family, he remains in the trade from habit, notwithstanding the competition of the power-loom ; but in the other provinces there is little inducement to go out of the way to learn a business in which the wages are so low. The same friction that prevents its departure from Ulster tends to prevent its establishment in Munster.

On the whole, the changes are favourable to the other provinces ; but Ulster retains some advantage in the skill acquired by long experience, and in the possession of those establishments in which flax is prepared or manufactured. It remains to be seen whether flax can be successfully cultivated in the south and west of Ireland. Some say that it can, others say that it cannot ; and the accounts are usually furnished in such a manner as not to give the information that might settle the dispute.

They ought to state the extent and value of the land, the quantity and price of the seed, the number of men, women, and children employed on each operation, and for what number of days, and the wages paid to each. The quantity of flax at the commencement and end of each operation should be stated, and the quantity in the final state in which it is sold, and the price received for it. If this is done, it will be seen at once why one loses and another gains. It will be seen what processes are carried on at too great expense or too much waste of material.

Flax is an exhausting crop, and does not enter conveniently into any course of rotation. It is most suitable for small farmers, as it finds employment for their families. Any person who watches the operations before the scutching, that is, before it becomes a manufacture, will probably come to the conclusion that if he paid even moderate wages to the workers he would not find it easy to make any profit out of a field of flax.

The cultivation of madder, and of sugar-beet, has been recommended, and they may be tried by any one who can afford the experiment ; but it is easier to learn how to improve the cultivation of the known crops than how to raise a new crop profitably.

If the produce of the soil could be doubled, it would not diminish the discontent of the Irish tenantry. Their complaint is, not that the land is unproductive, but that it is not theirs. It is a dispute for property, and at present any increase in the productive powers of the land would only embitter the contest by enhancing the value of the prize.

As the evils presented themselves to my mind, I could not forbear from considering whether any remedies could be found. I considered that the following principles should be kept in view :—

1st. There should be no injustice nor confiscation of property.

2nd. There should be no interference with freedom of contract, and the law should do nothing to encourage those modes of dealing which are least beneficial to the nation. An apparently immaterial law in constant operation may have an important effect in moulding the habits of the people. It is even possible that the relation between landlord and tenant may have been influenced by the fact that a stamp is necessary for a lease, but no stamp is required on a notice to quit.

3rd. The landlord, subject to all express or implied contracts, and to all equities arising from past transactions, is entitled to the present value of the land, and to all increase in its value which does not arise from the acts of the tenants. Independent of the injustice, it would be impolitic to deprive the landlord of all interest in his estate, and to remove him from his natural position as the guide and friend and assistant of the tenant in the management of his farm. It would produce extensive absenteeism, by converting the landlords into mere receivers of fixed rents, without any interests in their estates. They would be an idle, useless, unhappy body of men, without any incentive to work, or any special duty or occupation.

4th. Although the tenant should not get his landlord's property for nothing, he ought not to be deprived of anything for which he paid with the concurrence of the landlord, although he may have trusted to the rules of natural equity, instead of complying with all the formalities required by a highly artificial state of the law.

Lastly, although men cannot be compelled to perform duties of imperfect obligation, they ought not to be permitted by any contract or promises to put the performance of those duties out of their power. Thus no settlement or incumbrance should prevent the landlord while in the enjoyment of his estate from dealing in a liberal spirit with his tenantry. Every landlord ought to have it in his power to give either a parliamentary tenant right, or a lease of forty-one years at a reasonable rent, and to make an agreement to compensate a tenant for his improvements.

It may be thought by many that in suggesting forty-one years I have named too long a term, and that a lease of twenty-one years would give a tenant sufficient enjoyment to compensate him for any improvement, except buildings, that he might make on his farm. To this it may be answered that, generally, the Irish tenant is not of this opinion, and that a lease of twenty-one

G 2

years would not induce him to improve. That a lease
for forty-one years is much shorter than a lease for three
lives, which is commonly permitted by marriage settlements, and that it is not the length of the lease at its
commencement, but the length of the term when the
tenant is about to improve that is the operative inducement.   A prudent tenant will not make any change
immediately on his obtaining possession of his farm.   He
will wait until experience has made him intimately
acquainted with its wants and capabilities.   If all leases
were granted for terms of twenty-one years, the unexpired terms would be of the average length of only ten
and a half years, and if they were granted for terms of
forty-one years, the average unexpired terms would be
six months less than twenty-one years.

With such an extension of leasing powers to the landlord, and with a right to the tenant to get compensation
for his improvements, and a parliamentary tenant right
whenever he has fairly earned it, the chief grievances
would be remedied without any violent interference with
the rights of property.

But if a man voluntarily enters into a contract to take
land with a precarious tenure, he has no right to demand
to have it made permanent until he has done something
to earn an enlargement of his estate.   To accede to such
a demand might do a serious injury, not to himself indeed,
but to his class.   If the rights arising from mere occupation are made too strong, men who have land in their
possession will be very careful not to let a new occupier
get possession, and the poor will be relegated to densely-
packed villages.   The owner of land may be disposed
to give a labourer the occupation of a comfortable cottage
and garden.   This will be a great benefit to the labourer
at a very slight loss or inconvenience to the landowner;
but it is essential that the occupation should be precarious, so as to prevent the labourer from making that
occupation a source of great discomfort to the landlord.
If the labourer neglects his work, or has ill-conducted
children, or harbours persons of bad character, or even
keeps pigs and poultry, frequently trespassing on the

landlord's property, it will be necessary to resume possession from him. There may be many other cases, which I need not enumerate here. Call the landlord's conduct capricious, arbitrary, tyrannical, or by any other epithet of abuse, it is necessary that he should have the power of removing the cottier on a reasonable notice, or he will not put any cottier in possession of any land. The option in future will not be between a fixed and a precarious occupation, but between a precarious tenure and nothing.

The same loss to the labourer will ensue if the landlord cannot obtain possession without expense at law, or being held up to public odium as a tyrant and oppressor. He will consider all the consequences which are likely to result from the reception of a cottier tenant, and if either law or custom makes those consequences grievous to him, he will be so much the less willing to give accommodation to the labourer.

CHAPTER X.

PROPERTY in land differs in its origin from property in any commodity produced by human labour. The product of labour naturally belongs to the labourer who produced it. If he works for wages, his employer is entitled to the product as assignee of the labourer. The substance of the contract is, that the employer pays a certain present sum as wages in exchange for the future uncertain product of the labour.

But the same argument does not apply to land, which is not the product of labour, but is the gift of the Creator of the world to mankind. Every argument used to give an ethical foundation for the exclusive right of property in land has a latent fallacy. It omits a portion of the value which ought not to be left out of consideration. I shall call attention to one or two of them.

First comes the argument founded on the rights of labour. Land, it is said, is worthless until it is cleared and cultivated, and it properly belongs to the man who has improved it, or brought it into cultivation. There would be some force in this argument if land was worth nothing beyond the value of the labour laid out upon it; but if this is not the case, the argument is subject to this objection, that it permits one man to improve another man's estate, and then hold it as his own. This is what is called improving a man out of his property. Here is some land very convenient and suitable as a site for building, it belongs to no person as private property, and therefore I, as a member of the community, am a part owner of it. Another person takes possession and builds a valuable house on it, and then claims the land as exclusive property on account of his buildings and improvements; am not I thereby improved out of my estate? I was a part owner once, and now I have no interest whatever in it. Land of very indifferent quality in the neighbourhood of a town frequently is sold or let for a large sum as a site for building, before a single penny has been laid out in reclaiming it. Although it is of no present use, still its capacity for being built on gives it a present value.

In this case the original value can be estimated, and in fact it is often separated from the additional value which the land derives from the buildings placed on it. It is the ground-rent which a tenant would be willing to pay on condition of getting a grant of the land in perpetuity.

But without any reference to building-land, it is easy to find large quantities of land in Ireland of which the value cannot be attributed to any labour expended on them. Indeed, some of the land is probably of less value than if it had been left in a state of nature; and yet it is private property.

It might at first appear as if the argument against the right to property in land as founded on labour applied equally to the case of manufactured articles. The raw material did belong to the community, which is deprived of it by the individual who manufactures it, and converts it into his own exclusive property. This objection would be valid if the raw material was in limited quantities; and if the labourer, for the purpose of the manufacture, seized upon a greater proportion than his share would be as a member of the general community. But this never happens. As a matter of fact, the value as well as the right of property in a manufactured article is derived from the labour employed in producing it; and the title could generally be shown through the most important stages. It is equally certain that neither the title to property in land nor the chief part of its value is founded upon labour. It was in general claimed as property before any labour was laid out on it. The right arising from the first discovery is sometimes alluded to as a possible foundation for the right of property in land. But this must refer to the right of the whole community, and not to the right of any private individual. When once a party lands upon an island, the whole island is substantially discovered. They all know the land is there, although they have not actually walked over every foot of it. But suppose the case of a discovery made by an individual. A party of men and women discover an uninhabited island, and take possession of it. Good water for drinking is scarce, and different persons go in various directions. One man, either by superior intelligence or better fortune, discovers a well which yields an ample supply. This does not give him a right to exclude the rest of the party. They must possess the same natural right which they had before the discovery, to use the well if they can find it. The right of the first discoverer is merely to keep his secret, or to sell it to the community for the best price which he can obtain for it.

The case bears some analogy to the patent laws, and therefore I may allude to an argument which is sometimes used in their defence. A man invents some process, and it is said that if the public makes use of this process he is deprived of the fruits of his industry and inventive talent. But this assumes the very point in dispute: it assumes that one of the natural fruits of a discovery is the right to prohibit every other person from doing the same thing. This is not a well-founded assumption. His natural right is only to use it himself. The first man who broke a cocoa-nut and found the inside eatable would have a right to eat it himself, but he would have no right to insist that no other man in the world should ever eat any other cocoa-nut without his permission.

The fact of possession is sometimes given as the origin of private property in land. The man who gets first under the shade of a tree has a right to remain there undisturbed. He cannot be removed without a breach of the peace; and this right seems to be acknowledged by the inferior animals. It is sometimes added, that the mere fact of taking possession is of itself an act of labour, and therefore that the right of property thereby conferred is within the general rule, that labour creates a right to property.

To this it may be replied, that this right, if it existed, would only last as long as the possession in which it originated. It could not extend over a large estate, nor be transferred to another person. As to the acknowledgment of the right by the lower animals; even if we were disposed to learn ethics from their example, there is great reason to doubt the fact. It probably exists only so far as the beast in possession has sufficient strength to make it inconvenient for any other beast to disturb him.

When it is said that the mere taking of possession is an act of labour, it should be noticed that even if it deserves the name of labour, it is not of that sort which can confer a title to property. The only labour which can give a title to property is that labour which has created the value of the property that it claims.

The foundation of the right to property in land is not ethical but political. Its origin is expediency. In order that it may be cultivated to the most advantage, it is necessary that the cultivator should be secured in the enjoyment of the fruits of his intended industry. For this purpose it is necessary that the person who is permitted to use the land should be permitted to enjoy it for a certain length of time, to make it his interest to cultivate it in the most productive manner. This period varies with the increase of forsesight and agricultural knowledge.

It is easy to conceive a state of things in which men did not look beyond the passing year. They sowed and they reaped without any knowledge or care whether the land is left in a better or worse condition.

But the inconvenience of a frequent repartition of land is quickly perceived, and this is best avoided by permitting land to be held in absolute ownership, subject to such taxes and regulations as the State shall from time to time think it reasonable to impose.

It seems just that land should be charged with the

duty of maintaining the poor, so that no man should be destitute on account of the existence of private property in land.   Those who are able to support themselves owe that power to that general wealth and civilization which could not have existed without the establishment of private property in land ; and those who are not able to support themselves, receive from the poor-rates a better subsistence than they could extract from their share of the land of the country if undivided and unreclaimed.

But the rights of the present owners do not depend upon the truth of any theory respecting the origin of proprietorial rights.   It is a rule of natural justice that says that, if I encourage a stranger to buy from a wrongful owner property that is really mine, I cannot justly press my own claims against the purchaser.   This is the case with land in every settled country.   The present owners either themselves purchased the land, or derive their rights under those who purchased it with the sanction of the community, represented by the authority of the State.   In many cases, the State itself received part of the purchase money from stamp-duties on the purchase deeds.

In this manner, the title of the landlord appears to be perfect as well against the nation at large as against every member of it.   But there is one person in particular who cannot claim the land without the most shameless dishonesty ; and that is the tenant who has obtained a temporary possession of the land by means of a contract with the landlord.

I wish for a farm.   I see one that suits me.   I apply to the person in possession, who claims to be the owner, and I agree to take a lease of it for twenty-one years, or as tenant from year to year at a rent of 50*l.* a year, and to give him back the farm when the lease expires. Nothing can be clearer than that I can claim no right to that land beyond what is given to me by the lease.   It either belongs to the landlord who bought, or to the nation at large, but certainly not to me.   If it belongs to the landlord, I can claim nothing but my bargain, viz., possession for twenty-one years.   If it belongs to the community at large, my right is still less.   It would be strange that I should claim more than my bargain, because I made the bargain with the wrongful owner.

I have put the case of a tenant obtaining the possession of land by a contract with the landlord, and on that possession, on that contract, resting his claim to hold the land for a larger period or at a smaller rent. But there are other cases in which the tenant has done something more, and in which he has some equitable rights, which, although they are rather vague, are yet, I think, capable of being ascertained, settled, and conceded by carefully-considered legislation. The two chief cases are—first, where the tenant has made such permanent improvements on the land as were necessary for its efficient cultivation, or for his decent and wholesome habitation; secondly, where the tenant has to the reasonable knowledge of the landlord paid the outgoing tenant money for his interest in the farm.

In the former case, it must be supposed that the tenant made the improvements, or erected the buildings, in the belief that he would be permitted to enjoy them. It is incredible that any man should build a house if he was assured that another should enjoy all the benefit, either by turning him out, or by charging him rent for it. The same argument applies to the case of a purchase of a precarious interest. The landlord who permits the purchase of a mere tenancy-at-will must be considered as encouraging the belief that the purchaser thereby acquires a substantial interest in the land.

A third case in which the tenant seems to be entitled to something more than the law gives him, is where he has made a reasonable bargain with the apparent owner of the land. There is a common-sense distinction between a purchaser and a tenant which the law does not sufficiently recognize. The man who buys an estate, and the man who takes a farm in order to earn his bread by its cultivation, are treated by law in the same manner, and are subject to the complicated laws of real property. These laws are troublesome and inconvenient so far as they affect purchasers, but are oppressive and unjust where they disturb the title of a tenant.

It may be said that it is not easy to distinguish
between a tenant and a purchaser. A man takes a lease
of land for a thousand years at a rent of a penny an
acre. Is he not to be considered a purchaser, although
he takes the land for a limited term and is subject to a
rent? Add a penny to his rent, and take a year away
from his term, he is still a purchaser. Continue this
process, and you may have him paying a rent of 4*l*. 2*s*. 6*d*.
an acre, and with a term of only ten years. He is then
clearly a tenant. At what step in the process did his
position change from a purchaser to a tenant?

Such an argument has no practical force. It must be
met by drawing an arbitrary line at some reasonable
point. Say that a tenant, whose rent is not less than
three-fourths of the value, and whose term does not
exceed forty-one years, shall not be disturbed in consequence of any settlement or incumbrance affecting his
landlord's interests.

It is inconsistent with justice that a man should hold
land at a certain rent, and for a certain term, without
any claim except that he took the land for a different
term and for a different rent. A man takes a farm to-
day, and demands that a law shall be made which would
enable him to sell his lease next day for several hundred
pounds. This is to give him a property which he did
not purchase or earn, merely because he threatens to
commit murder if he is kept to his engagements.

However, no demand founded in justice ought to be
refused, merely on account of the improper manner in
which it is demanded. I must not refuse to pay a creditor
because he presents his account or demands payment in
an uncivil manner.

I have made these observations on the origin of property in land in order to show that the State retains the
power of modifying it from time in accordance with the
general interests of the community. This right of private
property in land is a political not a natural institution.
"Nam propriæ telluris herum, natura neque illum, Nec
me, nec quenquam statuit."

What justice requires is that changes in the law

should not be directed against any particular persons, but that all who are in similar circumstances should be treated in the same manner. A land-tax of ten per cent. would not be unjust if it was thought necessary for the security of the kingdom ; and there would be as little injustice in a law which modified the rights of property for the same object, even although the result should be equivalent to a tax by causing some diminution in the value of the property.

It is sometimes supposed that a change in the law would be unjust to purchasers under the Landed Estates Court. I see no grounds for that opinion. The Act of Parliament which constituted the Court did not give a guarantee against future legislation. To do that is beyond the power of Parliament. What the conveyance of the judges gives is the perfect right to the land, subject only to the adverse rights mentioned in the deed, and to such obligations as may afterwards be imposed, either by the purchaser or by the authority of Parliament. It may almost be said that the latter comes within the former case, as the House of Commons is the lawful representative of the purchaser.

It could hardly be contended that the purchaser with a parliamentary title should be exempt from all Acts passed for the relief of the poor, or that the area of poor-law taxation should not be altered, and yet such changes might have the effect of giving his poorer tenants a substantial interest in his estate.

What the purchaser has a right to insist on is, that no law shall be specially directed against him, and that no rights shall be set up which were in existence at the time of his purchase, but were omitted from the deed of conveyance. But in common with all the subjects of the realm, he must take subject to all regulations that may be made by lawful authority, whether they increase or diminish the value of his property. The purchaser, by the fact of his purchases, places himself in a new relation to a certain number of persons, which imposes on him some very important duties, and it is for the State to determine whether those duties shall be enforced by law or trusted to his own conscience for their fulfilment.

The following changes might be made in the law of real property, and they do not violate any natural or political right.

First, the law of primogeniture should be abolished, and all the children of the same parents, and their descendants should have equal rights to the land of their direct or collateral ancestor. Under the influence of this new law absenteeism would quickly disappear. Some of the children of an absentee would sell the estate which descended on them, and for which, not having seen it, they could entertain no special affection.

No lease nor agreement between landlord and tenant should be liable to any stamp-duty.

No settlement or encumbrance should prevent the owner of land in possession from having the following power :—First,—He may make any lease for any term not exceeding forty-one years at a rent not less than three-fourths of the full value, or competition rent. Second,—He may take a fine on granting a lease. Third,—He may agree that the tenant shall be entitled to tenant right as above defined. Fourth,—He may agree with his tenant to give him compensation for improvements.

If a lease is made for a shorter term than forty-one years, the landlord should not be permitted to distrain for rent.

If a lease is made for a shorter term than forty-one years, and without tenant right, all poor-rate and county cess should be borne by the landlord.

No proceedings should be taken to recover any arrear of rent which accrued more than a year before the commencement of the proceeding.

In the absence of a written agreement, the tenancy should determine on the first of November, and require a year's notice to quit.

The arbitrator should have power to award parliamentary tenant right to any tenant who had fairly earned it by his outlay.

The tenant should be entitled to the trees he planted, without the necessity of registering them.

II.

THE LAND-LAWS OF ENGLAND.

By C. Wren Hoskyns, M.P.

MORE than a generation has passed away since a late
Professor of Geology, in addressing the Royal Agricultural Society at their first country-meeting, held
at Oxford, arrested the attention of his landed and
farming auditory by the remark, that the perfect model
of a Plough, and of a Ship, still furnished to the world
of science matter of unsatisfied inquiry and speculation.
The speaker cited these familiar instances,—and he
could hardly have made a more skilful choice,—to
illustrate the proposition that some of the deepest
problems underlie our commonest uses, problems that
seem never to wear out or to grow old by time, but
reappear from age to age, linking the old world and the
new, by questions that equally defy the decision of
authority and the conquest of science.

In the interval that has elapsed since the words were
uttered, in all the confidence of knowledge that continues
to mark each "ignorant present time" of the world's
history—it will be admitted that the advances made by
the "audax Iapeti genus" in the forms that plough both
land and ocean, have given to them a force little
intended, or even dreamt of, by the speaker: yet the
challenge still remains that seemed almost antiquated
then, and perhaps the words conveying it are but the
formula for an equally pregnant future.   Why it is that
the most enduring questions should seem to link themselves often with what is most familiar to our daily

practice, is a matter of inquiry beyond the present purpose; but there are few experienced minds whose thoughts do not bear testimony to the existence of what may be termed standing difficulties in common things.

One of these, holding a place anterior to most—if not in point of time, yet certainly in importance—connected as it is with the history of our common inheritance, is that of the Laws of the Soil, the individual right to use, to hold, to dispose of it, by gift, or sale, to others, to transmit it by descent, or will, to the next generation,—and, resulting out of all these, its general distribution amongst the various classes and members of the community.

Old as the subject is—for it must be nearly coeval with man's social existence,—and worn as much by modern treatment as by mere age, yet it can hardly be denied that it comes to us little simplified, if not rather complicated by time, and the usage it has found among the various families of our race, who have, in truth, exhibited few differences more characteristic, more ethnologically marked, than those arising out of national habits in reference to the soil.

The grazier, the sportsman, even that picturesque terror of our childhood, now rarely seen, the encamped gipsy,—has each his ancient prototype in tribes and races having this feature in common, that to each of them the earth presented simply so much space to move in, and to use as suited their temporary wants or convenience. No law of *meum* and *tuum* was written upon the Waste, or grew out of it, for those to whom not even a fixed habitation had yet suggested the idea of 'property' in the land.

But as soon as *tillage* comes upon the scene, even in its earliest and rudest form, a very different claim to that implied in the mere surface use begins to develop itself. It needs no abstract description: we have it in familiar shape before our eyes, in the settlements of our own race in America and Australasia—where, in the dealings with some of the non-cultivating native races, the idea of purchase—as a contract of *permanent* and exclusive right— of irredeemable alienation—was almost as unintelligible on one side as its violation was on the other.

It can hardly with reason be doubted that the laws of the soil, including the first idea of permanent proprietary right (for even the hunter of the Prairie claims a temporary sole possession) owed their very birth to tillage. Land does not become *soil* till cultivation has made it so : the process, when accomplished, is as much a manufacture as the implement that effected it, —as the plough-beam shaped from the timber, or the coulter from the smelted iron. If it could only be *carried away* after the conversion, it would have spared the world some ingenious arguments on both sides of the question of exclusive property. Had the agricultural fact been kept in view that a Seed-bed (always excepting the one primeval example on the banks of Father Nile) is as strictly an artificial production of labour as any that is wrought by man's hand upon Nature's materials, the political economist might perhaps have had a lighter task. The claim of him who before he can reap any return must invest a long expenditure in time, and seed, and labour, and tools, might vindicate a year's possession, and a freshly earned one year by year (and the four or six-course farmer perhaps could urge a still more protracted suit) against that ideal claim of his brother man which has been quaintly described as " the right that belongs to all to take that which belongs to none."* But the more complicated question lies waiting for us yet one stage

* The words of Locke are as follows : "Though the earth, and all inferior creatures, be common to all men, yet every man hath a property in his own person : this nobody has a right to but himself. The labour of his body and the work of his hands, we may say, are properly his. Whatever, then, he removes out of the state that Nature hath provided and left it in, he hath mixed his labour with, and joined to it something that *is* his own, and thereby makes it his property. It being by him removed from the common state Nature hath placed it in, it hath by this labour something annexed to it that excludes the common right of other men. For, this labour being the unquestionable property of the labourer, no man but he can have a right to what that is once joined to, at least when there is enough and as good left in common for others."

H

further: namely, when the phenomenon begins to be
witnessed of the severance of ownership from occupation;
when the fact stands patent of a process having taken
place which has enabled the occupier to *transfer* the
right he held to *another*, either wholly,—by sale or gift,
and the still more potential act of transmission by
heritage, or by will,—or partially, by lease, or other
temporary assignment.   In every fully-peopled country
a long unwritten history has been acted out, of
the gradual acquisition of such rights over the soil;
and in most of them there has come, in the natural
course of events, a time when the unlanded portion of
the growing community have begun to inquire into the
cause of their own exclusion, and the ' title ' of those who
have been before them in the race, and have got possession.

The student of early Roman history is often puzzled
by the reiterated occurrence of some mysterious struggles
between the richer and poorer citizens which appear
never to reach any final settlement; marking the growth
and predominating power of a landed caste whose domains
extending around the city for miles, gave, in a population so dense and concentrated as that of Rome, a special
severity to the Agrarian question, by leaving for the increasing numbers of the State only the more distant and
worthless portions of the unappropriated "public land."
So, in the Greek States, " every accession to the number
of citizens was followed by a call for a fresh division of
the public land; and as this involved the sacrifice of
many encroachments that had grown into vested interests,
it was regarded with horror by the old citizens as an act
of revolutionary violence.   For though the land was the
undoubted property of the State, and although the
occupiers of it were to the State mere tenants at will,
yet it is in human nature that a long possession should
give a feeling of ownership, the more so, as while the
State's claim lay dormant, the *possessor* was to all
appearance the *proprietor;* and the land would thus be
repeatedly passing by regular sale from one occupier to
another." *

* Arnold. ' Hist. of Rome,' vol. i.   Dr. Arnold shows that the law of real

The same tale which finds such faltering expression in those nations that had historians, has worked out its silent but not less actual history in every cultivating nation of the world. Increase of population; decrease of public land; the vehement claim of participation on the one hand, the fierce and jealous tenacity of prescriptive rights on the other.

Probably in no other country of Europe so much as in our own—partly owing to its island character, and partly to the succession of distinct races that has gone to form its people and its laws—have the history of the land and the institutions connected with it been more truly, in every sense, a history. The forced introduction by the Norman kings of the most oppressive incidents of feudalism, without its better features, broke in upon an ancient landed system which had been growing up for centuries, disjointedly, but steadily, in Saxon England, having its roots in the imperishable principles of Roman jurisprudence, that had prevailed here for nearly four centuries, and of which it has been truly said that it "was never permanently lost in any country in which it was once established."* Under the subsequent rule of such men as Egbert, Alfred, Athelstan, and Canute, there are surviving proofs that the laws and distribution of land had reached a stage of advancement that embodied, with the remains of that Roman polity which "had graven itself in our land,"† some of the most

property in Rome was more advanced than the Feudal system in many important features. The proprietor of land was the absolute owner during his life-time, and could bestow it absolutely at his death.

* Creasy. 'Hist. of England.' During the intervening centuries, from A. D. 82 when Agricola reduced the island to A. D. 463 when the Legions were withdrawn, the judicial tribunals of the Province of Britain were fashioned on the Roman models. The corporations invented by Roman Jurists were the origin of our municipal institutions by which England has always been distinguished. Papinian, the celebrated Roman jurist under Septimius Severus, presided in the Forum Eboraci (York); Ulpian and Paulus are considered by Selden to have occupied the functions of 'Assessores' in the tribunals of Roman Britain.

† Pearson. 'England in the Early and Middle Ages,' vol. i., chap. ii. "It is scarcely too much to say," writes Mr. Pearson (p. 51), "that we owe a vantage-ground of six centuries of inherited Law and Culture to our Roman conquerors."

sterling elements of the old Saxon character and institutions.

We must not forget that it is from the pens of Norman writers that most of the ideas we entertain of our native English forefathers at the time of the Conquest have been derived: but ample traces that have escaped the distorting profile of the historian, tend to show that whatever the comparison may seem to us between the personal habits of the conquering and of the conquered race in other points, it would be far from the truth to suppose that the English of the eleventh century had much, if anything, to learn from their Norman invaders, in the laws of the soil. "Norman literature before the Conquest is worthless; their law-courts have nothing to match the splendid series of Anglo-Saxon charters."* There is much that is primitive and simple to be met with, but (apart from the personal habits of the age) nothing of barbarism in the land institutions of Saxon England, unless, indeed, an excessive love for it, and an almost exaggerated deference for its possession may be so classed. In an age when freedom was the exceptional condition, the ownership of land was the mark of a free man, and ample territory the inseparable appanage of rank. The modern Conveyancer's broad separation between 'real' and 'personal' estate was strongly marked in the practices of Saxon life, but with far better reason, when the rareness and insignificance of other forms of property gave truth and meaning to the distinction. No amount of gold or 'chattel' property conferred the franchise: land alone was recognised as the vehicle of all personal privilege, and the basis of civil rank. "There is no trace of such a qualification as constituted citizenship at Athens or Rome; among our Saxon forefathers the exclusive idea of the city had no sway."† In this they only inherited the national character of their continental ancestors pictured by the Roman annalist with such expressive brevity. "It is well known that the German race inhabit not cities, nor care even to join

* Pearson. Vol. i. p. 401.
† Kemble. 'Saxons in England.'

house to house. They dwell independently, and apart, as the stream, the meadow, or the grove may guide their choice."* Centuries have not obliterated these features in their descendants to this day; the love of land, its estimation above all other forms of property, and its political preponderance. It long held, and still in a measure holds, with us, the dangerous prerogative of being its own lawgiver, a power hardly to be trusted to any human hands, without check or counterweight; for, even justice and conscience are not always gifted with that reflex intelligence that can see in the claims of others the portraiture of the same rights which they defend for themselves.

The characteristics of the English land system before the Conquest are worth careful notice, not only as being the earliest contributions to the history of the land in this country, but as embracing original types of national law and custom, from which it would be difficult to say how large a share of that unwritten code known to our familiar use as 'Common Law' is derived. If the materials are not as abundant as those of later time, they are yet so hand-marked as to make up for want of detail by the significance of a few broad outlines. In the first place it embraced (though with some variations in different parts of the country) those three important rights which together may be said to form the very test of land freedom. 1. The right of alienation, or transfer by sale, or gift. 2. The power of disposal by will. 3. That of transmission by inheritance. This is the more observable, at that early period of our national life, because under the Feudal rule which succeeded the Conquest, the two first were abrogated, and the third completely changed from its original character, so as to subserve only the feudal purposes.

In the next place, there existed in a very distinct form that remarkable reservation of public right which found expression in the word "Folc-land," or land of the people, and embodied "the principle of a direct

* Tacitus. De Mor. Germ. c. xvi. The passage is as characteristic of the writer as of the people he describes.

ownership by the community, not in theory only but to
some extent in practice : private property in its more
perfect form obtained only over those portions which
were granted to individuals by charter, and hence were
called ' boc-land ' "* (book-land). This distinction seems
almost identical with the ' publica terra ' and ' privatus
ager ' of the Romans, and marks, with other evidence,
the extent to which the principles of Roman law still
subsisted. " It was only with the consent of his Witan
that the king could make grants of the public domains of
the Folc-land. The theory that the sovereign is the
paramount proprietor of all land, was utterly alien to
Saxon ideas and institutions. Such state domains, like
the *ager publicus* of the Romans, might be held by individuals as tenants of the Commonwealth, till it was
formally made over as private property."† But still,
after such appropriation, and accompanying every private
estate, *all land* remained subject to three inevitable
public charges (' Trinoda necessitas ')—1. Military service
in (but not always confined to) defensive war. 2. The
repair of bridges, and 3, of royal fortresses.

The land-owning class consisted of the Eorls or
larger owners who held under the crown, and the Ceorls,
a much more numerous but independent class.‡ " They
are the root," says Hallam, " of a noble plant; the free
socage tenants, or English yeomanry, whose independence
stamped with peculiar features both our constitution and
our national character."§ The limits of land were defined with scrupulous accuracy, and a Register of deeds
and decisions, including mortgages, was kept in the
superior courts.‖ The form of alienation, or transfer,

---

* See Mr. C. Neate's ' Lecture on the History and Conditions of Landed
Property,' p. 19.
† Creasy. ' Hist. of England.' " The feebleness of the resistance of so brave
a people as the English at the Battle of Hastings is attributed by Mr. Kemble
to the discontent and depression of the middle class at the gradual absorption
of all the public lands by the great owners of that day."
‡ The Eorl and Ceorl (words whose terminal sound often coupled them in a
sort of civil apposition) nearly corresponded to the Squire and Yeoman of a
later day. The Thegnes (Thanes) were of a higher order, yet hardly equivalent
to the nobleman of the present.
§ ' Middle Ages,' ii. 386.
‖ Kelham's ' Domesday Book,' p. 242, note 1.

was very simple ; but its efficacy was secured *by publicity.*
" Before the Conquest, grants of land were enrolled in the
Shire-book, after proclamation made, in public Shire-mote,
for any to come in that could claim the lands conveyed ;
and this was as irreversible as the modern Fine with pro-
clamations, or Recovery."* It might almost shame a
reader of our Blue-books on ' Sale and transfer of
Land,' to find a ' Registry of Title,' and, what was then
almost its equivalent, a ' Register of Assurances ' existing
in the ancient English county courts, while the age of
Christendom was yet written in three figures.

The power of disposition by Will appears to have
been unrestricted, extending even to oral declaration if
formally made in the presence of a sufficient number
of witnesses,† of whom eight or ten were usually required ; and all wills had to be established in the County
court. The right of hereditary succession extended—in

---

* Gurdon on ' Courts Baron.'

† Hallam's ' Middle Ages,' ii. p. 393.   He gives a very ancient and
characteristic Saxon instrument, published by Hickes, recording a suit in a
county court.

" It is made known by this writing that in the Shire-gemot (county court),
held at Agelnothestane (Aylston, in Herefordshire), in the reign of Cnute,
there sat Athelstan the bishop, and Ranig the alderman, and Edwin his son,
and Leofwin, Wulfig's son ; and Thurkil the White, and Tofig, came there on
the king's business ; and there were Bryning the sheriff, and Athelweard of
Frome, and Leofwin of Frome, and Goodric of Stoke, and all the Thegns of
Herefordshire.   Then came to the mote Edwin, son of Enneawne, and sued
his mother for some lands, called Weolintun and Cyrdeslea.   Then the
bishop asked, who would answer for his mother.   Then answered Thurkil the
White, and said that he would, if he knew the facts, which he did not.
Then were seen in the mote three Thegns, that belonged to Feligly (Fawley,
five miles from Aylston), Leofwin of Frome, Ægelwig the Red, and Thinsig
Stœgthman : and they went to her, and inquired what she had to say about
the lands which her son claimed.   She said that she had no land that belonged
to him, and fell into a noble passion against her son, and calling for Leofleda
her kinswoman, the wife of Thurkil, thus spake to her before them : ' This
is Leofleda my kinswoman, to whom *I give my lands, money, clothes, and
whatever I possess after my life ;*' and this said, she then spake to the Thegns :
' Behave like Thegns, and bear my message to all the good men in the mote,
and tell them to whom I have given my lands, and all my possessions, and
nothing to my son ;' and bade them to be witnesses to this.   And thus they
did, rode to the mote, and told all the good men what she had enjoined them.
Then Thurkil the White addressed the mote, and requested all the Thegns
to let his wife have the lands which her kinswoman had given her ; and thus
they did, and Thurkil rode to the church of St. Ethelbert, with the leave and
witness of all the people, and *had this inserted in a book in the church.*"

A Nuncupative Will is recorded also in the Domesday of Worcestershire.
Consuetudines, Gale, vol. iii. p. 768.

accordance with the custom of Gavel-kind—to all the children,* differing in this respect from that introduced after the Conquest, which has ever since prevailed in this country. To the ante-Norman Englishman the claim of primogeniture seems to have been unknown.† A practice curiously the converse of it existed, however, in some districts, under the name of 'Borough-English,' by which the *youngest* son succeeded to the inheritance;‡ the reason assigned for this preference being that the elder sons would be more surely provided for during the father's lifetime; a ground that may stand comparison with some of the arguments used for our law of succession of the eldest.

It may also be noticed that, upon the death of the son without issue, the father inherited. " By our common law he is absolutely and in every case excluded," writes Mr. Hallam, in the year 1829, just before this principle was restored to our law, after an interval of eight centuries, thus leaving only one of the ancient English land-institutions unredeemed from feudal change.§

Several features of the Saxon land laws, the relation of lord and 'vassal,'‖ the obligation of military service, and the reverting of some lands to the State on the failure of male heirs, have led to the belief that an inchoate form of feudalism existed in England before the Norman invasion; and the question has been contested by high authority on both sides. Some negative evidence for the assertion is found in the fact that no new *code of law* appears to have ever been promulgated by the Conqueror, who had sworn at his coronation to observe the laws of his new subjects. But the question is chiefly of antiquarian interest. A sovereign who not

* Females were sometimes excluded.

† William the Conqueror's charter to London provides (as for a point on which there might be apprehension) that the children of an Intestate shall inherit equally. As late as Hen. I. the eldest son only inherited the Fief; Boc-land went to the family.

‡ This practice has lasted down to historical times in this country; and seems to have been transplanted from England to Brittany.

§ See Freeman's ' Conquest,' vol. i. p. 597 ; note, on the use of the word ' English.'

‖ This word is used by Asserius, a contemporary of Alfred. ' Middle Ages,' vol. ii. p. 413.

only employed his own justiciaries, using a foreign language not understood by the people, but provided the land itself with *new owners*, could afford—and would be not unlikely—to omit the ceremony of a new code. But the opposite opinion seems to be now generally received ; and it is strongly supported by the facts of the land having been transferable *inter vivos*, devisable by will, and the inheritance equally shared by the children, features all so opposed to the principles of feudal tenure that they render the question, for the present purpose, unimportant.

These and most other free and distinctive features of the native land laws were swept away and entirely abolished at the Conquest. William's grants made no distinction of public and private land, and were all made by his own sole will as absolute sovereign, unshared by any Council, and to be held directly and solely of himself as feudal lord. "He formally established the doctrine of the universal supremacy of the Crown, and he exacted the solemn acknowledgment of it by all the landowners of England, at the great assembly which he convened at Salisbury in 1086."*

But he did much more than this. The same system which, on the Continent, formed a kind of social network of alternate sub-infeudation, shared by the nobles, took the shape in England of an oppressive tyranny of one sole monarch, felt chiefly in the exasperating incidents of 'relief' and 'wardship' which the Norman kings in succession inflicted upon their English subjects† in place of the free and systematised land-institutions, which they had before enjoyed from the time of the great Alfred, and which found their attestation, with their death-blow, in the terrible record of 'Domesday Book.' That extraordinary work, which, as it sprang from the fiat of the Conqueror, has been attributed to his genius and power, seems, however, to have owed the possibility of its production—accomplished as it was in the course

---

* Creasy. 'Hist. of England.' Freeman's 'Conquest of England.'
† Hallam seems to be of opinion that several of the most oppressive incidents formed no parts of the system, but were invented as well as introduced by the "rapacious Norman tyrants." ['Mid. Ages,' ii. 415.]

of a few months by the commissioners who compiled it*—
to the organization which they found ready to their hand
in every county and hundred of the kingdom ; an organization framed upon the accurate definitions of land in
Anglo-Saxon charters, and county court Registries, both
based on ancient principles of public right and record (of
which the County Court was the local centre), and
justifying the bitter regrets with which the nation, after
it had bowed to the exactions of its Norman rulers for
a hundred and fifty years, down to the reign of Henry III.,
still looked back to its ancient land freedom, under the
never-forgotten title of "The Laws of Edward the Con-
fessor."

"It is remarkable," says Hallam, "that although the
feudal system established in England upon the Conquest
broke in very much upon our ancient Saxon liberties,
though it was attended with harsher servitude than in
any other country, yet it has been treated with more
favour by English than French writers." The explanation
of the paradox is to be found in the concurrent history
of two things that would seem incompatible; one, the
grandest code of personal and civil liberty, the other, the
most complicate and technical system of land laws, ever
exemplified in the same country.

As the Conqueror had constituted himself sole lord of
the land, and denied to his nobles all the participation
which on the Continent made each lord a petty sovereign
and tyrant, the barons of England were gradually drawn
into sympathy with the demands of the People, as Magna
Charta soon nobly attested; and from that time the
real sting of feudalism ceased to be personally felt by the
English commonalty. But as all law proceedings, and
all clerkly learning, were in a foreign tongue—the
Norman French—none of the learned class was willing,

---

* The orders for it were given by the court held at Gloucester, Christmas, A. D. 1085, and the returns were brought to the court at Winchester,
at Easter following. The same commissioners did not act for all England.
They proceeded by summoning before them the sheriffs, lords of manors,
parish priests, bailiffs, &c., to give an exact account of the land, whether
wood, pasture, or tillage, &c. In some cases the live-stock were enumerated.

and no layman was able, to draw comparisons in favour of the ancient landed liberties, against the system in which they were now taught, and to which all their learning and all their prejudices leaned. And thus, while in matters affecting the general liberty of the realm, the commonalty profited by the power, and shared many of the privileges, of the nobles—wrung from William's successors, and strengthened by repeated confirmations of the Great Charter,—the evil seed of landed feudalism planted by his hand, and screened by its language from popular intelligence, produced its evil fruit; and the tyranny of 'relief' and 'wardship' continued, through successive centuries, to generate a systematic growth of "legal legerdemain," to escape their burdens,—a complete science of fiction and evasion,—which still, unhappily, characterises the laws that govern real property in this country.

But as " virtue cannot so inoculate our old stock but we shall relish of it," the vestiges of English liberty and the perseverance of English resistance contrived to retain a large portion of the land under the modified and freer tenure called ' common socage,' in which, though the feudal bond existed, its exactions were pecuniary, instead of personal and military. This form of tenure was preferable in so far as it altered the character, though without getting rid of, that feudal dependence whose essential element was *an enduring personal relation which no time released or affected as between the lord and his heirs on the one side, and the tenant and his successors on the other*. The power of alienation was, however, withheld, and the primogenitary succession substituted, though not so universally, for that of equal inheritance. Indeed that mode of land-succession was the keystone of feudal tenure; for, the power of alienation *during life*, by the tenant in tail, though nominally forbidden, was in the smaller fiefs connived at, on the condition that the lord was not deprived of his rights. Provided there was an eldest son to succeed to the duties and services of the fief, it did not greatly matter *whose* eldest son it was; and the practice grew up of bespeaking the acceptance by the lord of the new tenant, during the life of the old one who wished to retire.

This practice did not extend to the tenants of the crown (*in capite*), but it became sufficiently general to lead to the enactment of two important and well-known statutes passed in the reign of Edward I.; one (*de Donis conditionalibus*) which prohibited the collusive alienation of ' estates tail,' by which the lords had been deprived of their forfeitures on the failure of heirs ; the other (*Quia Emptores*), passed five years afterwards, which, while appearing to legalise alienation, reclaimed the right of the superior lord against the attempts of the tenant to substitute *himself* as lord to the new purchaser, and reimposed on the land the same rights of lordship to which it had been subject in the hands of the vendor.

These two statutes for nearly two centuries crushed the growing effort to emancipate land from its feudal fetters, at least by open alienation ; and had the further mischievous effect of making the position of the unfortunate tenant in agriculture more insecure than ever, as no leasing power of one tenant-in-tail was binding on his successor. Thence, all good farming betook itself to the monastic houses, whose Mortmain lands became the fixed asylum of agricultural knowledge and improvement. Certainty of tenure out of doors, and the classical writers on husbandry studied and transcribed within, told powerfully upon the soil, and were draining and redeeming into cultivation the fens and marshes of Lincoln, and Somerset, and Sussex, while elsewhere the pressure of feudal exaction upon the fee-simple proprietor, and the insecurity of the farming tenant, even under lease, reduced cultivation to its most precarious and servile condition, and dwarfed the agricultural growth of the kingdom. The remedy for the effects of these statutes was gradually found, in a practice which drew from the machinery of the law the instrument of its own evasion by means of what was called a " Common Recovery."

This ingenious but surreptitious mode of transfer seems to have owed its invention to the churchmen, in

order to evade the statute against Mortmain appended
to the reissue of the Great Charter in the ninth year of
Henry III., and consisted in the artifice of inducing
liberal or superstitious landowners to become defendants
in collusive lawsuits, in which the ecclesiastical plaintiffs
sued for and recovered the lands as their own, no defence
being made to their claim : and these mockeries of law,
as well as justice, received the sanction of the courts,
equally to the disgrace of the clergy who instituted, and
the judges who allowed them.

But of all the manifold inventions which grew up
under the pressure of feudalism, the most fertile of am-
biguity was that by which the ownership of land, while
nominally vested in the hands of several proprietors, was
secretly transferred to the ' use ' of another person, who
was thus enabled to enjoy the beneficiary ownership
without being liable to forfeiture, or the onerous charges
of relief and wardship.   Down to the time of Henry VIII.
this practice had so increased that, by its means, a considerable part of the kingdom had contrived to get
rid of some of the worst inconveniences of feudal
tenure.*

One evasion generates another ; and the adoption of
' uses ' was out-manœuvred in its turn by a statute
passed in the twenty-seventh year of that reign, by which
the beneficiary owner of the ' use ' was drawn from his
retreat, by the two estates being thrown into one, that is,
by investing the owner of the Use with the ' legal
estate.'   And henceforward the machinery that had
been employed in the creation of the Use was adopted for
the transfer of land by *Deed without publicity or registration.*   Thus our whole present system of unregistered
conveyances is derived from an original fraudulent evasion
of the law ; " an objection of no great weight," observes

* In the courts of Common Law the ' use ' was a nonentity ; and so it
escaped the Mortmain Statutes.   But the Chancellors (who were almost invariably ecclesiastics), acting upon the fiduciary principle introduced into
Roman jurisprudence (to escape the harshness of the Voconian law U.C. 584),
gave it validity, as binding on the conscience (" fidei commissa:") and on
the same principle, ' *Cestuique Trust* ' afterwards succeeded to ' *Cestuique
Use.*'

Mr. Neate, "as so much of the law of real property rests on no better foundation."*

Nominally, this solidification of the Use into a tangible 'legal estate' again subjected the land to its old feudal liabilities. But that iron grasp which, rising out of the decay of Roman power, had reached over the greater part of Europe, holding the mind and liberties of nations with a force so wonderfully concentrated— wonderful even when looked at from the advanced social organization of our own day—had begun to relax its hold. No better proof of this can be seen than in the fact that only five years after the Statute of Uses, the Act was passed (32 Hen. VIII.) which is commonly said to have given, but in truth *restored*, the power to devise lands by Will. As this power, which had freely existed before the Norman rule, was extinguished by the practice of primogenitary descent—with which it was of course incompatible—it would have been right that, on its restoration, the ancient English rule of equal division in case of intestacy should be also restored, as the system of exclusive heredity, though no longer required for feudal objects, could now be created at pleasure by Will. This, however, will be more fully considered presently. After an attempt to resuscitate the feudal claim of the sovereign by Charles I. in his struggle with the Parliament, military tenure was finally abolished in the first year (legally the twelfth) of Charles II.

What then was the actual condition in which the formal extinction of feudal tenures left those laws that govern Land in all that is implied in its modern relation to the uses of society? This is the anxious question, above all others, of the agricultural Owner, and Occupier, whose interests are so fundamentally, yet often obscurely, affected by the silent operation of the principles which regulate the distribution of the Soil. And first of all, what was the condition of the law especially in the three points before named—the power of Alienation, of disposal by Will, and of Inheritance?

* 'History and Conditions of Landed Property.'

With regard to the first, the early simplicity of transfer accompanied by public registry, and even the later forms of Seisin and Enfeoffment, had become substituted by secret conveyance, through the instrumentality of private deeds, whose language was cast in the forms and phraseology derived from the reiterated struggles of ecclesiastical and legal ingenuity against feudal and statutory restrictions.

'Fine and recovery,' 'conveyance to uses,' 'lease and release,' all the circuitous shapes that evasion had been compelled to assume, survived, together with the whole storehouse of factitious science that had grown up around them. Once launched into existence, the system of private and unregistered conveyance had generated a science and vocabulary applicable to the numberless 'estates' created in land, which made every 'title' a matter of intricate *personal* history; hence arose the necessity of investigations requiring the most practised and recondite knowledge of the whole body of statute law, which feudalism, though extinct, had left behind it; and demanding a long train of evidence, traced in full upon the instrument of conveyance, of all the 'dealings' that had occurred to the 'estate' of the vendor, for, at least, the period of human life; indeed, the right of bringing 'real actions' (suits for the recovery of land) far exceeded this limit.

It would be a hopeless and presumptuous task to attempt to present, in a mere popular essay, even a sketch of the history of all the various 'estates' upon which land was held, each a study in itself, and which necessarily entered into the question of title, when once that was divorced from the public evidence which had guarded its simplicity and security. The mere epitome of all the various doctrines of legal and equitable estates, of seisins, of uses, of trusts executed and executory, of powers at common law, and in equity, of terms of years outstanding and assigned, of mortgages, of all the complex interests, often fictitious, and even contradictory—by which "the same person may be at one side of Westminster Hall the *owner*, and at the other a *trespasser*"—

which form the Real Property Law of this country, would awaken in the mind of the reader a kind of despair that might well take the form of Rasselas's exclamation after hearing Imlac's catalogue of the requisites to make a Poet. "Enough! no man can be a Vendor or a Purchaser; or a *Conveyancer!* proceed with thy narrative." Those who are most deeply versed in the intricate science that grew out of so many centuries of conflict between land in its feudal sense, and land in its modern development as the basis of all industry, the source of all wealth, will, perhaps, least wonder at the slow and partial emancipation witnessed even to our own day, from that state in which the extinction of military tenures left it two centuries ago.

Five bulky volumes of blue-books, reaching from 1829 to nearly the present date, record the labours of the Real Property Commissioners, who from time to time have entered upon this Herculean task. The limitation of 'Real actions,' the earliest result of their inquiry, and which held out the promise of a title by twenty years' possession,* reserving the five exempted cases of infancy, coverture, idiotcy, lunacy, and beyond seas, proved, for practical purposes, a failure. No conveyancing skill or human foresight could insure a purchaser against the eventualities that might be lurking in the ten years' reservation accorded to this formidable list of excepted claims. Capital is proverbially timid; and the fear that indulges itself at another's cost, and not without advantage to the prudent alarmist, is more easily awakened than allayed. The abolition of Fines and Recoveries,† of the assignment of Outstanding Terms,‡ and of the Lease and release,§ have done something to simplify the form and language of the deed of conveyance, but not much towards the shortening of titles, from which conveyancing practice abates little if any of its claim for the exhibition of a title on the part of a Vendor, or Mortgagor, for a period equivalent to the life of two generations.

* 3 and 4 Wm. IV. c. 27.   † Ibid. c. 74.
‡ 8 and 9 Vict. c. 106.   § Ibid. c. 112.

So early as at the time of the Restoration this uncertainty of the titles to estates was stated as " one cause of the decay of rents and value of lands,"* and at the date of the report of the Commissioners on the Registration of Title (1857), upwards of twenty bills had within twenty years been brought into Parliament in order to establish a system of Registration ; and a Select Committee of the House of Lords appointed to inquire into the burthens upon land, attributed the diminution of its marketable value to the tedious and expensive process attending its transfer, and asked for a " thorough revision of the whole subject of conveyancing, and the disuse of the present prolix and vexatious system."

The problem has not been suffered to sleep, and has been taken up by Chancellor after Chancellor, as if the highest station of the legal profession had come to recognise the task as a challenge to its corporate conscience ; and the names of Cairns, of Westbury, and of Hatherley are each associated with the noblest efforts to remove an evil, of which neither the existing Land Register in England, nor the Landed Estates Court in Ireland, have furnished any permanent abatement. Individual practice defeats in detail the permissive operation, in the former case, of an Act which was soon found to offer a remedy that, like Inoculation, has *too much of the original disease* for safe or profitable use ; and titles gather again the parasitic evils from which they were temporarily freed, (once for all as it was vainly hoped,) in the latter. The same disproportionate cost, delay, and repeated investigation for every fresh transaction of sale or mortgage remain practically as they were ; impressing the public mind with the feeling that he who enters upon the sale or purchase of land must do so under the warning that he is indulging in something that has many of the features of a *Law-suit,* of uncertain cost, duration and result, through the operation of a system as opposed to the simple forms of antiquity, as it is to the broad stream of modern thought and procedure in all the transactions of business, and of social life.

* 1669, Lords' Journals, vol. xii. 273.

It would be incredible, if it were not true, that at a time when personal property changes hands at the Bankers' clearing house in London at the rate of three and a half *Billions* sterling in the twelvemonth, the title to land, which of all things on the face of the earth—being itself a definite portion of that face—ought to be capable of the most clear and patent evidence, is locked up in private boxes and stowed away in uninsured offices, to be doubtfully educed from the perishable evidence of MS. deeds, written (in the fifth century since the invention of printing) in language requiring sometimes the translation, sometimes the deciphering, but always the interpretation, of an expert.

But the transfer of land is beset by a class of difficulties more deep-rooted in obstructive power than those presented by prolixity of deeds, or the fossil forms of an extinct system and vocabulary, or even the growing canker of unregistered title. The early history of Entail, as it insidiously grew under the pressure of feudal exactions and forfeitures, though checked by the device of Recoveries, and shattered for a season by Henry the Eighth's Statute of Fines, stood forth when feudal tenure had disappeared, in the form of a perfected plan and science, around which had gathered an elaborate network of factitious rules and principles, woven by the subtle machinery of evasion. The scaffolding fell away only to reveal an edifice that had been growing up within, shaped for the accomplishment of a self-renewing perpetuity by means of what has been called "a dualism of proprietorship." By this system the property in land was divided out to several persons with estates ' for life,' and in ' remainder,' so as to prevent the possibility of alienation until not only the whole of the lives existing at the time of making the settlement, or will, had dropped, but until the *unborn child* of one who was then an infant had attained twenty-one years of age ; so, in fact, as to extend the entail ordinarily for fifty, but possibly for eighty or even ninety years. In common parlance—for the practice is that now in force—estates in land may be settled upon any number of lives in being, *and twenty-one years afterwards.*

It is needless to say that this posthumous power of entail, which is now almost peculiar to this country, is looked upon with as many differences of opinion as there are points of view from which it may be regarded. Lord St. Leonards, describing it from the lawyer's standpoint, says, " The present plan of a strict settlement, within reasonable limit enables the owner to transmit his land *to all his posterity,* and from its very nature leads to successive settlements ;" in another passage he remarks that, " our law admits no dispositions which *tend to perpetuity.*" The apparent contradiction resolves itself into the meaning of a word. That which is tied up to all posterity *from within,* is effectual as a perpetuity to all except the settlor (or testator) and his successors.

" One would suppose," writes Mr. Fowler, " that the law of England, instead of 'abhorring perpetuities'—to quote its quaint language—really cherished them with a peculiar vene-ration, . . . in so far as the law permits a man, by his will, or by deed made in his life, to direct how his property shall be held when he is resting in his grave. Viewed in the abstract, the existence of such a power is a strange thing. . . . But those who most highly approve of giving an owner this power must admit that it should have a limit, and that it would be intolerable that the dead man should speak for ever. . . . In practice the usual custom is to settle an estate on the father for life, then on the son for life, with remainder in tail to the unborn child of the son. When the grandson comes of age the land can be again settled, and his interest changed to a tenancy for life, with remainder to his unborn child, as before. By this system of settlement and resettlement it is obvious that a property can be retained in the same family generation after generation, the owner in possession being, in general, only tenant for life, with no power of disposing of the family estate."[*]

Another writer, referring to this family settlement and resettlement, in a vein of caustic irony characterises the practice as a " solemn appeal from one generation to the next ;" observing that even in such a case, " the common interest of the nation would be unrepresented in

* ' Thoughts on Free Trade in Land,' by William Fowler, LL.D., M.P.

the more than diplomatic privacy of this negotiation between father and son.   But, on closer examination, the supposed solemn appeal to each generation dwindles to a hasty compact dictated by somewhat sordid considerations of a momentary interest, to which the law lends the sanction of irrevocability."*

The worst ground of complaint, however, is not that the law should sanction the settled transmission of wealth within the statutory limits, but that the medium of the posthumous settlement should be an article of limited supply, upon which the nation has a just claim that its capabilities should not be dwarfed by that contraction of its possessory powers which settlement usually implies.

The important question which the demands of agricultural progress, since the great expansion given to it by the changes that have followed upon free trade, have of late years brought into prominent discussion, is how far this system is beneficial to all the parties interested in the soil, including the Landowner himself, the agricultural Tenant, the Labourer, and lastly the Community at large, to whom none will deny an interest in the productiveness of the land, as well as a reasonable claim in respect of its freedom of purchase.

It will be convenient to consider these under their separate heads.

With regard to the first—that of the Landowner—the act of resettlement is thus described by Lord St. Leonards :—

"Where there are younger children, the father is always anxious to have the estate resettled on them and their issue, in case of failure of issue of the first son.   This he cannot accomplish without the concurrence of the son ; and as the son, upon his establishment in life in his father's lifetime, requires an immediate provision, the father generally secures to him a provision during their joint lives, as a consideration for the resettlement of the estate in remainder upon the younger sons. Thus are estates quickly resettled."

This is the abstract view of the matter, as it appears to the eye of the lawyer, and, in point of form, com-

* 'The Land Laws,' by W. L. Newman, Esq.

monly occurs. It is right, however, in the interest of those most nearly concerned, that the practical operation of the system should be viewed from all sides.

"Take the case," writes Mr. Cliffe Leslie, "of an ante-nuptial settlement in which the son joins with the father. It is commonly supposed that the son acts with his eyes open, and with a special eye to the contingencies of the future, and of family life. But what are the real facts of the case? Before the future owner of the land has come into possession—before he has any experience of his property, or of what is best to do, or what he can do, in regard of it—before the exigencies of the future, or his own real position are known to him—before the character, number, and wants of his children are learned, or the claims of parental affection and duty can make themselves felt, and while still very much at the mercy of a predecessor desirous of posthumous greatness and power, he enters into an irrevocable disposition, by which he parts with the rights of a proprietor over his future property for ever, and settles its devolution, burdened with charges, upon an unborn heir."[*]

The same features have been thus described by another writer :—

"No sooner does a Tenant in tail come of age, than in numerous instances he is urged, by those whose influence is irresistible, to cut off the entail, to resettle the estate, and to fasten upon it the debts of his ancestors. In fact, he is invited to pay for the extravagance of a father or grandfather, who has often done worse than nothing for the condition of the family property. . . . It may be fairly made a question, whether so young a person should be by law capable of binding himself in so important a transaction. This law is open to two serious objections; one, that a young man executes a solemn act, deeply compromising his fortune, when as yet he cannot understand its consequences: the other, that the weight of hereditary debts, which he thus fixes upon himself, may crush all his efforts and disappoint all his intentions to improve the cultivation of his estate."[†]

The words of one more writer shall be quoted, who has had better opportunity than most men of forming a practical judgment from eye-witness experience through-

[*] ' Fraser's Magazine,' February, 1867.
[†] Letter to the Right Hon. Sir Charles Wood, Bart., by Frederick Calvert, Esq., Q.C.

out the length and breadth of the land, as to the effects of long entail upon the proprietary classes of this country.

"Much of the land of England," says Mr. Caird, writing just after the conclusion of his survey through the agricultural districts in 1851—"a far greater proportion of it than is generally believed—" (by the evidence before Mr. Pusey's committee the estates under settlement were estimated as exceeding two-thirds of the kingdom) "is in the possession of tenants for life so heavily burthened with settlement encumbrances that they have not the means of improving the land which they are obliged to hold. It would be a waste of space to dilate on the public and private disadvantages thus occasioned; for they are acknowledged by all who have studied the subject, and seriously felt by those who are affected by it. A neglected property in this country, the *nominal owner* of which is incapable from his embarrassments of improving it, will not be looked at by tenants of capital; and tenants of limited means on such a property must be overborne in unrestricted competition with farmers of capital, cultivating land where every convenience and accommodation which an unencumbered landlord finds it his interest to give has been supplied."

The reactive and life-like nature of the soil makes it a tell-tale, in the long run, of the laws under which it is placed, and by which it is governed. And it cannot be made the subject of unwise legislation in the hands of the Owner, any more than of bad husbandry in those of the Tenant, without developing results which reach, unhappily, beyond these classes, to the injury of all connected with or employed upon it, though innocent (as in the case of the labourer) and even ignorant of the originating cause of the mischief. The trust which its ownership brings, as well as its occupation (if these are divided), is enforced by penalties as inexorable as those of natural law. The pressure of the responsibility increases with every step in agricultural advancement, till the rights of one age become the wrongs of another. Modes of settlement, carving out the proprietary interest into a series of limited estates ' for life,' and ' in remainder,' each in succession barren of power and of motive to meet the wants, the improvements, the discoveries of the time, present a very different aspect to the same thing before the rivalry of the farm was a world struggle. The increased energy and activity of the tenant demand the outlay of capital by the landlord before his own can be safely thrown into the partnership; for such the relation practically is in England, and such it must become wherever the English system prevails. The ' expenses ' of land are the familiar theme of every man of business. Nothing is more common than to hear the wealthy and unfettered fee-simple owner complain of the voracious demands of his *landed* property, for buildings, draining, cottages, and other necessary improvements exacted by the time : and those who give most attention to the debtor and creditor history of their estates are best alive to the fact that landed property has become more like a Business than a mere Income. It is so : and, in a certain sense, it ought to be so. The soil was not meant for idle enjoyment even by its unoccupying owner. The dilemma of land without the capital to meet its claims exactly opposes the original object of ' the Settlement,' for it harnesses the fettered with the free, and endangers a catastrophe by the very links that were forged to prevent it. Yet this must inevitably be the case under a system where entail, extending to the unborn, permits, and may even be said to encourage, the inconsistent practice of at once burthening the estate with all the charges of ' the family,' ' the creditor,' and its own expenses, and tying up the hand of the heir upon whom the whole administration must devolve.

It is difficult under such circumstances to resist the conclusion which declares itself against that part of the practice of entail which launches the " daring creation of an impossible foresight " upon a cruise into futurity in search of *the unborn.* ' Any number of lives *in being* ' is a phrase that suggests the obvious limit of human prudence ; and, in the settlement of land, has the advantage of presenting the principle of a natural term,

where the responsibility, and with it the right of each
generation ends.

That the practice of Entail should be reconciled with
the best principles of estate management is of the utmost
importance, if only because it constitutes the modern
substitute for the feudal rule which devolved the inheritance of land upon the eldest male. This law has survived the system to which it owed its introduction into
this country ; operating, indeed, only in cases of intestacy
or disputed claim, but exercising a far more mischievous
influence in propping up the barrier which the great in-
novator Time renders every day more artificial and absurd
between ' real ' and ' personal ' estate, and dishonouring
an old and favoured national *custom* by the retention of
an exclusive and invidious law in the case of land, in the
face of equal division in every other form of property.

So long as land, in its feudal relations, was a thing
out of commerce altogether, when Commerce itself had
scarcely an existence, no special inconvenience resulted
from laws restricting its alienation or its succession ; but
when, in the progress of national wealth, it has lost its
speciality as the only ' property,' and has become simply
one of the forms of invested wealth, the incoherence of
two principles of succession, one of which recognises no
difference of sex or order of birth, like our law of personal
intestacy, while the other devolves the whole inheritance
upon the first-born male, produces endless litigation,
intricacy of legal distinction,* and even uncertainty of

---

* See the case of Ackroyd and Smithson. Brown's Chancery Cases, Vol. i.
p. 505. See also Jarman's Powell, 77-78, *et seq.*

The following is Lord Eldon's own account of the judgment in the celebrated
case which has governed so many nice questions of " real " and " personal "
property.

" Might I ask you, Lord Eldon," said Mr. Farrer, " whether Ackroyd and
Smithson was not the first case in which you distinguished yourself ?"—" Did
I never tell you the history of that case ? You must know (he replied) that
the testator had directed his *real* estates to be sold, and the residue to be
divided into fifteen parts, which he gave to fifteen persons named in his Will.
One died in the testator's lifetime. A bill was filed by the *next of kin*, claiming the lapsed share. A brief was given me to *consent* for *the heir-at-law.*
* * * So I went into Court, and when Lord Thurlow asked who was to
appear for the heir-at-law, I rose and said modestly that I was : and as I could
not but think that my client had the right to the property, if his Lordship
would give me leave I would argue it. And I argued that the testator had

decision, that will hereafter be looked upon as one of the most curious episodes in the juridical history of this country. "No human laws," says Blackstone, "are or any validity if contrary to the law of nature; and such or them as are valid derive all their authority mediately or immediately from this original." But next to a law based on no principle at all, the worst conceivable is one that attempts to embody two conflicting principles into one code, confusing the public sense of right; for, what is law if it be not a Rule of Right, its index-finger clear for all to read, and not pointing two ways?

Volumes have been written, the highest authorities in political economy appealed to, proposals made Session after Session in the House of Commons, the practice of every civilised country in the world cited (with one or two exceptions, which fortify the rule they seem to infringe), in order to remove this straggling relic of an extinct system from our law. The prevailing influence which has deferred its removal has been the fear of the subdivision of land, by the breaking-up of estates. As things suggest their extreme opposites by a well-known natural law, this fear has been intensified by that portion of the Code Napoléon which, on the other side of the English Channel, has parcelled out French soil by a law which subjects the testamentary power of the parent to the number of his children, dividing his estate accordingly. This arbitrary *morcellement* is pictured as the inevitable alternative; as though the interspace of freedom and true principle which lies, broad as the channel itself, between the two, were lost to sight, or had no existence. Hasty and unfounded assumptions of evil results from 'peasant proprietaries' are readily accepted, which if true would be immaterial to the question of the removal

---

ordered this fifteenth share to be converted into *personal property*, for the benefit of one particular individual, and that therefore he never contemplated its coming into possession of either the next of kin, or the residuary legatee; but *being land* at the death of the individual, it came to the *heir-at-law*. Well, Thurlow *took three days to consider*, and then delivered his judgment in accordance with my speech."

Twiss's Life of Lord Eldon, I., 119.

of a law which, anomalous itself, can only come into
operation by intestacies, which its abrogation would
render still more rare ; a law which, when it does operate,
" makes a will for a man which any one of its supporters
would deem it an insult to be accused of making for
himself."*   They who really value the *Custom* of primogeniture—a practice in this country centuries older than
that law, and likely long to survive it—should, in true
consistency, banish from public view its hideous effigy,
which presents the hard lineaments of exclusive heredity
in the most revolting form—that of disinheritance to all
but one, leaving the widow, the helpless daughters, and the
other sons destitute. Its condemnation is pronounced by
nothing more strikingly than by the practice of the primogenitary class, for no well-drawn settlement ever omits to
make provision for the widow, and the younger children.

It is the unfortunate peculiarity of laws governing the
distribution of land, that their effect upon the life and
welfare of the community, unlike those causes which
directly touch the personal freedom or convenience of
individuals, is often obscure, lying remote from their consequences; like that class of poisons which, received
into the circulation, enter the tissues of the body without
detection, to be recognised only in the concrete form
of diseased structure. The evils are slow of cure that
reach men thus indirectly, and have to wait upon opinion.
Such is the character of this law. It passes innocuously
through the upper stratum of large proprietors, where
the absence of family entail—its almost universal substitute—is extremely rare ; where it alights, when it does
so, is generally upon those small and unpretending
acreages, whose owners have found it possible to marry
without a settlement and die without a will, a class
of proprietors upon whose surviving families it works the
greatest hardship, and who are often as ignorant of its
existence as they are innocent of primogenitary intention. The instances of singular hardship among such
intestates cited by Mr. Locke King in his repeated
introduction of the Bill to the House of Commons have

* Mr. W. L. Newman on the Land Laws.

been sometimes met by the trite reply that 'extreme cases make bad law.' The converse is the truth here; it is the bad law, and only the *law*, that makes the extreme cases; and its extinction would obviate a scandal to our landed system which rarely, if ever, arises under the operation of the custom of primogeniture as arising by deed or will.

It may be hoped that the majority obtained in the House of Commons during the last session in favour of the Bill which Mr. Locke King has so consistently kept before the legislature indicates a change of view not confined to the mere narrow issue involved in the clauses of the Bill. The popular arguments which enter into the debate have often obscured the far more important question that is involved, forming, as this law does, the basis of the obsolete distinction expressed in the words 'real' and 'personal,' a distinction more correctly indicated by the terms movable and immovable, which have passed from the Roman law into other European systems.

But if the limited ownership resulting from our system of entail be unfavourable to the investment of capital by the Proprietor, it is yet commonly thought that under the security of a Lease there is nothing to prevent it on the part of the occupying Tenant. Most well-drawn settlements contain leasing powers extending to twenty-one years ; and it is often said that the freedom of contract between the owner and occupier leaves the parties at liberty to make what arrangements they please. But even here one of the worst vestiges of feudal law meets us again. By the statute of Gloucester (6 Edw. I.) the maxim was established, *Quicquid plantatur solo, solo cedit,* which took away all claim of the tenant over every addition he had annexed to or incorporated with the land the moment that his interest, whether yearly or by lease, expired. Under the misapplied name of 'Waste,' he was even forbidden to erect any building upon land where there was none before, or to convert one kind of edifice into another, even of improved value to the estate.

Exceptions were soon made, after the passing of the statute, in favour of Trade ; and Lord Holt is reported to have said that trade fixtures were even recoverable by Common Law.* But the statute has always operated with full severity against the tenant in agriculture, whose property is thus confiscated in any engine or machine annexed to the soil, though for the express purposes of the farm, and without which it could not be profitably occupied. It would be difficult to conceive a law more injurious to the very party in whose favour it was made ; and probably there is none in the whole range of land legislation by which *the proprietor* has suffered more loss than by this. The temptation to outlay upon land by the occupier even under short leases is always disproportionately great—far beyond what the tenure seems to justify ; and, generally speaking, no one knows so well as himself what is required. A law the very opposite to that above referred to, and encouraging a regular system of valuation for addition and improvement by the tenant, would be the most salutary for the interests of all parties, and would have added millions sterling to the landed wealth of the country. It would hardly be too much to say of this statute that it has lain like a cankerworm at the root of the whole question of landlord and tenant, wherever that question indicates adverse instead of united interests. It is obvious almost to a truism that, next to the occupation of the owner himself, the occupation that *most resembles ownership* must, by the imperative laws of the soil, and equally of human instinct, be the most profitable to both parties by the *uninterrupted* progress of improvement and addition to the land. The expense of keeping up a high state of cultivation is small, compared with that of *restoring* it ; and the national loss is almost incalculable which the 'beggaring out' of farms has occasioned under the influence of the motives brought into action by this law. No tenant even under lease would lay out money in improvements which he must

* Elwes *v.* Mawe. 2 Smith L. C. and Notes. See also the Judgment of Lord Hardwicke in Lawton *v.* Lawton, and of Lord Kenyon in Penton *v.* Robart, 2 East 90.

leave behind him, on the estate of another, unless he felt sure of such increased profits during his term as would repay him ; and therefore it is that under short leases and yearly tenancies the land is rarely cultivated to its full extent. Moderation of charge in case of actual change of tenancy would be generally insured by the fact that every addition made by the occupier is far more valuable *in situ* than after removal. The recommendation of the Real-Property Committee of the Law Amendment Society was strongly in favour of an alteration of the law in this particular. The words of their Report on this point state—

"That the law with respect to things affixed to the freehold is different, and more beneficial to the tenant, as regards the annexations made for the purposes of *trade* than those made for the purposes of *agriculture*; an outgoing tenant being permitted in many cases to remove the former when erected by himself, but not the latter."

The practical effect of what may be called the feudal law of Fixtures, as still subsisting, is that the parties to the supposed contract meet each other scarcely upon fair and equal terms. A lease even for twenty-one years underlain by a law that confiscates to the lessor whatever is left unremoved or (to adopt the infelicitous expression of common use) *unexhausted* upon the land by the lessee is somewhat deceptive in operation, because it includes in the term those years near its effluxion during which productive outlay has to be withdrawn, and the ' mill works half time ;' and of necessity restricts all investment to that which can be withdrawn within the term. The evidence of one of the witnesses (Mr. Owen, a Berkshire land agent) given before Mr. Pusey's committee on Agricultural Customs put this matter in a true light :—

"I am convinced of this, that where landlords cannot make improvements, there are so many cases where the tenant has the means of making them, that he could make them very much to his advantage, and very much to the landlord's advantage ; because I consider that, under the present system in our country of letting farms, farms are what we call ' beggared out.'

There is not a farm that I have re-let, but every tenant who has quitted has taken everything out of the farm that he possibly could.   If a system could be laid down where that never could be allowed to be done, and any outlay that the tenant had made upon that property, whether they were improvements by building or manure, he should have the certainty of being repaid for them, I think the benefit would be immense, both to the landlord, and the tenant, and the public."

Under the existing system operating over the greater part of the land in this kingdom, it is a difficult matter to say who there really is possessing such an interest in the soil as to enable or even justify the full amount of profitable investment.   The ostensible owner, usually a tenant for life, cannot make it for the reasons before noticed ; the remainder-man cannot make it, because he is not in possession.   The ' tenant-farmer ' cannot do it, because he, at best, is only a holder for a term of years, which every year brings nearer to its conclusion.   The whole system of landed settlement is founded upon laws and habits unconnected with the needs of modern agriculture.

To an occupier, whether of lands or tenements, life-tenure is the one which offers the highest inducement to make every necessary outlay and improvement.   The uncertainty of life is one which each individual construes favourably to himself, under the influence of that useful feeling, which has been said, with as much truth as poetry, to make " all men think all men mortal but themselves."   But to the owner who is *not* the occupier, the case is exactly reversed : here the calculation of life operates for the avoidance of all that diminishes the *annual return* ; and even necessary repairs are apt to be postponed.   On the other hand, a lease for years, even though the term may exceed the probable duration of the life of the lessee, is always looked upon in reference to its effluxion ; the average ' expectation ' (to use a technical expression) of a 21 years' lease is only 10½ years.

Now, by the system pursued in agricultural tenure both these principles of action are violated.   The occupier, holding for a period which the law recognises

only as a chattel interest, is dissociated from that desire
of improvement common in the case of a life interest;
and the life-*owner*, uninterested in the occupation, finds
his account to lie in a direction equally negative to permanent investment.

Such is the formal position of the parties. The
varieties of circumstance and locality modify it greatly;
and the ordinary amount of capital employed in farming,
where drainage and other improvements are not required, enables the system to work smoothly enough
to hide the defects of the machinery. But where heavy
outlay is required, as where embankments, arterial and
other drainage, inclosure, expensive irrigation, road-
making, and other permanent additions are needed,
the want of a capitalist soon discloses itself. It would
be impossible, under such circumstances, to undertake
any work of heavy and protracted outlay where the
annual returns did not, as in a farm, meet, if not far
exceed, the current outlay. Government drainage-grants
and land-improvement Companies thus rose up, in
evidence, that life-tenure forbids the employment of
capital upon settled estates.

The immediate benefit conferred by the machinery
of these grants is no proof of the political wisdom of
the system. The work is done; but the relief, like
that known to medical science under the name of local
remedy, is followed by a recurring ' local liability.' The
power to follow up the enlarged business growing out of
the loaned investment will, in most cases, devolve upon
the tenant. That a public company, itself borrowing
public money, should have to be invoked to help a landowner to carry on the business of his own estate would
offer a singular commentary upon the state of the
English land-laws, to a person uninformed of the cause.
And of this we may be sure, that wherever a series of
supplementary devices manifests itself, in order to meet
a state of things at variance with the progress of the
day, it indicates the undercurrent of a law struggling
against worn-out barriers that will not long be able to
withstand it.

In no other country is there known to exist any
parallel to the system of land tenancy prevailing so
commonly in England, by which the relations between
the owner and occupier are comprehended in the expressive phrase, 'a good understanding.' It has been
construed severely by some as a compact of selfish
interests ; politics, and game, on one side, undisturbed
tenure and rent on the other, and stigmatised as a sorry
substitute for Leases.   More favourable critics have seen
and eulogised in it the evidence of a mutual trust rarely
exampled, and equally honourable to both parties in the
unwritten contract.   It scarcely merits either the blame
or the praise.   Leases were common upon most English
estates down to the period of the War at the close of the
last century, when the extraordinary and rapid rise in the
prices of produce and value of land took place, and
continued to advance throughout the war, causing a
complete disruption of all previous calculations.   The
collapse that occurred at the close of the war in 1815,
followed by the extreme uncertainty which marked the
Corn Law period of the next thirty years, sustained the
interruption, though from an opposite cause.   Yearly
tenancy thus became, for more than half a century,
the almost inevitable alternative of a period when
agricultural prices, and political apprehensions, alike
uncertain, scarcely allowed of any but provisional
terms ; and tenants as well as owners were willing to
stand loose from permanent engagements, not knowing
what a year might bring forth ; believing that no skill
or foresight could reduce future prospects to calculation,
for the fixed and unelastic terms of a Lease.   The Corn
Law question is gone ; but the 'good understanding'
survives the causes that gave it origin.   It has, however,
this defect, that as it offers no banking security, it
increases the dependence of the English as compared
with the Scotch tenant, and the analogy which in this
respect exists between his own holding and that of the
owner who, has to play the banker's part.   In both, the
nature of the tenure discourages the outlay of private
capital by those who possess it, and prevents the

employment of loaned capital by those who would borrow it. The effect of this upon the condition of the Labourer will be presently noticed.

In Scotland, the predominance of leases, though not of earlier date, has been more systematic, and was preserved with less interruption during the period affected by the circumstances above named, than in England. Several distinct causes have conduced to this: the difference resulting from a climate less favourable to speculative excess in the growth of grain, and less influenced therefore by a system of legislation based on the market value of that produce; a more diffused education giving clearer views of the practical value of leases, coupled with their available use, and recognition by bankers, as security for advances of capital to the leaseholder; the power to heirs of entail (under the Montgomery Act) to charge the estates for their own improvement—all these causes combined have produced a very characteristic difference in the land system of our northern neighbours, and a more commercial and business-like independence in the general economy of landed and farm management.

In Ireland the land question has a history of its own — a history that presents the most deplorable and in some respects the strangest issues that ever in any country have darkened the problem of the vicarial occupation of land.

It is too much forgotten that this relation of man with man is one for which nature has made no provision. No appeal lies to any innate sense, as in that of the parental, filial, or fraternal instinct, in aid of the tie, conjunctive or disjunctive, as the case may prove, that unites—or confronts—the interests of men under the factitious relation of proprietor and occupier. It is one that bows to no sentiment, nor tolerates even the unsound ring of a faulty metaphor. "We pull in the same boat," said the English landlord to his tenant, when rents hung quivering upon the Corn Law Debates: "Yes, but in opposite directions," was the humorous retort. There was a vein of truth in the reply, that is

K

ever at hand, to show itself on the surface when occasion
calls. "The land laws of Ireland," it is often remarked,
"are the same as those of England;"—where large
estates have made large farms, and large farms have in
their turn produced a gigantic manufacture of machines
and labour-saving implements, unknown to former times
or other countries, itself reacting upon a system whose
broad-scale cultivation is finally quoted, perhaps too
exclusively, as the perfection of agriculture.

It is true that the laws are the same. But there is
an old adage of authority, that "indifferent laws well
administered are better than good laws badly administered." If England has exemplified the first category,
in the sister island has been seen the worst of both.

By the presence of the wealthy English proprietor
amongst his tenants, by the example—sometimes the
warning—of his own experimental farm, by the introduction of the last 'new and improved' machine, and the
best blood, by the intelligent and kindly intercourse
(not confined to the "stumpy courtesies of males") per-
vading the estate as from a central focus, by his heavy
bills for farm repairs, constantly occasioning some visita-
tion of his own, be the mason and carpenter never so
alert, or the steward never so ubiquitous; by these mere
commonplaces of an English landlord's life, what laws,
however awkward and rusty, could fail to move lightly
on well-oiled hinges? What does the tenant, in such a
case, think or care about the 'land laws?' What are
they to him more than the night-wind that whistles
through the keyhole of his well-warmed dwelling, erected
—like everything else upon the farm except the very
corn-ricks—by his landlord, and at a cost whose yearly
interest, exclusive of repairs, is a running item 'written
off' by the hand of Time, in the silent partnership
that meets his own investment in the soil.

Now take away all this; substitute, one cannot say
its 'opposite'—the picture of its mere *absence*—in every
particular; open the Pandora's box, and let out all the
ills that follow the "curse of absenteeism,"—the rack-rent,
the often unfurnished farm, with its lean kine, and fossil

implements, the dismal dirty cabin; and let the same wind blow upon the scene—upon " this picture and on that." Would it be possible, out of the same bare elements, to create a greater contrast? under the " same laws " to produce more opposite effects ?

But a contrast no less striking lies in this, that whilst in England the aggregation of land under the influence of entails has tended to create large farms ; on the other hand, it has been under these very laws that the worst evils that have ever been associated with small holdings of land, as seen in the cottier system of Ireland, have grown up ; and led to results that reached their climax in the Encumbered Estates Court, and the Potato Famine : whilst no such results have been ever exemplified or heard of in those countries, and they are many, whose laws are favourable instead of adverse to the distribution of land (in the sense understood by political economy). Yet that which looks so like a paradox, is as due to the simple laws of cause and effect as anything can be which the history of land teaches.

The solution lies in the well-known fact that men treat what is their own in one way, and what is another man's in another way ; that what is a man's own teaches him *care* and *economy*, while in dealing with that which is another's he learns indifference and waste.

Let Ireland on the one hand, and Belgium (or Prussia, since the introduction of Stein's system), on the other, be taken as illustrations. In the former were to be seen immense estates held, and let at second hand, by ' middle men ;' and let and sublet again, like a sporadic growth generating its kind, till it reached, if it *did* reach, its unit in the potato-patch. In the latter, the law which facilitates and cheapens purchase, to the small equally with the large buyer, beginning, *at the small end*, so to speak, sets at work the self-interest, and care, and prudence, of every individual who can buy, no matter what the quantity. The result shows itself in the conduct and character of a whole people. In each case, the land reflects like a mirror the motives set to work upon it. Take away the individual sense of property, and the opposite result is seen. Arthur Young's often-quoted words underlie the whole question. Those who attribute the results experienced in Ireland to national character, find in Ireland examples which contradict the judgment, even were it not nullified by the impossibility of distinguishing between cause and effect. In his speech on the second reading of the Irish Church Bill the Bishop of Lichfield (late Bishop of New Zealand) said:

"In New Zealand, Englishmen, Scotchmen, and Irishmen, live together upon the best terms. The qualities of each particular class become blended with each other to the improvement of all. No dissension as to tenant right can arise, *because every tenant has the right of purchasing the land he holds at a fixed price.* Under these circumstances the tenants, instead of being lazy and drunken, strain every nerve in order to save the money which will enable them to become the proprietors of the land they occupy. In this way it happens that the most irregular people of the Irish race become steady and industrious, acquiring property, and losing all their wandering habits, until it becomes almost impossible to distinguish between the comparative value of the character of Irish and Scotch elements.

"Of their loyalty to the Crown I can speak from my own observation, for the only regiment that is employed in keeping order in New Zealand is *Her Majesty's Royal Irish.*"

But if this be true in New Zealand, it is not less exemplified at home, where the impartial pen of the Times' correspondent in Ireland has exhibited instances of estates as well managed by *resident proprietors*, and in some cases by intelligent agents, and a tenantry as satisfied, prosperous, and attached, as in any part of England. The description given of the Bessborough tenantry might be taken as an exemplar of small farming. Where the same ameliorating causes are present the same results are found to follow ; but these are exceptions, and will continue to be so wherever the English land laws prevail unmodified by the hand of the resident proprietor, and the resources presented in a wealthy manufacturing country where the displaced agricultural population can find employment in the towns. It is not under such modifying conditions that our land laws work out their natural consequences. What we have to consider when examining *a system* are its absolute elements and structure, not the dress it may be made to wear under special circumstances, or in the lap of customs invented and adapted to relieve its pressure. Ireland has furnished the test and criterion of the naked action of laws, writing of which Lord St. Leonards, the most professional, not to say technical apologist they have ever had, acknowledges that "no young state ought ever to be entangled in the complication of our law of real property." Such an acknowledgment from such a quarter leaves little unsaid ; it would be difficult to frame a heavier indictment. Our colonies have, one and all, wisely shrunk from their imposition ; the United States rejected and repealed them as soon as they were free to choose, and there is now (with one, and that only a partial exception), not a country of the civilised world in which they survive. Ireland alone—not a colony, not a dependency, but an integral part of the United Kingdom—is involved in the unwelcome partnership of laws which we inflict upon ourselves in the teeth of our own Commissioners' Reports and the testimony of our greatest lawyers and economists.

"Committees and commissions," writes Mr. Booth, in answer to the Real Property Commissioners,* "composed of men of capacity and experience of all parties, have, over and over and over again, patiently and ably investigated the causes of the distresses, difficulties, and misfortunes peculiar to Ireland, and there has been an almost general concurrence of opinion in their numerous reports, as also in the writings of other able men, including those in the periodical press of the whole kingdom, that the system of Transfer of Land requires simplification and amendment. The whole subject has, in short, been so exhausted in these publications, that it is scarcely possible to suggest an idea upon it which has not been clearly expressed before.

"Simple absolute ownership of land is the condition most favourable to its improvement ; but, nearly up to the present time, such ownership has been very limited in Ireland. The land has been almost wholly held by tenants for life, often

* 'Report of the Commissioners for Registration of Title,' p. 411. Communication from Mr. William Booth, C.B. (Ordnance Office), Dublin.

liable to the payment of heavy annual charges for incumbrances, or by men holding under such circumstances of tenure as deprived them of that stimulus to the expenditure of labour and capital which accompanies a full ownership of land. The personal interest of the absolute owner is, that his land shall become as valuable in every respect as he can make it; that of the mere life annuitant, or of the man having any other limited interest in it, is merely that his own rent shall be as high as can be obtained. Millions of the public money have been lavishly squandered in the vain endeavour to put down evils which would have had no existence under a better state of the laws of property; disturbances and insurrections, with all their attendant misfortunes and crimes, have, until very recently, for a century past existed in Ireland as a chronic disease, clearly traceable to the anomalous state of ownership and tenure of land.

" So many difficulties beset the man who has any dealings with land, that some persons erroneously believe they were contrived expressly to deter men from becoming the owners of real property. There could not have arisen such universal dissatisfaction with the existing laws, or such general approbation of that most salutary measure, the Encumbered Estates Act, unless the evils of the ordinary system had become almost intolerable.

"The people of Ireland of the inferior classes are very shrewd and intelligent. I have often heard men of that class make use of a common saying, 'A pennyworth of land, a pound's worth of law.' Since the passing of the Encumbered Estates Act another expression has become common : ' It was the best thing ever done for Ireland.'

" There can be no doubt that Ireland, by means of its existing Registry of deeds, its complete Ordnance survey, and uniform public valuation, and the machinery formed under the Encumbered Estates Act, possesses obvious facilities for the introduction of some permanent system to facilitate the sale and transfer of land."

The Encumbered Estates Act did all that a temporary remedy could do for a permanent disease ; but it " scotched the snake, not killed it." It probed the wound and showed where the mischief lay. It even created wealth in Ireland, and a taste of prosperity which has flushed the cry for a constitutional cure, for land laws that shall not drift the country again into the renewed need of such a measure.

The treatment of the Irish land disease will hardly be

found out by ignoring its cause, lest the discovery should present us with the home motto, " Physician, cure thyself." Nor will the cure be hastened by indulging the selfish nationality that expects from another people the race-characteristics that do not belong to them. It may be startling to the English experience that prefers tenancy to ownership, or to the Scotch intelligence that has brought leasehold to a science, to find their panacea imperfectly appreciated by a people whose native attachment is to the land more than to forms of tenure, or even length of lease.

But statesmanship embraces all nationalities; and if the utmost freedom of land purchase,—which all authorities on the wealth of nations have pronounced to be one of the first of national benefits,—contain, as proved in other countries, the permanent cure for agrarian difficulty, the day may be nearer than it is thought,—and near it is, if there be truth in the maxim that a complete diagnosis is half a cure—when the long-running issue of Ireland's greatest trouble shall be dried up. But the malady of centuries' growth is not cured in a year.

Hitherto the points of view from which the history of our land laws has been considered have comprehended only the interests of the Owner, and the Occupier, whose individual and relative positions it has been attempted to trace.

The two classes that remain—the Labourer, and that large portion of the public who have no direct participation in the ownership or tenancy of land—seem to fall under a different field of inquiry. It is true, we commonly hear our agricultural system spoken of as comprehending the Landlord, the Tenant, and the Labourer, and so in a certain sense it does; but no one who considers the position of the labourer in English agriculture will assert that he has any fixed personal tie within the structure—that he stands to it in any relation but that of an auxiliary, more or less in demand at different seasons of the year, subject to the precarious vicissitudes of that demand, no longer indeed as in

former times, *adscriptus glebæ*—free to go and come as he
pleases, but without part or parcel in the land he helps
to cultivate, or any certain abode upon it, near it, or in
connection with it, for himself or for his family.

This is no overdrawn picture : neither are the facts
stated due to any surviving hardship of feudal habits
which modern legislation has forgotten to correct.   On
the contrary, the labourer was, till recent times, the
recognised inmate of the farmer's house, and still farther
back than this, the bond that tied him to the soil, the
badge of his servitude, was yet the link which connected
his life and social state with that of his employer, who
was usually the Owner of the land he tilled.   Time has
changed all this; and, for most other classes, for the
better.   But the same English reign that awarded to the
labourer his freedom, marks the origin of our Poor-
Law system—an ominous association—and his present
disconnection from all that is known as the " progress of
society," constitutes not only the reproach of our agricultural advancement, but an acknowledged blot upon
our social system.

It would be a libel upon any class of the generation
to which we belong to charge upon it the isolated
phenomenon which the agricultural labourer presents in
the midst of the growing wealth, and the growing poverty,
that are separating the modern life of this country into
the problem of two gigantic masses widening from each
other, and both rapidly augmenting : " Constantly increasing rates, constantly increasing pauperism, millions
of money spent, yet without satisfaction, and—infinitely
worse—millions of human beings whose very name
implies a degradation even in their own eyes as re-
cipients of parochial relief " * on the one side, and on the
other, on a scale never before exemplified, " the most
conclusive evidence that the production of wealth in
this country is so vast and so rapidly augmenting, that
it is idle to say poverty exists because enough wealth is
not produced."†

---

* Speech of the President of the Poor Law Board, December 20, 1868.
† Fawcett. 'Economic Position of the British Labourer,' p. 6.

An anomaly within this wider anomaly is presented in the farm-labourer; for while in every other feature of progress—in machinery, in skill, in applied science, and in scale of profit, the business to which his labour belongs has advanced at a ratio never before witnessed, his position has been, except in a few favoured districts, nearly stationary. Mr. Caird's tour, in 1850, through the counties of England, established that " while in the purely agricultural counties the rent of land, and the rent of a labourer's cottage had risen since the tour of Arthur Young, 100 per cent., the price of butter 100 per cent., and of meat 70 per cent., the rise in the labourer's wages was but 14 per cent." Over the south and west of England, the description given by Mr. Fawcett of those whose daily toil is on the land, is still applicable. " Theirs is a life of incessant toil for wages too scanty to give them a sufficient supply even of the first necessaries of life. No hope cheers their monotonous career : a life of constant labour brings them no other prospect than that when their strength is exhausted they must crave as suppliant mendicants a pittance from parish relief. Many classes of labourers have still to work as long, and for as little remuneration as they received in past times ; and one out of every twenty inhabitants of England is sunk so deep in pauperism that he has to be supported by parochial relief."*

Comparisons are sometimes drawn between the agricultural labourer in England, and in other countries ; but little reliance can be placed upon parallels made by travellers from hasty generalisation, mostly in accordance with foregone conclusions, and which contradict each other : the true and honest comparison in all countries is that which arises in measuring the relative advance of class with class at home. And here the state of the agricultural labourer presents itself as that of one thrown out of participation by the very system which his toil helps to build. The manual labour of an arable farm forms at least a third of the entire cost of production ; nothing is more common than to hear the

* Fawcett. ' Economic Position of the British Labourer,' p. 6

complaint of the great costliness of this element in the
year's accounts.   In his useful little essay Mr. Bailey
Denton remarks, " The only way to justify an increase of
the labourer's wages will be by rendering the value of
the labour greater than it now is."*   Yet its energy and
power are wasted, almost without a thought, even in the
mere element of *distance*,—which has been aptly compared
to the day's march of a soldier,—between the toiler and
his work ; coupled with a neglect of his comfort, of his
spirit, and of his intelligence, that diminishes its value
as much as the waste of physical power.

But effects do not arise without causes, and the condition of the labourer will derive no permanent change
from the mere suggestions of philanthropy.   It must be
studied in conjunction with the system of which it is a
part.   The law of Parish Settlement swept away Cottages, and the Union Chargeability Act has done
nothing to restore them.   Whose interest is it under
our universal system of tenancy, to provide the
labourer with a home that may connect him with his
work ?   The farming tenant cannot do so ; the land is
not his to build on, nor the permanent interest his, to
care to sprinkle the land with dwellings that might
furnish hands for acres to those who come after, or
even, it may be, for next year ; for who can tell what
change to himself a year may bring forth ?   And the
landlord cannot do it ; for what, under our system, is
his interest ?   He lets his land for the return that
another man's capital and skill can make of it, by any
means not forbidden in the agreement or lease.   It
is the tenant's natural endeavour—it is his business—to
make the most that he can, and within a certain time ;
and if he could cultivate his farm entirely by machinery,
without employing a single labourer upon it, it would
be worth his while to purchase a saving so economical to himself, placed as he is in the position of an
occupier to whose point of view each cottage is a
standing threat upon the rates, subject to *the whole* of
which he rents his farm.   Under our land-tenure system

* 'The Agricultural Labourer,' by J. Bailey Denton, Esq.

—that of the life owner under settlement, and the yearly tenant farming the land for the largest profit that can be made from it, by the most compendious machinery, with the least outlay of manual labour—the interest of the labourer in the soil, his relation to it, or to either of the other parties, is one admitting of strange definition. He is *not* his landlord's workman, and he is *not* his employer's tenant ;—the man who employs cannot house, and the man who could house does not employ him. Dependence has its advantages, and independence its charms ; but his lot is so cast as to derive the minimum of benefit from either.

The improvement of his present condition by education belongs to a great and solemn question of the day : but education which quickens the sense of hardship, also happily tends to emancipate the subject of it ; and an *educated* farm-labourer becomes, in too many cases now, a farm-labourer no longer.   When we are considering how to improve the nest, it hardly helps the inquiry to show how the birds may learn to fly out of it.   The question as to his cottage accommodation becomes, under our system, one of those detached problems that fall into the waste-basket of pure philanthropy.   Whence he comes in the morning to his work, or whither he goes in the evening when he has done it, provided he has done it, his employer, who has no cottage to give him nor means of building one, may vainly inquire ; and if it presses lightly upon him, still more remotely does it touch the landlord, who is ill prepared to spend the portions of his younger children in making questionable additions to the inheritance of his eldest, by erecting a class of buildings that have the worst reputation of all as an investment ; thereupon the Government is invoked to lend the public money—through " land improvement companies " empowered by Act of Parliament to furnish gentlemen's estates with Cottages, and to help " Tenant for life " out of the dilemma between younger children and philanthropy ; and public capital is invited to join an indirect scheme for keeping public capital out of the land-market.

Dr. Hunter, the medical officer of the Privy Council, inquires, " whether all land *which requires labour* ought not to be held liable to the obligation of containing a certain proportion of labourers' dwellings ;"* and so we go on putting legislative props under this decaying branch, and under that ; the last thought that occurs being that of examining what it is that *ails the circulation*,—what is the matter at the root ;—whether the defect be not in the system itself, which has been instrumental in bringing the condition of the farm labourer to be preached at as a standing subject for charity, philanthropy, state grants, and emigration, as if it was an isolated effect without a cause ? The question has been brought so frequently of late before the public, the facts have been so fully and forcibly stated, of the housing, and condition, and prospects, of the agricultural labourer, that it is useless to repeat the description. The point we have here to consider is its connection with the landed system of which it forms a part, a part thrown out, indeed, like the slag from the working of the furnace, and yet a part.

The striking defect of the system is that of his entire separation from all interest and share in the results of his own labour. " The worst-paid workmen in this country," says Mr. Fawcett, " are so thoroughly reckless that they seldom show any foresight for the future ; and even higher wages effect no permanent improvement in the condition of the poor. They do not save their increased earnings, but spend their money either in drink or luxurious living. That this should be the case can be a matter of no surprise whatever. There is no effect of ignorance more certain than an almost entire absence of foresight ; and the life of a hired labourer can exert no influence whatever towards cultivating any of the habits of prudence. . . . How much more powerfully would prudence be stimulated, if a definite prospect were held out, that a labourer might in the course of time, by means of his saving, secure a small landed property ! The value of such an acquisition

* Seventh Report.

is not to be estimated by the amount of wealth with
which it enriches him. It makes him, in fact, a different
man; it raises him from the position of a mere labourer,
and calls forth all those active qualities of mind which
are sure to be exerted when a man has the consciousness
that he is working on his own account."

The proposal contained in this last paragraph has been
looked upon in some quarters as if it was chimerical.
The circumstances of 'landed property' have with us
become so thoroughly exceptional, that the very idea of
what may be described as its *proportional* acquisition or
enjoyment has ceased to be regarded as a possible reality.
Such is the effect of habit and custom on many minds that
they come to regard conventional impediments sanctioned
by the law as if they were natural impossibilities. The
effect becomes a cause, and the obstacles that artificially
exist are the lions in the path of their own removal;
and the argument goes into a circle.

Mr. Bailey Denton, in his essay before referred to,
observes : " An agricultural labourer, if he is fortunate
enough to have—what he ought invariably to have—a
rood of garden ground as part of his occupation, which he
may cultivate after he has done his wage-paid work,
will grow upon it vegetables sufficient to yield him a
return, after payment of rent and for seed, of at least
4*l.* a year, which is rather more than 1*s.* 6*d.* a week.
. . . If I am right, the labourer makes from his garden
ground a profit equivalent to the rent of his cottage."
And in a previous page he says : " As newly-built cottages
are now usually placed so as to reduce to a minimum
the distance the labourer has to walk, whereby time and
sinew are saved, the advantages to the employer are, in
the aggregate, equal to the difference between the return
due to the condemned hovel and that due to the improved
cottage ; and thus, in point of fact, the farm labourer
receives in a better home an equivalent to increased
wages."

A consummation devoutly to be wished. But meantime (with some striking exceptions in the eastern counties) there is not a living animal connected with the

farm, from the Draught-Team down to the Sheep-dog, that
is not better lodged and looked after than the labourer
and his family. And it is curious enough that the
omission of the Farm is stereotyped in the omission of
the Legislature, which has conceded every loan-claim
that fettered ownership has asked for but this one, which
really forms the most notable deficiency in the "Furniture" of almost every English farm.

The last point, the one last thought of, yet immeasurably the most important of all, is the effect of our land
laws on the whole of that class who have no participation
in the soil, who look upon its ownership from a distance
as a thing that has long grown out of the reach of the
great bulk of the community by its costliness of purchase, and the still more discouraging prospect of its
continuing costliness *to hold*; who see it gathering year
by year into larger territorial acreages, beyond the
reach, as beyond the prudence of moderate or small
investments, who are jauntily assured that henceforward
in this country land is to be regarded as the "pleasure-
ground" of the rich, and that whatever political economy
may say about the distribution of wealth, at least when
it takes this form, it is neither profitable nor desirable
that it should be owned in any but the largest quantities—estates that will support their lawyer and their
land-agent without sensible diminution of the rental.
Of the actual inducement offered by our present system
of transfer to buy small quantities of land, the two
following Tables will furnish some idea.* The first is
that of purchases over, and the second of purchases at
or under 1000*l.*, during a period of four years :—

* 'List of Purchaser's expenses, furnished by Mr. George Sweet, Barrister
(Conveyancer) to the Commission for Registration of Title,' p. 381.

TABLE 1.

Purchase Money.	Purchaser's Expenses, irrespective of Stamp Duty, &c.		
£	£	s.	d.
1,800	24	0	10
4,667	54	5	4
2,300	52	0	4
1,260	17	2	8
2,662	39	0	0
1,340	40	9	2
1,695	21	10	0
1,835	32	0	10
1,248	46	12	2
1,895	54	8	0
2,274	72	4	6
£22,976	£453	13	10

TABLE 2.

Purchase Money.	Purchaser's Expenses irrespective of Stamp Duty, &c.		
£	£	s.	d.
1,000	46	12	0
956	23	19	0
746	48	12	6
600	31	10	0
500	15	6	8
230	39	13	3
225	15	7	0
100	23	14	3
£4,357	£244	14	8

These Tables show an average of $2\frac{1}{2}$ per cent., or five times the ad valorem stamp duty, which alone is a heavy tax. But an average gives no evidence of the burthen in individual cases. Thus in Table 2, taken alone, the average expense of the purchaser is nearly 6, and in the last case 23 per cent.! The vendor's expenses would be in every case much higher.

It is not to be wondered at that under such discouragement attending the mere initiatory step, and irrespective of all the after-circumstances attending the ownership of land, it should gradually cease to enter into the thoughts of the great bulk of small and middle-class investors, and come to be looked upon as the expensive plaything only of the largest fortunes. It is beyond the power of judgment or calculation to estimate the effect, upon a saving and industrious community, of this denial of the most natural and preferred of all forms of investment—the purchase of land. We see the picture of its alternative, in speculations of the wildest and most wasteful character entered upon by the public under sanguine views, often equalled only by the ignorance of the

very nature of the objects undertaken ; where thousands
of small capitals which, employed upon the land under
the influence of a very small share of the *auri sacra
fames* that vents itself to no purpose upon useless or deceptive schemes, would set to work tens of thousands of
agricultural labourers.   It would be difficult to paint the
portrait of a folly more cruel and suicidal than that
which, by home-made obstruction, purely artificial and
conventional, intercepts the inward flow of capital, and
drives it from our shores in pursuit of objects far more il-
lusory and worthless than the conversion of the most impracticable moor or bog that ever was turned into an
example-farm.

In the very "madness" of such home investment there
lies a "method" which belongs to the birthright of
the labourer.   To him first, and to the home consumer
secondly, there arises benefit upon schemes of land
restoration and improvement that might have remained
for centuries neglected, if the returns of the capitalist
had been the only point of calculation.   Every cause
that interferes with the transfer—with the free circulation—of land is laden with this heavy responsibility, one
that operates in the same or a like degree upon no other
form that wealth can take.

The mischief of artificial laws is not simply, or even
primarily, the evil they set up, but the *good they prevent,*
by interfering with those natural laws whose salutary
action they intercept.   It ought to be superfluous to say
that what is wholesomest for every country, is that
wealth, whatever form it takes, should exist in both large
and small, and every intermediate proportion without
hindrance from the agency of factitious rules and
theories.   The rule applies unchanged to that which
takes the form of land.   It is not true that small estates
or that large estates are evils ; but it is true that
artificial restrictions, and exceptional laws directed to
produce either extreme, whether in England or any other
country, are an evil, more mischievous than is commonly
supposed.   They not only affect injuriously the immediate
subject of their operation, but disturb all the relations

naturally connected with it. And of nothing is this so true as of the land. There is not a class of society unaffected by the laws that govern it.

If this proposition appear too sweeping, let it be borne in mind that the earth is literally *the leaf we feed on,* the original source of all wealth, and of the whole machinery of human action consequent thereon. Let it be asked whether it is probable that an error in the laws that govern it should be a trifling matter, a mere mistake, of small moment, or limited action, involving no consequences that interpenetrate the social action of the community : whether it is safe or prudent to indulge theories *in favour of* small estates, or large estates in land ; when the trodden experience of life ought sufficiently to demonstrate that the mere tendency of a " law " to produce either extreme is its condemnation.

The comparison of large and small holdings in land is useful in so far as it brings into practical view their relative advantages, and limits, both in mode of culture and speciality of produce, their adaptation to peculiarities of soil and climate, and to the varying genius of race (for the differences of national aptitude and bent are evident and unquestionable) ; but, as a matter of controversy, it is unpractical and inconclusive, since no result of argument can bring it within the proper sphere of legislation, or under any human tribunal. The laws have no such office, and custom will take care of itself. All that the hand of legislation can do is to remove every obstruction to the wholesome operation of the natural laws which regulate the distribution of land, and its response to the causes that affect it, under laws as inflexible as those that govern the tides. The Anglo-Danish monarch might have reversed the throne that his courtiers set for him on the sea-shore, and with equal wisdom have again apostrophised the littleness of human power when it attempts to govern the laws that govern *the land.*

The real property laws of this country, from the period immediately succeeding the Conquest down to the present

L

time, present a history consistent with itself in one
particular, that of a perpetual struggle of rival interests.
The parties to the conflict have differed in successive
periods; the feudal sovereign, the baron, the churchman,
the lawyer, and the landowner have each entered into
the strife in turn, each as the pressure of adverse power
or of selfish interest impelled them.   The result of all
these struggles was the system bequeathed two centuries
ago, and under which, with but slight modification, the
business of the country is still carried on.   But in those
struggles there are two voices that were never heard—
two interests little thought of—those of the Political
Economist, and the Agriculturist.   Can it be wondered
at, if the state of those laws be found productive of
results injurious to the best practices of the one, and
violating the first principles of the other?   There is
probably in the history of this country no instance to be
found in which the ripened and intelligent desire of the
community, clearly and repeatedly expressed through the
most public, the most able, the most learned channels,
upon a subject which has received prolonged and exhaustive investigation by a succession of Royal Commissions—has waited so long and so patiently upon the
hand of legislation as that which has asked for the reform
of our law of Real Property, especially as affecting the
transfer of land.   Whether the subject be looked at from
the point of view of the Jurist as a question of law-reform,
in the restoration of simple and inexpensive, instead of
complicated and costly procedure, or from that of the
Agriculturist in respect of the influence that this branch
of the law exercises over our most important home-
industry, or from that of the Political Economist pleading
for the rights of the community in the distribution of
public wealth,—the cry is still the same, " Free the land;"
release it from the shackles in which time, and customs,
and interests—long passed away—have entangled it,
obstructing its adaptation to the uses of modern life, and
presenting it as an anachronism upon the face of our
institutions.

It is almost idle to expect—from those whose professional education and whose daily practice have been engaged upon the traditional forms and technical framework of a system which comes to their hands sanctioned by the usages and stamped by the learning of centuries,— from them to expect the initiative of that emancipation of land which the necessities of modern life, agricultural and commercial, demand, from restrictions imposed during historical periods, when those interests had no representative in the State.

The land has parted with protection in the disposal of its produce, and confronts the rivalry of the world. In that rivalry it encounters the laws which govern the productive powers of other States, laws resting upon the diffusion, not the concentration of land, or the contraction of its resources.

The testimony of a host of witnesses who have communicated their views personally or by writing, to the Royal Commissions that have sat from time to time during the last *forty years,* and of writers, professional and otherwise, whose very pamphlets, if collected, would form an encyclopædia of real-property-law reform, might be cited to show that the rendering *effectual* the Registry of title, based upon an authorised map on the cadastral (6 inch) scale, and free of stamp-duty for the first five years—restriction of Entail to lives in being at the date of the Settlement, or death of the Testator, -- the assimilation of the law of landed Intestacy to that in the case of personalty, the fusion of Legal and Equitable estates, and the assimilation of the law of agricultural to that of trade Fixtures, would do more to advance the interests of those concerned in the land, and those dependent on them, than all the cumbrous mechanism which the law now lavishes upon forms that operate by withdrawing from each ownership in turn that fertilising power and action in the present, which experience has shown to be the best protection of the Future.

III.

THE TENURE OF LAND IN INDIA.

By George Campbell.

CONTENTS.

TENURES PREVIOUS TO BRITISH RULE.

IT is sometimes said that India is composed of so many different countries that we can never speak of it as a whole. I do not think that is the case in the full sense in which the statement is made. Probably, six or eight hundred years ago, in the European countries which had been conquered and ruled first by the Romans and then by the Germanic peoples, there was a greater similarity of institutions and manners than in modern days. Similarly it has happened that, however different may have been the aborigines of different provinces of India, they have been covered by successive waves, first of Hindoo populations, and then of Mahommedan conquerors, and so have been assimilated in perhaps a greater degree than ever were European countries.

We have no historical record of the advances of the Hindoo peoples, but much still remains, in the ethnography and institutions of the country, to show that they may be divided into at least two classes, the earlier Brahminical Hindoos, and the later tribes of more democratic character and more nearly allied to the Germans, who preceded the Mahommedans in the rule of the country. After all that has passed, the institutions of these Hindoo races still survive in almost every Indian village.

The Mahommedan conquest and dominion was more complete and more centralized than that of any power which has ruled in Europe since the Romans. Twice have Mahommedan empires ruled over the whole of India, with little exception. In the interval between these two universal empires the country was not lost to the Mahommedans, but was for the most part divided among several Mahommedan dynasties, very similar to one another in character. The last great Mahommedan empire, which welded all India into one country, was in its zenith no longer ago than the beginning of the last century. Its rule was highly centralised, and from Peshawur to Cape Comorin on the one side, and to Chittagong on the other, much of its official system, and almost all its official language, survive to the present day.

My view then is that, although the present circumstances of the various provinces of India infinitely vary, their institutions may be traced to very similar sources. We may say that very varied forms have been built up on various plans, but that the materials are in the main the same. I would first try to explain the conditions of landed tenures which we found in existence, and then would exhibit the different phases which they have assumed in different provinces under British administration.

The long-disputed question, whether private property in land existed in India before the British rule, is one which can never be satisfactorily settled, because it is, like many disputed matters, principally a question of the meaning to be applied to words. Those who deny the existence of this property mean property in one sense; those who affirm its existence mean property in another sense. We are too apt to forget that property in land, as a transferable mercantile commodity absolutely owned and passing from hand to hand like any chattel, is not an ancient institution but a modern development, reached only in a few very advanced countries. In the greater part of the world the right of cultivating particular portions of the earth is rather a privilege than a property; a privilege first of a whole people, then of a particular tribe or a particular village community, and finally, of particular individuals of the community. In this last stage the land is partitioned off to these individuals as a matter of mutual convenience, but not in unconditional property; it long remains subject to certain conditions and to reversionary interests of the community, which prevent its uncontrolled alienation, and attach to it certain common rights and common burdens.

A still more important distinction is this, that in countries which have been conquered by immigrant races from predecessors who had already cultivated the soil (that is, in almost all the countries of the old world), the dominant arms-bearers generally cannot cultivate the whole of the land themselves, and do not attempt to cultivate through others on the modern capitalist farmer and labourer system; they willingly leave in actual possession of the greater part of the soil the people who cultivated it and who are attached to it by many bonds. Hence we have a very widely-prevailing distinction between the privilege of levying the customary rent and the privilege of occupying the soil. In India the rent was generally levied by the State or the immediate

assignees and representatives of the State; but, nevertheless, there was frequently to be found in the village
communities a privilege or property in the occupation
and management of the soil, which constituted as strong
a form of property as can anywhere be found short of
our modern form of landed property. I do not here
refer to the disputed question of the right of occupancy
as between landlord and ryot, which is the latest phase
of Indian land questions, but to the rights of some
of those whom we now put in the proprietory class.
I cannot imagine a more distinct privilege-property
than that of some of the strong Jat villages in the
Punjab territories, many of which were rather tributary
republics than subjects or tenants. In the sense, then,
of the right of holding the land subject to the payment
of customary rents, I think that private property in
land has existed in many parts of India from time immemorial.

The feudal system I believe to be no invention of the
middle ages, but the almost necessary result of the hereditary character of Indo-Germanic institutions, when the
tribes take the position of dominant conquerors. They
form, in fact, a hereditary army with that gradation of
fealty from the commander-in-chief to the private soldier,
which is essential to military operations. Accordingly
we find that among all the tribes of Indo-Germanic blood
which have conquered and ruled Indian provinces, the
tendency is to establish a feudal system extremely
similar to that which prevailed in Europe. In Rajpootana, the system is still in full force. The Mahrattas
and Sikhs had both established a similar system. In
my early days it existed in great perfection in some
parts of the Cis-Sutlej Sikh States. But the Mahommedan system is quite non-hereditary—I may say, anti-
hereditary. The genius of their centralized government
was entirely opposed to the feudal system; and wherever
they have completely ruled, they have swept it away.
Hence it has only survived in those Rajpoot States
which were indulgently permitted to retain a self-governed
position as tributaries, and among some border tribes

never thoroughly subdued. It had been but partially redeveloped in the Hindoo States which had a brief independent existence between the fall of the Mahommedan and the rise of British power. Rajpootana then not being British territory, and the surviving Mahratta and Sikh Jaghardeers being in most instances rather rulers than subjects, it may be said that, notwithstanding the feudal genius of the people, the feudal system does not prevail in our territories. There are a good many tributary chiefs and sub-holders under them in the wilder parts of the country, and several gradations of tenure may still be found in some provinces; but no great province is organized on a regular feudal system.

There are, however, numerous grants of the revenue due from particular tracts or plots of land, and to these revenue-free holdings only do the Mahommedans apply the term "milk," or property. They are very frequently granted by the ruler for the time being in terms importing perpetuity; but being almost always assigned for some particular purpose—the support of a particular religious institution—for a particular service of some kind—or for the livelihood of a particular family—they may be considered as being property entailed and inalienable. In practice they were always resumable at the pleasure of the ruler of the day; and under native rule there was a continual process of resuming old grants, and granting new ones. In the confusion attending the downfall of dynasties, many grants of this kind were made by subordinates of insufficient authority; many were set up by fraud and usurpation; and the known tenderness of British rule for anything bearing the appearance of property, as well as our foreign ignorance, greatly encouraged such claims and usurpations, in the provinces which first came into our hands. The sifting of these grants, and distinguishing the good from the bad, and those made for purposes still subsisting from those for services no longer rendered, is a process which always requires early attention. We have treated them under very liberal rules. Renouncing the arbitrary de facto powers of native princes, we have recognised, as valid and binding, all grants made by any authority which was at the time competent to make them, and have given the grantees a complete and certain tenure, instead of the precarious tenure at the pleasure of the prince for the time being. All incomplete tenures having some show of long possession or other equitable claim, we have treated very tenderly, either maintaining them, or giving them terms of very easy compromise. We have not only professed this indulgent treatment, but we have embodied these lenient rules in public laws, and have opened the courts of justice to all who wish to appeal to them from the decisions of the executive officers. Altogether, so far, nothing could be more equitable and indulgent than the treatment of the whole subject. But it unfortunately happened that in some of our older provinces, the investigations necessary to apply the rules were long delayed—the most fraudulent and unfounded tenures acquired a certain prescription of possession—and when the inquiry was at last made, there was a good deal of bitterness and outcry, which led to still more indulgent compromises. I believe that these investigations have now been entirely or almost completed in every province, and that the whole matter is finally set at rest.

The permanent revenue-free holdings thus created, though large in the aggregate, are in most districts very inferior in extent to the lands which remain subject to the public revenue, and may therefore be put aside as exceptional.

In the course of the general investigation of titles, which forms part of what we call a settlement, it is determined whether the grant-holders have a complete title to the land, or are only entitled to the public rent or revenue. In very many cases—in almost all the larger holdings—they are but revenue receivers, while the land is actually held by others whose privileges are similar to those held under Government. In other cases, especially in the smaller holdings, the grantee either held the land before it was made revenue-free, or has in some manner obtained possession of it.

In that case, he is the complete owner. A large proportion of the grants are, as I have said, held for specific trusts; but many (too many, in my opinion) have evaded such obligations. These latter are now freely alienable, and they constitute the only complete landed property in the English sense which exists in India.

Having disposed of the revenue-free tenures once for all, I return to the normal condition of land in India; that is, when it pays rent or revenue to the State, but is occupied and managed by individuals. The whole question whether we consider the State to have been the superior proprietor, may be narrowed to the question whether we are to call the State receipts revenue or rent; and that again may be got over by showing what the dues of the State really are, and leaving it to every man to give them what name he chooses.

The original form of the due received by the State from the land was certainly a share of the produce. When the crop is reaped the State is entitled to a proportion of the grain, regulated according to the custom of the locality. That is a very old institution. In very ancient times the proportions were less than in modern times—one-tenth or one-eighth—and I am unable to say whether the subsequent enhancement of the State share is chiefly owing to greater demand for land to feed a larger population, and consequent natural increase of rent, or whether it is rather owing to enhancement of taxation on the part of successive conquerors. But this is certain, that in modern times, and indeed for centuries past, the share taken has been so large as to be no mere tax, but substantially to absorb the rent. It has amounted, in fact, to a customary rent raised to the highest point to which it can be raised without causing the people to emigrate or rebel, and so defeating its own end. It seems to me that the distinction between a tax and a rent is merely matter of amount; and that if a land tax is so high as to absorb the rent, it becomes in fact rent. In this view the State in India may be considered to have been the superior proprietor, in the same sense as any other proprietor who is entitled to receive customary rents, but does not cultivate or manage the land.

In no part of India, and under no form of government, did the State undertake these latter functions, or any others analogous to those of an English landlord. Except in the assignment of waste land to be cultivated on the customary tenure, there never was any system of interference with the immediate possession of the soil; no letting it by competition to the highest bidder, or anything of that kind. Those in possession of the village area were left in possession, and were allowed to manage their own affairs, subject only to the State right to receive its dues before the crops were carried from the ground.

The State, then, generally took very nearly, if not quite a full rent; but, so far as my knowledge goes, there was seldom in India any systematic attempt on a large scale to go beyond this point, by chaining the people to the soil, and so exacting from them a customary rent larger than the real rent, as was the case in Europe when free trade in tenants was put a stop to by the system of serfage. The people have never been adscripti glebæ. I cannot say whether this is due to the large population and cheap labour, rendering anything like agricultural slavery unprofitable, or to equitable laws. The Hindoo system was one of small States, or when there have been large feudal organisations the territory was divided among different chiefs. I should judge that in a country abounding in great open plains, and where personal property is in small compass and light, it would have been scarcely possible to prevent the escape of a dissatisfied ryot to another jurisdiction. To the present day we have sometimes complaints that a tenant has decamped in the night without paying his rent, and carried his house with him. Under the more centralised Mahommedan rule, the equitable Mahommedan laws did not permit any excessive tyranny of the great and rich over the poor. And so it has happened that under all governments, notwithstanding many hardships, the people have always in India enjoyed a great amount of individual freedom.

To this extent only it may be said that, in the times immediately preceding our rule, the Government rent was not unfrequently driven beyond a full rent, viz., that the settled ryots, the ancient inhabitants attached to the soil by the bonds of affection, habit, and property, were sometimes made to pay heavier rates than the mere temporary sojourners who were induced to come from elsewhere, and to take up, on exceptionally favourable terms, the lands left uncultivated for want of hands, at times when the country had been depopulated by wars and famines. The old inhabitants no doubt had the first choice of the best land, but still I believe that the result of the system was, that in hard times grasping rulers took from them both the fullest rent, and anything more that they could be induced to pay, rather than abandon their household gods, and the wells and other improvements which they had made.

It must not be supposed that the customary rent consisted of a uniform share of the produce levied equally on all crops, and under all circumstances. On the contrary, the system was to a remarkable degree adapted to the circumstances, with much regard to principles which we should call political economy. Not only did the share taken vary in different parts of the country, but it also varied in respect of different kinds of crops, and different modes of cultivation. For instance, crops raised by artificial irrigation (not supplied from Government works), usually rendered a smaller proportion than those raised without irrigation, because in the former case a larger proportion was due to the labour and capital of the cultivator. The more valuable products, as sugar-cane, cotton, vegetables, &c., paid money rates according to the measurement of the land—the produce not being divided. The proportion of grain crops taken as rent or revenue may be said in modern times to have varied from one-fourth to one-half, one-fourth being a decidedly light assessment—one-half the heaviest. One-third and two-fifths were, I should say, the most common rates. The grain only was divided, the cultivator usually retaining the straw. In ordinary

agricultural villages he also had free grazing for his
cattle on the village common, but in parts of the country
where a large proportion of the land was given to
grazing, a cess per head was levied on the cattle.

I am not aware that the rent was in any part of India
paid in labour as in Europe ; but in addition to the
proper rent, it was a common arrangement that the
villagers furnished a regulated number of unpaid
labourers for the service of the rajah.   These labourers
were men of the servile classes, who received a small but
exactly regulated proportion of the grain from the
threshing floor, as their remuneration for this and other
labour.   When the labour was not exacted, its value
was charged to the village, and formed a regular item
in the accounts.

Most frequently the grain is not actually taken in
kind, but being weighed at the threshing-floor, the value
of the Government share is charged at the market rate,
and paid in cash.

Another mode is to estimate the produce of the crops
on the ground before they are cut, and to charge the
value of the proportions derived from the estimate ; but
in this case, allowance being made for over-estimate and
the risk which the farmer runs, the proportion is calculated at a lower rate than when the grain is actually
divided ; for instance, if the division rate is one-third, the
estimate rate will be one-fourth.

In each locality, then, there is a regular and exact
scale of rates and charges established by long practice.
I know no mode by which these rates can be altered in
a constitutional manner : to make a radical alteration of
this kind would be a revolutionary measure such as
would only be effected by a very strong Government;
perhaps by a conqueror making new arrangements for
the first time.   But in another way native governments
generally contrive to squeeze their subjects a little more,
viz., by the system of cesses, dues, and benevolences so
well known in Europe.   These are generally not taken
in an altogether uncertain manner ; there is much
system in all these arrangements, and the various cesses

are for the most part regularly entered in the revenue accounts and uniformly levied ; the peculiarity, however, being that a rate once made for a temporary purpose very soon acquires, in the ruler's eyes, the sanction of custom, and is continued long after the necessity for it has ceased. Thus, then, a native revenue account exhibits, besides the main rent, a succession of small charges— perquisites of various officials—perquisites of the rajah's wife—contributions to the marriage expenses of the rajah's son—and so on.

Previous to our rule, the Government share of the crop had been in some parts of the country commuted into money rates, classified according to the most prominent descriptions of soil, and the nature of the crops grown. These money rates were equally subject to the extra cesses which I have mentioned.

Besides the Government dues made up of the aggregate of the assessment on each individual, there were frequently charges upon the whole village, such as the value of forced labour already mentioned—benevolences levied in the lump—fines and compensations for value of property plundered in the village limits—and such like ; and these charges were partitioned among the individual members of the community, according to fractional shares or other form of account, representing the interests of each.

The village is the well-known unit of all revenue arrangements, and it may be said of all landed tenures in India. I use the word not to signify a village in our sense, but rather the area of land occupied by a community who generally reside together in a village. In the plain and thickly-populated country it may be said that all the land cultivated and uncultivated belongs to one village or another. The country is, in fact, partitioned off into villages ; the village boundaries are known (if they are not the subject of feuds), and where one village ends another begins.

When I speak of a village "community," I use this latter word in our ordinary English sense, and not to signify the actual holding of property in common.

Nothing can be a greater mistake than to attribute to the Indian village system any of the features of communism. It is true that in early times, before communities have settled down to fixed cultivation, the land is held to a great degree in common for grazing purposes, private property being in cattle, not in land ; and even after it has been distributed for the purposes of cultivation, the custom of periodically adjusting inequalities by redistribution has not unfrequently subsisted to a much later time. But even in this latter case the land was never equally distributed, but was only reparted according to the recognised ancestral shares, casual inequalities and usurpations being redressed. As communities become more and more fixed and settled, this practice of redistribution dies out ; and it may be said that in modern communities, in civilized parts of the country, it no longer exists. Encroachments may of course be resisted and redressed, but inequalities founded on possession of long standing are redressed by redistribution of the burdens, not by redistribution of the land.

The bond which keeps together a village community is, then, rather municipal than a community of property. The cultivated land is held by individuals, and the common interest in common property is scarcely greater than that which exists among the commoners of an English manor. The waste land and grazing ground is held in common, certain common receipts are brought to a common fund, certain common charges are charged against the same fund, and distributed in a cess on individuals according to their holdings. There is a system of municipal management, and the community claims to exercise a certain limited control over its members, and to have a reversionary right to the land of members who cease to cultivate or fail to pay ; but beyond this there is complete individual freedom.

The Indian village is best known in England by the descriptions which have been given by Elphinstone and others of the Deccan village ; but in my view that is a somewhat decayed form of the true village of the stronger Hindu tribes, and we must look for the strongest and most perfect village form in the more complete and more democratic communities, such as we find in the Punjab territory. It is these which I have cited as exhibiting the strongest form of Peasant property.

A Jat village community consists of a body of free-men of one caste, and who traditionally derive from a common ancestor—clansmen, in fact. A village may be divided into two or three parts, held by different castes or tribes, but I describe a simple village. Every man has his share, which is generally in the Punjab expressed in plough lands. A plough land is not a uniform quantity of land, but a share in the particular village. There may be sixty-four or a hundred and twenty-eight, or any other number of shares; one man has two ploughs, another a plough and a half, another half a plough, and each holds land representing his share.

The community is managed by a council of elders, who rule it so long as they retain the confidence of the people, and who conduct all negotiations with the Government. In such a village, then, the body of the cultivators consider themselves to be proprietors. They are united, and very strong; they certainly exercise rights of property; and no one would dream of attempting to disturb them.

Most republics have been in some degree served by some inferior race, and in these Indian communities a smaller body of the servile tribes is almost invariably attached to the village; not slaves, but servile labourers. They may cultivate small portions of land, but they have no part in the village management, and would not, I think, be considered to have rights of property. Again, persons of better condition, but not members of the proprietary tribe, may have settled in the village and obtained land. The Government dues being such as to leave scarcely any margin between rent and revenue, we almost always find that all these people pay the same rates as the original proprietors. It may be that they are not admitted to a voice in the manage-ment, or to share in certain common receipts or per-quisites levied by the headmen; but the distinction

M

between an original proprietor and a cultivator long settled in the community, and in a great degree adopted into it, frequently became very shadowy in native times.*

Where we have strong communities, there is little difficulty in dealing with the community. But more frequently we have phases of land tenure which are much more doubtful. In some provinces, where the Indo-German tribes have not fully penetrated, the village constitutions perhaps never were so complete as those which I have described. My impression is that the ancient Brahminical institutions were by no means so democratic. Both in Lower Bengal and in Cashmere the villages have much less cohesion.

Again, in great parts of the country, war, desolation, and famine have, during the last century, obliterated many communities, and their place on the land has been taken by casual cultivators, hanging loosely together, and who can claim no ancient rights in the soil.

A still more common phase is the following :—The older proprietary tribes have been exhausted by prosperity, promotion, military service, misfortune, and the many vicissitudes of Indian history ; they have ceased to hold their original position. But a small remnant partially occupies the place where once they were dominant ; and the land which they have ceased to till has been occupied by others. This has frequently happened to Rajpoot communities in the north-west provinces, and to other tribes in the south of India. The reduced representatives of the old tribe will generally be found to assert claims which the others do not always admit. The Government officers take their dues from the old inhabitants and new comers indifferently, and looking to revenue will not permit the former to keep others out of that which they cannot cultivate themselves. The old families may or may not furnish the headman through whom the Government

---

* For facility of reference, I give in this Paper a short account of the indigenous village communities, &c.; but some years ago I published details on the subject. *Modern India*, chap. iii.—G. C.

collects its dues; they may or may not receive some of the old perquisites for duties which they may or may not perform. But I think I may say that the relation between the old and the new occupants never, under native rule, takes the form of landlord and tenant. There is no such thing as an old family letting the lands to tenants at its pleasure, and making its profit of the rents. Wherever they have the management, it is as headmen accounting to the Government for their collections. And wherever they have certain dues, it is in the shape of perquisites, not of rent.

In all cases in which there was not a democratic body electing their own headmen, there was a headman whose functions were partly those of a Government officer, and partly those of the head of a quasi-municipality. This headman was called the Mokaddum in the more northern and eastern provinces; Potail in western and central India and in the Maratta Deccan; and Gauda in some other parts of the south. The office was semi-hereditary, as almost all Hindoo offices are, that is, the fittest member of the late official's family succeeds, with the sanction of the ruling power, some preference being given to seniority combined with approved fitness. The Potail accounted for the revenue collections, receiving the perquisites and percentages which were the accustomed dues of the office. Then there was an accountant, who held on a similar tenure, and sometimes combined with it the functions of village banker; and there were other officers, each paid by the established perquisites. The whole constitute the form of community described by authors who have written of the Deccan and other provinces similarly situated.

What, if any, were the rights of the cultivators of comparatively recent settlement who do not come within the category of village proprietors, is a question which has been raised into great importance of recent years, since there has been discussion of the relative rights of landlords and tenants, but to which no definite answer can be given. It is and must remain a mere matter of opinion whether the facts establish a claim to consideration or not. There was no law to determine such rights, and no standard by which they could be measured. It is certain that, as a rule, such cultivators were not dispossessed so long as they wished to hold their fields ; but it may equally be asserted that if any individual for any reason were dispossessed, there was little chance of any remedy available to him. We have no details of the social arrangements of any former period when India was so settled and so well cultivated that cultivators had difficulty in obtaining land in one place or other. During the prosperous period of the Mahommedan empire, the cultivators were no doubt in some sort protected. All the Mahommedan Regulations aim at that object. But during the century of anarchy which preceded our settled dominion, there was for them only the protection which circumstances afforded. In fact, the depopulation and reduction of cultivated area, resulting from a long anarchy had almost everywhere occasioned a demand for cultivators, which, as soon as peace was restored in any province, rendered the position of the ryot in some respects favourable. Instead of being obliged to compete for land, he found that there was a competition for ryots. A ruler's strength and wealth, under a system of customary rents, depended on the number of his ryots and the extent of their cultivation ; and a man not embarrassed by local ties could generally make favourable terms.

As no one was evicted, the question of compensation for improvements never arose. It is not, however, altogether lost to sight. Wherever there is a question between the representatives of a declining body still claiming to be owners of the land, but not fully occupying it, and strangers holding it on terms not yet admitted to be permanent, the making of an improvement which cannot be removed—the building of a well, or even the planting of a tree—is always regarded with jealousy, as an act involving ownership or at least permanent occupancy. The Indian law does not, as with us, give to the proprietor everything that is put upon the land ; it remains the property of the man who put it

there. An Indian proprietor, therefore, does not claim
a right to benefit by another man's improvement; he
objects to his making the improvement, as involving a
property inseparable from the soil. I have had such
complaints in modern days. If an improvement of a
solid immovable kind be made, I think the right of
occupancy would be admitted. But unless a well be built
or a grove planted, the ordinary agricultural requirements
are so few as to give rise to little question of compensation. The house is built of mud, which is of no value,
and the wood used for the roof is taken away by an
outgoing ryot. The principal expenditure in the way of
improvement is in bringing jungle into cultivation, and
many of the recently-settled ryots had established that
claim to permanency.

The general result seems to be that there was no
definite law giving a right of occupancy to nonpro-
prietary cultivators, and that the equitable claims of
these men varied infinitely in degree. But there was in
the general language of the country a distinction between
ryots settled as permanent inhabitants of and cultivators
in a village who had given pledges by building and
clearing and establishing themselves, and had accepted a
share of common obligations, and those other ryots who
were avowedly mere temporary sojourners, or who, without sojourning at all, came from some other village to
cultivate patches of land. The former were called
" Khoodkasht," or " own cultivating," " Chapper bund,"
or " house tied," and sometimes " Mooroossee," or " hereditary ;" while the latter were called " Pye-kasht," a
term implying that they come and go at pleasure. The
sentiment and feeling of the country was certainly in
favour of the moral claim of the former class to hold the
land as long as they cultivated and paid their rent.
Some think that our Government might be justified in
treating these men as tenants-at-will, and turning them
over to landlords in that character ; some think that they
could not with justice be so treated. The latter was
the view taken in the early days of our rule ; the other is
that held by those who in these days favour the idea of

capitalist landlords. But either party would, I think, admit that in most parts of the country there was nothing to prevent the Government from recognising the position of the ryots and improving their status, if it was minded so to do at the time of the first settlement of rights, and before incompatible rights were conferred on others.

In small native states the ruler very frequently collects his dues direct from the cultivators, with the assistance of the established headmen and accountants. The alternative mode of management is to farm out the right of receiving the state dues to mercantile speculators. In disturbed times, again, when it was not easy to collect dues in detail, it sometimes happened that the ruling power for the time being compromised with the villagers by agreeing to take from them a lump sum in lieu of all claims, and the villagers themselves allocated the burden according to holdings.

In these various ways were the land revenues collected by native rulers. But it is well known that, in some of the greater dominions, persons were found intermediate between the villagers and the Government, whose position had become more or less hereditary, and whose claims and treatment have given rise to much discussion. We must then examine the origin of these hereditary middlemen. First, however, we should be clear about the meaning in which we use the words "zemeendar," and "ryot."

"Zemeendar" is a Persian word, signifying literally "land-holder." It has been, however, very variously applied to different classes connected with the land. The Mahommedans seem originally to have used it very much as we use the term "native," applying it to the people of the land. But eventually they applied it to the holders of the tributary tenures not brought under complete subjection. Under the Moguls the semi-independent territories are always called the Zemeendarees. Great Rajpoot chiefs and others were known as "Zemeendars." In Bengal and other districts the term came to be applied to the great middlemen, who rose to power in the decline of the empire ; and the name may have had some weight

in bringing about the policy which made them proprietors. But a little farther north we find the same
name applied to the small village proprietors; and farther
north again in the Punjab the term is universally applied
to simple peasants. I have often asked a man on the
road-side, " Who are you?" and got for answer, " Oh, a
poor man—a Zemeendar!" And as the Jats are the
great cultivating tribe in the Punjab, the terms have come
to be used as synonymous; and a man will often tell
you he is a Zemeendar by Caste, meaning a Jat.

I shall try to use the word as much as possible in its
ordinary English acceptation of a holder between the
State and the actual cultivator.

"Ryot" is a word which is much more mis-used. It
is Arabic, but no doubt comes through the Persian. It
means " protected one," " subject," or " commoner," as
distinguished from " Raees," or " noble." In a native
mouth, to the present day, it is used in this sense, and
not in that of " tenant." Not only all classes of cultivators, those who claim the strongest rights equally with
those who claim none, but also weavers, carpenters, and
labourers, call themselves ryots. To simplify matters I
shall apply the term to cultivators of the land, proprietary or non-proprietary, as distinguished from the
holder intermediate between the ryot and the State. It
is very important to note the meaning of this word,
because the persons on whom very strong rights are
conferred by the early regulations or by subsequent laws,
are officially called " ryots," and by merely translating the
word " tenants," it is assumed that rights were arbitrarily
bestowed on persons holding the position of English
tenants.

In the ancient Braminical accounts of Hindoo institutions as they ought to be, we find mention of district
officers who seem to have filled much the same position
in larger areas which the village headmen fill in villages. They were lords of one thousand, of one hundred,
or of ten villages, and were apparently hereditary officers.
I do not know whether the Marattas derive similar offices
direct from earlier times, or whether they have been re-

invented by the Maratta Bramins, but we certainly found in Maratta countries an established system of " Deshmooks,"—officers exercising a jurisdiction in considerable tracts—and " Deshpandyas "—district accountants for similar areas. A proprietary character has, however, never been attributed to these men, and they have been for the most part pensioned off.

In the days when the Mahommedan rule was vigorous, there was little intermediate tenure between the state and the people ; but in proportion as the central power declined, smaller authorities rose. In the long period of anarchy there was, under a nominal imperial rule, a partial return in many parts of the country to native rule and to the Hindoo system of petty chiefships. Out of these it may be said that the larger modern Zemeendarees have sprung.

I would trace them to the following principal origins :—

First. Old tributary rajas, who have been gradually reduced to the position of subjects, but have never lost the management of their ancient territories, which they hold rather as native rulers than as proprietors. These are chiefly found in outlying border districts and jungly semi-civilised countries.

Second. Native leaders, sometimes leading men of Hindoo clans, sometimes mere adventurers, who have risen to power as guerilla plunderers, levying black mail, and eventually, coming to terms with the Government, have established themselves, under the titles of Zemeendars, Polygars, &c., in the control of tracts of country for which they pay a revenue or tribute, uncertain under a weak power, but which becomes a regular land revenue when a strong power is established. This is a very common origin of many of the most considerable modern families, both in the north and in the south. To our ideas there is a wide gulf between a robber and a landlord, but not so in native view. It is wonderful how much, in times such as those of the last century, the robber, the raja, and the Zemeendar run into one another.

Third. The officers whose business it is to collect and
account for the revenue have frequently, in disturbed
times, gained such a footing that their rendering of an
account becomes almost nominal, and practically they
pay the sum which the ruling power is willing to accept,
and make the most of their charges.

Fourth. I have alluded to mercantile contracts for the
dues payable by the ryots, held by persons in the
position of Farmers-General. To a weak Government
this system is very tempting, and in the decadence of
the Mogul empire enterprising bankers and other
speculators, taking contracts of this kind, exercised great
authority, and handed it down to their successors.

There are infinite varieties of the phases which the
matter may assume, one of these characters passing into
the other, so that a Zemeendar may have sprung partly
from one and partly from another of these sources.

The tendency of everything Hindoo is to become
hereditary. The son becomes, by the mere fact of his
birth, the partner of his father, and so a family interest
is established in everything. Thus contracts and other
holdings passed from father to son, and when we found
them well established, the holders have passed into the
category of Zemeendars.

Where there is a recognised chiefship or office, it
is understood that, as it cannot be divided, one man
must hold it. Great Zemeendarees have therefore generally descended to that member of the family who was
best fitted, and of whom the superior power approved.
There was something corresponding to primogeniture,
modified by circumstances.

With the usual tendency of Hindoo institutions to a
feudal character, we constantly find that, under great
Zemeendars, sub-holders have sprung up, sub-chiefs of
the original raja, or the original robber; inferior
officers, sub-contractors; and these acquiring permanence
in a manner similar to their chiefs, have sometimes
survived when the chief has fallen, or are sometimes
found holding under him.

Whatever the character of these various classes of

hereditary or semi-hereditary middlemen, one thing may
broadly be said of them all, that they were the representatives of the governing powers, the delegates of the
Government, receiving the dues of Government. The
status of the cultivators was not altered. Where there
were strong village proprietors they held the same
position under the Zemeendar ; where their position was
not so strong, the Zemeendar exercised the functions
which the Government officers would have exercised.
This only may be said, that a small ruler may exercise
a more minute interference than a great ruler. But still
the relation was between governor and governed, or at
most between payer and payee of the customary rent ;
there was nothing like our relation of landlord and
tenant.

Under native rule the rights in the land, whatever
they may be, are not bought and sold in the market.
As regards the occupancy of the peasants, the rent
which gives the real value going to the Government, and
the claim of the peasant being rather a privilege, deriving
its value from sentiment affection and habit, than a
property capable of being estimated in money, there
was little room for mercantile dealings. Nor was there
any margin of profit which admitted of systematic
sub-letting. Transfer from one hand to another did
occur, but the communities claimed a right of veto, and
would not permit the entrance by purchase of a
stranger disagreeable to them. The general feeling
prevented a man from alienating his land for ever.
Hence, if the occupant was unable to cultivate his land
or to pay the revenue, when he did not simply run
away, the ordinary form of alienation was, not by
selling or letting, but by mortgaging, if the term can
properly be applied to the transaction. The mortgagee,
or depositary, undertook to discharge what was due upon
the land, and obtained the use of it, while the original
owner retained an almost indefinite right of reclaiming
it on repaying the mortgagee. Nothing has been more
difficult to settle than the adverse claims of persons
long in possession, and of others claiming to be very

ancient mortgagors. As respects the superior tenures, they were so entirely of a personal and official character that they were in no degree transferable by ordinary sale.

It may be said then of all landed tenures in India previous to our rule, that they were practically not transferable by sale ; and that only certain classes of the better-defined claims were to some extent transferable by mortgage. The seizure and sale of land for private debt was wholly and utterly unknown,—such an idea had never entered into the native imagination.

THE BENGAL SYSTEM.

Bengal proper was the first considerable province which came under British Administration. The later northern tribes had scarcely penetrated into that country, and the village institutions were not of that democratic independent self-supporting character which gives facilities for dealing direct with the people. The servants of the East India Company were then quite without experience of civil administration. Middlemen, more or less hereditary, Zemeendars, Choudrees, Talookdars, &c., were found in existence, and it was natural that foreigners attempting so new a task should avail themselves of the services of these men. No proprietary character was then attributed to them. It was quite understood that they were liable to be displaced for inefficiency or misconduct, and in fact they frequently were displaced. There was no well-established rule of inheritance. But still if a man did well, another of the family was generally permitted to succeed him. In the course of the various experiments which were made, these men may sometimes have had contracts for the revenue ; but their recognized position was that of men bound to account to the British Government for their collections ; and in the Regulations of 1793, it is stated that up to that time their right was to take a perquisite of ten per cent. on the revenue ; or, as it is expressed, they were bound to pay into the Treasury ten-elevenths of their collections.

It would be foreign to the purpose of this paper to attempt to trace the various systems of land administrations which were tried from the assumption of the Deewance of Bengal and Bahar,* to the time of the Permanent Settlement. All our modern history dates from the Regulations of 1793, establishing the latter measure and the code of laws which accompanied it. The circumstances and character of the Permanent Settlement of Bengal have been a good deal misapprehended.† It has been supposed that we were very new to, and ignorant of Indian administration; that the British administrators mistook tax-collectors for landed proprietors, and by the laws then passed conferred upon them absolute property in the soil to the entire exclusion of the rights and claims of the inferior holders. Such views of the matter are very wide of the truth. British officers had administered Bengal for a whole generation. Circumstances make men, and in the papers of a much earlier period, I have been greatly struck by the breadth of view and public spirit of many of the local administrators of those early days. At the time of the Permanent Settlement, Lord Cornwallis was surrounded by men of ripe experience and knowledge. The preambles to the Bengal Regulations sufficiently attest that these men quite understood and did not over-estimate the real position of the Zemeendars, who were made proprietors, not in recognition of a right, but in pursuance of a deliberate policy. The unsatisfactory result of the systems of administration already tried had led to the belief that what was most wanted was permanence and security of tenure, and a grand experiment was made in that direction. I pass over here the sin against posterity (and so far I think that

* The imperial grant was of the Deewance of Bengal, Bahar, and Orissa; but Orissa was in the possession of the Nagpore Marattas, and we only acquired it from them in the beginning of the present century.

† I must confess to have been under a misapprehension myself, and to have to some extent taken part in misleading others on this point, when I published "Modern India." At that time I had had no official connection with Bengal proper, and adopted the popular view. I have since spent some years of my life in dealing officially and judicially with the land tenures of Bengal, and give the present statement in correction of that which I previously made.—G. C.

there was a financial mistake) which was committed in
fixing the revenue demand for ever, instead of for a
long period.   As respects the tenure of the land, it
seems to me that there was not so much error as is
generally supposed.   The Government having found the
uncertainty of tenure of the Zemeendars and others to
be attended with much evil, made the Zemeendars in
one sense proprietors.   As between the Government
and the Zemeendars the claims of the former were
strictly limited, and the Zemeendars became proprietors,
instead of mere revenue officers; but they were by
no means made sole and absolute proprietors.   As one
of the English lawyers on the bench of the High
Court at Calcutta said of the original enactment in his
judgment on the great Rent Case (decided in 1865),
" This Regulation teems with provisions quite incompatible with any notion of the Zemeendar being absolute
proprietor."   These provisions may be said in brief to
have given, so far as the theory of the law goes, to all
under-holders down to the ryots, the same security of
tenure as against the Zemeendar, which the Zemeendar
had as against the Government.   Subholders of Talookas and other divisions, under the Zemeendars, were
recognised and protected in their holding, subject to the
payment of the established dues.   As respects the ryots,
the main provisions were these : All extra cesses and
exactions were abolished, and the Zemeendars were
required to specify, in writing, the original rent payable
by each ryot at the pergunnah or established rates.   If
any dispute arose regarding the rates to be so entered,
the question was to be " *determined in the Dewany-*
Adawlut (Civil Court) of the Zillah in which the lands
were situated, according to the rates established in the per-
gunnah for lands of the same description and quality as
those respecting which the dispute arose."   It was farther
provided that no Zemeendar should have power to
cancel the pottahs (or specifications of rent) except on
the ground that they had been obtained by collusion,
at rates below the established rates ; and that the resident
ryots should always be entitled to renewed pottahs at those

rates. Even on a sale for arrear of revenue (which cancelled all superior rights), the purchaser was to have no power to evict any resident ryot unless he refused a pottah at the established pergunnah rate. Thus, in fact, fixity of tenure and fixity of rent rates were secured to the ryots by law. In Bengal proper, the proportion of the produce had very generally been converted into money rates, and thus these fixed rates were, in fact, fixed rents. Provision was at the same time made for the maintenance both of the Canoongoes or district registrars, and of Patwarees, or official village accountants, an object of whose appointment was declared to be "to prevent oppression of the persons paying rent."

In addition to these specific provisions, there was the general provision, often quoted, reserving a power of future interference in behalf of the inferior holders. "The Governor-General in Council will, whenever he may deem it proper, enact such regulations as he may think necessary for the protection of the dependent talookdars, ryots, and other cultivators of the soil."

As the early Regulations were construed by the judicial tribunals, the law was settled to be that, under the general provisions in favour of subholders, every man, whether ryot or of any other class, who had held for twelve years before the permanent settlement (that being the Indian term of prescription) at a uniform rent, was entitled to hold for ever at that rent, whether it was or was not below the established rates; other resident ryots were entitled to hold at the established rates, but if holding below the customary rate, could be enhanced up to that point.

The Zemeendars were authorised to appropriate to their own use the difference between the sum which they engaged to pay the Government and the established rates, "which formed the unalterable due of the Government according to the ancient and established usage of the country." They were, moreover, encouraged to exert themselves to bring the waste lands into cultivation, and to induce the ryots to cultivate more valuable articles of produce, by the assurance that all that was thus

added to the rent-roll should be their own. The whole of
the waste lands were thrown into the holdings of the
Zemeendars without additional charge, except in the case
of some remote parts of the country, uncultivated and
unpopulated, where there were none to claim the land or
pay revenue for it.

So far as I can judge, I should say that the recognition of the position of the Bengal Zemeendars was not
more than would have been to some extent done in
modern days in any part of India in which the
Ryotwar system, pure and simple, was not adopted.
There was a time when their claims might have been
more rigorously scrutinised, and in Bahar (which,
though attached to Bengal, is quite a Hindostanee province) the claims of the chiefs prevailed over those of
village holders to a much greater degree than would
have been the case when the present north-west provinces
were settled. But in Bengal proper, where the village
system had so little cohesion, I doubt whether at any period
of our administration we should have quite set aside the
Zemeendars. They not only had a certain position and
certain claims when we assumed the administration, but
we had ourselves dealt with them and used them for
upwards of a generation. To set them aside altogether
would have been a very strong measure.

In fact, the settlement was by no means made with
the great Zemeendars exclusively : when holders of
smaller degree were thought to have stronger claims, it
was made with them. There were many such small
holders ; and in one or two of the eastern districts of
Bengal the mere cultivators were found to have the best
claim, and the settlement is, for the most part, to all
intents and purposes Ryotwar.

As respects revenue, the Zemeendars were subjected
to immediate terms very much harder than those which
are now accorded. The Government demand was fixed
at ten-elevenths of the then rent-roll.

On the whole, my impression is that (perpetuity of
revenue apart) the principles of the permanent settlement
of Bengal were in the main good and sound, and that

the ground for subsequent complaints is to be found not so much in those principles as in the failure properly to carry them out, and in the ideas which afterwards arose from a misinterpretation of them.

The original intention of the framers of the permanent settlement was to record all rights. The Canoongoes and Patwarees were to register all holdings, all transfers, all rent-rolls, and all receipts and payments ; and every five years there was to be filed in the public offices a complete register of all land tenures. But the task was a difficult one : there was delay in carrying it out. English ideas of the rights of a landlord, and of the advantage of non-interference, began more and more to prevail in Bengal. The executive more and more abnegated the functions of recording rights and protecting the inferior holders, and left everything to the judicial tribunals. The Patwarees fell into disuse, or became the mere servants of the Zemeendars : the Canoongoes were abolished. No record of the rights of the Ryots and inferior holders was ever made, and even the quinquennial register of superior rights, which was maintained for a time, fell into disuse. When a regular police was established, the Zemeendars were in practice freed from any effective responsibility for the suppression of crime or other administrative functions. They became in every sense mere rent-receivers. The Bengal principle of non-interference on the part of Government was pushed to the point which may be said to have culminated in the recent famine, when the authorities so long refused to interfere, not because the Zemeendars did anything for the people, but because, according to the Bengal theory, they ought to do so.

At the same time that property in land was recognized by the Regulations of 1793, it was made freely transferable by sale, and in every respect put on the footing of property. The original code declared the custom of descent to a single heir, existing in certain large estates, to have been an invention of the Mahommedans for revenue purposes, and abolished it, laying down that the descent of all estates was to be regulated by the ordinary

Hindoo and Mahommedan laws, applicable to any other property. But a subsequent regulation modified this provision, and permitted the rule of primogeniture in some jungle and other districts, where it was well established. To this day I believe that it is not very clear what estates do, and what do not descend to a single heir ; but the matter is not so important, because the courts have recognized the power of Hindoos to make wills. The Hindoo laws say nothing of wills, and it is very doubtful whether they should have been admitted ; but the courts, acting on English precedents, having once admitted them, this curious result has followed, that, in the absence of any provisions to limit them, the power of a Hindoo in Bengal to tie up his property by will seems to be almost unlimited.

A creditor has the most summary power of selling all the landed rights of his debtor in satisfaction of debts of any kind. And it was part of the system that permanent rights of property being once recognized, and the revenue being so fixed that the Government could no longer demand any increase, the reserved rent of Government must be paid with unfailing regularity. Failing payment on the appointed day, the estate is put up to auction, and knocked down to the highest bidder, with a clear and complete title against all comers. In the first years after the settlement, this provision was very operative, and a large proportion of the newly-created proprietors were sold out. Subsequently the Zemeendars have learned punctuality ; but sales for debt are always constant. It may be said, then, that from the very first an encumbered estates court has been sitting in permanence in every district.

It has been epigrammatically said that Lord Cornwallis designed to make English landlords in Bengal, and only succeeded in making Irish landlords. This, however, hardly expresses the truth. He certainly sanguinely hoped that security of tenure would induce the Zemeendars to perform duties in the way of improvement in which they have entirely failed ; but it has been shown that nothing was farther from the thoughts of Lord Corn-

N

wallis and his advisers than to create absolute landlords
after the English pattern. The design was rather to
create something like what model Irish landlords ought
to be. The theory and intention of the Cornwallis administration was to do for Bengal exactly what James I.
did for Ireland—to secure all parties, great landholders
and cultivators alike, in their rights according to their
degree. The subsequent sales of the rights conferred on
the Zemeendars, and the failure to record the inferior
rights, produced in practice in Bengal something of the
same state of things which resulted in Ireland from
Cromwell's confiscation of the rights conferred by James,
followed as it was by the de facto restoration of the Irish
cultivators to their holdings. In Bengal, as in Ireland,
the cultivators were protected by custom and public
opinion rather than by an efficient administration of the
law. The landholders were men who did nothing for
the land, but only received (generally through middlemen) the customary rents from the cultivators who
tilled old fields or cleared new ones. Still there were
not in Bengal the differences of race and politics which
have embittered the social state in Ireland ; and religious
differences do not lead to the same bad blood. Hindoo
and Mahommedan generally live in an amity which
Roman Catholic and Protestant may well imitate. So far,
then, Bengal has been in a much better state than Ireland.

The margin of profit left to the Zemeendars was at
first so narrow, and habits were still so native, that it is
scarcely surprising that for many years there were complaints of the illegal levy of the cesses and imposts
so universal under native rule, and of exactions from the
ryots still poor and abject. But as, with peace and
prosperity and the rise of prices, the condition of the
ryots has improved, the rates levied by the Zemeendars
have not increased in an equal degree. The Bengallee
is not a very pushing landlord ; he is generally content
to take what he can claim according to the custom, with
such additions as his agents can quietly manage ; and for
the rest he is satisfied with the enormous increase of
income which the, as it were spontaneous, increase of

cultivation has given him. On the whole, then, the relation of landlord and tenant has not been unfriendly. The Zemeendar scarcely ever sought to take into his own hands more land than his old "seer" or demesne. Population had not yet reached the point when there is a severe struggle among cultivators for land ; and there was no such thing as any desire to evict tenants. The mass of the ryots in Bengal proper came at last to be tolerably well off, sitting at pretty easy rents, which gave them some margin of profit and attached a certain value to their holdings.

In order to prevent the fraudulent or improvident disposal of the assets from which the revenue was to be paid, the Zemeendars were at first prohibited from giving leases of any parts of their estates for terms exceeding ten years ; but some years later this restriction was withdrawn. In Bahar, where there are many large estates which descend undivided, they are let in portions for short terms of years to mercantile speculators, who make the most of the ryot—an arrangement almost universal under such circumstances. The mercantile class of those parts are a pushing set of men, but having no permanent interest in the soil, the practice has all the disadvantages of the middleman system. The ryots have not even the advantage of a landlord who has some interest in keeping them alive ; and in that part of the country they are much more rack-rented than in Lower Bengal.

In Bengal proper, where there is less of the mercantile spirit, the custom has sprung up of giving sub-leases in perpetuity for a consideration. The great estates have thus been split up by a system of sub-infeudation ; and it may be said that practically most of the land in Bengal is now in the hands of permanent landowners of moderate calibre. Many ryots and other smaller holders, even when they cannot prove a title from the permanent settlement, have obtained perpetuities by payment of a fine. And so it happens that under the shadow of the permanent settlement, a very widespread system of perpetuities of all grades has sprung up.

N 2

Perpetuities are always transferable, and the inferior like the superior tenures can be summarily sold for arrears of rent.   Where there is a mere right of occupancy at the customary rates, the sanction of the superior holder is ordinarily required to a transfer by sale; but in some districts the Zemeendars interfered so little, and were so glad to have the security for their rents afforded by saleable tenures, that the ryots' tenures have become by custom entirely transferable, and the state of things is very similar to that prevailing in the north of Ireland.

The Hindoo laws and customs divide property among all the sons or other agnates.   Failing sons, a widow succeeds on a very limited tenure ; and in Bengal daughters and other female relations also succeed after the widow, when there are no sons.   The Mahommedan law of inheritance is extremely complicated, and creates a great complication of shares.   The result of the operation of these laws for several generations has been the creation of a very large number of interests, present and contingent, in almost every estate.   The law gives to every shareholder the right of partitioning off his share ; but where there is no survey and no record, and no machinery in the hands of the executive Government, the attempt to divide through the courts an estate not in possession of the parties, but held by ryots, and of which the parties themselves scarcely know more than the rent-roll, is in practice attended with enormous difficulties. The process is seldom attempted in Bengal, and still seldomer brought to a successful issue.   Thus then almost all estates are held in undivided shares by several, or many people—and many others have reversionary rights.   It is very singular how many of the higher classes of Hindoos die childless, and how many widows' life tenures result.   The tenure of Hindoo widows is peculiar in the extreme.   They have no power to administer for useful purposes, so as to give leases, &c., beyond their own lives, but under Bramin-made laws they can do many things in favour of Bramins, and for superstitious purposes.   They are constantly in the hands of Bramins, and constantly trying to make away with the estates for the benefit of their own relations, or of their Bramin friends, to the prejudice of the husbands' heirs. Altogether the tenure is a most noxious one, and gives rise to half the litigation in Bengal.

When we have then concurrently, a system of inheritance leading to constant subdivision of rights, without division of tenures; a vast system of sub-infeudation in every form and degree, and on every condition, at the unrestrained pleasure of the parties; and then perplexing and injurious widow holdings coming as constant faults to disturb the course of every tenure; all this overlaid on a system originally complicated and unrecorded, it may be supposed that there is an ample field for litigation in the courts. To this it must be added that our judicial system has encouraged to the utmost the worst technicalities of law, and a practice under which witnesses have been numbered rather than weighed. To such an extent has the habit of playing at law been carried, that it has become the common practice to purchase and hold land in any fictitious name rather than a man's own. The most respectable man feels that if he has not need to cheat any one at present, he may some day have occasion to do so, and it is the custom of the country; so he puts his estate in the name of his wife's grandmother under a secret trust. If he is pressed by creditors, or opposing suitors, it is not his; if his wife's grandmother plays him false, he brings a suit to declare the trust. To any one who should follow any land suit, taken at random from the files of our courts, in its inception, origin, and progress through many appeals to a final decree, and then should observe how the attempt to carry out the decree breeds half a dozen new suits, the wonder must be how any people can tolerate such a state of things. It is, however, remarkable how the world adapts itself to circumstances. The apparent evils are mitigated by two considerations; first, the litigation of nearly a century has produced a certain record of rights in the shape of recorded decisions, which give a certain solid basis for future proceedings; and second, litigation is to a Bengallee what alcohol and stock-jobbing together are to our countrymen, and opium and the opium trade to the Chinese—it is his stimulant, and his form of gambling; and in some sense he likes it. Every Bengallee, high and low, treasures as his Lares and Penates an endless assortment of decrees of court and other processes, which he unfolds to every one who will listen to him.

The grand difficulty in purchasing land in Bengal is to make a title. A purchaser can never be sure that some one will not start up and declare the seller to have been a mere man of straw. In truth, too often a litigious person buys from a man of straw a nominal property which is not in his possession. The only safe title is a purchase under a sale for arrear of revenue.

Notwithstanding all drawbacks, the desire to possess landed rights is so great, and so much money has accumulated during a hundred years of peace, for which there is great want of means of safe investment, that land has come to bear a very high price indeed. The profits of the superior holders are now very high, and the prices paid are such as to yield but a small rate of interest on the money invested.

It would be sufficient subject for a separate treatise to discover why it is that the evils attending joint holdings much subdivided (without corresponding facility of partition and transfer), which are so evident in all tenures above those of the cultivators, are not so marked as respects the holdings of the cultivating ryots. Their tenure is simpler; being at the bottom, there are seldom complications under them; they are on better terms with one another, and less skilled in law. They, too, have generally had a good deal of litigation; but if they can only settle their rights, as between them and their landlords, they sometimes settle their own family affairs out of court. Up to this time the process of absorbing the waste has been going on, and there has not been complaint of the too minute division of farms, and the impossibility of supporting life upon them. A large proportion of the holdings are certainly very small; but except in time of general failure of crops and universal famine, the people support themselves without poor laws

and do not trouble us. We really know wonderfully
little of the social arrangements of the lower classes.
They are independent, and that is enough for us. I
think I may say, once for all, that the Irish form of
difficulty, over population and insufficiency of land, has
not yet troubled us. But the population is certainly
much increasing, and this phase of the question may
not be far off.

I have alluded to the failure of the Bengal Zemeendars
to perform the duties of landlords. In fact, to expect
of them the duties of an English landlord, to build, and
plant, and introduce improved agriculture, and improved
machinery, if it ever was expected, was a mere chimera,
and not reasonably to be looked for under the circumstances. Those are not the functions of a native landlord. If a man encourages and protects the ryots who
break up his waste and till his lands, and deals faith-
fully and equitably by them, he is considered to do his
duty. If he further acts the part of a capitalist money-
lender, and advances money and seed, to be repaid with
interest at harvest time, he does something more; and if
the interest exacted is not too exorbitant, he is a model
landlord. In the very large estates the intervention of
middlemen renders it impossible for the landlord to
perform these functions, and he does not do so. In
moderate estates he might do so, but in Bengal the
complications of existing and contingent titles are so
great that few have the power, if they have the will,
and they are generally little disposed to do much. The
virtues of a Bengallee landlord are rather negative than
positive. I have said that generally he is not very
exacting. Perhaps the ryots might fare worse than
under his King Log sort of rule.

In India, as in Ireland and many other countries, the
tenure of land affects the happiness and determines the
content or discontent of the people more than all other
laws and administrative acts put together, and a main
test of the success of the land system is to be found in
the political feelings of the people. The advocates of
the Bengal system of management are wont to quote the

quiet and loyalty of the people of Bengal during the
mutiny, as a proof of the excellence of their system.
It is impossible to compare a country far from the scene
of the military outbreak, and inhabited by an unwarlike
people utterly alien to the Sepoys (whom they personally
detest), with countries which were the immediate scenes
of the mutiny and the home of the Sepoys; but still no
doubt those days, when the British power seemed to be
for a time almost in abeyance, afforded great opportunity
for the outbreak of discontent in any part of India.
The population of Eastern Bengal is chiefly Mahommedan, and there are many of those reformed Mahommedans whom a little persistent persecution may
make our enemies. Although Bahar was much disturbed,
Bengal certainly remained perfectly quiet throughout the
mutiny; and when, towards the end of the crisis, a Sepoy
party stationed in Eastern Bengal threw off their allegiance, they were even actively opposed by the people.
Without, then, admitting that the system is in all
respects good, I think it may be said that the people
were not seriously discontented with our rule.

I reserve to a subsequent part of this Paper a notice of
recent legislation affecting the tenure of the land.

THE SYSTEM OF THE NORTH-WEST PROVINCES.

For some years subsequent to 1793 the views which had
led to the permanent settlement of Bengal still prevailed.
A part of the Madras presidency was permanently
settled with great Zemeendars. Under that administration, however, ryotwar principles having eventually
prevailed, the rights of the ryots under these Zemeendars
were secured by record and the active intervention of
the Government. The permanent settlement was also
extended to the Benares province, but there, too, in consequence of its being attached to the north-west provinces, where a different system prevailed, a complete
record of inferior rights has been made.

In the early years of the present century, the obligations towards us of our ally the Nawab of Oude were

settled by a partition of his country, half being retained by the Nawab, and half made over to the British Government. About the same time a considerable territory in the same part of India, which had been overrun by the Marattas, was acquired by their repulse. We thus obtained the command of the upper Gangetic valley, or rather plain—the proper Hindoostan ; and the territories so acquired are those known as the north-west provinces.

Soon after their acquisition the Government proclaimed its intention of making a permanent settlement on the Bengal pattern—a declaration which is still referred to as an embarrassing pledge. But other counsels soon prevailed. Great doubts were thrown on the advantage of the permanent settlement system ; the settlement of the north-west provinces on the same system was first postponed, and then altogether abandoned. Thus it has happened that, while in the lower provinces of Bengal and Bahar the system has been, as I have explained, exaggerated and intensified in one direction, the northern provinces have fallen into a different groove, and the land policy has taken quite another direction.

The doubts and differences of opinion which prevailed led to a succession of short temporary and provisional settlements of the new territories, without any minute investigation of rights. Short leases were given to the parties most easily accessible ; and where there seemed to be none possessed of any hereditary or quasi-proprietary claims, the villages were let to farmers. Wherever there was any appearance of rights they were ruthlessly sold when the revenue fell into arrears, and great abuses resulted, to the profit of our subordinate officials and their confederates, who acquired much of the land which they brought to sale. A special commission subsequently inquired into and partially redressed these abuses, but it was felt that some more settled system was necessary. This state of things led to the famous Regulation VII. of 1822, which is the basis of all subsequent land arrangements in all parts of Northern India. The system of fixing the land revenue in perpetuity was abandoned, settlements for long periods being substituted ; but

private property in the land was none the less to be as
fully acknowledged as in Bengal.   The landholders were
in fact to have long leases, with a right of renewal at
a revaluation at the end of the leases.   Their rights were
to be freely transferable, and completely regulated by
law.   No class was to be arbitrarily invested with these
rights, but an exact survey and complete inquiry was to
be made ; the parties best entitled to proprietary rights
were to be ascertained, and with them the Government
revenue was to be settled ; while at the same time all
inferior rights of every description were also to be fully
ascertained, described, and recorded.   A very important
provision was this, that where two or more parties,
superior and inferior, were found to be possessed of concurrent rights in the same land, the Government officers
were empowered either to settle directly with the
superior, and to make a subsettlement between the
superior and inferior holders, or to pension off one party
with a percentage (in compensation for the rights which
he had heretofore exercised), and to make the settlement
with the other.

The ryots were to be divided into old settled ryots
having a right of occupancy so long as they paid a fair
rent, and ryots who had acquired no such rights ; but
the tests by which this right was to be determined,
and the standards by which the rent was to be fixed
from time to time, were not defined with such accuracy
as might have been desired.

There was, however, to be a general record of the
rules and customs of every village available for future
reference.

Minute calculations were to be made of the value of
agricultural produce, and of the share of that produce to
which Government was entitled, and from these calculations money rates were to be deduced, from which, after
due allowance for the expenses and profits of the proprietors, the Government revenue was to be calculated
and fixed.

I think that one error to some extent pervades these
excellent provisions, and has embarrassed all the opera-

tions founded on them, —I mean the assumption that distinct proprietary rights everywhere exist, which we have only to ascertain and record. The fact is that, as I have before tried to show, such rights exist in a strong form only in certain parts of the country ; in others they are but inchoate and rudimentary ; in others they have fallen into decay and almost into abeyance ; in some they hardly exist at all. The consequence was that the function of the settlement officers has been to a great degree not only to ascertain rights but also to create a class of rights which did not exist before, or at any rate to give them a form and substance which they did not before possess. Great scope was thus left for individual discretion ; and in the absence of distinct provision for the cases in which that which did not exist could not be ascertained, individual prejudices were carried a long way in one direction or other. Much difference of opinion, and many official battles have resulted. I think it would have been better if the Government had boldly recognized the fact that to arrive at complete private property a great creation of rights was indispensable, and had distinctly determined on whom and in what degree those rights were to be conferred, what was to be given to great Zemeendars, what to village headmen, and what to the ryots, instead of leaving those questions to be fought out by the local officers in every case. As it is, there has generally been (as in most matters in which Englishmen are concerned) an aristocratic party and a party of the people ; a party which would give as much as possible to the rich and gentlemanlike natives, the descendants of ancient rajas or sons of modern farmers-general, and trust to them to rule the people ; another, which, considering that it is our function to protect the people from the tyranny of native rulers, would give as much as possible to the people, and restrict the aristocracy to their actual rights. Either course is possible under the law, for by putting the people to the proof, and giving them no more than they can prove a right to, all the rest falls to the aristocrats ; by putting the aristocrats to the proof, and giving them no more than *they* can prove a title to, there is ample room to give the people very large rights.

On one point all administrators in all the provinces which have been administered by the Bengal Civil Service (the name is applied to the whole service, which comprises the separate Bengal and North-Western branches), or by officers associated with them under the Government of India, have agreed, viz., that under no circumstances whatever will the Government deal direct with the individual ryots, as in Madras and Bombay. If there is no intermediate proprietor, or office holder of some kind who can be taken as such, and the villagers have not a complete constitution enabling them to deal with the Government in a body through their representatives for a lump sum to be paid jointly, a proprietor must be found or created. To this day in Bengal the estates which have in any way lapsed as Government property are sold to the highest bidder, rather than settled with the ryots under a system which Bengal officers do not accept as admissible. They cannot get rid of the small tenures of Eastern Bengal, but will allow no others where they can help it.

In the North-West Provinces every village is settled in the lump with some one.

For some years the proceedings under Reg. VII. of 1822 did not progress satisfactorily. It turned out that the machinery at the disposal of Government was quite inadequate to the vastness of the work which had been undertaken; and the attempt to obtain reliable revenue rates by a calculation of the value of produce and cost of production was found to be fallacious and impossible. In 1833 the requisite machinery was supplied by the employment of natives in posts hitherto confined to Europeans; and it was determined to calculate the revenue of each village in the gross, with reference to actual past receipts, and to allow the parties interested to distribute it under the superintendence of the settlement officers. An energetic settlement school sprung up; and in the course of the following eight or nine years the whole of the North-West Provinces, yielding an annual revenue of some 4,000,000*l.*, was settled, and all rights and holdings of every kind were voluminously recorded in great detail.

This settlement was mainly carried out under the superintendence of Mr. Robert Mertins Bird, Mr. Thomason being one of his most active subordinates; but as it afterwards fell to Mr. Thomason, during a long incumbency as Lieutenant-Governor, to administer the system, it is popularly associated with his name.

The battle between the officers who supported the claims of the aristocracy and those who took the more popular view raged with intensity in the course of the settlement. Neither one nor the other entirely prevailed; but it is not to be denied that the party which looked with disfavour on aristocratic claims had eventually more support of authority than the other. Many large Zemeendars were maintained in their position; but in many cases, where they had hitherto held from Government, village proprietors were found to have claims to a sub-settlement under them; and in some instances they were altogether set aside with an allowance, and the settlement was made with the sub-proprietors, under the provision for such cases which I have mentioned.

The supporters of the aristocracy assert that in some places village claims which had been long ago overridden and trodden out, during the troublous times which preceded our rule, were arbitrarily revived, to the prejudice of the great landlords, who had exercised complete authority.

On the whole subject of this settlement it must, however, be understood that the settlement officers and the Government under whom they acted had no arbitrary powers; the civil courts were open to all, to contest and bring to a judicial decision the justice of their awards; and by the higher classes especially that remedy was freely resorted to.

The proprietary rights having been determined, the principle followed was to take two-thirds of the then rental as Government revenue, leaving to the proprietors the remaining third, and all future increase during the

term of the settlement, which was fixed at thirty years.
A proprietor objecting to the assessment fixed may
decline the engagement, in which case the village is let
to a farmer, and he has a small percentage—a good
check on over-assessment. The waste lands were demar-
cated with the village boundaries, and included in the
settlement. The survey was most minute. Every field,
however small, was measured and mapped, with the
name of the occupant and the rent.

Perhaps the part of the settlement which was least
guided by any uniform rules was that which distinguished between hereditary occupancy ryots and tenants-
at-will. The fact is that there was no contest on the
point. The ryots hardly understood the distinction,
the question of eviction never having been raised ; and
the Zemeendars did not press any claim to evict so long
as they got their rents. It was thus left to the settlement officers to do very much as they liked on this
point. A practice sprang up—it is not clear how—to
consider that all cultivating ryots who had been in uninterrupted possession for twelve years, without special
contract, should be taken to have a right of occupancy ;
and in most districts that rule was followed. No doubt,
as matter of prescription, the holding of a tenant-at-will
or from year to year is not adverse to his landlord, and
so far there was no legal justification for the rule. But
in the absence of any other rule, and in the absence of
contest, the rule was probably as good as any other
which could have been suggested, and had some support
from the analogy of judicial decisions in the case of the
Bengal ryots. If the Government, when conferring such
great benefits upon those who were made proprietors,
had in so many words established by law this rule in
favour of the ryots, there would have been no complaint ; but since the rights of the proprietors have been
established, and are taken for granted, it has in recent
days been said that the settlement officers gave occupancy rights to ryots who had no sufficient title.

Nothing was declared as to the power of the Zemeendars to raise the rents of occupancy ryots for any cause

during the term of the settlement. The power to realise
rent by summary proceedings before the collector was
restricted to the recorded rent heretofore payable; but
it was eventually decided in the civil courts that a
Zemeendar was entitled, on showing that causes independent of the exertions of the ryot had raised the value
of the land, to obtain by regular suit an increase of
rent. The course of procedure was, however, difficult,
the right hardly known; and I think it may be said
that in practice the occupancy ryots held at unvaried
rents, till the introduction of the new rent law, to
which I shall come presently.

The result of the settlement of proprietary rights in
the North-West Provinces was to create a great variety
of landholders of many different classes. I have said
that many large Zemeendars retained great estates. In
some parts of the country the settlement was made with
cultivating village communities; but as the proper
villages of this class are principally in the territory
about Delhi, since transferred to the Punjab, I may
leave them till I come to that province. In the greater
part of the North-West Provinces the settlement was
most frequently made with small landholders and village
proprietors, a class intermediate between the great
Zemeendars and the true cultivating communities. The
country is chiefly that in which the Rajpoots were at
one time predominant; and a large proportion of the
villages were of that class, to which I have before referred, where the original Rajpoot community or other
similar body was considerably reduced in numbers, and
did not cultivate the whole village, but still maintained
a position of greater or less superiority over the ordinary
ryots by whom they were surrounded. The proprietary
rights of these families or groups of families were very
generally recognised. The system is that they cultivate
the lands in their own possession, and collect on common
account the rents payable by the other ryots. The
common receipts are applied to the payment of the
revenue, and any deficiency is supplied by a rate on the
lands of the proprietors. Where a small family holds,

and the rents of the ryots exceed the revenue and expenses, the surplus is similarly divided according to shares.

In the many villages where neither great Zemeendars nor old proprietary families established claims, it being necessary to find some proprietors, a good headman or solvent farmer, or some other person of some sort, was established as proprietor.

The facility of sale and transfer afforded by the establishment of saleable property and authentic register of rights, with the frequency of compulsory sales through the civil courts, have brought into possession of many landed properties men of the mercantile and capitalist classes. These men are in Northern India very enterprising, and some of them have really done much to plant ryots and develop the resources of the country in the native way.

The normal tenure of the North-West Provinces may be said then to be that of moderate proprietors, of fair position and character, with many ryots under them who possess a right of occupancy at a fair rent. The security of tenure resulting from the settlement gave a great impulse to agriculture ; there was peace and prosperity ; the country flourished ; property in land acquired a high value ; and for a long period the settlement of the North-West Provinces was held out as the perfection of Indian management.

In a great degree these praises were well deserved ; yet there are some drawbacks. The immense records, pushed on rapidly to completion, were sometimes found to contain a good many errors, and required some revision and correction. Considerable inequalities no doubt occurred in the assessment of the revenue. The main drawbacks are, however, I think the following :

The establishment of property gave facility for obtaining credit, while the facility of resort to sale of landed rights in satisfaction of debts, and the strictness of the collectors' demands, rendered alienations very frequent. Those who most suffered in this way were the somewhat improvident classes—the old Rajpoot and such-like families—who were constantly sold out. If there was often

economic gain in this process, there was political weakness, for the old proprietors—the most martial class in
the country—remained on the land in great numbers,
reduced to the position of needy and discontented cultivators, holding under those whom they contemned as
mere shopkeepers, and who were only kept in their
position by the strength of British power.

Then, as the old headmen and others, who had been
made proprietors of so many villages on account of
their merits and prominence, died out, their properties
often fell to people who had not their capacity ; and they
have been much subdivided under the laws of inheritance.
The tendency in many of the small estates which at first
seemed all that could be desired is, I think, to the gradual
creation of a small proprietary class, above cultivating
themselves, and not efficient as landlords.

Finally, as land became valuable and competition
arose, it was found that the position of the ryots had not
been sufficiently defined.

The North-West Provinces were the principal scene of
the mutiny. The Sepoys were almost all Hindostanees.
For several months, the British power was, it may be
said, absolutely and wholly extinct throughout the length
and breadth of these provinces. Anarchy, of course,
resulted ; it could not have been otherwise. To expect
that a grateful people would keep the country for us
under such circumstances, when they had seen their
British masters slaughtered and driven away, would be
too much. The old robber tribes resorted again to robbery ; the strong took advantage of the weak ; old feuds
were fought out ; every man's hand was against his neighbour. The judicial records containing obnoxious decrees
were in some instances burnt. Yet I can speak with
some authority when I say that there was nothing like a
general popular war against ourselves ; for I marched
the whole length of the provinces as civil commissioner
with the first column which came down after the fall of
Dehli, and can say that there was not a symptom of popular
resistance or hostility. With the exception of opposition
from one or two considerable chiefs and Zemeendars, we

o

everywhere walked into the villages and met the people as if nothing had happened. The moment our military power was re-established, they quieted down as a matter of course. While, then, this paper is designed rather to state facts than to offer opinions, I cannot but testify, as matter of fact, to the want of foundation for the suggestion at one time put forward in some quarters, that the events of the mutiny showed the unsoundness of the settlement system of Northern India. On every occasion of great calamity there is a disposition to say that whatever is, is wrong, and it was so on this occasion. It has been some-times said in the public prints that the people took the opportunity of rushing back to allegiance to their old masters, the great Zemeendars ; but no particulars of places or circumstances are given, and the statement is quite without foundation. Putting aside Oude, which had only been a few months annexed, and to which I shall presently come, I venture to say that great Zemeen-dars, who had long ceased to exercise their functions, nowhere regained authority. It is true that, in this time of anarchy, good Zemeendars of large means and con-siderable power were able to maintain a nearer approach to order than existed elsewhere ; but, on the other hand, several men of that class took the opportunity of rebel-ling. What did very generally happen was this, that the ousted *village* Zemeendars, the families and com-munities of the arm-bearing castes, who had been recog-nised at the settlement but had been sold out (princi-pally by the civil courts), took the opportunity of driving away the unmilitary purchasers, and resuming what they still considered to be theirs. This it was which was mistaken for a voluntary return of the people to the dominion of their ancient chiefs.

While, then, I have said that the North-West settlement is not, in all respects, the piece of absolute perfection which it was at one time represented to be, on the other hand I say that nothing occurred in the mutiny to give the slightest ground for suggesting that it had failed or was founded on wrong principles. It was only made apparent that the subsequent action of the courts, in too

summarily alienating the rights of the village proprietors
who had been properly recognised at the settlement, was
a source of political weakness; and that lesson is one
which has been borne in mind.

THE PUNJAB.

Much of the Cis-Sutlej Sikh country, and the Jullunder
Doab, were annexed in 1846, and the Punjab became
British territory in 1849. To these were added the
Dehli territory, and the whole form the present Punjab
Government. The Punjab was settled on precisely the
same principles as the North-West Provinces. Lord
Lawrence was bred a settlement officer under Mr. Bird,
and the system was fully introduced. The differences
caused by local circumstances are chiefly the following:
Although there are found in the Punjab, as in all
provinces settled under Reg. VII. of 1822, a considerable
variety of tenures, the majority are the complete village
communities which I have described in the first part of
this paper. These, then, may be taken as the normal
Punjab type, on which the Punjab system is founded.
The proprietary rights of the communities are fully
acknowledged, and the settlement is made with them,
each village undertaking the payment, through its representative council of elders, of the revenue assessed
upon it, which again is distributed upon the individual
members, in proportion to the land held and cultivated
by them. Thus we recognise the proprietary right of
the mass of the freemen—constituting, I should say, in
most cases an actual majority of the population, and
certainly almost the whole strength of the country.
Practically, the settlement made with a community is
very nearly ryotwar, with the difference that Government
deals with the united body, and not directly with each
individual separately.
Most of the Punjab people are far better cultivators
and much more provident than the Rajpoots and similar tribes, and the Government officers have been more
considerate; hence the sale of rights, in consequence of

the non-payment of revenue, is almost unknown. The revenue is paid with extreme punctuality.

Another most important distinction, as compared with the North-West Provinces, is this, that in the first instance the unlimited interference of civil courts administering technical law on the principle of "fiat justitia ruat cœlum" was not permitted. In those days it was considered that in the new countries, called non-regulation, the ruling authorities had, in the absence of specific law restraining them, something of the old despotic power of the rulers to whom they succeeded. There were no independent judicial tribunals. The executive officers were vested with judicial powers; and there was at most only an appeal from Philip drunk to Philip sober. It was distinctly laid down as the rule of the country that landed property was not liable, as a matter of course, to summary sale in satisfaction of simple debts, such sales being only permitted with the special sanction of the higher authorities; and that was only accorded on a full consideration of the circumstances of the tenure and of the case, when it was considered that the course was both just and expedient. These conditions being made fully known, no injustice was done to those who chose to lend money on such security as they could get. There was also in all cases of sale of individual rights, a right of pre-emption in the other members of the same village community.

A large Sepoy army was quartered in the Punjab in 1857; and all the regiments which were not disarmed in time and guarded almost as prisoners broke into mutiny and rebellion. It may be admitted that the Punjab people had no love for the Sepoys. But still most of the European troops having marched to Dehli, an almost complete opportunity was afforded to a war-like and independent people only a few years conquered. It is impossible to suppose that if there had been discontent it must not have then burst forth. Yet it is well known that the people not only did not rebel, but gave us the most active assistance. We put arms in their hands; they fought the rebel Sepoys; the villagers hunted them down ; troops hastily organised in the Punjab largely contributed to take Dehli. It may then very confidently be asserted that the system pursued in the Punjab had given satisfaction to the people.

It is constantly said, as matter of theory, by those who follow other systems, that the joint responsibility which the system of joint engagements involves must be bad ; that it is a system which makes the good pay for the bad, the provident for the improvident. But, in fact, this is not so. The assessments are calculated to give, and do in fact give, much value to the land ; if a man breaks down, others are always found most ready to take his land and pay up his arrears ; it is generally not even necessary absolutely to transfer the land of the defaulter (although this may be done) ; the feeling of the country is rather in favour of transfer in the way of native mortgage, which gives the defaulter a sufficient period to recover his inheritance, on paying the amount advanced, if he can obtain the means by military service or otherwise. The theory of the northern settlement system gives every shareholder the right to have his land and his liabilities partitioned, if he likes to incur the necessary expense; but the privileges and advantages of membership of these communities are such that the shareholders seldom seek to carry the division farther than the partition of cultivated lands, which is the essence of the system. In course of time we shall probably come to entirely separate properties ; but there is no need to hurry the process.*

Even if it be conceded that there might be some economical objection to the system of joint tenure, the main point is this, that by the indigenous system of joint engagements the Government is enabled at once to deal with the body of the cultivators, and to acknow-

---

* The most curious proof that the natives do not necessarily prefer the separate to the joint system, is found in the fact, published in some of the official papers of the Madras Presidency, that in that country villages were found which for half a century had submitted to the farce of a Government assessment on each individual, but had year by year lumped the individual assessments together, and redivided the total in their own way among the members of the community.

ledge and enlarge their rights, to the satisfaction of the people and advantage of the administration. It can do this without incurring the much more serious evils and drawbacks which have always been found to attend the attempt of a great foreign Government to deal separately with each petty holder, till, at least, many years and much experience have enabled it to do so in a way which is impossible in the first generation under our rule.

I will not delay to enter into farther details; but I believe it must be admitted on all hands that in practice the Punjab system has been eminently successful. No one can have passed through the country without feeling that.

THE RYOTWAR SYSTEMS OF MADRAS AND BOMBAY.

The system known as the " ryotwar " is that of dealing separately with each ryot without joint responsibility. It has been mentioned that a part of the Madras territory was permanently settled with the great Zemeendars. In another part, on the western coast, there are peculiar tenures nearly amounting to complete property; but my space will not admit of going into details; and, in treating of Madras, I shall keep to the normal system of the greater part of the Madras territory, the ryotwar.

As soon as the orders for adopting the Bengal system were relaxed, the Madras authorities returned to their own system of management. They considered the Zemeendars and Polygars to be no better than robbers and tyrants, from whom we had delivered the people. Most of these men had been swept away in the wars of our early days, and those who remained were put aside. The Madras authorities not only dealt direct with the people; but, insisting on strict economic justice in every individual case, they rejected the old system of joint village responsibility.

It is singular how much Englishmen, educated in the same way, and dealing with very similar institutions, have fallen into different grooves when separated in different localities in a foreign country. Perhaps no two sets of men bred in different planets could have diverged more widely than Bengal and Madras civilians on the land question. The fact seems to be that the country to which the rule of India has fallen is that of all the countries of Europe in which there is least that is analogous to Oriental institutions. And Englishmen, set down amid scenes entirely new to them, are very amenable to local influences. Local schools being once established, men isolated, and coming little into personal contact with those following other systems, maintain their own views with a persistence and intolerance which we do not find when men are brought more together.

It has been said that the different schools of Bengal civilians agree in this, that under no circumstances shall the Government deal direct with the individual ryots. The Madras civilians, on the other hand, have made it the root and foundation of their faith that under no circumstances shall the Government deal with the land in any other way. Much of the country was really in that state which suggested the ryotwar system, there being none who could claim the character of proprietors, unless they had been created, as would have been the case in Bengal or the North-West. But it is abundantly clear, from the descriptions of the early administrators, that in some parts of the south there were village communities just as completely constituted as those of the Punjab, and well accustomed to pay the revenue in the lump, and manage their own affairs. The system was rejected as unjust and inexpedient; and, by the force of the Government, the communities were generally dissolved into the individual units, each man being separately assessed for the land which he held; although in some instances the villages maintained their system in spite of the Government.

In the early years of vigorous ryotwar management, a measurement and classification was made, in native fashion, of the whole lands of the country; every field was recorded, with the Government dues payable for it. Every ryot in possession is secured so long as he pays the revenue so assessed. He may give up any field if he likes, and may take any unoccupied field. For long, a certain distinction was drawn between the meerasdars or hereditary and proprietary ryots, who had more fixed and positive rights, and the simple ryots, whose tenure was rather one of permission to hold than an acknowledged property ; but, by a system of levelling up, this distinction may be said to have been eventually effaced in the ryotwar countries, and the ryots' holdings have become complete property so long as the revenue is paid.

A very important difference between a ryotwar system and the others which have been described is this, that in the ryotwar provinces all the waste and unoccupied lands are considered to be Government property, and, being separately assessed in fields or survey plots, are available to the first comer, native of the village or stranger, who chooses to take them upon the prescribed terms. Whether the settlement be made with the Bengal Zemeendar or with the Punjab village community, the lump sum assessed includes all the lands of each village area, cultivated and uncultivated ; and the proprietors may make their own arrangements for cultivating the waste without increase of revenue, except when there is a new settlement. In Madras and Bombay it is not so ; there for every new field cultivated the Government has an additional revenue. Where, as is still the case in some parts of Madras, the revenue is payable in the old native fashion (a proportion of the grain crop, varying rates for different kinds of crops, and so on), the Government also benefits by the increase of prices and spread of valuable products.

The advantages and disadvantages of the ryotwar system have been made very apparent in Madras. There is no tyranny of grasping proprietors over poor ryots. The revenue is adjusted according to circumstances. When peace brought down war prices, it somewhat fell off; since the expenditure of British capital, and other recent circumstances, have enhanced prices and increased resources, it has greatly risen. But too much was attempted in the first instance. The survey was very rough, and the rates were certainly too high; so that there has not, till quite recently, been any sufficient margin to enable the ryots generally to attain an easy and independent position.

The survey and assessment have not been revised, as was necessary. In the greater part of the presidency there is still nothing more recent than the days of Sir Thomas Monro. The assessment once fixed was never altered; and it has frequently happened that the best fields remained uncultivated, as being too highly assessed. The chief evil is this, that it is impossible to work a most complicated system, and to collect from many hundreds of thousands of ryots a revenue, expressed in a multitude of items, without the intervention of a host of native subordinates. The revenue could never be exactly collected; the grant of remissions to individuals who can show some excuse for non-payment is still a recognised part of the system; and as it is totally impossible that the collector can really master every such case, many abuses necessarily result.

In Bombay, when the territory was acquired from the Marattas, Mountstuart Elphinstone was altogether in favour of the village system; but eventually the Madras pattern of ryotwar management was that more generally adopted. Subsequently, when the successful settlement of the north-western provinces had called attention to these matters, a knot of able and energetic Bombay officers devised an improved ryotwar system, which has been very successfully carried out. A new and exact survey and valuation is made by much improved methods. The land is permanently marked out by substantial boundary marks in convenient fields or small blocks, and the revenue is systematically assessed on each in money, and fixed for a period of thirty years. The rates are extremely low—many people say too low —but that is now generally considered to be a fault on the right side; and although there was at first a disposition to rush from old lands to lightly-assessed new ones, and to take up more than a man could properly cultivate, I believe that, the great demand for cotton and consequent flow of money largely aiding, there has been a very great increase of substantial and permanent cultivation and a great development of agricultural enterprise. A man may still give up each field at his pleasure, or take any new one that is unoccupied; but all land in possession is declared to be complete and absolute property, and has acquired such a value that it is now seldom surrendered. The rates being so low, the revenue is punctually exacted, and the tenures are held liable for its payment.

I believe that, sufficient pains being taken, and a sufficient machinery employed, and circumstances favouring, the ryotwar system has really been worked out to a very successful issue in Bombay, and that the revenue has been benefited as well as the people.*

The mode of assessment was originally too artificial and minute; but I suppose that in practice the great object has been to make a reasonable assessment in some way, at rates so low that minor inequalities are comparatively immaterial. The Bombay territory is small: the officers employed were zealous and energetic; and the object aimed at has been effected. It must, however, be understood that the thing has not been done without something of the same lump system to which objection is taken as regards the practice of Northern India. The unit is not the village, but a smaller unit; still that unit is to some degree arbitrary and artificial. The assessment is not imposed on each actual petty field, but on an artificial field, often ten or twelve acres or more. When there are several holders in this block, a certain joint responsibility is imposed. If one cultivator surrenders his portion, he who remains must take the whole or give up the whole. And he is not permitted to subdivide it again for revenue purposes.

Subject to the undivided responsibility for each revenue block, there is no prohibition of subdivision by inherit-

* I am compelled to be brief as regards Bombay and Madras, but I have given fuller details of the systems there followed in ' Modern India,' chap. vii.—G. C.

ance, &c., as among the people themselves ; but there being much facility for taking up new land on the one hand, and great demand for labour for railways, manufactories, &c., on the other, I understand that the tendency has been rather to consolidation, and not to subdivision of farms, taking the country generally. I am told that there has not been much sub-letting, and that the evils sometimes said to attend small properties have not yet been largely experienced in Bombay.

My visits to Bombay districts have impressed me very favourably. I can say that all that we can hear from the people of the adjoining villages of the central provinces goes to show that the Bombay system is extremely popular. And the highest authorities connected with the Bombay Administration assure me that the social results are so far altogether good.

The success of the Bombay system led to measures for a similar revision and reconstruction of the ryot-war system in Madras ; but the same successful result has not yet been obtained. The reasons of this failure are not clear ; this only is certain, that the territory is larger, and the task heavier than in Bombay. Madras men used to say that it would be very easy to give as much satisfaction if the revenue were as completely sacrificed as it had been in Bombay ; but since the Bombay revenue has been recouped, that argument can hardly hold. I suspect that a dislike servilely to follow the Bombay, or any other pattern, has something to do with it. And I should rather think, from the papers I have seen, that the Madras officers have fallen into the same error which at first rendered Reg. VII. of 1822 inoperative, that is, they attempt too minute calculations of produce, and too scientific deductions of rates, as the basis of their settlements, instead of cutting the knot by a rough and ready assessment at rates so low as to be safe, some inequalities notwithstanding. I have not been in the Madras territories since 1864, and Madras revenue affairs have always been a kind of sacred mystery to the outside world, the whole system is so full of native complications, and all the reports so bristle with hopelessly unintelligible technicalities. The popularised settlement reports which have been elsewhere so much in vogue, have not been generally imitated in Madras. The official documents are such that I, an expert of many provinces, shrink from them : an ordinary Englishman might as well attempt to read an arrow-headed inscription.

The Madras authorities used to be loud in praise of their own system, but of late years they seem to have run to the other extreme of pessimism.

After years of discussing and minuting, a resolution intended to inaugurate a new survey and settlement was recorded by the Madras Government, on 14th August, 1855. According to this document everything was bad. With little exception, no part of the presidency had been in British possession for less than half a century, yet it stood alone among British provinces, as that in which there had been no proper survey and settlement. The old survey was wholly defective, a mere measurement and valuation made in haste by persons wholly ignorant of any correct methods of measuring, and under no effective control. There were no maps and no permanent boundaries. The records, such as they were, had been imperfectly preserved, and in many instances had been grossly tampered with. There were many districts in which there had been no pretence of measurement, and where at that day " the land revenue demand is based merely on the unchecked statement of the Curnum, who has thus vast opportunity both of making exactions on the ryots, and in collusion with them of defrauding Government."

The general result of the system was stated to be that not only was the revenue injuriously affected, but the poorer and less influential classes suffered for the benefit of the wealthy ; to all, both rich and poor, property was rendered uncertain, and they were placed in dependence on grasping and unscrupulous men, and diverted from the pursuits of honest industry.

The moral of this dreadfully black picture was that the Supreme Government must give the money necessary for a new survey and settlement; but still there was too much truth in it; and the new settlement was resolved on. Elaborate details regarding the system to be followed are to be found in the papers.

The Madras Government wished to settle the revenue at money rates, calculated on the average prices of produce, which were to be revised every seven or ten years; but the Government at home decided that it would be better to fix low money rates once for all, and to make the settlement at these rates for thirty years.

When I visited the Madras presidency in 1859, Sir C. Trevelyan being Governor, the settlement was being actively discussed, and it was apparently in train to be fully carried out. In 1864 I could not find that anything substantial had been done, and since that time I had been unable to learn anything tangible regarding the progress of the settlement. On applying for information, I have now received, as the latest intelligence, a paper which seems to put things in a very unfavourable light. It is a report made in the present year, 1869, to the Board of Revenue by an officer specially deputed to inquire into the matter, and himself formerly deputy director of settlements. The Board simply request the director of settlements to favour them with his views, and I suppose that it is a tolerably reliable document. It appears that, excepting the districts where a new system of irrigation rendered a resettlement indispensable, scarcely any settlements have yet been completed. A conference, it is stated, was held on settlement subjects in Sir Charles Trevelyan's time, in 1859, but, says the report, "The result of the conference was never officially notified; for Sir Charles Trevelyan soon after left the country, and from that day to this the Settlement Department has continued to work without any specific instructions, on a sort of semi-organised footing, doing a little here and there, in an uncertain and unconnected manner." That is a very extraordinary statement. The report goes on to say, that as things are managed the system still works badly, "The bulk of the people are paupers. They can just pay their cess in a

good year, and fail altogether when the season is bad.
Remissions have to be made perhaps every third year
in most districts.   There is a bad year in some one
district or group of districts every year."

It is stated that the Government have gradually
abolished a vast number of vexatious and petty native
items of assessment, but that there are still nineteen
different systems in the nineteen districts, and many
anomalies; *e.g.*, " A man grows tobacco in his garden
and is charged eighteen rupees an acre, while his neighbour grows millet and is charged three rupees an acre.
Single crop lands are charged double crop rates, and
double crop lands single crop rates.   Two or more rates
of assessment are imposed on different parts of the same
field.   Certain lands in this village are charged eight
rupees, and precisely similar lands in a neighbouring
village, four rupees an acre."   These and many other
anomalies are said to exist ; but it is asked, Are the advantages of a new settlement worth the outlay of a
million sterling on establishment and working expenses,
and a certain loss of revenue which it will take time to
recoup ?   In fact, says the reporter, two millions must
be spared to carry out the settlement, or the system
must be abandoned.

I believe that, notwithstanding the pessimism of the
reports which I have quoted, there has been of late years
a considerable increase of prosperity and wealth in Madras.
Still the failure to put the great interests connected with
the land on a proper footing seems very bad.   That is
no consequence of the ryotwar system ; on the contrary,
the adoption of that system is just what renders a minute
survey and valuation much more indispensably necessary
than in provinces where we deal with the people in a
body, or through intermediate proprietors, and leave
them to settle their own affairs.   The omission to carry
out a proper system can only be considered to be an
administrative failure.

RECENT LEGISLATION AND SETTLEMENTS.

I have explained the very good footing on which the

Bengal ryots of the time of the permanent settlement were put by the laws of that day, record only being wanting ; but I have scarcely alluded to the ryots who came into land subsequent to the settlement. In truth, till recent legislation dealt with the whole subject, their position was very obscure and doubtful. The Regulations giving the Zemeendars power to deal with the waste land would have enabled them to introduce, in so much of their estates, an English contract system ; to have retained the complete and absolute property in their own hands—to have built and improved, and let the improved lands to tenants. But, in fact, they did nothing of the sort. Exactly the same thing happened which has happened in Ireland, that is to say, the Zemeendars and those holding under them permitted ryots to reclaim the land, settle themselves, put up houses, and do all that was required for agricultural purposes, on the understanding that when it was reclaimed they were to pay the usual rents.

There was, however, this material difference from the state of things in Ireland, that no circumstances arose leading the Zemeendars to think of attempting to evict tenants. And the mass of the old tenants not being liable to eviction, those who came in subsequently, on similar customary terms, probably considered that they also were not to be evicted so long as they paid their rents. In course of time, indeed, the distinction between the old and new ryots would necessarily become very difficult to trace; it became hard to say who had held from before the settlement, and who had come in subsequently, the apparent tenure being precisely the same. At any rate the question of occupancy rights was not raised between the Zemeendars and ryots, both parties being content that things should remain as they were. Under a legal system where the greatest force is given to custom, it was at least doubtful whether it might not be held that, according to the custom and understanding of the country, any man who occupied land as a resident ryot, and invested his labour and money in it, ipso facto acquired a right of occupancy subject to the customary rent.

The old Regulations, in fact, seem hardly to contemplate any other than the ordinary native method of managing these things; and there are in them expressions which would seem to imply that no more is to be taken from any class of ryots, old or new, than the customary rates of the neighbourhood. Special contracts would probably override these general provisions; but it is certain that in the whole course of litigation, from 1793 to 1859, there was no case in which any ryot's rent had been raised by the agency of the courts, on any other ground than that it was below the customary rates of the neighbourhood, and should be raised to that standard. The logical inference would be that as there was no mode of raising the general established rates of a locality all round, and individual holdings could not be raised beyond those rates, they must have remained unaltered all along. The fact, however, is not exactly so. Zemeendars, like other native rulers, have a good deal of irregular power; as prices rose and expenses increased, they had some equitable claim to an increase of rent. Cesses and extra items were added to the rent-roll: then on special occasions new measurements were made, and claims of one kind and another were sometimes compromised by an agreement to add something to the previous rates. Thus in an irregular way, but more or less by mutual consent, the old Pergunnah rates were changed into very various local rates, and the tendency was always towards increase; there being in this respect little distinction between ancient and modern ryots, except in the case of the formally acknowledged holders of perpetuities at a quit rent. Once the body of the ryots had submitted to any increase, individuals could be made to pay the local rates thus established. Still there was no general system of rapid enhancement, and, as I have already said, the increase of rents did not keep pace with the increased value of the land.

A few years ago it was found that the increase of knowledge and of the mercantile spirit were bringing about a state of things when it would be no longer safe to rely on the undefined customs which were daily becoming more varied and indistinct, and that a revision of the Bengal rent laws was necessary. In the north-west provinces, also, it was felt that the settlement proceedings had left the rights and liabilities of the ryots in a some-what inaccurate state. And it was determined to pass a new law applicable to both provinces. This was the famous Act X. of 1859, by which the respective rights of landlords and ryots are now regulated. ·

The first provisions are applicable to the permanently settled provinces only, and do little more than confirm the rights of the old ryots conferred on them by the original laws. Ryots who have held from the time of the permanent settlement at fixed rates of rent which had never been changed are entitled to hold at those rents for ever. The effect is that those of the ancient ryots who have clung to their rights and submitted to no increase keep them still; but those who have, as matter of fact, submitted to any increase, just or unjust, fall down into a lower class, to be presently mentioned.

Then, to get over the want of record and the difficulty or impossibility of proving an ancient invariable hold-ing, it was provided that when any ryot can prove that his rent has not been changed for twenty years, it shall be presumed that the land has been held at the same rate from the time of the permanent settlement, *unless the Zemeendar shows to the contrary.* This is by no means giving perpetuity to all ryots of twenty years' standing, but is a mere adjustment of the burden of proof. There has been a great disposition to be very strict in the proof required of the twenty years' holding at a fixed rent. It has not been thought enough that some sort of proof should be given, and it should be accepted if uncontradicted by evidence on the other side. Very specific and exact proof has been required, which is not always forthcoming, the provision not having been anticipated, and there being no official record. This deficiency has often been met in native method by forging the receipts which were wanting. The result, I fear, is that it very much depends on the idiosyncrasy of the individual judge, whether claims to hold at a fixed

P

rent are admitted wholesale or rejected wholesale; and there is a painful uncertainty as to every tenure which has not passed the ordeal of the courts.

These, however, are judicial difficulties; the general equity of the law is so far not disputed. The provision which has since led to much discussion, and to a cry that the rights of landlords have been confiscated, is the next, which declares a right of occupancy at a fair rent (subject to enhancement from time to time) to belong to every ryot who has held land for a period of twelve years and upwards, with two important exceptions. First, the law is not to affect the terms of any written contract, so that a man holding, on contract only, a terminable lease does not benefit by the provision. And second, it does not apply to the "seer" or demesne lands of the proprietors. Lands which have once borne that character, although let for the time, can be resumed at any time.

Tenants having a right of occupancy are liable to enhancement of rent on the following grounds, and on these only:—

That the land is found by measurement to be in excess of the quantity paid for.

That the rate of rent is below the prevailing rates paid by the same class of ryots for similar lands in the places adjacent.

That the value of the produce or the productive powers of the land have been increased otherwise than by the agency or at the expense of the ryot.

Facilities were given to the Zemeendars to put in force claims under these provisions in special revenue courts of easy access.

The following incidents of the occupancy tenures are established by law or by judicial decisions. So long as the ryot pays the rent he may do what he likes with the land (provided he does not absolutely destroy it); and may sublet it temporarily. It also descends by inheritance, and there is no actual restriction upon subdivision as regards the rights of the heirs among themselves. But the Zemeendar is not bound to recognise any subdivision; so long as he does not accept separate tenants he is entitled to hold the whole tenure liable for the whole rent, and can sell the tenure or eject the ryots when any part of the rent is in arrear. The question whether the tenures are or are not saleable is left to be determined by the custom of each district or locality.

The right of occupancy having been secured to so large a body of the tenants, there is no provision for compensation for improvements; but an outgoing tenant is entitled to carry away everything which he has placed on the land if he can remove it, and generally either sells or removes the woodwork in his house, and anything else not actually sunk in the soil.

It has been said that the twelve years' rule of occupancy is an arbitrary rule, borne out by no native law or custom; and there is some truth in that statement. But then very much was to be said for the still wider rule which would have given every resident ryot a right of occupancy, as his due under the custom and an implied contract. In fact the law, as originally drawn for Bengal, gave all resident ryots the right to hold at the prevailing rates. It was, however, pointed out by the authorities of the north-west provinces, that in modern times, since the cessation of the external pressure which in troubled times made every man necessarily reside in a village as a member of a community united for many purposes, the distinction between resident and non-resident ryots could hardly be maintained, and they suggested their own twelve years' rule, which was adopted accordingly, as a compromise of a doubtful question. Be the abstract merits of the occupancy question what they may, the consideration which I think takes away all ground of complaint is that the law declaring the occupancy right of the mass of ryots was passed without the slightest opposition on the part of the Zemeendars; it may almost be said with their tacit consent. Modern Indian laws are not passed as mere edicts; they are published and fully discussed in an open legislative council, the proceedings of which are reported day by day. The Bengallee Zemeendars are a highly educated class, with English newspapers, and

abundant organs; they are the last people to submit
without complaint to any infringement of their rights.
But on this occasion they did not complain. It is true that
the twelve years'-limit was, I believe, put in somewhat
hurriedly, towards the latter stages of the bill; but then
it was, as I have said, substituted for a much wider rule,
which had been long published. The fact is, that to
native ideas the rule was one to which it did not occur to
them to object. Native Zemeendars generally prefer fixed
ryots to those who may run away any day.

At the same time that the twelve years' rule was introduced, there was also inserted the third of the grounds for
enhancement of rent which I have mentioned; one previously unknown in Bengal, and not practically operative
in the north-west provinces, which gave the Zemeendars a
right to enhance on the ground of increase in the value of
the produce or in the productive powers of the land.
That was a great gain to them. In the north-west provinces, where no class of ryots have a right to hold at fixed
rents, and the right of occupancy was already secured,
the result of this provision is that the Rent Act, taken
as a whole, benefits the Zemeendars, and renders the
ryots much more subject to enhancement of rent than
before. In Bengal, the settlement in favour of the ryots
of a doubtful right of occupancy is counterbalanced by
the new rule of enhancement. But the Zemeendars did
not show a disposition to press it much; and so far as the
natives, superior and inferior, were concerned, the new
law might have worked quietly enough in Bengal. A
storm, however, soon after arose from an unexpected
quarter.

The oldest and perhaps the most successful European
industrial enterprise in India is that of the Bengal indigo
planters. They used generally to buy the indigo plant
from the ryots, and to manufacture the indigo themselves.
For facility of obtaining indigo, they had acquired possession of considerable estates, generally as sub-holders or
middlemen, under the Zemeendars. Holding thus towards the ryots a double relation as landlords and merchants, the landlord influence was brought to bear on

the cultivation and delivery of the plant. And, as so often happens in India, the matter came to be regulated rather by custom than by proper mercantile principles. The planters did not attempt to make profit by the rents; the ryots were allowed to sit at the old easy rents; but they were required to deliver a tale of indigo plant, and the price paid was fixed by custom and not by competition. As was shown when a Commission investigated the matter, the planters had adopted some high-handed ways, in the absence of sufficient Government authority in the interior of Bengal; but, after all, natives will bear a great deal in that way, so long as they are in the main tolerably well off; and through the planters much European money circulated among them. It was when the increase of prices of all produce and general rise of values made it apparent that the old customary prices paid for the indigo plant were very unprofitable, that there arose serious discontent, terminating in a sort of rebellion against the indigo planters. The whole matter was inquired into by a Commission, and it was made evident that the old state of things could not continue, and that if the planters wanted indigo, they must pay market value for the plant.

They then said, "We have let you sit at easy rents because you gave us indigo; but since you object to give indigo on the old terms, we will raise your rents." So far the planters had entirely right on their side; and if they had on the one hand offered a reasonably increased price for the indigo plant, and on the other claimed a reasonable increase of rent, the matter might probably have been settled. In fact, however, the planters who tried the question did not at first take this moderate course. They rather sought to conquer the ryots and to bring them to their own terms with respect to indigo, by demanding an extravagant and penal increase of rent. They proposed to treble and quadruple the rents all round at one blow. The case came before the Chief Justice, Sir Barnes Peacock, who decided that the ryots were bound to pay a fair rent in the sense of the highest rent obtainable, and that, an increase of the value of produce being shown, there was no limit to the increase demandable but the net profit of the cultivator or rack-rent. Entering into a calculation of the value of produce and costs of production, and deducting the one from the other, he found that the difference left a profit greater than the rent claimed by the planter, and accordingly decreed the full claim.

The ryots, however, still declined either to grow indigo on the old terms or to pay the rents so greatly increased, and the case eventually came before the full High Court of fifteen judges, who decided by fourteen to one (the Chief Justice still maintaining his opinion) that as the landlord could only enhance for a certain cause, he could only enhance in the same degree or in the same proportion in which that cause operated. It being shown that the value of agricultural produce has increased in a certain proportion since the last adjustment of rent, the rent will be increased in the same proportion ; *e.g.*, if prices have risen fifty per cent. the rent will also be raised fifty per cent. That is the final decision in what is called the Great Rent Case.

I believe that under this decision things have settled down quietly enough. The planters are enabled considerably to raise their rents, they have been obliged to pay higher for the indigo plant, and things go on upon a better footing than before. The native Zemeendars have to some extent followed the example of claiming enhanced rents ; but I do not think that in Bengal they have done so to an excessive degree, or that there is any considerable war of classes there.

The thirty years' settlement of the north-western provinces having expired, a new settlement has been for some time in progress. It has been determined to follow in all new settlements a more moderate rule of assessment than in former days. Instead of taking two-thirds of the rent, the Government is now to take only half of the present rents, leaving the other half to the landholder for his expenses and profits, besides future increase. There are several cesses for roads, schools, &c.,

to be paid out of the landholders' portion; but still the profit left to him is very large. The increase of rental since the last settlement being counterbalanced by the lower rate of assessment, I believe that the Government will scarcely profit by the revision.

Of late years there had been a reaction of opinion in favour of permanent settlement of the land revenue, and orders were sent out by the Secretary of State that in every estate where the land might be considered to be sufficiently cultivated (the proportion of untilled land not being in excess of that required for grazing and other reasonable purposes) the assessment should be declared to be perpetual.

It is evident, however, that a permanent assessment on the basis of half present assets is a much more liberal arrangement than any hitherto made, and that as the land revenue forms in India so large a proportion of the total revenue of the country, if it is stereotyped we must seek for other sources of income. There is much reason to suppose that the value of money and produce are rapidly altering, and that great changes are likely to occur in the next few years. An opinion has also sprung up that the resources of the country are as yet insufficiently developed, and that it is for the Government, as superior landlord, to do much in the way of irrigation works and similar improvements, about which there will be difficulty if it is debarred from increase of land revenue. Hence I think there has again been some reaction of feeling. Orders have been issued that where there is a probability of irrigation works being undertaken we are not to commit ourselves to permanency of the land revenue. Altogether the question seems to be still in an unsettled state.

It is to be noted that the recent orders for permanent settlements in the north-western provinces contain no provisions for extending the benefit of permanency to the inferior class possessed of acknowledged rights in the land (the old occupancy ryots) such as were contained in Lord Cornwallis's Regulations, and are repeated (as regards the old permanently settled provinces) in Act X.

of 1859. As matters now stand they would still remain subject to constant increase of rent.

The first settlements in the Punjab were made for shorter terms than those adopted in older provinces, and a revised settlement has been for some time in progress here. The proceedings have led to one of those lamentable official battles which so much interfere with progress.

I have mentioned that the normal tenure of the Punjab is that under which the same persons, as members of village communities, are proprietors and cultivators at the same time. Still there are also in parts a good many non-cultivating landholders of the same classes as those of the north-west provinces, and many cultivators holding under them. The distinction between hereditary or occupancy ryots and tenants-at-will had certainly been very loosely made in the first settlements (as was also the case in the north-west provinces), there being little or no contest at a time when the distinction between revenue and rent rates was hardly known to the people; and the landholders were sometimes ready enough to let others share the burden of the fixed money revenue then for the first time imposed on them. Some settlement officers had followed the old north-west practice of considering all who had held for twelve years to have a right of occupancy ; but the more correct rule afterwards laid down by Sir J. Lawrence was " to consider the nature quite as much as the length of occupancy, and to pay entire regard to local customs and the opinions of the agriculturists." In the original settlement very large numbers of inferior holders were recorded as having right of occupancy.

Act X. of 1859 has never been extended to the Punjab, so that its provisions do not settle the matter.

Soon after the commencement of the new settlement operations the officer at the head of the department represented that the old settlement was very frequently wrong in attributing occupancy rights to mere tenants-at-will ; that many of these men themselves admitted this to be so ; and he asked if he might re-open the matter and correct the erroneous entries.

Beyond an order enjoining on him extreme caution in his inquiries, no definite instructions were issued. Unhappily this question of the rights of the cultivators was then the subject of hot controversy in several parts of India, and the dispute was taken up by opposing parties among the Punjab officials. The highest authorities differed, and nothing was settled.

Meantime the settlement commissioner, being himself very strongly of the party which denied the rights of ryots, went on in his own way, and very many thousands of the occupancy ryots of the old settlement were put down as tenants-at-will under the new settlement.

An independent chief court has now been established in the Punjab, and some of the proceedings of the settlement commissioner coming before the court, were declared to be not warranted by law. All parties were then agreed as to the necessity of legislation of some sort. After much discussion a new Land Act was passed for the Punjab last year, the provisions of which, as regards the disputed point, are these :—

Every person entered in the records of settlements previously completed and sanctioned, as having a right of occupancy, shall be presumed to have such right, unless it shall be proved by regular suit brought by the landlord—

1. That he has admitted before a settlement officer that he has no such right ; or,
2. That within thirty years tenants of the same class, in the same or adjacent villages, have ordinarily been ejected at the will of the landlord.

Revised rent-laws have also been passed in Madras and Bombay, settling all doubts which had there arisen.

During recent years much attention has been paid to the land affairs of new provinces, which I shall separately notice.

THE LAND QUESTION IN OUDE.

The partition of the Oude territory at the beginning of the century has been mentioned. The division, in a plain country with no natural boundaries, was purely

political. The people of the country left to the Nawab
were almost absolutely identical with those of the
districts taken by the British, in race, language, and
institutions, being Hindoostanees of the regular Hindoo-
stanee type.

The first use made by the Nawab of the power which
a strong British contingent gave him was to bring to
complete obedience the subjects who were left to him,
and to put down most of the Jagheerdars and Talookdars.
But under his successors, the interference of British
forces in their internal affairs being no longer permitted,
a very different state of things grew up. A great degree
of anarchy prevailed ; local chiefs constantly set the
Government at defiance, and from the death of Nawab
Saadat Allee, to the time of the annexation of Oude,
these men acquired more and more power. This is the
period of the rise of the modern Talookdars. Some of
them are members of old leading families, and a few of
these are in some sense chiefs of clans ; many others are
mere modern revenue collectors or contractors who have
obtained a hold over the districts intrusted to them.
In all cases the power has gone to the strongest or most
astute in each family, not to the man who had the most
legitimate claims by seniority.

Take as an example the family of the present leader
of the Talookdars, known to the English public as " chief
of the barons of Oude," Maharajah Sir Man Sing, K.S.I.
They are not Oude men at all. The uncle of the present
Maharajah, a native of the old British province of Bahar,
and a Bramin by caste, was a trooper in one of the
Company's regiments of regular cavalry. Being quartered
at Lucknow, he entered the Oude service and rose to
high office. He introduced his brother, the father of the
Maharajah. Up to the time of annexation the family
rose higher and higher in the Oude administration, and
acquired a great estate. The eldest son has held
great places, but is notorious for having almost ruined
by tyranny the districts beyond the Gogra, and has
been prudently kept in the background since British
rule. Another son is a man of literary tastes, who does

not care for politics; and the family is now represented by the youngest son, the present Maharajah, an extremely clever person, thoroughly versed in political affairs.

I have no doubt that the example of the British districts by which they were surrounded had much to do with the disposition shown by the Talookdars to acquire, by fair means or foul, not only the rule over, but something like proprietary right in as many villages as possible. Certain it is that a continual process of absorption of the independent villages into the Talookas, and suppression of those men who would have been considered village proprietors under the north-west system, went on up to the time of annexation; so that at last the greater part of Oude was held by the large Talookdars, corresponding to the Zemeendars of Bengal.

Not only were the Talookdars constantly in arms against the Government, but the Talookas were also torn by intestine feuds. If we look to the succession of the great chiefships, we shall generally find that the ruler for the time had murdered his uncle and supplanted his cousins, and that the cousins or cousins' sons formed an opposition, ready to supplant him on the first opportunity. The *outs* constantly harassed the *ins* by predatory attacks. When I was magistrate of a British border district, I had repeated remonstrances, through the British resident, regarding the atrocities of a man who was represented as a common robber and dacoit of the vilest description, sheltered by British subjects; and after some blood had been spilt in an attempt of my police to capture him, I was quietly told that I need not trouble myself any longer, as he had made terms with his Government, and was installed as Talookdar.

The ryots, too, were often almost necessarily involved on the side of one faction or other, and were plundered and oppressed when the opposite faction triumphed. The British border was sometimes full of them. Yet they seemed seldom to care to settle there; they only encamped, and were generally ready to return on a favourable opportunity. The fact is that the system had its compensations for them; the exercise of despotic

power by the superior implies the possession of the
sacred right of rebellion by the inferior; and if they were
illused by one man, they generally soon found the means
of paying him off by adhering to some opposition chief;
so that either party would at last make some sort of
terms with them.

The general result, however, of the state of anarchy
which prevailed, was that all tenures and all rights had
been very much shaken and shuffled in the generation
preceding our rule; and under a nominal Government at
Lucknow, the country was in great degree held by semi-
independent Talookdars, rather tributary than subject.

Both the official reports and the Anglo-Indian newspapers were constantly full of the tyrannies and oppres-
sions of the Talookdars. Colonel Sleeman, the British
resident, made an official tour through the country, and
wrote a book full of their misdeeds. It was solely and
wholly on the ground of the inability of the native
Government to control them and protect the people that,
in the year 1856, under orders issued contrary to the
opinion of Lord Dalhousie, we dethroned the representative of the family who had been our oldest allies
and for a hundred years thoroughly faithful to us, and
annexed the country.

Under these circumstances, it is scarcely surprising
that the first orders issued on the annexation gave somewhat scant justice to the Talookdars, who had caused all
the mischief. They amounted in brief to this: that our
officers should deal primarily with the village communities, leaving the Talookdars to prove their right to
superior tenures, if they had any.

In practice, however, these orders could not be fully
carried out. The Talookdars had too complete a hold
of much of their possessions to leave it possible to ignore
them altogether. Many of their more recent acquisitions
were taken from them and restored to village proprietors;
but they still remained possessed of great estates, and had
not been deprived of their forts, guns, and followers when
the mutiny broke out, in the year immediately following
the annexation. Oude was, as is well known, one of the

chief scenes of the mutiny. It was almost exclusively held by Sepoy troops, very many of whom were natives of the country; and when they rose the small British force was besieged in the Residency. The Talookdars did not behave excessively ill. Some of them assisted our fugitive officers to escape, and for a time they generally temporized, and did not take a very decided part. From the time, however, when the attempted relief by Havelock and Outram failed, and the relievers were shut up along with the original besieged, the great body of the Talookdars identified themselves with the Sepoy cause, went into full rebellion, and took part in the siege of the Residency.

As soon as the military strength of the rebellion was completely broken, Lord Canning came out with his famous proclamation, confiscating all the lands of Oude. As there has been so much discussion on this subject, I may state that, being then in immediate communication with Lord Canning, he showed me the original draft of the proclamation in his own handwriting, and I then had it from his own lips (before the proclamation was published) that his object was not really to confiscate finally the rights of the Talookdars, but to get rid of all the engagements into which we had entered after annexation, and to obtain a " tabula rasa " which would enable him to restore the great landowners, and redress the injustice which he thought they had suffered, on condition of their full and complete allegiance. In fact, the step was taken in pursuance of a policy the opposite of that which had before prevailed, and in order to clear the ground for the new system.

The advice which I ventured to tender to Lord Canning was, that it would be better to avoid the appearance of extreme severity on the one hand, and the extreme of concession to those who had rebelled on the other; that it would be enough to assure the Talookdars that bygones should be bygones—that their property and reasonable claims should be respected—that the whole question of landed rights should be again gone into, and that any injustice of which they could fairly complain

should be redressed.   But the Governor-General had
taken his course.   The proclamation was accordingly
issued, and the Talookdars were immediately informed,
that on their submission they should have re-grants of
all that they had held before the annexation.   They
were at first very suspicious and incredulous about the
extreme goodness of the terms offered ; but they had no
choice but to come in or go off to the hills as fugitives;
they almost all came in and received English grants of
all the villages which they had in any shape or in any
way brought under their dominion before the annexation of the country.

Thus Lord Canning did in Oude precisely what Queen
Elizabeth did in Ireland, when the surrender of the Irish
chiefs was accepted and their possessions were re-granted
on English titles.

Soon after the pacification of the country, a revenue
settlement was undertaken, and then there arose the
question whether any inferior rights were to be recognised in subordination to those of the Talookdars, just as
the same question arose when a settlement of Ireland
was made under James I.   The advocates of the extreme
landlord theory at first said that the confiscation swept
away everything, and that the Talookdars had now complete and absolute titles, to the exclusion of every one
else.   But it was shown that Lord Canning had reserved
subordinate rights, proved to have been in active existence at the time of annexation, and any such which can
be made out are maintained.

Views unfavourable to rights of ryots were then
held by many, and Sir Barnes Peacock's decision in
favour of the landlord had just come out.   As respects
the ryots, then, it was at first said that the old hereditary
ryots had a bare right of occupancy, but that there was
no limit to the rent which might be demanded, save the
highest rack-rent of the day.   A little later, the Chief
Commissioner declared that he had been misled by the
prejudices of his education in the north-west provinces, and
that, correcting himself, he now said that there was no
such thing as a right of occupancy ; he therefore directed

that no distinction should be made in the records between tenants-at-will and any other class of ryots, except in case of leases under voluntary contract.

Of these orders the Governor-General, Sir John Lawrence, disapproved, and there was a special inquiry on the subject.

It turned out that most of the ryots did not care to claim fixity of tenure. Even the grant of proprietary rights under our system, accompanied by fixed burdens punctually exacted, are scarcely ever appreciated in the earliest years of our rule ; and perhaps, seeing how often the first possessors of such dangerous rights have been sold out and reduced far below their original position, the natives are not so far wrong as we suppose. It is, then, hardly surprising that most of the Oude ryots, who had so long looked on the free right of rebelling and running away as their best safeguard, did not much like anything which seemed to bind them down, and wholly rejected the leases which it was sometimes attempted to thrust upon them. There was also no standard of law and right ; and though the ryots said that a Talookdar ought not to turn them out, when asked whether he formerly had the power to do so, they said, " Of course he had—the man in power could do anything." The general result of the inquiry was that neither the ryots proved a right to stay in, nor did the Talookdars prove a right to turn them out ; but the Talookdars being taken as primâ facie owners under the grants, and the onus of proof being thrown upon the ryots, it may be said that the ryots generally failed of the proof necessary to give them any legal status. All depends on the way the burden of proof is put.

Eventually a compromise was effected, under which a comparatively small number of the highest class of ryots, the descendants of old proprietors and dominant families, have been admitted to a right of occupancy at rates (to be fixed from time to time) slightly below the full rack-rents of the day, while all the other ryots become tenants-at-will.

Thus the Oude Talookdars are much more complete

owners of the soil than any superior landholders in any
other province—infinitely more so than those of Bengal
ever were.

Since the Oude inquiry it has been said that the result
conclusively proves the whole system of ryots' rights
hitherto obtaining in so many provinces to have been a
mistake—that ryots' rights are a fiction of the British
imagination, and that the less they are fostered the
better.

It may, I think, be admitted that wherever the strong
communities of the Punjab type are not found, if the
burden of proving a legal title be thrown wholly on the
ryots, in countries where there are no laws, and before
custom has had time to crystallize into shape under
British rule, most of them would fail to prove any titles.
Even putting out of view the disturbance of all titles in
Oude in the half century between our annexation of the
first half and that of the second half of the territory, I
believe that if, in the first years of our rule, the ryots of the
districts of the north-west provinces had been subjected to
the same ordeal as the Oude ryots, the result would not
have been very different. But it by no means follows,
that when landed rights are to be created or enlarged, it
may not be equitable to give some share of that which is
to be given to the ryots ; or that, if time be allowed
before the question is raised, it will not be found that
native feeling and custom have given them a position
which ought to be recognised. It may be, in fact, that
without any formal declaration they would crystallize
into copyholders, as did English villeins.

The Oude system is still on its trial. The Talookdars
were taken under the special protection of Lord Canning.
They have had a remarkably light assessment of the
revenue, and every advantage. English newspapers have
been started as their organs with every sort of enlightened
ideas. As many virtues have been attributed to them
as formerly were vices. As usual, the truth will probably be found to be somewhere midway. But already
we hear of their free use of the power of raising rents
without restriction which has been conferred on them,

and even of the service of notices of ejectment in large numbers; and, on the other hand, of combinations of ryots to resist these proceedings. Class questions seem to be prematurely arising which have not been reached in other provinces in several generations. And it has been necessary for the Government to come to the assistance of the aristocratic system, by lending the Talookdars money, not to improve their estates but to stave off their creditors.

THE CENTRAL PROVINCES.

Till a recent period, the British territories in India have been completely separated from one another, the mass of native States in the centre dividing them into very unequal portions. The great sub-Himalayan plain, running upwards of fifteen hundred miles from the Bay of Bengal to the Affghan hills, contains one hundred millions of British subjects, and comprises the four administrations of Bengal, the North-west Provinces, Oude, and the Punjab. Madras occupies the south of the Peninsula, with twenty-four millions of inhabitants, and Bombay, the west, with thirteen millions. The annexation of the Nagpore territories, in the very centre of India, and the assigument to British use of the Nizam's Berar territory, gave us a link uniting the different British Provinces, and taking a little here and a little there, the central provinces were formed.

The oldest portion of these provinces is what was called the Saugor and Nerbudda territory, a large country on either side of the Nerbudda, and extending from Bundlecund and the north-west provinces on one side, to the Nagpore limits on the other. This territory, taken from the Marattas in the last great Maratta war, but not in population a Maratta country, had been long under a separate commissioner, but was for a time attached to the north-west provinces. Then there was the Nagpore territory, principally occupied by a Maratta-speaking population. And there were thrown in, on the west, some minor districts adjoining the Bombay territory, on the east some outlying districts of Bengal, the river Godavery transferred from Madras, and the great wild semi-independent territory between the Godavery and the Bengal frontiers.

Contrasts of administration heretofore veiled by distance have been brought into prominence by this arrangement of a territory uniting all the others. It seemed strange that salt coming to the central provinces from one quarter should be charged one rate of duty, and from another quarter three times that rate. And the Bombay officers who had been unable to see any trace of proprietary rights above those of the ryots, in the lands of Candeish and similar districts, looked with wonder on a system which, in adjacent villages, inhabited by the same races, under the same native institutions, found or created proprietors of a higher degree. Yet in respect of land tenure the system of the central provinces is in some sense intermediate.

The Saugor and Nerbudda territories contained some trace of the north-west form of village proprietary, and something of more southern institutions. The system followed had been to acknowledge no proprietary rights, but to farm out the villages for terms to farmers, who were as much as possible selected from the local headmen or from persons having local claims and influence. The holdings of the farmers were allowed to descend in the semi-hereditary manner of Indian offices, a good and efficient member of a deceased farmer's family being put in his place; and it was understood that good farmers would have a renewal of lease on re-settlement. Still, property not being admitted, the Civil Courts could not interfere. Private transfers were occasionally sanctioned; but if a man broke down, the tenure was not sold; the Government officer selected some other good man to put in his place; and the subdivision of interests in the farms, or other dealings with them in a way which might be prejudicial to efficient management, or dangerous to the security of the revenue, was not permitted.

The rents to be paid by the ryots were adjusted by the Government officers, and the farmers had no power

to raise them or to turn out the ryots, although they
benefited by the increase of cultivation during the terms
of their leases.

This system had its advantages.   The ryots were
completely protected, and the Government officers were
able to secure efficient men in the grade between themselves and the ryots, instead of being subject to the
inconveniences resulting from the introduction of ineffi-
cient or grasping men, and divided, limited, or complicated
tenures, by the action of the laws of inheritance and the
civil courts ; while at the same time a confidence in the
regular and considerate action of the Government as
superior landlord gave a substantial security of tenure,
which was an incitement to improvement in the native
fashion.   The result was that the north-west authorities
found the villages in possession of semi-hereditary farmers,
a few of whom were really of the same class who had
been recognised as village proprietors in the north-west ;
while many more, with no original claims to the character
of proprietors, had old hereditary connection with the
villages ; and a good many, owing to failures and changes,
were farmers of more recent introduction.

The north-west authorities, in pursuance of the ideas
prevailing in that part of India, considered that full property must be established ; but in consideration of the
peculiar circumstances of this territory, and the exceptionally favourable position which had been enjoyed by
the ryots for upwards of forty years, a reasonable
compromise was made in the orders issued for a regular
settlement.

The rules to be followed were these :—Wherever a
real proprietary right could be shown by any of the
persons hitherto called farmers, they were to be recognised as proprietors, and the ryots were to be treated
exactly as in the north-west provinces.   But in other
cases the old hereditary ryots were to be maintained in
their former position, being treated as a sort of sub-
proprietors of their holdings, subject to rent-rates somewhat in excess of revenue rates, which could not be
altered during the term of settlement ; while the farmers

were made village proprietors with the right of collecting from the ryots, and having as their profit both the difference between the rent-rates of the old ryots and the revenue-rates, and all that they could make by raising the rent of recent ryots, and promoting the cultivation of the waste lands attached to the village areas.

It may be mentioned, too, that in this settlement a compromise has been made between the northern system of including all waste in the settled areas, and the Madras-Bombay system, of charging additional revenue for all waste brought into cultivation. There is a great excess of uncultivated land in all this country. Liberal areas of waste have been assigned to each village, and included in the settlement, so as to give room for the extension of the cultivation, and by way of compromise of indefinite claims to grazing, wood, and water; while all beyond these areas has been reserved as Government property to be afterwards dealt with. The best forest lands are preserved for the growth and supply of timber.

It was found that in none of the districts received from different quarters had the Government made pledges which precluded the adoption of a similar system; and the rules above mentioned as originally laid down for the Nerbudda territories were applied to the whole of the central provinces.

It may be mentioned that in Orissa (which was ceded by the Marattas in the beginning of the present century, and most of which has never been permanently settled) the tenure is almost identical with that which has been described in the central provinces. The ancient "Thanee" ryots were secured by titles held direct from Government, under an old thirty year settlement; while they paid through hereditary farmers called "Surberakars," or managers. The Bengal revenue authorities made a strong effort to break down the ryots on the expiry of the settlement, and to reduce them to the level of ordinary ryots under the farmers turned into proprietors—but the matter was brought to the notice of the Government, and they have been confirmed at the old rent for another thirty years.

SUMMARY OF TENURES.

The present distribution of tenures in the different provinces may then be stated to be (speaking generally) as follows : Oude being at one extreme with an aristocratic system, which gives the land to nobles ; Madras and Bombay at the other, with a system which gives the land to the people.

Oude.—Great Zemeendars, almost complete owners, with few subordinate rights.

North-west Provinces.—Moderate proprietors ; the old ryots have fixity of tenure at a fair rent.

Punjab.—Very small and very numerous proprietors ; old ryots have also a measure of fixity of tenure at fair rent.

Bengal.—Great Zemeendars, whose rights are limited. Numerous sub-proprietors of several grades under them. Ancient ryots who have both fixity of tenure and fixity of rent. Other old ryots who have fixity of tenure at fair rent, variable from time to time.

Central Provinces.—Moderate proprietors. Ancient ryots who are sub-proprietors of their holdings at rents fixed for the term of each settlement. Other old ryots have fixity of tenure at a fair rent.

Madras and Bombay.—The ryots are complete proprietors of the soil, subject only to payment of revenue.

GRANT OF WASTE LANDS IN FEE SIMPLE.

An account of Indian land tenures would not be complete without noticing the system of granting waste lands in fee simple at a low price, which has been recently adopted.

There was formerly a liberal system of clearance leases, under which jungle tracts were freely given to enterprising individuals, on condition of clearance ; nothing being paid the first few years—then very light rates—and finally, ordinary revenue rates. Thus the progress of the country and the progress of the revenue is secured at the same time, and in dealing with natives and native products, the system is probably the best that can be adopted.

But when there seemed to be a prospect that some of the tracts of country and ranges of hills, hitherto almost waste, might be turned to account for the cultivation of new and valuable products introduced by Europeans, and possibly might be made to some degree the seats of European colonies, it was felt that these objects were amply sufficient to outweigh the remote prospect of deriving any considerable land revenue from such lands; and it was deemed that a fee-simple tenure cheaply accessible would be more suitable to European settlers, and more agreeable to them than conditional grants, the terms of which it might be difficult to enforce. It was, therefore, decided that all the uncultivated and unassessed lands in the Himalayas, in the tea districts of Assam and Cachar, in the coffee districts of the Neilgherries and the south-western ghats, in Central India, and elsewhere, should be offered to all who chose to take them at a low upset price, ranging from two shillings an acre in most districts to sixpence an acre in some parts of Central India.

The original orders were loosely drawn, and left a door to some abuse. Most of the waste land in India has been waste because, owing to inaccessibility, want of population, or unhealthiness, it has hitherto been unprofitable to cultivate it. But there were a few valuable small tracts in the settled country, or in the immediate neighbourhood of Hill Stations, which were rather untilled than waste, having been reserved for grazing, or firewood, or because nothing had been settled as to the disposal of the land. The original orders contained a proviso that when there were more than two applicants for the same land, it should be put up to auction; but some of the local authorities seem to have considered that such applications must be made at the identically same time, and that once an application had been received, the door might be shut to all others. Hence, in some few instances, easily accessible lands were given to the first comers at the upset price, when they would have

fetched many times that price in an open market. Lord
Halifax, therefore, ordered that all land applied for
should be put up to the highest bidder at or above the
upset price, and some lands, given away without compliance with the terms of the original rules, were resumed
and sold for vastly larger prices.

The legality of this last proceeding has been un-
successfully contested in the courts. And there has
been a good deal of complaint, not without some show
of reason, that it is hard that the industry of the man
who has discovered a good plot of land should be lost
by permitting a richer man to outbid him. On the
other hand, it must be remembered that the really
valuable waste lands are for the most part very limited.
And the facilities offered have been such as to lead to
some symptoms of the practice of land-jobbing so well
known in the colonies. Low as is the upset price,
purchasers have been allowed to take possession on payment of a small percentage, leaving the rest secured on
the land, to be paid up afterwards. In some instances
great tracts, which the purchasers had never seen, have
been secured on a mere deposit of a nominal sum towards
expenses of measurement. People have been said to get
into the way in order to be paid for getting out of it.
And more frequently the object has been to get up one
of the tea, or other companies, lately so much in vogue,
and to sell, at a great price, the land taken up on a
very trifling payment. Since the company mania has
collapsed, much of the land has been thrown back on
the hands of Government, by parties who are unable to
fulfil the terms of the purchase.

On the whole, then, I do not think it can be fairly
said that the Indian Government has failed to offer
the waste lands to European settlers on sufficiently
favourable terms. The bonâ fide tea and coffee estates
are held in fee simple on payment of a very small price.

IV.

THE LAND SYSTEM OF BELGIUM AND HOLLAND.

Emile De Laveleye.

CONTENTS.

§ 1. I do not propose to give here an account of the state of agriculture in Belgium and Holland, having done so else-

where; what I seek is to point out facts relative to both
countries, calculated to throw some light upon the following question, What is the agrarian constitution (*i.e.*, the
system of ownership and tenure of land) most conducive
to the progress of agriculture and to the welfare of
mankind ?

A preliminary observation is requisite. Thirty years
ago economists were in the habit of considering only the
production of wealth, paying hardly any attention to its
distribution, which they thought to be regulated by
inexorable natural laws; the system which yielded the
largest produce being of course thought the best. But
modern improvements in machinery having doubled, nay,
trebled the production without adding to the welfare of
all those who seemed to be entitled to it by their
industry, endeavours are now made to devise means of
better distributing the produce ; and there are now those
who think that of two systems of agrarian organisation,
the one which leads to the more equitable distribution of
the produce is the one to be preferred.

For example, let us suppose a certain area of land to
yield a produce of one thousand, distributed thus :—

One landlord	200 parts.
One tenant	100 „
14 labourers, at the rate of fifty .	700 „
	1,000 parts.

Suppose, on the other hand, the same area of land,
worked by 16 small owners, to yield but 960, yet to give
60 to each of them, for my part, I should consider the
second organisation superior to the first.

Neither extreme poverty nor extreme opulence is the
thing to be desired. Pauperism and divitism alike are
the parents of vice in private, and revolution in public
life.

§ 2. In England, a contrast is often drawn between
Flanders and Ireland, and the former is said to enjoy agricultural advantages not possessed by Ireland, such as

great markets, a better climate, abundance of manure, more manufactures.   This is a point on which some light should be thrown.

Flanders does enjoy certain advantages, but they are equally accessible to the Irish, derived, as they are, from human industry; whereas the advantages possessed by Ireland, coming, as they do, from nature, are not within the reach of the Flemish.

Let us look, first, at climate and soil.   The climate of Ireland is damper and less warm in summer, but less cold in winter.   In Flanders, it rains 175 days in a year, in Ireland, 220 days.   On this account, the Irish climate is more favourable to the growth of grass, forage, and roots, but less so to the *ripening* of cereals; yet the Fleming would be but too happy had he such a climate, cereals being but of secondary importance with him, and often used as food for his cattle.   He seeks only abundance of food for his cows, knowing that the value of live stock goes on increasing, while that of cereals remains stationary.   Butter, flax, colza, and chicory are the staple articles of his wealth, and the climate of Ireland is at least as well suited to the production of these as that of Flanders.

As for the soil of Ireland, it produces excellent pasture *spontaneously*, whilst that of Flanders hardly permits of the natural growth of heather and furze.   It is the worst soil in all Europe; sterile sand, like that of La Campine and of Brandenburg.   A few miles from Antwerp, land sells for 20 francs (16s.) an acre, and those who buy it for the purpose of cultivation get ruined.   Having been fertilised by ten centuries of laborious husbandry, it does not yield a single crop without being manured, a fact unique in Europe.

If in a Flemish farm of 25 acres there were but five or six acres of Irish soil, forming good natural pasture, it would be worth one-third more.   Not a blade of grass grows in Flanders without manure.   Irish soil might be bought to fertilise the soil of the Fleming.   The ideal, the dream of the Flemish farmer—is a few acres of good grass.   In Ireland, nature supplies grass in abundance.

But it may be said that Flanders is well supplied
with manure. Doubtless it is; but it is got only by
returning to the earth all that has been taken from it.
The Flemish farmer scrupulously collects every atom of
sewage from the towns; he guards his manure like a
treasure, putting a roof over it to prevent the rain and
sunshine from spoiling it. He gathers mud from rivers
and canals, the excretions of animals along the high roads,
and their bones for conversion into phosphate. With
cows' urine gathered in tanks he waters turnips which
would not come up without it; and he spends incredible
sums in the purchase of guano and artificial manures.

True, it may be said, he must have money for that,
and the Irishman has none. But where does the
Fleming's money come from ? From his flax, colza, hops,
and chicory; crops which he sells at the rate of from
600 to 1500 francs (24*l.* to 60*l.*) per hectare; and why
cannot the Irishman go and do likewise ? The Irishman,
it may be answered, must grow food for himself. But so
does the Fleming; for, in fact, apart from the special
crops referred to, he grows enough to support a
population relatively twice as large as that of Ireland.
It has indeed been argued that the special crops for
which Flanders is famous would be out of the question
save for access to markets which are not within the
reach of the Irishman.* But this argument seems to me
to have small validity. The chief market for the agricultural produce of Belgium is England. And is London
nearer to Ostend and Antwerp than Dublin and Cork
are to Liverpool and Manchester ? Friesland and Hol-
stein send cattle and butter to England, and Galicia ships
oxen by way of Vigo, across that dangerous Bay of
Biscay ; why cannot Ireland do the same ?

Flanders exports prepared chicory to Germany, to
Holland, to all parts of the world, and chicory roots as
far as Warsaw ; hops to Paris, London, and Scotland ;
flax to France, England, and even to Ireland itself ; tobacco to America ; colza and poppy-seed oils to the very
south of France ; while, on the other hand, it imports

* See Lord Dufferin on ' Irish Tenure,' p. 167.

corn from Hungary by land, and from Iowa or Wisconsin by lake, canal, railway, and ocean shipping. It is plain, therefore, that produce worth three or four times as much might well be exported from Ireland to England. But there are manufacturers in Flanders, is it said, and none in Ireland, or only in Ulster. Now on this point it is important to draw a distinction. Flanders possesses undoubtedly a number of small local industries, but they are the consequences not the cause of her good husbandry ; and any country possessing the latter would be in possession of the former. The great industries of Belgium are situated in the Walloon country, not in Flanders. Complete proof of this is afforded by the following table :—

1866.	Stationary Engines.	Horse-power.
West Flanders . . . East Flanders . .	307 806 } 1,113 {	3,110 12,984 } 16,094
Hainaut . . . . . Liège	2,546 1,608 } 4,154 {	73,157 39,929 }113,086

Thus the two industrial provinces of the Walloon country have seven times as much steam-power as Flanders. Then, again, Flanders has but one great centre of manufacture, Ghent, with 120,000 inhabitants ; whilst Belfast has a population of over 150,000, and is increasing much more rapidly than the capital of Flanders.

On the whole, for carrying farming to a high pitch of perfection, Ireland enjoys far greater advantages than Flanders, the land being much superior, the climate equally favourable to the growth of valuable crops, and the same markets being at hand. Unfortunately the Irish farmer has not the same agricultural traditions as the Fleming. And, of course, these wholesome traditions, being the work of centuries, cannot be acquired in a day. In every country, the progress of husbandry is slow at first, on the one hand, because the peasant has received little education ; and on the other, because the processes resorted to elsewhere cannot be simply copied in agriculture as they are in manufactures ; they must be modified in accordance with the nature of the soil and the climate, and that is an *art*. The knowledge and practice of that art in Flanders is of very ancient date, and it may not be thought out of place to say something of its early history.

§ 3. The most ancient historical records tend to show that the cultivation of the soil was always in a high state of perfection in Flanders. As far back as the time of the Romans, inscriptions on tumuli prove that the inhabitants of the borders of the Scheldt used to resort to England for marl to improve their infertile soil. From one of Eginhard's letters it appears that in the ninth century, flax and vines were grown at the same time that cloth was manufactured in the environs of Ghent. Numerous documents in the middle ages, such as registers of monasteries, donations and leases, reveal the existence of processes of farming almost as elaborate as those in use at the present day ; manure in abundance, fields carefully enclosed with magnificent hedgerows, alternate crops, forage and roots for cattle.* Rural manufactures arose from the progress of husbandry ; linen and woollen fabrics were woven, which ere long became famous. The weavers first lived in the open country, and subsequently flocked into towns ; and exportation led to the development of urban manufactures and the growth of a great urban population. It was wealth originating in the good cultivation of the country which created cities, such as Ghent, Bruges, Ypres, Louvain, Brussels, and Antwerp. In turn, the wealth of the cities fostered the progress of agriculture and rural civilisation.

One fact alone is sufficient to show the degree of advancement the Flemish villages of the middle ages had reached. As far back as the year 1400, dramatic performances took place in the villages, the pieces being written, got up, and performed exclusively by persons belonging to the country.† Most of the villages had

* *Vide* the Author's 'Economie Rurale de la Belgique,' chap. i. and Appendix No. 1.

† *Vide* Mr. Vanderstraeten's Essay in the ' Annales de la Société historique d'Ypres,' vol. iv.

their *Sociétés de Rhetorique,* forming so many focuses of intellectual life. In the sixteenth century, these societies adopted most of the ideas of the Reformation, and on this account were suppressed by the Spaniards. Industry was killed by war and persecution; and agriculture and civilisation were arrested and even thrown back. Happily the traditions of the past were too deep to be extirpated, and to them Flanders is indebted for her present wealth.

The question arises, can arts of such ancient birth in Flanders be diffused through such a country without the same early traditions and training? It is a problem fraught with difficulties. Something, doubtless, might be done in the way of agricultural instruction, were all persons in an influential position, such as magistrates, landowners, clergymen, to exert themselves for its diffusion, and themselves to supply practical examples of it. But examples of more weight with small farmers would be the spectacle of some of the latter class, enriching themselves by an improved system of husbandry. Were two or three intelligent farmers in each district in Ireland, having become landowners or hereditary tenants, to borrow from Flemish agriculture such processes as are applicable to the soil and climate of Ireland, a complete transformation of Irish farming might ensue. In the Belgian province of Hainaut, the example of a single farmer adopting the Flemish rotation was sufficient to bring about the suppression of the fallow throughout the whole region.* Could nothing be done to produce the same result in Ireland?†

§ 4. One most important fact in considering land systems, is that the country itself and not the town is naturally the chief market for agricultural produce. It is a great error to suppose that agriculture, in order to thrive, must have a market in great cities for its productions. The cultivators, on the contrary, may constitute

---

* 'Economie Rurale de la Belgique,' p. 148.

† I have hardly ever met with an answer to the important question: Does the Irish small *proprietor* exhaust his land as much as the small tenant?

a market for themselves. Let them produce plenty of corn, animals of various kinds, milk, butter, cheese, and vegetables, and interchange their produce, and they will be well fed, to begin. But furthermore, they will have the means of supporting a number of artificers; they may thus be well housed, furnished, and clothed, without any external market. For this, however, they must be proprietors of the soil they cultivate, and have all its fruits for themselves. If they are but tenants who have a rent to pay and no permanent interest in the soil, they certainly require a market to make money. In a country whose cultivators are all tenants, an external market for their produce is indispensable; it is not so in a country of freeholders: all the latter requires is that agriculture should be carried on with the energy and intelligence which the diffusion of property is sure to arouse in a people.

The province of Groningen was the best cultivated of Holland before ever it exported any of its products to England, and yet there are no large towns in it; but, thanks to its peculiar system of hereditary leases, the farmers could keep almost the entire produce of their labour to themselves.

Suppose that by the stroke of a magic wand, the whole of the tenant farmers of Flanders were to become possessed of the fee-simple of their lands, what would be the result? They would then themselves consume the milk, butter, and meat which they are now obliged to sell, and in consequence have to dispense with animal food and to resort almost exclusively to the vegetable kingdom for their support; then they would no longer have to send what they do to an English market. Would they be the worse off for that?

Look at Switzerland. In proportion to her population, she has more horned cattle than Flanders; i.e., 35 head to every 100 inhabitants, against 24 in Flanders. Yet while the latter exports butter, oxen, rabbits, &c., to France and England, Switzerland actually *imports* butter, cattle, corn, &c. The consequence is that Switzerland consumes twice as much animal food as Flanders; viz.,

22 kilos of meat, 12 kilos of cheese, 5 of butter, and 182 of milk per head per annum. Of the Swiss, indeed, we may say what Cæsar said of the ancient Britons,— *Lacte et carne vivunt.*

How is it that the Swiss peasant is much more substantially fed than the Flemish? Because the former is nearly always an owner of the soil, while the latter is but too often only an occupier. The Swiss has not for his market the insatiable stomach of the London market which the poor Fleming contributes to feed; he has a better one than that, namely, his own.

Thus, Switzerland and Groningen prove that agriculture does not stand in need of a large foreign market to make progress. A peasant proprietary is the best of all markets.*

§ 5. On the 1st of January, 1865, there were in West Flanders, on an area of 323,466 hectares, 89,297 proprietors and 693,904 " parcels " of land; in East Flanders, 155,381 proprietors and 845,220 parcels, towns and villages included; in the entire kingdom of Belgium there were 1,069,327 owners and 6,207,512 parcels. In 1846, the enumeration showed 758,512 proprietors and 5,500,000 parcels of land. Thus it appears that the number of landowners and of parcels has considerably increased.

In Belgium, I have never heard a complaint of the present state of things, nor any expression of alarm for the future, such as one used to hear in France before economists of eminence such as De Lavergne, Wolowski, and Passy had undertaken the labour of demonstrating the chimerical nature of the fears that the soil would be crumbled to bits.

As regards Belgium, and more especially Flanders, foreigners should not be misled by the great number of *parcels.* The parcels enumerated are *cadastral* parcels for the purposes of the survey; and very often the

* Is another proof needed? No vines are better cared for than those of the Canton of Vaud, being the agricultural wonder of the Lake of Geneva. Is the wine grown there exported like champagne, claret, or port? Not at all; the Vaudois drink it themselves. Does it not do them more good?

R

surface of the soil shows not the least trace of any such
divisions.   Not only do many parcels often belong to one
and the same proprietor, but a single estate or farm of ten
or twelve hectares generally consists of many of them.
The land is divided into farms of different sizes in proportion to the capitals of the cultivators; for example,
fifty hectares to four horses, twenty-five to two, twelve
for one horse, five or six hectares to a family without
beasts of burden, and a little plot for a labourer. When
large farms are subdivided it is done on economical
grounds, viz., because they fetch higher prices when sold
in lots: they are hardly ever divided in consequence of
the law of succession. The peasant attaches too much
value to the proper outline of a field to break it into
pieces; he would rather sell it altogether.

Hitherto, the consequence of the progressive subdivision of land in Flanders has only been to raise at
once the rental, the gross produce, and the value of the
soil; at the same time that the number of landowners
has increased, the condition of the cultivators has improved.

In Flanders you do not find the land subdivided in the
way it is in Ireland, according to Lord Dufferin, who
has shown the evils of the kind of subdivision practised
there;* from his description it appears that in Ireland, at
the death of any holder and often even during his lifetime, the children divide the land among themselves,
each of them building a cottage on it; or, if the tenant
has no children, he sublets his land to several small
farmers, and allows them to settle on it, notwithstanding
the stipulations of the lease. Such breaking-up of the
land must lead to the most wretched kind of farming, and
to pauperism on the part of the tenants. As long as the
Irish farmer has no better understanding than that, of
his own interest and of the requirements of a sound
economical system, no agricultural policy, neither fixity
of tenure nor even ownership in fee-simple could improve
his condition. Although the population of Flanders is
twice as dense as that of Ireland, a Flemish peasant

* *Vide* Lord Dufferin on 'Irish Tenure,' chap. iii.

would never think of dividing the farm he cultivates among his children ; and the idea of allowing a stranger to settle and build a house on it, and farm a portion of it, would appear altogether monstrous to him. On the contrary, he will submit to extraordinary sacrifices to give his farm the size and typical shape it should have.

How is it that the Fleming and the Irishman hold such different points of view? I think it is partly due to the difference of race, and partly to circumstances. The Celt being more sociable, thinks most of the requirements of members of his family, whilst the Teuton thinks more of the requirements of the soil and of good cultivation. Nowhere to my knowledge does the Celt show himself a cultivator of the first order (cultivateur d'élite) ; it is to the German, the Fleming, the Englishman that agriculture is indebted for its greatest improvements. The Celt has in several countries subdivided the soil for the sake of his family, without regard to the requirements of national husbandry. Throughout Germany,* law and custom alike have always been opposed to the division of farms. In Upper Bavaria this is carried so far that almost all the land is in the hands of wealthy peasants, keeping up a kind of entail by always bequeathing the whole of their property to one of their children, a small pittance being given to the others. But supposing the Irishman to become the absolute owner of his farm, would he learn and comply with the requirements of the land? A Flemish farmer's son always wants to have a good farm of his own ; he would not put up with a hovel improvised on a potato field. Could the Irishman but be brought to practise agriculture as an art, and not as a mere means of bringing a subsistence from the soil, he would soon abandon the miserable system of subdivision which he has adhered to so long. But how is this taste for agriculture as an art to be imparted to him? To extinguish the influence of instincts or tendencies, whether inherent in the race or the historical product of centuries, would it suffice to introduce an agrarian constitution in Ireland similar to that of Flanders, or, better still, of Switzerland?

* *Vide* W. Roscher, 'Nationalökonomik des Ackerbaues,' p. 229.

These are questions which I confess myself not in a position to answer; but they are questions which those who have the Irish land question to solve ought to face, when considering the land system of Flanders.

I think it useful to subjoin a tabulated statement, giving an idea of the number of farms (*exploitations*) and their relative sizes. These results date as far back as 1846, no returns having been published since :—

PROVINCES.	PROPORTIONATE NUMBER OF FARMS OF FROM									
	50 Ares and less. i.e. half an hectare.	51 Ares to 1 hectare.	1 to 5 Hectares.	5 to 10 Hectares.	10 to 15 Hectares.	15 to 20 Hectares.	20 to 25 Hectares.	25 to 50 Hectares.	50 to 100 Hectares.	100 Hectares and upwards.
Antwerp . . .	43·53	8·62	26·90	10·38	4·97	2·26	1·18	1·52	0·14	0·0?
Brabant . . .	34·11	17·24	36·20	6·18	2·30	1 15	0·17	1·42	0·53	0·1?
Flanders, West .	57·42	7·35	19·24	6·27	2·66	2·10	1·72	2·7?	0·53	0·0?
Flanders, East .	44·68	10·08	31·50	7·63	2·77	1·38	0·81	1·02	0·12	0·0?
Hainaut . . .	53·46	11·99	23·92	4·83	2·06	1·09	0·66	1·32	0 56	0·11
Liège	45 72	13·81	25 76	7·10	2·91	1·35	0·73	1·40	0·91	0·2?
Limbourg . . .	30·41	11·97	32·62	13·34	5·64	2·50	1·1?	1·78	0·47	0·1?
Luxembourg .	18·92	12·75	41·88	12·67	5·28	2·75	1·48	2·78	1·10	0·9?
Namur . . .	33·87	18·97	32·92	6·26	2·40	1·19	0·76	1·60	1·44	0·7?
Average of Kingdom	43·24	12·30	28·99	7·46	3·04	1·59	0·98	1·64	0·58	0·1?

§ 6. It has often been asserted that the peasant properties of Flanders are burdened with debts, and that loans on them are raised at ruinous rates of interest.

The following table shows that the truth lies in the opposite direction. In the remarkable return of the Census of 1846, the Government published an instructive table, showing which are the provinces of Belgium where loans are raised at highest rates of interest (page 240).

Thus while in East Flanders no more than five per cent. of the loans are raised on usurious interest, in the province of Luxembourg as much as eighty-two per cent. of the loans bear interest at five per cent. and upwards.

Were a statement drawn up of the debts with which land property is burdened in the various parts of Europe, it would be seen that large estates are generally more encumbered than small ones.

PROVINCES.		Proportion of Capital bearing interest at the rate of 5 per cent. and upwards to tho aggregate Loans.	
Antwerp . . . . Flanders, West . . . Flanders, East . . .	Small farms	15 per cent. 23 ,, 5 ,,	
Brabant . . . . . Limbourg	Middle-size farms	33 per cent. 40 ,,	
Hainaut . . . . . Liège . . . . . Namur . . . . . Luxembourg . . .	Large farms	71 per cent. 39 ,, 76 ,, 82 ,,	

In England, the mortgages are reported to amount to fifty-eight per cent. of the value of the land ; in France only to ten per cent., according to Messrs. Passy and Wolowski. In Prussia the eastern provinces with their large estates show greater indebtedness than those of the west with their small farms.* In Lombardy, the total landed debt amounts to twenty-five per cent. of the value of land, and in the province of Sondria, where the farms are small, they represent no more than one-and-a-half per cent. of that value.

§ 7. Every one knows La Fontaine's story of Perette going to the market to buy eggs ; the eggs are hatched into chickens ; the chickens produce a pig and then a calf, and the calf becomes a cow. This dream of Perette's is daily realized by the Flemish small farmer.

We are often told that agriculture stands in need of capital ; that institutions in aid of agricultural credit are wanting : I reply, good husbandry itself creates the capital needed.

In agriculture, the capital most needed is live stock, to furnish the manure by which rich harvests are secured.

The Flemish small farmer picks up grass and manure along the roads. He raises rabbits, and with the money

* *Vide* the excellent work by President Adolph Lette : ' Die Vertheilung des Grundeigenthums.'

they fetch he buys first a goat, then a pig, next a calf,
by which he gets a cow producing calves in her turn.
But of course he must find food for them, and this he
does by staking all on fodder and roots ; and in this way
the farmer grows rich, and so does the land.   The institution in Flanders, in aid of agricultural credit is the
manure-merchant, who has founded it in the best of
forms ; for money lent may be spent in a public-house,
but a loan of manure must be laid out on the land.

The poor labourer goes with his wheelbarrow to the
dealer in the village to buy a sack or two of guano,
undertaking to pay for it after the harvest.   The dealer
trusts him and gives him credit, having a lien on the
crop produced by the aid of his manure.   In November
he gets his money : the produce has been doubled, and
the land improved.   The small farmer does as the
labourer does ; each opens an account with the manure-
dealer, who is the best of all bankers.

The large farmers of Hainaut and Namur do not buy
manure, fancying they would ruin themselves by doing
so.   The Flemish small farmers invest from fifteen to
twenty millions of francs in guano every year, and quite
as much in other kinds of manure.   Where does large
farming make such advances ?

§ 8. The chief objection made to *la petite culture* is, however, that it does not admit of the use of machinery,
being reduced, as it is alleged, to the employment of the
most primitive implements of husbandry, and never raising
itself above the first stage of cultivation in that respect.
This has been put forward as an incontestable axiom,
baffling refutation, and I believe is so regarded in England.

To disprove this, I need not point out that to Flanders
are due the best forms of the spade, the harrow, the cart,
and the plough—Brabant ploughs having for a long
time been imported from Flanders into England.   It
may be said that these are primitive and not very costly
implements.   I need only reply, look at what is going
on in Flanders at the present day.

The most costly agricultural machine in general use

in England is the locomotive steam threshing-machine. Well, this machine is to be found everywhere in Flanders. Some farmers will club together to purchase one, and use it in turn ; or else a villager, often the miller, buys one, and goes round threshing for the small farmers, on their own ground, at so much per day, and per hundred kilos of corn. The same thing takes place with the steam-plough as soon as the use of it becomes *remunerative*.

To keep hops in good condition, very expensive machines are required to press it. At Poperinghe, in the centre of the hop country, the *commune* has purchased the machines, and the farmers pay a fixed rate for having their hops pressed—which is at once an advantage to them and a source of revenue to the town.

The example of Flanders proves, therefore, that the division of land forms no obstacle to mechanical economy in farming. Moreover, the subdivision of the soil is perfectly compatible with the methods of *la grande culture* itself ; the operations of husbandry may all be on a great scale, while the land is held in shares by a number of persons, like shares in a railway. I see no practical impossibility in such a solution of the problem how to combine the land system of Flanders with all the improvements of the age.

§ 9. It is often asserted that poor lands can be brought into cultivation only by large and wealthy owners. This is exactly the reverse of the truth—at least as regards the most intractable soils.

In Belgium there are lands so sterile by nature that one-half of all the capital sunk in them is either lost or yields hardly any returns—so that it is not in the interest of any capitalist to work them. In La Campine, all those who have attempted to set up large farms, were they ever so well managed, have ruined themselves, or, at any rate, lost money by it.

It is the small cultivator only who, spade in hand, can fertilize the waste, and perform prodigies which nothing but his love of the land could enable him to accomplish.

His day's work he counts for nothing; he spares no exertion, and shuns no trouble; and by doing double the work, he produces double the result he would do if he worked for hire.   Thus he has made fertile farms of the dunes and quicksands which border our dangerous coast.   Penetrating into the interior of these dunes in the neighbourhood of Nieuport, you observe little cottages with a few acres of rye and potatoes around them. Their owners succeed in keeping a few cows, which the children take out to graze wherever a blade of salt grass can be found.   With the manure of their cattle they mix seaweed and whatever animal matter the sea throws up, and thus they raise crops of first-rate potatoes and vegetables.   La Veluwe—the Campine of Holland— has been reclaimed in like manner inch by inch by the peasantry.   I have elsewhere given an account of the rise of one of these sand villages within recent years.[*]

In Savoy, in Switzerland, in Lombardy, in all mountainous countries, land has been reclaimed by *la petite culture*, which large landowners could not have broached without loss.   In those highlands man makes the very soil.   He builds terraces along steep inclines, lining them with blocks of stone, and then carrying earth to them on his back, in which he plants a mulberry or walnut tree, or a vine, or raises a little corn or maize.[†] Whoever, after paying for the labour, should take a lease of the ground thus created would not get one half per cent. from his outlay, and therefore a capitalist will never do it.   But the small cultivator *does* it; and thus the mountain and the rock become transformed.   So too under *la petite culture*, even when aided not by proprietorship, but only the kind of tenure to which the name of *emphyteusis* has been given, and which corresponds to a long lease, the most ungrateful land has been reclaimed in Flanders.   The tenant, being secure of the future, builds a house, clears the ground, manures and fertilizes the rebellious soil; and though he will not reap the same benefit from it that a peasant pro-

[*] *Vide* ' Economie Rurale de la Néerland,' p 212.
[†] *Vide* my ' Economie Rurale de la Suisse et de la Lombardie,' p. 71.

prietor would, he reaps much more than either a large
farmer or a large proprietor would.

§ 10. Notwithstanding all the arguments of the
most distinguished economists in England, especially
Mr. John Stuart Mill, to the contrary, peasant property
in land seems still to be regarded there as synonymous
with wretched cultivation, and large estates with rich
and improved farming. The reason is obvious; the
English are accustomed to compare the farming of their
own country with that of Ireland. In fact, however, both
England and Ireland are exceptions, one on the right, the
other on the wrong side. In England there exists a class
of well-to-do and intelligent tenant farmers such as are
not to be found anywhere else. In Ireland, on the
contrary, there is no peasant property, but only large
estates in combination with small tenure, often with a
middleman between the landlord and the cultivator—of
all agrarian systems the most wretched. Added to this,
many centuries of oppression and misgovernment made
the Irish people more improvident than the inhabitants
of any other country in the civilized world ; thus, what
with a land system of the worst kind, and the general condition of the country, the case of Ireland is surely an
exceptional one. All over the continent of Europe there
is more live stock kept, more capital owned, more produce
and income yielded by small farms than by large estates.

Look at Flanders, for an example. The soil is de-
testable, as we have seen ; and it is unhappily a country
where a multitude of small farms are held by tenants, as
in Ireland ; but happily the peasant proprietor exists by
the side of the small tenant.

The working capital of a farm, which in England is
estimated at from 10*l.* to 12*l.*, amounts here to 500
francs (20*l.*). The gross produce may be taken at 600
francs (24*l.*) per hectare. As regards live stock, there
were to be found in 1846, 55 heads of horned cattle, 12
horses, and 8 sheep on every 100 hectares superficial area.

For England (not including Ireland and Scotland)
M. de Lavergne gives the following averages for the same

year:—33 heads of horned cattle, 6 horses, and 200 sheep per 100 hectares.

Bringing these figures down to the common standard of heads of great cattle,* we find 64 heads in England and 68 in Flanders; the land of Flanders being at the same time worse than any in England. The average rent of land in Flanders is 100 francs (4*l*.) per hectare, and the value or selling price varies from 3500 to 4000 francs (140*l*. to 160*l*.). Rents and selling prices have doubled since 1830. These results are not equalled in any other part of Europe.

§ 11. The fact that the Flemish husbandman derives such abundant produce from a soil naturally so poor, is due to the following reasons, viz. :—

1. The perfection of both plough and spade work.

2. Each field has the perfection of shape given to it, to facilitate cultivation and drainage.

3. Most careful husbanding of manure. None is wasted either in town or country, and all farmers, down to the poorest tenants and labourers, purchase manure from the dealers.

4. The great variety of crops, especially of industrial plants, *e.g.*, colza, flax, tobacco, hops, chicory, &c., yielding large returns and admitting of exportation to the most distant countries.

5. Second, or "stolen" crops, such as turnips and carrots, after the cereals, of English clover, spurry, &c., whereby the cultivated area is in effect increased one-third.

6. Abundance of food for cattle. Although the soil is not favourable to permanent meadows, yet, taking the second crops into account, one-half of the available superfices is devoted to the keeping of live stock. Hence the rise of rents, although the price of corn has hardly increased.

7. House feeding of the cattle, by which the cows give both more milk and more manure.

8. Minute weeding.†

---

* In reducing sheep to great cattle, we have adopted the proportion of 8 : 1, instead of the usual one of 10 : 1, the English sheep being exceptionally superior as regards flesh and wool.

† *Vide* my ' Economie Rurale de la Belgique.' The reader will pardon my

Many of these agricultural practices are possibly only where there is a large agricultural population ; for which, on the other hand, work is found at the same time by these very practices.

§ 12. The following table shows the amount of labour employed in the cultivation of the soil in Belgium.

PROVINCES.	Area in acres for every 100 inhabitants.	Number of field hands* per 100 inhabitants.	Number of women† to every 100 men.	Number of women among the holders,‡ to every 100 men.	Number of labourers per 100 hectares of productive land.	Beasts of burden per 100 hectares of husbandable land.	Number of hectares per holder.	Number of owners, farmers, and tenants.	Number of labourers of both sexes, above 12 years of age.
Antwerp	70	26	74	84	83	17	4·76	47,935	106,080
Brabant.	47	27	64	78	86	18	3·46	83,130	183,522
Flanders, W. . . .	50	23	57	56	65	13	3·86	78,498	149,668
Flanders, E. . . .	38	26	60	57	103	14	2·76	88,305	203,561
Hainaut.	52	22	70	57	67	23	3·14	105,977	157,071
Liège	64	17	64	69	46	20	4·49	55,347	76,290
Limbourg	130	37	55	61	58	19	6·72	32,170	69,158
Luxembourg . . .	237	37	77	71	51	30	11·35	36,244	69,537
Namur	68	26	50	57	42	19	7·42	44,944	68,714
Aggregate of Kingdom	68	25	61	65	97	19	4·55	572,550	1,083,60

* Comprising the farmers themselves, the farm labourers, and labourers proper.
† Being the proportion of women of the three preceding classes to 100 men.
‡ " Holders " includes both freehold and tenant farmers.

This table is taken from the official statistics published by the Belgian Government in 1850. Those published in 1861 relate to the year 1856, and are less detailed. In the following table I have given the data relative to the two Flanders, Namur, Luxembourg, and the entire kingdom, as derived from those statistics. Although the two tables are drawn up on different statistical plans, the returns are about the same, and therefore the data may be considered the more trustworthy.

referring him to a previous work of mine for particulars which need not be repeated here. Even in the writings of the best foreign authors errors occur with regard to Belgium. Thus Mr. Stuart Mill, in his 'Principles o Political Economy,' quotes a passage from MacCulloch in which Hainaut and the two Flanders are alluded to as being circumstanced alike—whereas, in fact, their conditions are different in every respect.

	FLANDERS, WEST.		FLANDERS, EAST.		LUXEMBOURG.	
—	Males.	Females.	Males.	Females.	Males.	Females.
Owners, tenants, managers and directors of farms .	32,617	28,132	79,207	35,812	19,223	4,671
Gardeners, kitchen-gardeners, horticulturists, arboriculturists, silkworm rearers, vintners	1,727	546	1,478	360	62	..
Shepherds, graziers, herdsmen . . .	304	4	432	..	532	46
Field hands and day labourers, farm-servants of both sexes . .	63,957	39,139	63,174	31,802	14,445	7,227
Wood-cutters and other wood labourers, gamekeepers and others . .	673	137	98)	1	580	3
	99,278	67,958	145,271	67,975	34,842	11,947

	NAMUR.		ENTIRE KINGDOM.		
—	Males.	Females.	Males.	Females.	Total.
Landowners and tenants, farmers and managers of estates . . .	15,226	982	300,473	122,630	423,103
Gardeners, kitchen-gardeners, horticulturists, arboriculturists, silkworm rearers, vintners	308	..	8,681	1,462	10,323
Shepherds, graziers, drovers . . .	627	5	4,811	396	5,207
Field hands and day labourers, farm-servants of both sexes . . .	28,621	11,347	388,312	228,115	616,427
Wood-cutters and other wood labourers, gamekeepers and others . .	1,059	2	6,757	298	7,055
	45,841	12,836	709,214	352,901	1.062,115

§ 13. It has often been argued from the example of Ireland that the subdivision of land must tend to produce an excessive increase of the population. Arthur Young prophesied that the subdivision of the soil would convert France into a rabbit warren.

Now the fact is, that in no other country, not actually in a state of decadency, is the increase of the population slower than in France. The same may be said of Flanders, where the population increases at a rate much inferior to that of the rest of the kingdom, viz. :—

—	POPULATION IN		Proportional Increase.
	1846.	1866.	
Flanders, West . . .	643,004	659,938	2·6 per cent.
Flanders, East . .	793,264	824,175	3·8 per cent.
Entire Kingdom . . .	4,337,196	4,984,351	15·1 per cent.

Yet in Flanders the soil is greatly subdivided, as shown by figures given above (§ 5).

§ 14. To prove the superiority of large farming, Arthur Young made the following calculation :—

To cultivate a district of 4000 hectares, divided into farms of a single plough, 666 men and 1000 horses would be required; whereas in farms of three ploughs apiece the same district would require only 545 men and 681 horses ; being a saving of 121 men and 319 horses, capable of other useful employment in the production of manufactured articles. Therefore the district with large farms will be better provided for than the one with small holdings, and consequently large farming is preferable to small farming.

Young's calculation is perfectly correct so far as it goes ; nevertheless only one thing is necessary to overthrow his conclusion, namely, that the smaller farms should yield more produce, and more valuable produce, than the large ones ; and this is precisely the case all over the continent of Europe, without a single exception that I know of, wherever *la petite* and *la grande propriété* are seen in competition. "At the present day," says M. Hippolyte Passy,* "on the same area and under equal circumstances, the largest clear produce is yielded by small farming, which, besides, by increasing the country population, opens a safe market to the products of manufacturing industry." Which are the richest and most productive provinces of France? Precisely those in which the small landowners are in the majority, especially Flanders and Alsace. In this respect I need but refer the reader to the works of M. Léonce de Lavergne.

In the Eastern provinces of Prussia (Prussia proper and Posen) there are hardly any but large estates, worked by the owners themselves. In Westphalia and the Rhenish provinces there are to be found peasant proprietors and small farmers. The Eastern provinces are inferior to those of the West, even with respect to live stock, as appears from the following table:—

There are to every square mile in the—

PROVINCES.	Metres of Road.	Inhabitants.	Heads of Large Cattle.
Posen	5,000 }	3,000	2,980
Prussia	4,000 }		
Westphalia	14,000 }	6,000	3,569
Rhineland . .	17,000 }		4,024

In the western provinces agricultural wages are double what they are in the eastern ones; and while in the latter there are nine inhabitants to every house, there are but five and a-half in the former.

As regards Saxony, Dr. Engel's well-known statistics have shown that small farms keep twice as much live stock as large ones.†

As to Italy, Mr. Kay expresses himself as follows in his 'Notes of a Traveller':—"In 1836, Tuscany contained

* Vide 'Mémoire de l'Académie des Sciences morales et politiques dans la Séance du 4 Janvier, 1845.'

† Vide 'Zeitschrift des Statistischen Bureau's des K. Sächsischen Ministe-ruims des Innern,' No. 1, February, 1857.

130,190 landed estates.   In the dominions of the Pope,
from the frontier of the Neapolitan to that of the Tuscan
state, the whole country is reckoned to be divided into
about 600 landed estates.   Compare the husbandry of
Tuscany, the perfect system of drainage, for instance, in
the straits of the Arno, by drains between every two beds
of land, all connected with a main drain—being our own
lately introduced furrow, till draining, but connected here
with the irrigation as well as the draining of land—compare the clean state of the growing crops, the variety and
succession of green crops for feeding cattle in the house
all the year round, the attention to collecting manure, the
garden-like cultivation of the whole face of the country—
compare this with the desert waste of the Roman
Maremma, or with the Papal country, of soil and productiveness as good as that of the Vale of the Arno, the
country about Foligno and Perugia—compare the well-
clothed busy people, the smart country girls at work
about their cows' food, or their silkworm leaves, with the
ragged, sallow, indolent population lounging about their
doors in the Papal dominions, starving, and with nothing
to do on the great estates ; nay, compare the agricultural
industry in this land of small farms, with the best of our
large farms districts, with Tweedside or East Lothian,
and snap your finger at the wisdom of our St. Johns and
all the host of our bookmakers on agriculture, who bleat
after each other that solemn saw that small farms are
incompatible with a high and perfect state of cultivation."

In Lombardy, in the province of Como, where *la
petite culture* prevails, the value of the cattle per hectare
in cultivation is 161 francs ; whilst in the province of
Mantua, with its large farms and fine pasture land, it
is but 94 francs.*

In Portugal there are in the large-farming province
of Alemtego but 329,277 inhabitants on an area of
2,454,062 hectares, with an annual production—
exclusive of cattle—worth 54,762,500 francs, or
22·72 francs per hectare.   On the contrary, in the small-

* *Vide* my 'Etudes d'Economie Rurale en Lombardie,' p. 112, and Signor
Tacini's beautiful book, ' La Proprietà fondiaria in Lombardia.'

farming province of Minho, there are on an area of 749,994 hectares, 915,400 inhabitants, producing—exclusive of cattle—37,756,250 francs per annum, or 50·34 francs per hectare, being more than twice the production of Alemtego.*

In Spain, compare Estremadura, the Castiles, or even Andalusia, with the kingdom of Valencia, and with Lower Catalonia. Where small farming prevails, the land is a garden ; where the estates are large, a desert.

In Belgium, the small-farm provinces, the Flanders, own more cattle, yield more produce, are more carefully cultivated, and have more agricultural capital than those in which large estates are predominant, as will be seen from the subjoined table. Here I have compared East Flanders with Namur ; and it is to be noticed that in the former province the land is poorer than in the latter.

	Namur.	Flanders, E.
Heads of cattle per 100 hectares . . .	35	68
Working capital per hectare . .	francs 250	francs 450
Produce per hectare	„ 300	„ 600
Rent per hectare	„ 50	„ 93
Average selling price of land per hectare	„ 1,804	„ 3,218
Number of Inhabitants per 100 hectares .	138	263

§ 15. Let us carry out the parallel drawn by Arthur

* With reference to Portugal, see the excellent work, ' Compendio de Economia rural,' by Senhor A. Rebello da Tilva, at present Colonial Minister of Portugal ; and J. Forrester's ' Portugal and its Capabilities,' in which we find the following passages :—" The Minho is justly termed the garden of Portugal." " The Alemtego is the largest, and perhaps naturally the richest, province of Portugal. Once the granary of Portugal, it is now the worst cultivated and most thinly populated of the entire kingdom. The reason of this change may be traced to the following fact. The fecundity of this province has been proverbial from the remotest times ; and people of substance relinquishing the North, came here, and united many small farms in a few extensive estates, which have descended from father to son undivided, undiminished, and through mismanagement and neglect are at this moment so many waste lands in the possession of proprietors who themselves have not the means of cultivating them, and who will not allow others to do so. Hence, there being no employment for agricultural labourers, the Transteganos have dispersed themselves over the other provinces, leaving the feudal lords in full possession of their land, their pride, and their poverty" (p. 102). Of the north of Portugal it may also be said, latifundia perdidere Lusitaniam.

Young between the results of small and large farming, by placing spade and plough side by side before us.

Throughout Flanders, and especially in the Waes country, the spade is often used to prepare the soil before sowing. To dig up one hectare with the spade, at the rate of 5 ares per diem, 20 days are required, and an outlay of 30 francs; whilst the same work done with the plough would cost no more than 6 or 7 francs, perhaps less. Thus, spade work costs five times as much as plough work, which is an enormous balance in favour of the latter.

Yet the Fleming persists in calling the spade a gold mine (*De Spa is de Goudmyn der Boeren*); and in Lombardy they have a proverb to the same effect: *Se l'aratro ha il vomero di ferro, la vanga ha la punta d'oro.* How is this to be accounted for? Is it routine or miscalculation? Neither; the peasant only means to say that a large increase in the returns is well worth a larger outlay.

In Lombardy, it has been computed that in two fields of the same quality, and manured in the same way, one being worked with the spade and the other with the plough, the returns of the former were to those of the latter as 66 to 28. Assume the produce to be but double, it will make up for twice the excess of expense.

In Flanders, this difference is not very considerable for cereals; but the Fleming does not grow corn alone. In the same year in which corn comes up in the rotation he has a second crop (récotte dérobée), which of itself is worth three or four times the excess of 25 francs in the cost of spade work; and if after this he lifts such crops as flax, chicory, tobacco, and colza, returning from 600 to 1200 francs per hectare, the excess in the preliminary outlay dwindles down to a mere nothing. Young, and most English writers on agriculture after him, reason just as if no other crops were grown than cereals; a mistake with respect to the nature and objects of *la petite culture* which vitiates all their conclusions.

I am fully aware that these second crops may be derived also from the plough, and so they are indeed by many Flemish farmers; but then, in the first place, the land is better prepared by the spade for receiving the seed; and secondly, to weed and to gather crops of this kind much more labour is required, and therefore a larger population by whom the spade-work too may be done.   All these things go hand in hand, there being an intimate connection between such economic factors as large population, minute labour, rich produce, small rural industries like flax steeping and peeling, preparation of chicory, tobacco and hops, oil pressing, &c.   It is a system which must be looked at as a whole; and it is one by which a country, one might say by nature incapable of cultivation, has become the garden of Europe.

Thus the example of Flanders shows that, as far as the production of wealth and even the clear produce are concerned, the spade ought to get a verdict in an action against the plough.   I admit at once that it would be well for the spadesman, could he have his work done for him by horses and steam engines, that his work is harder and his returns smaller than is good for man.   But would he be happier, wealthier, better, under a different land system, under which he would be a labourer for hire without prospect of elevation?   Especially would he be so on the barren sands of Flanders?

§ 16.   The system of tenure usual in Belgium is a lease. In the middle ages, there also existed the form of tenure known by the name of métayage, of which, however, traces are now to be found only in some of the *polders* along the coast of the German Ocean.   The cultivation of land by the intervention of a bailiff or steward, so common in Eastern Europe, is a rare exception in Belgium.

The leases are, as a rule, very short—nine years at most, as a rule; very seldom indeed for so much as eighteen years.   On the other hand, yearly tenancy and tenure-at-will are also very exceptional.   All who devote attention to agriculture, even the agricultural societies, though consisting almost exclusively of landowners, admit that the leases are too short.   The tenant is not encouraged to improve; and if he does make improvements, he can hardly be said to reap the benefit of them. The landlords will not grant longer leases, because they want, in the first place, to keep a hold upon their tenants; and secondly, to raise the rents when the leases expire. It may be said that throughout Belgium such increases of rent take place regularly and periodically.

The following table gives an idea of this continuous increase of rents since 1830 :—

PROVINCES.	INCREASE OF RENTS FROM					PRICE PER HECTARE.	
	1830 to 1835.	1835 to 1840.	1840 to 1846.	1846 to 1850.	1850 to 1856.	1830.	1856.
	Per cent.	Per cent.	Per cent.	Per cent.	Per cent.	Fr. c.	Fr. c.
Antwerp	7·06	10·22	6·32	8·33	15·38	47·50	75
Brabant . . .	7·62	12·48	5·05	2·41	17·65	66·27	100
Flanders, W. . .	8·10	6·93	5·20	4·05	16·90	60·00	83
Flanders, E. . .	13·96	11·39	2·85	0	21·84	71·40	106
Hainaut	8·94	15·58	7·48	1·05	14·58	69·79	110
Liège	7·50	14·72	8·11	7·41	16·09	62·35	101
Limbourg . . .	10·28	13·02	1·90	0	17·00	46·80	62
Luxembourg . .	5·14	7·73	4·17	3·03	14·71	28·78	39
Namur	9·87	15·35	7·66	10·00	16·36	36·77	64
Average of Kingdom	9·10	12·74	5·90	2·94	17·14	57·25	82

Since 1856, rents have risen even more in proportion than during the preceding period. It may be affirmed that, since 1830, the value of land and the rents have doubled. This is a further proof of the proposition so clearly set forth by Mr. Mill, that while the rate of profit and of interest has a downward tendency in a progressing community, rent, on the contrary, tends to rise incessantly. Thus, the landowners actually reap all the benefit resulting from the progress made by the entire community in various directions. Part of this progressive increase in rent may be traced to improvements made by the farmers in the cultivation of the soil. By raising the rent, the landlord lays hold of this advance in the value of the land.

The increase of the revenue the landlord derives from his land is not the result of improvements executed by

s 2

himself; and the fact adverted to is a general one, which
may be met with everywhere.   In whatever cases landlords have actually made improvements, they have got
the interest of the outlay in the shape of an additional
augmentation of their revenue.

For these reasons, I think that the increase of rent,
being due to the progress of society at large, and not to
the exertions of the landowners, ought not in justice to
benefit the latter alone.   It would be but fair to divide this
benefit.   For a portion of it the tenant should come in;
and this he would get if he had a longer lease.   Another
part of it should fall to the share of the community at
large, in the shape of an increase of the land-tax.

At the present day, the land-tax (*impôt foncier*) in
Belgium is permanently fixed, amounting to about 16
million francs (640,000*l*.).   It ought, on the contrary, to
increase in some proportion to the augmentation of rent,
so, however, as not to affect the revenue, which is the
reward of improvements; but some portion of that
general advance of rents, which is the result of the
general progress of the country, ought to be laid under
contribution.

All this applies with equal force to the British Isles,
but subject to some important restrictions, because, in
the first place, English and Irish landlords do not put on
the screw of a continual increase of rent with anything
like the harshness habitual with Belgian landowners.
In the second place, the local rates in England are high,
and are rising progressively.   Thirdly, rents have been
raised in England much less in proportion than they are
in Belgium.

Nevertheless, as regards the increase of rent, the
land system of Belgium is superior to that of England.
In both countries part of the clear profit of civilization
is sublimated, so to speak, and deposited in the shape of
increased rent in the landlord's exchequer, even though
he be an absentee or a do-nothing.   But where there
are a great many landowners a large proportion of its
inhabitants must come in for a share in the increased rent.
If, on the contrary, they are few in number, they mono-

polize the whole of the social benefit. In the former case the working of the economic law of increasing rent will be harsher than in the latter ; yet it will be acquiesced in when many benefit by it, while it must sooner or later arouse opposition where it tends to enrich a few families only. The system of rack-renting, which is so much censured in England, is generally practised in Flanders ; nevertheless, the tenant bears with it in all meekness, notwithstanding the sufferings it entails on him. In the United Kingdom the landlord would scruple to shear his tenants as they are shorn in Flanders, yet he does not escape reproach ; and this is easily explained by the fact that, for one landowner in England there are two hundred and fifty in Flanders. Still, on the whole, the system of tenure of land in Flanders is anything but worthy of imitation. There are too many tenant farmers, and too few peasant proprietors ; the leases are excessively short, and the rents excessively high.

Arthur Young has said : " *Give a farmer a nine years' lease of a garden and he will make a desert of it.*" It is to the honour of the small farmers of Flanders, and of *la petite culture*, that they have falsified this maxim.

§ 17. Among the various systems of tenure of land in the Belgian and Dutch Low Countries, there is none more interesting to the student of agriculture than the *Beklem-regt*, in the province of Groningen. This is a kind of hereditary lease, something like fixity of tenure. The landlord can never raise the tenant's annual rent. The tenant, on the contrary (called the *Beklem-meyer*), may bequeath his right of occupation, dispose of it, mortgage it, provided only he does not diminish the value of the land. The *Beklem-regt* is indivisible, and can be held only by one person. Whenever it changes hands the landlord is entitled to a fee called *propinen*, which amounts to one or two years' rent, and is fixed beforehand. This system dates from the middle ages, and is still constantly practised in Groningen, even on lands recently reclaimed, on polders, and on lands put in cultivation in the turf-bog region. It arises in

the following manner:—Some landowners being in want
of money, and not wishing to mortgage their lands, give
hereditary leases of them for a sum of money, thus
remaining nominally proprietors; they never part with
the fee-simple.   Moreover, when the land is sold, the
fee-simple and the *Beklem-regt* are disposed of separately,
and a higher price is thus realized.

All Dutch economists are alive to the advantages
of the *Beklem-regt*, of which the principal ones are as
follows :

1st. It gives the tenant absolute security for the future,
thus encouraging him to make improvements.

2nd. The tenant purchasing the right of occupation
has less to pay for it than he would for the fee-simple,
and yet acquires the same security.   The higher the
rent, the less money he pays.   In Ireland, on the contrary, no real right is obtained by purchasing the good-
will or tenant right, and the new tenant must pay
the same rent as others.   In Groningen, an hereditary
right of occupation is acquired, and the rent to be paid
is moderate and invariable.

3rd. The *Beklem-regt*, being indivisible, prevents
compulsory or injurious subdivision.   If the division is
beneficial, the landlord consents to it in consideration
of a share in the profits to be gained by it.

4th. The *Beklem-regt* precludes the immoderate increase of the population, because, on the one hand, it
limits the number of farms, and on the other, because
the farmer himself being in good circumstances, his sons
are not likely to allow themselves to fall into distress.

5th. By this mode of tenure a number of well-to-do
quasi-proprietors are made to reside in the country,
cultivating the land with capital and science, whereas if
the landlords were to hold the land themselves they
would go and live in the towns, and let their estates to
tenants at ruinous rents.

Thus, instead of tenants with the fear of losing their
holdings always before their eyes, and ground down by
ever-increasing rents, this system, derived from the
middle ages, has created a class of semi-proprietors,

independent, proud, simple, but withal eager for en-
lightenment, appreciating the advantages of education,
practising husbandry not by blind routine and as a mean
occupation, but as a noble profession by which they
acquire wealth, influence, and the consideration of their
fellow-men ; a class ready to submit to any sacrifice to
drain their lands, improve their farm-buildings and implements, and looking for their well-being to their own
energy and foresight alone.

Systems of tenure of land similar to the *Beklem-regt*
used to exist in the Channel Islands and in Brittany, by
the name of *domaine congéable*, in Lombardy by the
name of *contratto di livello*, and in Portugal by that
of *aforamento.** As long as the hereditary *tenants*
cultivate the land themselves the *Beklem-regt* is attended only with beneficial effects ; but as soon as they
sublet it becomes subject to the drawbacks of common
leases, with the difference that in that case the sub-
tenant must pay a double rent, viz., the fixed one to the
landlord, and a variable one to the hereditary tenant.

Could the *goodwill* in Ireland be converted into
Beklem-regt or *aforamento*, the country might perhaps be
saved by it. But then the Irish peasants would, in the
first place, have to respect the *indivisibility* of their
leaseholds and of the farms for which these are granted.
Moreover they would have to pay to the landlords
themselves, not to the outgoing tenants, the price of the
hereditary leases for which they would come in. One
must add, however, that it would in all probability be
very difficult to make them understand and appreciate
this mode of tenure. Even in the provinces adjoining
Groningen, where the wholesome effects of this system
are seen and appreciated, it is not adopted.

Lawyers, inspired with the ideas of uniformity and simplification of the French Revolution, are moreover opposed
to a system which formerly used to prevail in a great
part of Europe. It has likewise disappeared in many
countries by degenerating from its original form, or by
reason of being coupled with improper regulations. In

* *Vide* the note on *aforamento* at the end of this essay.

Lombardy the *contratto di livello*, enforcing certain payments in kind, prevented the hereditary farmer from
growing such crops as he liked, and thus formed an
obstacle to progress in husbandry. Instead of trying to
do away with this system, it should be preserved and
even brought into general use, with improvements in
its form.

§ 18. The Flemish *Pachters-regt*, or farmer's right,
consists in the liability of the incoming tenant to pay
the outgoing one for the value of the straw and manure
on the land, besides the manure in stock, and the
manure and crops on the ground ; being a compensation
for *unexhausted improvements*, but given on a more
systematic plan than in England.

The existence of this custom in Flanders dates as far
back as the middle ages, which is another instance of
the progress the country had achieved, even in those
remote days. At present the *Pachters-regt* varies according to districts, and the differences seem to coincide
with the areas occupied of old by the various German
tribes. In the neighbourhood of Ypres and Courtrai,
not more than one-third of the value of the manure from
which a crop has already been raised, is given ; near
Ghent, the indemnity amounts to one-half of that value ;
and in the Waes country a fixed rate of twenty-one francs
is paid per hectare for the manure sunk in the two foregoing years. The total amount of compensation varies
according to the state of cultivation of the land and the
time of taking possession of it.

In the southern districts, where the leases commence
in October, the *Pachters-regt* applies only to the half-
exhausted manure and the manure kept in tanks, and
does not exceed 70 or 80 francs per hectare on an
average ; whilst in the neighbourhood of Ghent, where
the farmers take possession at Christmas, or on the 1st
of March, the indemnity is paid for the crops in the
ground as well as the manure, and amounts to 400 or
500 francs for every hectare sown with corn (emblavé).*

* In an interesting manual for valuers of indemnities to be paid to outgoing

In Mr. Caird's 'Letters on English Agriculture,' it is stated that in the counties of Surrey and Essex an *inventory* is usually drawn up, similar to the Flemish *prizy*, which is an inventory of unexhausted improvements. However, Mr. Caird is not very much in favour of a custom which, in his opinion, is attended with the following two drawbacks :—

1st. Costly valuations, lawsuits, and law expenses.

2nd. The compensation for the inventory exhausts the resources of the incoming tenant.

Neither of these two drawbacks exists in Flanders, and neither ought to exist in England. The inventory is drawn up by experts, and frequently by the notary of the locality, at a trifling expense, and litigious proceedings hardly ever arise from this. Where the crop in the ground is to be valued, as in the neighbourhood of Ghent, the operation is indeed attended with some difficulties ; but where the new-comer takes possession in October, as in the environs of Courtrai, nothing need be valued except the farmyard manure (of which the cubic volume may be readily ascertained), and the half-exhausted manure ; and the inventory is taken with the greatest facility.

As regards the alleged diminution of the incoming tenant's resources, this charge is groundless; on the contrary, the *prizy* increases his capital. He pays for manure on the spot, which he would otherwise have to procure from some remote quarter. It is owing to the *prizy* that the outgoing farmer does not neglect the land even in the last year of his tenure, and the incoming tenant finds it in perfect condition, instead of its being exhausted and overgrown with weeds. No outlay is less regretted by the Flemish farmer than the one for the inventory. His saying is, *hoe hooger hoe beter*, the higher the better.*

---

tenants, entitled ' Het Pachters-regt ; door L. Delaruge en van Boekel,' I find valuations of compensations for lands sown with barley, colza, and wheat, amounting to from four hundred to five hundred francs per hectare ; of which upwards of three hundred francs are for manure.

* I need hardly add that nothing of all this applies to the Ulster tenant right as described by Lord Dufferin on ' Irish Tenure,' p. 116.

In Flanders all agricultural authorities agree that the *Pachters-regt* is indispensable to good culture.   They go so far as to demand, in the interest of rural economy, that the local customs relative to this right be systematized and regulated by law.   In fact, the land in Flanders is naturally so excessively poor that if the outgoing tenant neglects it during the last two years of his occupation the farm is ruined, and a great expenditure becomes necessary to put it into its proper condition again.

The Flemish *Pachters-regt* deserves to be introduced everywhere, for the following reasons :—

1. It is equitable, compensating, as it does, the farmer for his improvements and good cultivation.

2. It prevents the exhaustion of the land during the last two years of the lease.

3. It furnishes the incoming farmer with manure, which it is his interest to have.   Both the Flemish and the Chinese properly think that there is no better investment to be made than in manure.

§ 20.   Those who cultivate the soil are either landowners, tenants, or labourers.   Let us now examine the condition of each of these three classes in Flanders.

If the cultivator of the land is the owner of it at the same time, his condition is a happy one in Belgium, as everywhere else, unless the plot he holds is insufficient to support him, in which case he has to eke out his existence by becoming also a tenant or labourer.   But as a rule the peasant proprietor is well off, because, in the first place, he may consume the entire produce of his land; which being very large, especially in Flanders, his essential wants are amply satisfied.   Secondly, he is independent, having no apprehensions for the future; he need not fear being ejected from his farm, or having to pay more, in proportion as he improves the land by his labour.

Yet the mode of living of the landowner who is no *fine gentleman*, but a man who works as a peasant, differs very little from that of the tenant-farmer.   His food is about the same, except that he eats bacon more frequently, killing a pig or two for his own use, and that he drinks more beer.   His clothes, habits, and dwelling also resemble those of the other class, save that they denote rather easier circumstances.   He lays money by to purchase land and give his farm a better outliue; and it is owing to the competition of peasant proprietors in the land market that the value of real property is rising so rapidly.

What remains to be desired is not that the peasant proprietor should add to or refine his wants, for the progress of civilization is not co-extensive with that of epicureanism,* but that he should pay more attention to his own intellectual improvement, and to this a portion of his annual savings might very well be devoted.

The situation of the small Flemish tenant-farmers is, it must be owned, rather a sad one.   Owing to the shortness of their leases, they are incessantly exposed to having their rents raised or their farms taken from them. Enjoying no security as to the future, they live in perpetual anxiety.   So much does this fear of having their rents raised tell upon their minds, that they are afraid to answer any question about farming, fancying that an increase of rent would be the inevitable consequence.

Rack-rents leave the small farmer barely enough to subsist on.   I do not think his working capital returns three per cent., and he works himself like a labourer. However, he is always properly clothed, and on Sundays he dresses just like a *bourgeois.*   His wife and daughters, who work barefooted during the week, are stylishly dressed on Sunday, wearing crinolines, ornaments, and flowers in their hair.

It ought to be added that suitable farm buildings are almost always erected by the landlord, and remarkably well kept by the tenant; this is quite a traditional custom in Flanders, and has been so for many ages.   Every one is alive to and respects the requirements of good

* In my opinion it is a great mistake to consider the refinement of wants and luxury in private life as a *criterion* of civilization. In the best days of ancient Greece, private comfort was all but unknown. In ancient India and Judæa the men lived in quite a primitive way, whose minds conceived the ideas on which our moral life is based.

farming. The properties cultivated by the proprietors themselves, although in a minority, form a kind of model or type, and every one does his best to imitate them. They are looked upon as standards from which the peasants would be ashamed to depart very far. Their influence in this respect has been very forcibly pointed out by Mr. Cliffe Leslie in a remarkable article on ' The Farms and Peasantry of Belgium,'* in which he says : " As Falstaff could boast of being not only witty himself, but the cause of wit in other men, the peasant proprietor may boast that he is not only a good farmer himself, but the cause of good farming in other men."

Nothing gives a more charming idea of country life than the little farmhouses of Flanders, especially in the Pays de Waes. With an orchard in front, where the cows graze in the shadow of the apple trees, surrounded by well-kept hedges, the walls whitewashed, doors and window-frames painted in green, flowers behind the windows, the most perfect order everywhere, no manure lying about, the whole presents an appearance of neatness, and even of ease and comfort.

The reason why these small farmers are ground down by rack-rents is that there are too many of them. On 100 hectares, or one square kilometre (0·386 square mile), there are in West Flanders, 200, in East Flanders, 270 inhabitants, against 76 in France, and 136 in Lombardy. The peasants of Flanders unfortunately will not leave their own province, and their intense competition for farms raises the rents in a manner ruinous to themselves.

Above the small farmers there is a class of small proprietors, who profit without scruple by this competition. Having just enough to support themselves, they do not trouble themselves about the condition of the farmer or anything else, being anxious only to maintain "their position in the world," as they term it.

No parallel can be drawn between the Belgian and the English landowner. The latter, I believe, acts upon

* *Vide* ' Fraser's Magazine ' of December, 1867.

considerations unknown on the Continent, and no inference can therefore be drawn from so exceptional a case. Not that your Englishman is *intus et in cute* better than other men; but he is subject to a higher public opinion, and being a much wealthier man, he is not tempted to screw the last farthing out of his tenant. Hence the condition of the English tenant-farmer is a happier one than that of the Flemish.

As a rule, peasant property is an excellent thing wherever the proprietor is himself the cultivator; but where it exists side by side with leasehold farming in an over-populated country, the tenant farmer is placed in a worse condition than if the estates were large. But it is most important to bear in mind, in comparing the condition of the agricultural population in Flanders and England, that the small Flemish farmer who cultivates his land with his own hands corresponds, not to the English tenant farmer, but to the English farm labourer. Now our small farmer, though hardly better fed than the English agricultural labourer, has a decided advantage over the latter; he doubtless has the cares and responsibility his superior position entails, but on the other hand he acquires from it habits of providence and self-control, and the exercise of his intellectual faculties.

Let us next glance at the condition of the agricultural labourer in Flanders. His wages are very low, ranging from 1fr. 10c. to 1fr. 20c. per day, without board. In the Walloon country, in which are all the large centres of industry, the wages are about double of this, owing to the mines and manufactories competing with the land in the labour market. Some facts connected with this are almost incredible. In the environs of Liège, an agricultural labourer earns two francs a day, while near Hasselt, at a distance of no more than four leagues, he earns but one franc; the country is Flemish, and he is prevented by the difference of language from going to a Walloon district, in which he might earn much higher pay.

For breakfast the Flemish labourer has bread and butter, with chicory, coffee, and milk; for dinner,

potatoes, vegetables, and bread ; at 4 P.M., bread and
butter again, and for supper the same fare as for dinner;
very seldom a little bacon, and as for butchers' meat—
four or five times in a year.   Those who live with the
farmers get pork more frequently.

On the other hand, the farm-labourer is generally well
housed.   For himself and his family he always has a
house, with at least two, more frequently four rooms,
generally kept in good condition and having an acre or
half an acre of land belonging to it, where the man grows
vegetables, potatoes, and rye ; and there is besides a
goat which gives milk to the household.

NUMBER of FAMILIES for every 100 HOUSES in the RURAL DISTRICTS of

	1846.	1856.
Flanders, West	103	101
Flanders, East	104	102
The Entire Kingdom . . .	104	104

Thus, the number of houses in Flanders has increased
as compared with the rural population, who have by this
means found better accommodation.

No remarks need be made on the beneficial effect of a
good home on a man's morality and self-respect.   This
applies to the country as well as to towns, and accounts
for the fact that the Flemish population, badly fed and
little educated as it is, yet presents all the outward
appearance of well-being and civilization.

It may be affirmed that in normal years no pauperism
is to be found in the rural districts of Flanders.   The
labourers and small artisans live poorly ; yet having
nearly all of them a little plot of land to work, they are
at any rate kept from starving.   At the time machinery
supplanted hand-spinning, a severe crisis took place
indeed ; but the last traces of it have now disappeared.

A stranger visiting Flanders should guard against
rashly drawing unfavourable inferences from certain facts
arising from custom.   A Walloon, for instance, seeing

women working in the fields barefooted, is apt to consider it as a proof of extreme destitution. He is, however, in error—it is the custom of the country. A well-
to-do farmer's daughters, who are stylishly dressed on
Sundays, will work barefooted during the week. The
same observation applies to the rye-bread, which the
country people eat as a rule, simply because they have
done so for centuries, although they can often afford to
eat wheaten bread ; which, by-the-way, is coming into
more general use at present.

§ 20. In my work on the rural economy of Belgium, I
made some reflections on the indifferent condition of the
Flemish peasants, from which inferences adverse to
peasant proprietorship have been drawn. These conclusions are erroneous. The evil arises from the fact
that there are too few small proprietors and too many
small tenants among the peasantry of Flanders.

If you want to find a district in Belgium where the
peasants are well off, you must go to Lower Luxembourg.
There the land is divided out into a multitude of peasant
properties, almost the whole of which are cultivated by
the owners themselves. Each of these manages his own
farm, and under the shadow of his fruit-trees enjoys in
security what he earns by the sweat of his brow. This
is a kind of rural opulence, due not to the possession of
large capitals, but to the abundance of rural produce.
No one is rich enough to live in idleness ; none so poor
as to suffer from want. The peasant there is also more
enlightened than in Flanders, and more independent.
The situation is nearly the same as that of the Canton of
Grisons, in Switzerland.

A few figures will indicate the contrast between
Flanders and Luxembourg ; in each of the two provinces
I shall select a normal district.

Flanders. District of St. Nicholas, in the Pays de
Waes. Farm-labourer's wages, 1 franc 10 centimes per
day.

Area of land worked { by owners, 6,556 hectares.
{ by tenants, 31,689 hectares.

Luxembourg. Bouillon and Paliseal district.   Farm-labourer's wages, 2 francs per day.

Area of land worked $\begin{cases} \text{by owners, } 10,699 \text{ hectares.} \\ \text{by tenants, } 1,563 \text{ hectares.} \end{cases}$

Thus, in Lower Luxembourg the labourer's wages are double what they are in Flanders, although most articles of food, especially meat and potatoes, are cheaper in the former province.

§ 21. The farmers of Holland lead a comfortable, well-to-do, and cheerful life.   They are well housed and excellently clothed.   They have china ware and plate on their sideboards, tons of gold at their notaries', public securities in their safes, and in their stables excellent horses.   Their wives are bedecked with splendid corals and gold.   They do not work themselves to death.   On the ice in winter, at the kermesses in summer, they enjoy themselves with the zest of men whose minds are free from care.

The Belgian farmer, we have shown, is neither as rich as his Dutch neighbour, nor can he enjoy himself in the same way.

One reason is that in Holland the townspeople have at all times invested their savings in public securities, and generally left landed property alone, which has thus remained entirely in the hands of the peasants.   In Belgium, on the contrary, the nobility have retained large landed property, and capitalists have eagerly bought estates.   Hence a good number of the peasants have become mere tenants.

To meet with the ideal of rural life, you must look for it in Groningen or in Upper Bavaria.

§ 22. Pliny's saying, *latifundia perdidere Italiam*, has sounded like a warning voice across centuries.   The *latifundia* of the Roman aristocracy first devoured the small estates, then the small proprietors, and, when the Barbarians made their appearance, the empire had become a solitude.

The *Estados* of the grandees of Spain have also destroyed the small landowners, whose place has been taken by bandits, smugglers, beggars, and monks.

Tiberius Gracchus was the only Roman who understood the economic situation of his country. Had the laws proposed by him been adopted, the decline of the Republic might perhaps have been prevented.

It is the glory of England to have remained free from the consequences usually attending the large-property system. Great Britain possesses a class of landowners and tenants alive to the requirements of agriculture ; and her gigantic commerce has provided employment for the small freeholders whose lands have been swallowed up. But on the Continent the case is vastly different; and the reason of this is to be found in the facts noticed with reference to Belgium.

Here large farms are, as a rule, not so well cultivated as small ones, and this is easily accounted for. To work a farm of 200 hectares with as much capital as Flemish small farmers do, 100,000 francs (4000*l.*) would be required. Now a man who commands such a sum will not become a farmer ; he will either go and live in a town, become a functionary, or employ his capital in business ; hence the working capital of large farms is, as a rule, insufficient, and therefore the returns from these are smaller, and they let at less rent. Thus an additional stimulus is given to subdivision.

This being the case in Belgium, it must *à fortiori* be so in countries in which husbandry is more behindhand. In Eastern Europe, *e.g.*, in Hungary, Poland, and Prussia, large estates are farmed by the proprietors themselves, in the absence of tenants of sufficient capital.

Even in England, would not the land be more carefully cultivated were there a number of peasant proprietors ? and, supposing there were 200,000 small farmers more than there are now, might there not be 500,000 fewer paupers less to be supported ? I only put the question, not feeling myself competent to decide it.

§ 23. *Free trade in land.*—I borrow this title from an

T

interesting work published by Mr. W. Fowler, M.P.
In our western world it seems to me necessary that
there should be no obstacle to land changing hands, in
order that it may be distributed in conformity with the
laws of political economy, and become the property of
those who can turn it to the best account.

To this end, the first requisite is that all those
restrictions should be done away with by which landed
property is rendered immovable in the possession of
certain families; for example, primogeniture, entails, &c.
In the second place, every one ought to be able to
purchase a lot of land without heavy expenses, and with
perfect security. If the purchase of an estate involves
law-suits, risks of title, or considerable costs, then the
rich only can indulge in the luxury. The continuance
anywhere of so intolerable a state of things can only be
accounted for by the fact that it is the interest of
lawyers and of the wealthy to maintain it; the former
for the sake of the legal business it creates, the latter
because it keeps the land-market to themselves.

As regards the transfer of land and the law of
mortgage, Belgium may be considered a model country.
The following is a synopsis of the laws in force in this
respect :—

Since the passing of the Act of December 16, 1852,
modifying the then existing law, the sale of land takes
place by a deed executed before a notary, or else by
one under a private seal recognised in law. Deeds
under private seal used to give rise to irregularities, and
to serious dangers whenever the authenticity of the
signature was contested. By the following compulsory
forms of law the purchaser obtains perfect security with
regard to mortgages. His notary is bound to obtain a
certificate (état négatif) from the Registrar or Keeper
(Conservateur) of Mortgages, showing that there are
no outstanding charges against either the seller or the
former owners. The notary is personally responsible
for neglect to take this precaution, and the Registrar
of Mortgages would also be liable to an action for
damages were he to omit to give notice of any in-

cumbrances. If there be any incumbrances of this kind, they may be deducted from the selling price, and in that case the purchaser assumes the seller's liability; or else the purchaser may pay off the creditor, who then gives him a discharge of the debt.

The law of 1851 (1852?) has done away entirely with *hypothèques tacites ou légales.* All unregistered mortgages are invalid against the purchasers of an estate.

Along with the certificate against incumbrances an *état des mutations* must be obtained by the notary, *i. e.,* a statement of all the changes of hands the property has undergone since a fixed date prior to the sale, and establishing the title of the vendor. The notary must moreover take the precaution to obtain an extract from the *matrice cadastrale*, or otherwise a copy of the official survey. Notice is given of every transfer of landed property to the *administrateur du cadastre* by the offices of registration and succession duties, as well as by his own surveyors, who make periodical circuits and ascertain, *de visu*, what modifications the land has undergone. A good surveyor knows the " parcels " of his district just as well as a shepherd does his sheep.

The notary draws up the deed of sale, which is signed by the parties, two witnesses and himself. The *minute* or original of the deed is brought to the office of the Registrar (*receveur de l'enrégistrement*), who puts an abstract or summary of it on his register. By this formality the purchase and its date are fully authenticated ; but the primary object of it is to secure the Government duty, which amounts to 4 per cent., plus 30 *centimes additionnels*, altogether to 5 fr. 20 c. per cent. of the selling price.

After this the deed undergoes *transcription*. It is then no longer the minute that is lodged with the registrar of mortgages, but a duplicate duly executed. The registrar transcribes it in full; this transcription establishes the legal transfer of the property as far as third parties are concerned. Under the *Code Civil*, transcription was not required to validate a transfer. Under the present law, the purchaser who has been the first to have his

deed transcribed is the legal proprietor. The transcription is subject to a duty of 1 fr. 30 centimes per
cent., with some *centimes additionnels*. The notary's fees
vary according to the value of the property transferred.

The essential features of the process may be summed
up as follows :—

1st. A deed of transfer is executed before a public
officer (the notary), who is responsible for its proper
legal form. The original remains in the notary's hands
and forms the title-deed; and thus individuals are
secured against the loss of their title.

2nd. This document is transcribed on a public
register, with a statement of the mortgages, if any, on
the estate transferred. An extract from this register
may be had for a few francs, and thus any one may
readily ascertain to whom an estate belongs, by what
right it does so, and what incumbrances, if any, there
are on it; and all this without any uncertainty or
obscurity.

3rd. The official survey contains a plan of each township (*commune*), with the parcels, their areas, annual
values, and peculiarities marked on it; and in every
commune in the kingdom there is to be found a copy of
the plan of its territory, which may be referred to by
the inhabitants, and from which they may claim an
extract.

In Belgium the transfer duties (which are very high,
about seven per cent. of the selling price) are levied on
the property sold; but this tax is a bad one, impeding
free trade in land. In Prussia, where the same legislation exists, the tax amounts to no more than one-and-
a-half per cent., and the notary's fees are very low. If
the Government requires the amount of the tax, it had
better impose it on land directly, by increasing the land-
tax. It falls on the owners of land in either case, but
in the latter there would be the compensatory advantages
arising from unimpeded sale of their land. In other
respects the system is perfect. The *cadastre*, or official
survey, ascertains the areas, boundaries, and properties
of estates; the notary puts the deed of transfer into its

proper legal shape, and the transcription on a public register fixes the date of the transfer and publishes it to the world. There is, in short, absolute authenticity combined with full publicity, being just the two things needful. It is the duty of the State to make these formalities compulsory, a public and not merely a private interest being at stake.

It is of the highest public interest, in the first place, that landed property should easily get into those hands by which it can be turned to the best account; secondly, that the title to property in land should be secure, and incontestable; and, thirdly, that there should be no legal obstacles to the subdivision of land when the natural economy tends to it, so that the number of small landowners should not be artificially reduced by imperfection in the law.

The Belgian system is only an improvement on that of the French law, which has been successively adopted by almost all continental countries, on account of its conspicuous usefulness.

As long as England does not introduce security, publicity, facility of exchange, in fine, *free trade* into everything connected with property in land, there will ever be an insuperable obstacle to the establishment of an agrarian system in keeping with the wants of modern society. A reform in this particular branch of English law is, in my opinion, the most urgent of all.

§ 24. We have seen that much larger gross returns are everywhere obtained from the land by small than by large farming. This is certainly a great, but not the greatest, boon accruing from it.

The larger the number of landowners is in a country, the more free and independent citizens there are interested in the maintenance of public order. Property is the essential complement of liberty. Without property, man is not truly free. Whatever rights the political constitution may confer upon him, so long as he is a tenant he remains a dependent being. A free man politically, he is socially but a bondsman.

In Belgium most tenant-farmers enjoy both the municipal and parliamentary franchise. But this right, so far from raising them in the social scale, is but a source of mortification and humiliation to them, for they are forced to vote according to the dictate of the landlord, instead of following the dictates of their own inclinations and convictions. How can they feel any attachment to a constitution which, in conferring a new right, really at the same time rivets a new chain on them? The electoral franchise is but a mockery and a snare to the cultivator without either proprietorship or a long lease.

It may be thought a matter for surprise that, in Flanders, feelings hostile to social order nevertheless do not manifest themselves, and that agrarian outrages are never perpetrated as in Ireland, although I think it certain that, in consequence of excessive competitions, the Flemish farmer is much more ground down by his landlord than the Irish tenant. The fact that in Flanders, as in all countries in which landed property is distributed among a large number of owners, the ideas called socialist * in the bad sense of the word do not obtain, is to be accounted for as follows :—

The Flemish tenant, although ground down by the constant rise of rents, lives among his equals, peasants like himself who have tenants whom they use just as the large landowner does his. His father, his brother, perhaps the man himself, possesses something like an acre of land, which he lets at as high a rent as he can get. In the public-house peasant proprietors will boast of the high rents they get for their lands, just as they might boast of having sold their pigs or potatoes very dear. Letting at as high a rent as possible comes thus to seem to him to be quite a matter of course, and he never dreams of finding fault with either the landowners as a class or with property in land. His mind is not

---

* I think it is to be regretted that a disparaging meaning should attach to this word. Are not those who devote themselves to social science, socialists? When, in 1848, Proudhon was asked in the Committee of Inquiry, "What is socialism?" he replied, "A general desire for improvement." "Then we are all of us socialists," remarked the chairman of the Committee.

likely to dwell on the notion of a caste of domineering landlords, of "bloodthirsty tyrants," fattening on the sweat of impoverished tenants, and doing no work themselves ; for those who drive the hardest bargains are not the great landowners, but his own fellows. Thus the distribution of a number of small properties among the peasantry forms a kind of rampart and safeguard for the holders of large estates ; and peasant property may, without exaggeration, be called the lightning conductor that averts from society dangers which might otherwise lead to violent catastrophes.

The concentration of land in large estates among a small number of families is a sort of provocation of levelling legislative measures. The position of England, so enviable in many respects, seems to me to be in this respect full of danger for the future.*

§ 25. The idea that all men are equal, placed at the head of all modern constitutions, and announced as an axiom throughout the world is a new idea, the wholesome or baneful effects of which it is as yet impossible to foretell. The gospel proclaimed the equality and fraternity of all men ; but it was to Christians a heavenly ideal, which they did not feel called upon to realize in this world. The Reformation, the United States Constitution, and the French Revolution, made of it a terrestrial ideal, of which the consequences must be logically followed up ; it only remains to be seen to what extent these consequences are to be carried.

Tocqueville, in his book on Democracy, has admirably shown the effect of the equalitarian principle in politics ; but he has not pointed out with equal clearness the economic consequences it is likely to entail ; and these precisely absorb, at the present day, the attention of all those who can see and understand.

The idea that all men have equal rights, though proclaimed everywhere, has not yet taken root enough to become a living and earnest conviction, resolute on

---

* *Vide* Mr. Cliffe Leslie's remarkable Article on the Land System of England in ' Fraser's Magazine,' February, 1867.

action. To the upper strata of society this idea is like
a vague threat hanging over them; to the lower ones,
like a light of hope in a distant future; but being
incessantly repeated at workmen's congresses and meet-
ings, it is likely to diffuse itself through all classes, especially those whose interest it is to believe it to be true.

Now suppose this idea universally and ardently embraced in a country in which all the land is in few
hands, what sentiment is it likely to give birth to among
the masses? They will say : "If we are equal, how is it
that a caste has perpetual possession of all the land, and
that we are perpetually doomed to support this caste by
the produce of our labour? Has God made the land
only that a privileged few shall enjoy it? Property is
said to be the creature of labour. How is it, then, that
we ever behold idleness and opulence on one side, and
labour and destitution on the other? According to the
laws of nature, he who works ought to reap the fruits of
the earth, whilst he who lives in idleness should suffer
hunger; but does the perfection of social laws consist in
keeping the drone in abundance and the bee in distress?"

I will not carry the argument further; it will be
readily understood. This was precisely the language
held by the peasants who revolted in Germany when
Luther spoke of evangelical equality to the feudal society
of the sixteenth century. These ideas may be drowned
in blood, as they were on that occasion, as they were in
France at the time of the Jacqueries; but they will
always revive and redouble the danger to society in
countries where inequality appears like an institution
conspicuous to the sight of all.

It is a grave symptom of the emergency that the upper
classes themselves no longer remain inaccessible to
these ideas. A distinguished member of the British Parliament, to whom I pointed out that certain measures
proposed for Ireland looked remarkably like " confiscation," replied to me, " No doubt they do; but why should
they not? Is it not just that every one should have his
turn?" And really, if but a few are chosen to sit down

to the feast of life, why should these guests be always the same? This is in its crudity the idea which involuntarily rises in the mind. It is all very well for lawyers and economists to prove its absurdity, but one and the same argument produces a different effect on the man who is seated at table and the man who waits upon him; what may seem absurd to the man who has the good side of the present régime may appear perfectly right and proper to him who has come in for the bad side.

Travelling in Andalusia this year, I lighted upon peasants harvesting the crops on the lands of Spanish grandees, which they had shared among themselves. "Why," said they, "should these large estates remain almost uncultivated in the hands of people who have neither created nor improved them, but are ruining them by spending elsewhere the net produce they yield?" I am convinced, that were land more divided in those districts of Andalusia, where ideas of communion prevail at the present day, these would no longer find any adherents. In Belgium, socialism, though spreading among the working classes in manufacturing districts, does not penetrate into the country, where the small landowners block up its way.

Therefore I think the following propositions may be laid down as self-evident truths:—There are no measures more conservative, or more conducive to the maintenance of order in society, than those which facilitate the acquirement of property in land by those who cultivate it; there are none fraught with more danger for the future than those which concentrate the ownership of the soil in the hands of a small number of families.

APPENDIX.

ON THE AFORAMENTO IN PORTUGAL.

IN the following note are collected some highly interesting particulars of this mode of tenure, for which I am indebted to a Portuguese economist, Mr. Venancio Deslandes.

The *aforamento* is very much like the *Beklem-regt*, in Groningen, *i.e.*, an hereditary lease by which the right of occupation is granted indefinitely in consideration of an annual rent *fixed once for all, which the landlord can never increase.* This right passes on to the heirs, who, however, cannot subdivide the estate, the *aforamento* being essentially indivisible; therefore one of the heirs must take it as his share, and indemnify the others. Where this cannot be done, and the heirs do not agree, the *aforamento* is sold, and the purchaser then holds it subject to the same conditions as the seller. If there be no next of kin and no legatee, the *aforamento* expires, and the landlord re-enters into possession.

Again, if the hereditary tenant allows the land to deteriorate so as to reduce its value to one-fifth over and above the capitalized rent, the landlord resumes the right of possession without any compensation to the tenant.

Besides the yearly rent the landlord was formerly entitled to levy a duty, whenever the land changed hands, which was called *luctuosa*, if the change took place in consequence of a death, and *landemium*, if in consequence of a sale. The new civil code in force since July, 1867, which in many instances betrays, like its French prototype, a hostility to everything pertaining to the ancient *régime*, has done away with these dues as feudal charges.

Another and severer blow has been dealt to the *aforamento* system, by the new code prohibiting a holder from bequeathing the sole right of occupation to the one of his children he might designate. The division of all property into equal shares being made compulsory, and the *aforamento* being indivisible, a conflict arises between the two principles. The *aforamento* is then sold, and taken from the family who had held it perhaps for centuries.

The *aforamento* dates from the earliest times of the Portuguese monarchy. It was introduced by monastic orders, especially the Benedictines, on the lands they owned, and since then has gradually become general throughout Portugal north of the Tajo. Even down to this day, contracts of this kind are made between private parties; and if townships let common lands to the inhabitants, this is often done by *aforamento*.

Private persons let land at fixed rents, and in consideration of the fixity of tenure they grant, the payment of a certain sum of money is stipulated for, which represents the price of perpetual enjoyment by the tenant without increase of rent; by submitting to an immediate sacrifice, he gains perfect security for the future. The people used to have, and have even at this day, a great predilection for this kind of contract; both farmers and landlords agree in appreciating the great advantages it offers. These are especially evident in the province of Minho, so celebrated for the perfection of its husbandry, the well-being of its inhabitants, and the magnificent appearance of the country. There all lands are held by *aforamento*, and by this system of hereditary tenure its prosperity is accounted for.

I met with *aforamento* very frequently in the environs of Lisbon, especially in the magnificent country adjoining the Cintra Road.

Unfortunately legislation, prompted by French ideas, has declared war against this excellent system of tenure, with a view to carry out what is called the liberation of the land, *i.e.*, the reconstitution of absolute property, and the adoption of the common kind of lease. This is an error; for every institution is excellent which is calculated to give security of possession to him who cultivates the land.

V.

THE AGRARIAN LEGISLATION OF PRUSSIA DURING THE PRESENT CENTURY.

By R. B. D. Morier, C.B.

In treating of the agrarian legislation of Prussia during the present century, it is important to guard against a prevalent misconception, to the effect that this legislation is something " sui generis," and different in kind from that of any other European State. The contrary is the case—legislation similar to that we are about to describe has in some form or other marked the history of every German State during the last sixty years, and analogous legislation has marked our own history, and we may add that of every other State of Teutonic origin.

For every Teutonic community has been evolved out of a germ identical in its rudimental construction with that of every other, and therefore containing within itself the laws of a similar growth. The history of this growth is recorded in the history of the occupation of land ; for, in contradistinction to the *citizens* of the antique world, the Teutonic race is essentially a race of *landfolk.*

I. The original Teutonic community is an association of freemen, a " Gemeinde," a commonalty or commons (not common people in contradistinction to uncommon people, that is, a privileged class, but a body of men having property in common), amongst whom the private right of property in land is correlative to the public duty of military service and participation in the legislative and other political acts of the community. These public duties are of a comparatively simple kind ; the agricultural relations of the community, on the other hand, are of a comparatively complicated kind. The district, or Mark (*i.e.*, the geographical area *marked* out and appropriated by the community), consists of three distinct parts; first, the *Common Mark* (the Folcland of the Anglo-Saxons), owned jointly by the community; secondly, the *Arable Mark* (Feldmark), cut out of the Common Mark, and apportioned in equal lots to the members of the community (the Anglo-Saxon Boc land); and, lastly, the *Mark of the township* (Dorf, thorp, villa), also divided into equal lots, and individually appropriated.

The individual marksman, therefore, stands in a three-fold relation to the land occupied by the Gemeinde. He is a joint proprietor of the common land; he is an allottee in the arable mark, and he is a householder in the township. In the first case he owns "de indiviso," and his rights are strictly controlled by those of his co-marksmen. His cattle grazes on the common pasture, under the charge of the common herdsman; he hews wood in the forest, under the control of a communal officer.

In the Arable Mark he has a distinct inheritance, and can call a certain number of square roods his own; but he must cultivate his lot in concert with his associates, and the community at large determines on the mode of its cultivation. The whole Mark is divided into as many parts or *Fields* ("Fluren," "Campi") as the rotation of crops and the alternation between fallow and plough requires. Usually into three such "commonable" *Fields*, each *Field* lying fallow once in three years, the community having rights of pasturage on the fallow as well as on the stubbles of the land under the plough.* To obviate the possibility of the individual allottee finding

* It is these common rights of pasturage on the *Arable Mark* which it is of importance to note, for it was from these rights, and not from the right of pasturage on the *common pasture,* that mediæval agriculture derived its distinctive character. The obligatory cultivation on the "Three Field system," the *common temporary* enclosure of the commonable Field (not of the individual parcel), whilst the crop is growing, the removal of that enclosure after harvest, the prohibition against *permanent* and *individual* enclosures, are all of them results which flowed from the common right of pasture on the *fallow* and *stubbles.*

himself every third year without any land under cultivation, which would be the case if the lots lay in
undivided blocks, each lot is distributed in single parcels
over the three *Fields* of the arable mark, a subdivision
which renders cultivation in common still more necessary.

In the Common Mark, therefore, *and in the Arable
Mark*, the individual is everywhere controlled by his
peers, and by the minute customs and usages of the
community ; he is contained by and tethered to the
association. In his dwelling-house and its appurtenances
in the township the reverse is the case. Here he is
absolute lord and master. His fenced-in court-house or
manor (curtis, hof, mansus, manoir, manor) is in the
fullest sense his " own " (eigen). Over his family, over
the dependants (" Hörige " — " liti ") and slaves
(servi) domiciled within it he can dispose as seems
good to him. To them he is a lawgiver and a law
enforcer. Within his pale (septum) neither public nor
communal officer can enter otherwise than with his
sanction. It lies outside the community, and constitutes
an " immunity "—" *immunity* " and " *community* " thus
come to be opposed to each other. " Immunitas est
quod non communitas, immunis quod non communis."
In the eleventh century this is still the rule applicable
universally to the homestead of every freeman. " Omnis
domus, omnis area pacem infra septa sua habeat firmam.
Nullus invadat, nullus effringat, nullus *infra positos
temere inquirere*, aut violenter opprimere *præsumat*. Si
fugiens aliquis septum intraverit securus inibi sit."*
In the familiar saying, " Every Englishman's house is his
castle," we have a distant echo from those far-off times.

These two distinct aspects of the early Teutonic freeman as a " lord " and a " commoner " united in the same
person—the one when within the pale of his homestead,
the other when standing outside that pale in the economy
of the Mark—should not be lost sight of. In them are
reflected the two salient characteristics of the Teutonic
race, its spirit of individuality, and its spirit of associa-

---

* Juramentum pacis circa an. 1085, quoted in v. Maurer's ' Einleitung zur
Geschichte der Mark, Hof, Dorf und Stadt Verfassung,' p. 241.

tion ; and as the action and reaction upon each other of these two laws have determined the social and political history of the race, so, as the sequel will show, they have in an especial manner affected and determined its agricultural history.

Lastly, we should note a strange peculiarity apparently dating back to this period, viz., that the personal " status " of the occupant communicates itself to the walls of his domicile, and, as it were, adheres to them, sometimes reacting back upon the new occupant, and determining *his* status. The occupier privileges the manor occupied by him, and the manor thus privileged invests the later occupier with those privileges. In the same way the servile tenement renders the occupier servile.

This is the first period of the Teutonic community. Its characteristic features are, that there are two distinct communities—an *agricultural* community and a *political* community—inseparably identified with each other, the rights conferred by the one being correlative to the duties imposed by the other.

We may describe it as the period of *land-ownership* and *equal possession*, in which the freeman is a " miles " in virtue of being a land-*owner*.*

II. The second period can be described as the period of *land tenure*, and of *unequal possession*, in which the feudal tenant is not a " miles " in virtue of being a land-*owner*, but a land-*holder* in virtue of being a " miles."

The transition from the one state to the other is necessarily influenced by a great variety of circumstances in the different communities ; but there are certain fea-

---

* For the history of the constitution of the Mark we refer our readers to the numerous works of Ludwig George von Maurer. It would be impossible to cite our authorities for the statements made in the text in detail, for we have given the barest outline of a vast amount of learned investigation. The main features of the constitution of the Mark may be considered as having been now fairly won back to the domain of history, thanks to the labours of Maurer and many others, over the entire area of the primitive Teutonic settlements in Germany and Scandinavia.

It may seem pedantic, in treating of legislation in the nineteenth century, to go back to the institutions of the first century, but the agricultural features of the early Teutonic community have so indelibly engraved themselves on the entire subsequent history of Teutonic agriculture, especially in Germany (as any one who has seen the map of a German Gemeinde can testify), that we have found it impossible to dispense with this introduction.

tures connected with this transition common to all the communities.

1. Intertribal wars, the consequent subjugation of other communities, the appropriation of the land in the common marks of those communities, the unequal division of the lands so appropriated according to the amount of fighting work done by the associates, are among the earliest and most effective causes which break up the original equality of property, and lead to the accumulation of wealth in a few hands. The fines paid as blood-money (Wergeld) in accordance with a criminal system entirely based on fines, appears as another important cause leading to the same results.

2. The cessation of the political independence of the individual community, without, however, as yet a cessation of the political functions of the members of the community. This process takes place in two ways, first, by the gradual colonization of the *Common Mark* by communities sent forth from the original townships, in which case each new township receives an *Arable Mark* cut out from the *Common Mark*, but the *common mark* itself continues to be owned " de indiviso " by all the townships; secondly, by the agglomeration of a number of marks into a loose kind of confederacy, which, by degrees, assumes a greater consistency, and becomes in time a national unity.

In both cases the several communities retain in their own hands the management of the affairs of their own township, but national affairs are transacted in general assemblies. In both cases, however—and this is a point which it is of importance to note—a sort of embryo suzerainty or over-lordship is claimed, in the one case by one or other of the more important marks of which the confederacy is composed; in the other case by the original or mother township (Mutter Dorf), as it was termed, over the daughter townships.

3. The separation between executive and legislative functions, the establishment of permanent executive organs, and the gradual hereditariness of the executive office. Hitherto, the assembly of the community has

U

been all in all. In case of war, it elected a chief, a king
or Herzog, whose attributes were purely military, and
ceased when peace was concluded. When the assembly
sat as a court to try civil or criminal cases, it likewise
elected its president. From the earliest times, however,
in both cases, the choice appears to have been limited to
a certain number of families, who, in some especial
manner represented the blood of the tribe, and little by
little, though the forms of election continue, office becomes
practically hereditary. How this rule obtained in the
case of the Anglo-Saxon and Frankish kings is well
known; but it is necessary to note that this tendency is
universal throughout the Teutonic Kosmos, and applies
to all its institutions. Thus, as the king of the nation
is "de jure" elective "de facto" hereditary, so
also is the president of the court of the township, the
judge or *Schultheiss,* he who apportions unto a man his
debt or guilt, *i. e.,* who fixes and exacts the Wergeld.
This is a matter of extreme importance, as it is to the
hereditariness of this office and its identification with one
particular manor in each township, so that whosoever
owns the manor exercises the office, and whoever exercises
the office owns the manor, that we apparently owe the
origin of the manorial rights which afterwards become
the key-stone of the entire land system in feudal times,
and to this day affect in an important manner the agrarian
relations of many important countries in Europe, England
included. Our space does not admit of our entering upon
this subject here, and it must therefore suffice to say that
from the earliest times known to us—and we are now
speaking of times antecedent to the establishment of the
feudal system—we note in every Teutonic township one
manor (Hof), which thus becomes par excellence *the*
manor, raised above its fellows. This manor, afterwards
variously described as the " Salhof," " Frohnhof," " curtis
dominicalis," " curtis judicialis," " curia publica quæ
dicitur Frohnhof," receives dues and services from the
other manors in the township, *even where these manors
are the allodial property of freemen.* That these dues and
services were of the nature of public charges, and at a

time when all payments were made in kind represented the emoluments of the principal executive officer of the township seems now established beyond a doubt.*

The foregoing indications will suffice to point out the predisposing causes in the pure Teutonic society which led when that society came to conquer the Roman world to the establishment of the feudal system, a system made up of Teutonic and Roman elements, viz., on the one hand of the Teutonic idea of the correlation between possession of land and military service, of the Teutonic tendency to change public office into private right, and to transmit such rights by inheritance; lastly, of the Teutonic peculiarity of regarding " unfree" service rendered personally to the sovereign as in its nature honourable, though involving political disabilities (Thaneship, Dienstmannschaft, Hörigkeit, Ministerialität) ;† and, on the other hand, of the ideas of the Roman law regarding " beneficial uses," the difference between " possession " and " dominium," as well as the Roman practice connected with the agricultural colonisation of the provinces.

The application of the *feudal* ‡ system in Germany was necessarily a much slower process than in the Roman Provinces, where it was, as it were, called into life by the exigencies of conquest. In the one case, the raw material that it had to work up consisted of free *allodial* ‡

* Confer Landau Der Salhof, do. Die Territorien.

† Confer Freeman's account of Thaneship in his ' History of the Norman Conquest.'

‡ The etymology of *alodium* and *feodum* throws great light on the entire question of " ownership " versus " tenure."

The syllable *od*, in Old High German *ôt*, in Anglo-Saxon *ead*, signifying " possession," " wealth," " treasure," is common to both.

Allod, alodium, or, in its earliest form, *alodis* and *alaudes*, is that which is altogether my possession, or possession in all its fulness.

[Compare *Kleinod*, a jewel, *i.e.*, a small possession, or rather a possession dear to me, the diminutive being used to express endearment, as in the exactly analogous case of jewel, French *joyau*, *i.e.*, *gaudiculum*, a little joy.]

Feodum, if derived from Old High German *fihu* (modern German, Vieh), cattle, and *od*, possession, meant originally possession in cattle.

The early Teuton's land, *i.e.*, his lot in the Arable Mark and in the township, is altogether his own: it is possession in all its fulness. When he becomes acquainted with Roman " beneficial " possession, as distinct from " dominium." he expresses it by a distinction drawn between the land itself and the wealth which is on the land, and derived from the land, but separable from it ; viz., cattle (which, as in the English word *chattel*, becomes in time synonymous

proprietors, who deemed themselves the equals of the
king, and whose personal status was legally higher than
that of his proudest Thanes ; in the latter case it consisted
principally of conquered Romans and Provincials, who
were glad to get back their lands on any terms.

In Germany, therefore, it was an economical necessity
rather than a political convulsion which brought about the
change.   As population increased, more and more townships were settled on the common lands, the proportion
between pastoral as compared with agricultural wealth
decreased ; and the ordinary freeman was gradually
reduced to little more than what his lot in the arable
mark brought him in. Simultaneously with this diminution of his means rose the cost of his equipment for
the field, and the strain put upon his resources by
having to maintain himself during the long summer
and winter campaigns which were now the rule.
Soldiering under Charlemagne against the Saracens in
Spain, or the Huns on the Danube, was different work
from an autumn raid across the Rhine, after the harvest
was got in. Accordingly, as early as Dagobert's time, we
find the possession of five allotments to be the minimum
qualification required for a fully-armed " miles."

Hence, partly by his poverty—partly by the pressure.
often amounting to force, brought to bear upon him
by the lords who wished to increase their demesne
lands, the free owner was little by little reduced to the
condition of an unfree holder.

By "commending" himself ("comendatio," "traditio ")
to a superior lord, that is, by surrendering the " Dominium directum " of his " allodium " and receiving back

---

with moveable as distinct from immoveable property).   Thus the idea of
usufruct comes to be translated by the idea *cattle possession.*

This original conception of *feodum* remains the same, even if with Diez we
have to consider *feodum* as derived directly from Pro : *feu,* Italian *fio, i.e.,*
Old High German, *fihu,* and look upon the *d* as inserted for the sake of
euphony, as in *ladico* for *laico,* instead of seeing in it a remnant of the Old
High German *ôt.*

The idea of allodial ownership was lost in England from the moment the
whole of the soil came to be regarded as a demesne of the Crown, the only
allodial owner left being the sovereign.   For the etymologies in this Note we
are indebted to Professor Max Müller.

its "dominium utile," the freeman lost his personal rights, but obtained in return protection against the State, *i.e.*, against the public claims that could be made upon him in virtue of his being a full member of the political community.   According to the nature of his tenure, he had to render military service (no longer as a national duty but as a personal debt) to his superior, and in return was maintained by his lord when in the field : or, if his tenure was a purely agricultural one—and it is with these we are concerned—he was exempt from military service, and only rendered agricultural service.

In this way, as generation followed upon generation, the small free allodial owners disappeared and were replaced by unfree holders.   But the memory of their first estate long lived amongst the traditions of the German peasantry, and it required centuries before the free communities, who, out of dire necessity, had, by an act of their own, surrendered their liberties into the hands of the lords of the manor, sank to the level of the servile class settled upon their demesnes proper by the lords of the soil.   The glimpses we obtain of the Bauer in the 12th and 13th centuries* exhibit him to us as still a jovial, high-handed fellow, who holds his own with the folk from the castle, and is quick at retort both with his cudgel and his tongue.

In the peasant's war which followed on the Reformation, he made a desperate attempt to recover his lost liberties ; and in the record of grievances upon the basis of which he was ready to treat, he showed how accurate was his recollection of the past, and how well he knew the points on which the territorial lords had robbed him of his just rights.

The Thirty Years' War gave the final blow.   With exceptions here and there the tillers of the soil became a half servile caste, and were more and more estranged from the rest of the community, until, with the humanitarian revival at the close of last century, they became to philanthropists objects of the same kind of interest and

---

* Cfr. Freitag 'Neue Bilder aus dem Leben des deutschen Volks,' cap. 'Aus dem Leben des deutschen Bauers.'

inquiry which negroes have been to the same class of persons in our day.

Before we leave this second period we must allow ourselves a general observation, which is of importance both as regards this period and the next.

We described the earliest form of the Teutonic community as the union between an agricultural and a political community.

The second period is marked by the divorce between these two bodies. This divorce is accomplished when the power of the king has fully established itself, the result as regards Germany of the conquest of the Roman provinces and the foundation of the Frankish monarchy. Instead of the self-administered marks of a former age, the ancient " Gaue " now become " Gau Grafschaften," *i.e.*, counties governed by the " comites " of the king with a hierarchy of subordinate officials, " Vice comites," " Centgrafen " (Counts of the Hundred), &c. For a short while there is a real revival of the Roman Empire, and the structure which the genius of Charlemagne builds up and superposes over the Teutonic as well as over the Latin foundations of his monarchy, simple as are its classic outlines, contains all the appurtenances required for the government of a great centralized commonwealth.

After his death the structure, it is true, remains standing, and its external outlines can still be descried, but shooting upward from the ground and sidewards from every nook and crevice, the vigorous Teutonic vegetation, whose luxurious growth even the original architect had scarcely been able to restrain, spreads over the building and produces that marvellous but not unpicturesque monstrosity known as the Holy Roman Empire.

The Teutonizing of the Roman forms of administration was effected by a process precisely similar to that which had obtained in regard to the executive offices in the old free community. It was the same inveterate Teutonic tendency to treat public office as private property, and therefore as something that could be transmitted by inheritance, a hereditament, which ruled in the one case and the other. Thus as the office of king and Herzog, from being elective had become hereditary, so the Gau Graf, from being a prefect named by the Emperor to exercise royal prerogatives in his name, becomes a hereditary subregulus; the royal authority is decentralized, and the royal prerogative adscripted to the glebe, or rather identified with the person who is lord of the glebe. In the same way that the great territorial lords gradually possess themselves of the rights of the Gau Graf and transmit them to their posterity as part of their real estate, the lesser lords possess themselves of the attributes of the Cent-Graf, and so on down to the owners of *the* manor in the township. Now each of these offices, from the highest to the lowest, represents a jurisdiction, and each of these jurisdictions therefore comes to be identified with the possession of real estate. Consequently in the frightful chaos which resulted out of the feudal system we have nevertheless got a clue which enables us to unravel many difficulties. The idea of dominion, the rights of the "dominus" (Frohnherr, lord) are made up of public and private ingredients, but in inverse proportions to what they were in the first period. It is the turning topsy turvy of the ancient principle. Then private rights imposed public duties; now public duties breed private rights.

When the system has once been firmly established it is easy to note the different relation in which the community, the larger community of the mark as well as the smaller community of the township, comes to be placed in towards its executive officers. For a long period after the community has, by the consolidation of the kingly authority, ceased to be a political community in the sense of an independent and international unit, it continues in the general assemblies of the " Gau " to administer its local affairs, and in the same way the assembly of the township continues under the guidance of its quasi elected, but really hereditary magistrate, to administer its own affairs, and to sit as a civil and criminal court. During this intermediate stage the sovereign authority is still as it were emanating from below, and therefore the only jurisdiction to which freemen have to submit, is to that of their own peers. The president of the court is one of themselves, and in so far as he exercises executive authority, it is authority delegated by them.

With the establishment of the feudal system, the sovereign authority begins to flow from the contrary direction : it comes now from above, and no longer from below ; it is delegated by the king, and no longer by the commons. The owner of the manor now no longer exercises his functions as "primus inter pares;" he has obtained a jurisdiction over his former peers, and has become invested with a "dominium." From henceforth the township is administered partly as a political unit, partly as a private demesne, from the manor house. Public and private rights, public and private dues, get mixed up in inextricable confusion.

The divorce between the agricultural and the political community even in regard to local affairs (except in the most limited sense) is complete ; but the point which it is important to note is, that the agricultural community in Germany remains intact. The "Bauern Gemeinde" of the 19th century is in its essential points the micro-cosmic reproduction of the "Landes Gemeinde" of the 1st century, apart from the political rights and the cultivation in common. It is a corporation of free, allodial owners who are allottees in an arable mark, and co-partners in common lands. It is an administrative unit, managing its own private affairs, like any other body corporate, with some slight remnants of a jurisdiction which in Prussia is still exercised under the surveillance of the manor.

It is at this point that the agricultural history of England and Germany part asunder. In England the agricultural community, though traces of it are to be found much later than is generally supposed, traces which may even to this day be deciphered, from a very early period ceases to be conterminous with the self-governing body. Not the agricultural, but the ecclesiastical community, the parish, becomes with us the administrative unit, and the lord of the manor, except in regard of the freeholders who make up the court baron, finds himself face to face, not with a compact association and a recognised corporation, but with isolated individuals.

III. We have now arrived at the third and last period. It is that with which we have to deal in treating of the agrarian legislation of Prussia during the present century. It is marked by the demolition of the feudal edifice, and the removal of the materials of which it was built. *It can be described as the return to free ownership with unequal possession.*

The three principal incidents of the process can be classed as follows :—

1. Abolition of villeinage in so far as it affects the personal " status " of the villein.
2. Abolition of villein and other feudal tenures, and substitution in lieu thereof of allodial ownership.
3. Removal from the land thus allodially owned of all charges, whether of a public or private character, derived from the feudal forms of tenure and from the feudal organization of society.

The three great efforts made by the legislation of Prussia in 1807, in 1811, and 1850, respectively correspond to these three incidents.

From this it will be abundantly manifest that a similar process of legislation has marked the history of every State in which the feudal system has been established.

In England personal villeinage dies out at a comparatively early date, we hardly know how, so noiselessly does it disappear.

In the same noiseless way villein tenure loses its servile incidents and assumes the form of copyhold tenure, which tenure can by 15 and 16 Vict. c. 51 be commuted into freehold tenure at the instance of the lord of the manor or of the copyholder. By the statute 12 Car. II. c. 24 all forms of freehold tenure were practically reduced to the simple one of tenure by common socage.*

* For all practical purposes tenure by common socage is as good as allodial ownership, and therefore the statute of Charles II., taken in combination with the statutes of the present reign, enabling the transmutation of copyhold into freehold tenures, must be considered as the English equivalent of what we

It is not in any way our purpose, by calling attention to these analogies, to detract from the merits of the so-called Stein Hardenberg legislation. Those merits are of a transcendent kind, but it is to the accidents that accompanied the legislation, to the scale on which the measures were framed, to the spirit in which they were carried out, and not to the essence of the legislation, that those merits belong.*

---

have described as the second main incident of the Prussian agrarian legislation. For the purpose, however, of strict accuracy, it should be noted that in England, and in England alone, the feudal structure of society still exists on the statute book, with the further exceptional circumstance that the sovereign is lord paramount, and therefore, strictly speaking, the only real landowner, all his subjects being only tenants. Hence the inveterate use of the terms *freehold tenure*, and *freeholder*, when the idea intended to be conveyed is that of *allodial ownership*.

* We have felt it the more necessary to insist upon these points because, in a celebrated passage of a celebrated speech, Mr. Bright gives the received erroneous English account of the Prussian legislation in question. We most heartily sympathize with the object which Mr. Bright has in view, viz., the numerical increase of the landowning class in Ireland. No one can have lived abroad during the last twenty years without convincing himself that, in the present transition state of society, it is of vital importance that its one permanent conservative force, viz., landownership, should be so distributed as to exercise its steadying and restraining influence over a large area instead of a small area, over all classes instead of over one class. It is therefore with the greater regret that we notice the inaccuracy in question; but where so important a precedent is invoked on so important a matter, and by so great an authority, it appears to us of real moment that it should be correctly stated.

Mr. Bright is reported to have said : " If in this country fifty years ago, as in Prussia, there had arisen statesmen who would have taken one-third or one-half the land from the landowners of Ireland, and made it over to their tenants, I believe that the Irish landowner, great as would have been the injustice of which he might have complained, would, in all probability, have been richer and happier than he has been."

Now what the statesmen did in Prussia fifty, or rather sixty, years ago, was just the reverse. They took half or a third of the land possessed by the tenants of Prussia, and handed it over in full possession to the landlords of Prussia. The land occupied by these tenants was land on which, *except in case of devastation and in virtue of a judgment passed by a Court of Law*, the lord of the manor had no right of re-entry. What the law of 1811 did was to force the lord of the manor to sell his manorial overlordship to the copyholder for one-half, or one-third, of the copyhold. By this process he was put in possession of more land than he was possessed of before. What he was deprived of was labour. The tenant lost one-half or one-third of the land he possessed before, but obtained the " dominium directum," as well as the " dominium utile," over the remaining half or two-thirds ; what was, however, much more important, he got back the free use of his own labour. The landlord sold labour and bought land ; the tenant sold land and bought labour. All the essential features of the transaction would have remained the same even if the " dominium directum " of the landlord had not been passed over to the peasant, for an overlordship of this kind deprived of its material contents would have been

The Legislation of 1807.

In order to estimate what were the changes practically effected by the decree of 9th October, 1807, it is necessary to realize what was the state of things which that decree was intended to supersede.

At the period in question the entire land of Prussia (then, it must be remembered, consisting of the few provinces left to the King of Prussia by the peace of Tilsit) was distributed amongst three classes of society, carefully kept asunder, not by usage only, but by strict legal enactment—nobles, peasants, and burghers. In other words, it was held by knights' tenure, villein tenure, and a sort of civil tenure which had grown up out of the privileges of town municipalities. These classes were distinct castes—their personal status was reflected in the land held by them, and conversely the land held determined the status of the holder. The noble could follow no avocations but those of his caste. He could administer his estate, and serve the king either in a civil or military capacity. He could not occupy himself with trades or industries. He could acquire nobles' land, and therewith manorial rights over land held under villein tenure; but he could not acquire burgher land or the "dominium utile"—*i.e.*, the possession of peasant land.

The burgher had a monopoly of trades and industries, which with some very limited exceptions, such as the business of wheelwrights and smiths, were confined to the towns, and could not be exercised in the country. He could not acquire nobles' land or peasants' land. The military profession was closed to him, as well as the higher civil employments.

The condition of the peasant differed widely in the

---

a mere meaningless form, like the *dominium eminens* of the Crown in England. There was no injustice done of the kind supposed by Mr. Bright, any more than the act 15 and 16 Vict. c. 51 creates an injustice by compelling the lord of the manor to sell his copyhold rights to the copyholder. The only difference between the two transactions consists in the payment, in the one case being made in money, and in having, in the other, been made in land. One-half and one-third was a rough-and-ready calculation by which, in all probability, the lords of the manor, in some cases, got more than their share, the peasants less, and vice versâ.

different provinces, and in the different parts of the same
province.   It was a mirror in which almost every phase
of mediæval history was reflected.   There was this
feature, however, common to all peasant holdings—that
they were not isolated farms, but united in a "commonalty," and that these "commonalties" stood under
the jurisdiction of the manor.

The rural area of Prussia was consequently divided
into two kinds of districts.   The Gutsbezirk, or manorial
district proper, consisting of the demesne lands, cultivated
by the manorial proprietor, and in which he exercised
the functions of a police magistrate directly; and the
township of the peasant community, with its arable mark
and its common mark, in which a Schulze (contracted
from Schultheiss),* usually an hereditary office, or one
inseparable from a particular Hof, exercised the police
authority in the name of, and under the supervision and
control of the lord of the manor.   The community likewise managed its private affairs like any other corporation, but also under the guardianship of the manor.

The different communities held by different kinds of
tenure—varying in an ascending scale from those in
which the allottees were in a state of personal villeinage
with unlimited services to those in which they were free
settlers, who, though under the jurisdiction of the
manor, and paying dues to it in virtue of that jurisdiction,
were yet owners of their lots.   These distinctions generally
may be traced to the original difference in the nature of
the land held, adverted to in the first part of this essay.
In the one case, the communities had originally been
slave communities, settled upon the demesne lands
proper of large proprietors, and had gradually emerged
to the comparatively higher level of villeinage—or they
were communities of freemen or dependants, "liti,"
settled in the same way, who had gradually sunk to a
state of villeinage.   In the other case, they were originally
the allodial owners of the land held by them who had
surrendered their rights of full ownership to the manorial
lords on distinct stipulations, or they had retained the

* See supra, p. 284.

ownership of their land, and were only subject to the jurisdiction of the manor.

But there was another distinct class peculiar to Prussia, who owed their origin to the fact that the German race was in these parts a conquering race, and settled upon territory taken from another race. These were the free colonists colonized " more Teutonico," principally on the demesne land of the Crown. Contractors, termed "locatores," obtained grants of land, and brought with them, chiefly from Holland, communities of agriculturists, who, according to the old system of the mark, received their individual lots and likewise rights of coproprietorship in a certain amount of common lands. The contractor received a larger grant, free of services and dues, and was infeoffed in the office of Schulze. The colonists received their grants for ever, and were only bound to pay fixed and moderate dues in kind or money. These tenures may be considered as ready-made copyholds. The " tenants " were to all intents and purposes freeholders, with only a kind of shadowy "dominium directum" in the background.

The status of villeinage differed according as the villein was Leibeigen (*i.e.*, as his lord had rights of property in his body), or only " erbunterthänig," *i.e.*, in a state of hereditary subjection to the manor, "adscripti glebæ."

In its worst form the villein could be held to unlimited service, and could be deprived of his holding, and located in another. At his death, the whole or the largest portion of his personal estate fell to the lord. His children could not marry without the lord's consent, and could be kept an unlimited number of years as personal servants (Gesinde) in the service of the manor. He could receive corporal punishment to heighten his productive power, and to enforce respect, but his life was protected.

This extreme form was, however, the exception to the rule. It occurred mostly in the more remote provinces.*

* Stringent legislative enactments had been passed by Frederick the Great, regulating the personal " status " of the villein, and limiting the rights of his lord; but usage was stronger than law, and the greatest diversity in the " status " of the villein in the different parts of the monarchy is a characteristic feature of the agricultural system of Prussia at the commencement of the century.

The milder form differed from the former in the services to be performed and the dues to be paid, being limited by local custom, and in a greater freedom in the disposal of the holding. The villein knew what work he and his team would have to perform in the course of the year, the number of years his children would have to serve in the household of the lord, the tax he would have to pay on their marriage, the amount of the mortuary dues which at his death the lord would have a right to. He could also buy his freedom at a fixed price, and, with the permission of his lord, dispose of his holding.

The free peasant differed from the villein in having no personal dues to pay, and in his services and dues being usually recorded in writing in the grants made to him, and therefore bearing more directly the character of a legal contract. He could not, however, acquire by purchase or inheritance other than peasant land, nor could he change his position by changing his country life for a city life ; nor could he in the country exercise any trade or calling but that of agriculture.

The land cultivated by the peasant therefore was divided into two principal categories :

1. That in which he had rights of property ;
2. That in which he had only rights of usufruction.

In both cases services were rendered, and dues were paid in kind or money to the manor. But in the first case these services and dues may be considered as having had a public, in the latter case, a private origin.

As regards the land in which the peasant had only rights of usufruction, it was divided into two principal categories :

1. Land in which the peasant had hereditary rights of usufruction, and could transmit his holding to his descendants and his collaterals, according to the common law of inheritance ;
2. Land in which the occupier was only a tenant for life, or for a term of years, or at will.

In neither case, however, could the landlord re-enter on this land. The lords of the manor had been deprived

of this right,* if it ever existed, by various edicts of the
former Hohenzollern kings.   Frederick the Great imposed a fine of a hundred ducats on any landlord who appropriated to his own use any land held by his peasants.
At last, under his reign, a general law was passed on
the subject.   (Allgemeines Land Recht II. 7, §§ 14–16.)

The manors were respectively held by the Crown, by
corporations, lay and ecclesiastical, and by individual
nobles.   But whoever was the occupant, the functions of
the manor in the body politic remained the same.   The
term implied a house with farm buildings (*the* manor in
the community, the other manors having sunk to *mansi*,
" messuages ") : demesne lands cultivated by the labour
of the peasants under its jurisdiction : rights of various
kinds over the persons of these peasants and the lands
occupied by them : correlative duties in the way of main-

---

* No point connected with the mediæval history of land tenure presents
more difficulties than this question of what the manorial right of *Overlordship*
really amounted to, and whether or not it invested the lord with a right to
possess himself with the tenant's land.   Wherever in the Teutonic Kosmos we
meet with a manor and dependent " mansi," we are encountered by this
difficulty and by the difference between the " terra tenentium " and the
"*dominium* villenagium," *tenant* land and *demesne* land.   If the description
of the origin of manorial rights given in the early part of this essay is correct,
it would follow that what in feudal language are called " tenants " were
(except in the case of servile townships settled on the lord's " allodium ")
originally allodial owners, whose dues and services to the manor were of the
nature of public taxes, which could not invest the lord with rights of property
over the lands of the proprietors.   It is, however, certain that with the
establishment of the feudal system this original character was lost sight of,
and that the lords universally claimed the right to possess themselves of
tenant land.   Two forces came to the assistance of the tenant in his resistance
to this encroachment—

1. Wherever the royal authority was gaining the upper hand, the Crown
sided with the tenants against the lords.   A statute of William the Conqueror,
quoted in the work of Professor Nasse later on referred to (we have no means
of verifying the quotation), affords in this respect a remarkable analogy to the
edicts of Frederick the Great and his predecessors alluded to in the text.   It
forbids the lords " removere colonos a terris dummodo servitia persolvent;"
and it adds that if " domini terrarum non procurent idoneos cultores ad terras
suas colendas justiciarii hoc faciant."   This clearly refers to tenants' land.
On the other hand, Bracton defines " demesne land " (*dominium* villenagium)
as " item dicitur quod quis tempestive et intempestive resumere possit pro
voluntate suâ et revocare."

2. The Law Courts were the second force which came to the aid of the
tenants ; and here again Germany furnishes cases exactly analogous to the
celebrated decisions in the reign of Edward III. and Edward IV., by which
" customary tenure " was created, and the tenant obtained an action of trespass
against the lord.

taining paupers, furnishing wood for the building and repair of the peasants' farm-buildings, in some cases furnishing the stock of the farm, the building and endowing schools, the repairing of churches, &c., and, lastly, a police magistracy, and a court of first instance in civil and criminal matters, the so-called "Patrimonial Gerichtsbarkeit" (courtleet and customary court). It *did not* imply the right of re-entry on the lands occupied by the peasants.

The judicial functions were not exercised by the lord of the manor in person, but by his steward, who required to be a properly-trained lawyer.

Where the manor was the property of the Crown, or of a corporation, the rights of the manor were exercised by a bailiff.

Each manor had its own usages and customs, which amounted to a kind of microscopic customary law.

The manors situated on the demesne lands of the Crown were immeasurably in advance of those in private hands, both as to the position of the peasants and as to economical results.

Justice would not be done to the intricacy of these relations, did we not add that besides the rights above described, there were innumerable cross rights, servitudes, and easements, between the lords and the peasants (such as rights of pasturage by the lords on the common lands of the peasants, similar rights enjoyed by the peasants in the forests of the lords, &c.), as well as between the peasants of the same community "inter se," and between peasant communities belonging to different manors, and so on ad infinitum.

Lastly, the entire burdens of the State, as far as they rested on real estate, were borne by the peasant land.

Chaotic as this picture appears to us, it must not be supposed that chaos reigned in the monarchy of Frederick the Great. On the contrary, nothing could be more regular than the working of the wheels within wheels of this wonderful machinery—nothing more remarkable than the ledger-like beauty with which the productive forces

of the country were inventoried, and the debtor and
creditor account of its agricultural resources kept.
The Hohenzollerns had brought with them from
Nüremberg business habits, which have not a little
contributed to the greatness of the Prussian monarchy,
and Frederick the Great in this, as in other respects,
showed himself the representative man of his race.　He
was a strong advocate of the feudal system, such as he
understood it, not from any mediæval turn of mind, but
because it supplied him with a machinery which, in his
hands, could be made to produce great results.　The
political power of the Prussian nobility had long since
been broken.　They were docile instruments in the
hands of the Crown.　Sufficiently numerous to supply
the army with its officers, and therefore really rendering
knights' service in return for knights' fees, yet not so
numerous but that an indefatigable administrator like
Frederick II. could thoroughly acquaint himself with
the resources and capabilities of each of them, they
represented so many responsible centres of administration, whom the king made accountable, not only for the
public taxes and charges, but equally for the cultivation
and agricultural economy of the monarchy.

Frederick the Great knew exactly what every acre
of land, what every pair of hands, and what every yoke
of oxen, in his dominions were capable of producing, and
he took care not only that they should produce it, but
that they should be maintained in a state in which they
should continue capable of producing it.　He also knew
the economical value of justice between man and man,
and therefore, despite the tremendous strain put upon
the peasant class during his reign, and the scrupulous
maintenance of the manorial system, the peasants felt
that the great king was their friend ; and their material
condition was undoubtedly raised under his reign.　But
this very improvement only served to hasten the changes
which had become unavoidable.　Under the weak so-.
vereign who succeeded Frederick, it was seen that the
feudal system had long since been dead—that it had only
been galvanised into apparent vitality by the genius of

x

one man, and that the process of decomposition was
only the more rapid for the temporary interruption.

The Battle of Jena and the Peace of Tilsit sealed the
fate of the institution. The edict of October 9, 1807,
was its death-warrant.

Let us look with our own eyes at this great landmark
in the history of a great people.

" We, Frederick William, by the grace of God, &c.,
&c. Be it known unto all men that,

" Whereas, owing to the universal character of the
prevailing misery, it would surpass our means to relieve
each person individually, and, even if we could, the
objects we have at heart would not be fulfilled (loquitur
the mediæval Father of his people) ;

" And,

" Whereas, it is not only conformable to the ever-
lasting dictates of justice, but likewise to the principles
of a sound national economy, to remove all hindrances in
the way of the individual attaining to that measure of
material well-being which his capacities may enable him
to attain (loquitur Adam Smith) ;

" And,

" Whereas, the existing restrictions, partly on the
possession and enjoyment of landed property, partly in
connection with the personal condition of the agricultural
population, in an especial manner obstruct our benevolent intentions, and exercise a baneful influence, the
one by diminishing the value of landed property, and
impairing the credit of the landed proprietor, the other
by diminishing the value of labour ; we are minded that
both shall be restrained within the limits which the
public welfare requires, and therefore we decree and
ordain as follows :

" *Free Exchange of Real Property.*

" § 1. Every inhabitant of our dominions is, as far as
the State is concerned, henceforth free to acquire and
own landed property of every kind and description.
The noble, therefore, can acquire not only noble land

but burgher and peasant land, so also the burgher and the peasant can acquire not only burgher and peasant land, *i.e.*, land not noble, but likewise noble land.* Every such transfer of real estate must, however, continue, as before, to be notified to the authorities.

" *Freedom in regard to Choice of Occupation.*

" § 2. Every noble, without derogation to his rank, is henceforth free to exercise the trades and callings of the burgher—the burgher may become peasant, the peasant burgher.

" *In how far Rights of Pre-emption still exist.*

" § 3. (This paragraph is technical, and does not alter the principle of the measure.)

" *Division of Property.*

" § 4. All owners of real property, in its nature saleable, can after due notice to the provincial authority, sell the same piecemeal and in detail as well as in block. Co-proprietors can in the same way divide amongst them property owned in common.

" *Free power of Granting Leases.*

" § 5. Every proprietor, whether or not his property forms part of a fief or of any other kind of entailed property, is free to grant leases of any duration so long as the moneys received in payment of such leaseholds are used to pay off mortgages, and in the case of an entailed property, are capitalized for the benefit of the estate.

" *Extinction and Consolidation of Peasant Holdings.*

" § 6. When a landed proprietor is of opinion that he cannot restore to their former condition or keep up the several peasant establishments on his property, he may,

---

* §§ 6 and 7 restrict this right, which was only fully established by the 'Edict for the better Cultivation of the Land,' of the 14th September, 1811.

X 2

if the holdings have not got the character of hereditary tenures (*i. e.*, Anglicè, if they are not of the nature of copyhold or perpetual leaseholds), after the particular case has been inquired into by the Government of the province, and with the sanction of that Government, consolidate such holdings into one large peasant holding or incorporate them with demesne land.

"Special instructions as to the cases in which this process shall be permitted will be sent to the provincial Governments.

"§ 7. If, on the other hand, the tenures are of a hereditary kind, no change whatever can be effected without the previous acquisition by purchase, or in some other legal manner of the rights of the actual possessors. Such cases likewise require the formalities specified in § 6 (*i.e., the previous sanction of the Government*).

" *Facilities for Mortgaging Entailed Estates to pay Losses occasioned by War.*

"§ 8. (The provisions of this paragraph are of a temporary kind.)

" *Of the cutting off of Entails.*

"§ 9. Every entailed estate, whatever the nature of that entail, can be freed from the entail by the consent of the family.

" *Abolition of Villeinage.*

"§ 10. From the day of the publication of this edict no new relations of villeinage, either by birth, marriage, or acquisition of a villein holding can be created.

"§ 11. From the same date all peasants holding by hereditary tenures, cease, they and their wives and their children, to be villeins.

"§ 12. From Martinmas 1810, every remaining form of villeinage in all our dominions shall cease, and from that date there shall be none but freemen in our dominions, such as is already the case in our domains in all our provinces.* It is to be understood, however, that these freemen remain subject to all obligations flowing from the possession of land or from particular contracts to which, as freemen, they can be subjected.

"So Given at Memel, 9th October, 1807.

FRIEDERICH WILHELM,
SCHRÖTTER,
STEIN,
SCHRÖTTER II."

Such, with a few abbreviations and some unimportant omissions, is the text of the measure by which Prussia thoughtfully and deliberately stepped out of the mediæval past into the modern present.

Not the least interesting feature of the measure is its direct affiliation with the teaching of Adam Smith and its impregnation with the spirit of the Kantian philosophy.

The three persons more immediately concerned with the framing of the measure—Schön, Schrötter, and Auerswald—had all of them been students at Königsberg and pupils of Kraus, the great expounder of Adam Smith at that university, and one of that brilliant professorial body who, under the inspiration of Kant, were calling attention to the fact that man was a rational being, and that reason might be profitably consulted even in matters of State. It is this, we conceive, which has left so indelible a mark upon the Stein and Hardenberg legislation.

At a moment of universal chaos, when the old landmarks had been overthrown by the breaking up of the waters of the deep, when Europe was torn asunder by the wild passions evoked by the French Revolution, when to one party to be a reformer was to be a sansculotte, to the other party to maintain authority was to trample on the rights of man, a body of statesmen were found calm enough to take reason as their guide, and bold enough, in the teeth of the violent opposition of the privileged classes, to legislate à priori, and on general principles.

* Strange to say, this was an error; villeinage had at that time *not* ceased in all the domains of the Crown.

The interest which attaches to the edict of 1807 is greatly enhanced by an acquaintance with the deliberations of the commission from which it emanated. In that commission two parties had been hotly opposed to each other. The party of the pure economists, whose great object was to establish the most absolute freedom of exchange, both in land and labour, and who had an almost superstitious belief in the results which would flow from the application of capital to land as a consequence of this absolute freedom, and a party who, though equally zealous in their desire for reform, feared the disintegration which might result from this process, and were imbued with the Prussian traditions of the supremacy of the State over all the relations of its members, and impressed with the necessity of keeping intact the social foundations of the Prussian monarchy.

The disciples of Adam Smith, on the whole, carried the day, as the wording of the edict, every sentence of which breathes the spirit of free exchange and the liberation of productive forces, amply proves. On one point, however, connected with paragraphs 6 and 7, the opposite views, and this by the direct interposition of Stein, obtained a partial victory.

The point at issue in connection with this paragraph is one of great importance, as it involved one principal element of the controversy which raged in the commission, and is concerned with a principle on which opinion is at the present more than ever divided. It may, in its most abstract form, be thus stated. Should it be the object of the State to stimulate the community it represents to the production of the maximum of producible wealth irrespectively of the instruments by which it is produced, in other words, irrespectively of the distribution of that wealth; or should it have an eye to the distribution of that wealth as well as to its production? In the particular case under discussion it took this form: Should the State by its legislation stimulate the creation of large farms worked with corresponding capital, or should it, on the contrary, endeavour to retain the actual peasant cultivators, and only raise their personal status and increase their material well-being ?

The economists were imbued with the ideas of Arthur Young, and the English farming system was the ideal they had in view. Why, asks Schön, waste the productive force of four proprietors and sixteen horses to do that which one proprietor and six horses can do better? Because, was the answer probably returned, though the actual answer is not recorded, in a country like Prussia, whose existence depends on its fighting power, the wealth of the country could not for national purposes take a better form than that of the three additional proprietors and the ten additional horses.

The moment was singularly adapted for a change from the one system to the other. The whole country was suffering from the devastation caused by the French invasion. Whole villages were lying in ashes, whole tracts were depopulated. The landlords were bound to restore the farm-buildings of the peasantry to their former state. Now, therefore, was the moment for consolidation. Give them the right of re-entry on the peasant land, or, at all events, allow them to amalgamate small holdings into large.

Paragraph 6 of the edict admits the principle, thus abrogating the very stringent laws above referred to against the extinction of peasant holdings ; but confines its application to exceptional cases, the Provincial Government, and not the individual landlord being the judge in each particular case.

In the Instruction to the Provincial Governments, the rule was laid down that the permission to extinguish peasant holdings should only be given in regard to so-called new land : *i. e.*, land created peasants' land, that is, let out in peasant tenures during the last fifty years ; and that even in this case the permission should only be granted upon the condition that half the land proposed to be changed into demesne land should be made into comparatively large peasant holdings, and either given in fee simple to peasant holders, or let on perpetual leases.*

* It was necessary to call attention to this conflict between the statesmen

The Legislation of 1811.

The edict of 1807, great and incisive as had been its operation, was of a negative kind. It removed disabilities, undid the shackles which bound the peasant to the glebe, allowed such rights as existed to be used freely, and pulled down the walls which separated from each other the different classes of society. But it created no new forms of property ; it proclaimed freedom of exchange, but it did not provide the title-deeds required as the first condition of exchange. Peasants' land could now be held indiscriminately by all the citizens of the State ; but it was still held under the old forms of tenure; there were still two "dominia." The lord was still owner of the peasants' land, but had no right to its possession. The peasant was free, but was not master of his labour.

The legislation of 1811 stepped in to remedy this state of things, and applying to the monarchy generally the principles which during the last three years had proved in the highest degree successful when applied to the State

and the economists because it has been much commented upon and because the great name of Stein is immediately connected with it. Much misconception, however, exists on the subject. The prevalent idea is that it was by the direct interposition of the Prussian Government acting through the instrumentality of the instruction referred to in the text that the all-important class of peasant proprietors has been kept up. But this is wholly erroneous. The restrictions of the edict of 1807 remained in vigour for only a very short time, having been set aside by the edict of 1811. The point is one of great importance inasmuch as one of the most valuable precedents in favour of peasant proprietorship would lose its value if it could be established that these Prussian peasant proprietors had been artificially maintained by means of State interference. One of the commonest arguments used in England against small properties is that they cannot maintain themselves by the side of large properties, and that where free exchange in land is the rule, the large properties will invariably swallow up the small; consequently, that if small proprietors are a desideratum, there must be a law of compulsory division of property as in France, or some special State interference "ad hoc" as is supposed to exist in Prussia, in order to keep them up. The example of Prussia, on the contrary, tends to establish exactly the reverse, for there, with the most absolute rights of alienation on the part of the peasant proprietors, and with their immediate proximity to large and mostly curtailed estates, they have fully maintained their position. Strenuous attempts were made in 1824 and 1834 to curtail the liberty of alienation and dismemberment conferred by the edict of 1811, but the result of careful inquiries made into the subject by the Government triumphantly established the fact that none of the ill effects had arisen out of this freedom of exchange which its enemies supposed.

domains, it set itself to substitute allodial ownership for feudal tenure.

Its work was in the highest degree positive.

The legislation of 1811 mainly consists of two great edicts, both bearing the same date, that of the 14th of September. The one entitled, "Edict for the Regulation of the Relations between the Lords of the Manor and their Peasants."

The other, "Edict for the better Cultivation of the Land."

The first is concerned with the creation of new title-deeds for the peasant holders, and with the commutation of the services rendered in virtue of the old title-deeds.

The second surveys the whole field of agrarian reform, and introduces general measures of amelioration.

The preamble to the "Edict for the Regulation of the Relations between Landlord and Tenant" recites how "We, Frederick William, by the grace of God, King of Prussia, having convinced ourselves, both by personal experience in our own domains, and by that of many lords of manors, of the great advantages which have accrued both to the lord and to the peasant by the transformation of peasant holdings into property, and the commutation of the services and dues on the basis of a fair indemnity, and having consulted, in regard to this weighty matter, experienced farmers, and skilled persons of all kinds belonging to all our provinces, and to all ranks of our subjects, ordain and decree as follows:"

The edict then branches off into two main parts.

The first dealing with peasant holdings in which the tenant has hereditary rights; the second with holdings in which the tenant has no hereditary rights.

PART I.

All tenants of hereditary holdings—*i. e.*, holdings which are inherited according to the common law, or in which the lord of the manor is bound to select as tenant one or other of the heirs of the last tenant—*whatever the size of the holding,* shall by the present edict become the proprietors of their holdings, after paying to the landlord the indemnity fixed by this edict.

On the other hand, all claims of the peasant on the manor, for the keeping in repair of his farm-buildings, &c., shall cease.

We desire that landlords and tenants should of themselves come to terms of agreement, and give them two years from the date of this edict to do so. If within that time the work is not done, the State will undertake it.

The rights to be commuted may be thus generally classed :—

I. Rights of the landlord.
  1. Right of ownership (" dominium directum ").
  2. Claim to services.
  3. Dues in money and kind.
  4. Dead stock of the farms.
  5. Easements, or servitudes on the land held.

II. Rights of the tenant.*
  1. Claim to assistance in case of misfortune.
  2. Right to gather wood, and other forest rights, in the forest of the manor.
  3. Claim upon the landlord for repairs of buildings.
  4. Claim upon the landlord, in case tenant is unable to pay public taxes.
  5. Pasturage rights on demesne lands or forests.

Of these different rights only a few, viz., the dues paid in kind or money, the dead stock, and the servitudes, are capable of exact valuation.

The others can only be approximately estimated.

To obtain therefore a solid foundation for the work of commutation, and not to render it nugatory by difficulties

---

  * It is worthy of remark that the tenant's " dominium utile," or right of possession, is not recorded as a set-off against the dominium directum of the lord of the manor. The fact is, this right of possession is something so self-understood, that it never seems present to the mind of the legislator. The " dominium directum " is something quite different, for it represents an aggregation of all kinds of different rights. These rights he has to sell to the peasant, and the peasant buys them with the only thing he possesses, viz., his land.

impossible to be overcome, we deem it necessary to lay
down certain rules for arriving at this estimate, and to
deduce those rules from the general principles laid down
by the laws of the State.

These principles are :

1. That in the case of hereditary holdings, neither the
   services nor the dues can, under any circumstances, be raised.

2. That they must, on the contrary, be lowered if the
   holder cannot subsist at their actual rate.

3. That the holding must be maintained in a condition
   which will enable it to pay its dues to the State.

From these three constitutional principles, as well as
from the general principles of public law, it follows that
the right of the State, both to ordinary and extraordinary
taxes, takes precedence of every other right, and that
the services to the manor are limited by the obligation
which the latter is under to leave the tenant sufficient
means to subsist and to pay taxes.

We consider that both these conditions are fulfilled
when the sum-total of the dues and services rendered
to the manor do not exceed one-third of the total
revenue derived by an hereditary tenant from his holding.
Therefore, with the exceptions to be hereafter described,
the rule shall obtain :

That in the case of hereditary holdings the lords of
the manor shall be indemnified for their rights of ownership in the holding, and for the ordinary services and
dues attached to the holding, when the tenants shall have
surrendered one-third portion of all the lands held by
them, and shall have renounced their claims to all extraordinary assistance, as well as to the dead stock, to
repairs, and to the payment on their behalf of the dues
to the State when incapable of doing so.

The edict then goes on to lay down the rules to be
observed in applying this principle.

These rules presuppose the existence of the agricultural
community referred to in the earlier part of this Paper,
viz., equal allotments in an arable mark : the division
of the arable mark in which these several allotments are

situated into three " *Commonable Fields* " or " Fluren :"
a common system of cultivation obligatory on the community, in order to secure the community's right of
pasture on the fallow and stubbles : and common rights
of property in common lands occupied "de indiviso,"
mostly pasture lands, woods, &c., but sometimes also
in arable common lands.

As the rule, the lord of the manor is to acquire possession of one of the three Fields, or of one-third portion
of each field, and of one-third portion of the common
lands.

We have no space to enter into the details of the
arrangements which provide for the cases differing from
these.

As noted above, the lords and the peasants are left
free to make what arrangements they please, as long as
the proportion of one-third is maintained, *i.e.*, the indemnity may take the form of a payment of capital, cr
of a corn or money rent. Yet the rule to be followed (and
a departure from this rule must have a distinct motive)
is that the indemnity must be paid in land where the
holdings are over fifty " morgen,"* but in the shape of a
corn-rent where the holdings are under that size.

As a matter of practical convenience to both parties,
the absolute separation of proprietary rights suffers some
few exceptions : the first and most important is that the
lord retains the right of pasturing the manorial sheep on
two-thirds of the fallow and stubbles of the arable
mark ;† the peasant also continues to enjoy the right
of collecting as much firewood in the demesne as he requires for his personal use : for this right and for the
acquisition of his house and farm-buildings as well as
his garden-plot (his allotment in the mark of the township), he continues to render services to the lord of the
manor at times (*e. g.*, harvest) when extra hands are
wanted. These services are, however, restricted to a
maximum of ten days of team-work, and ten days of

* The Prussian acre is about equal to two-thirds of an English acre, an
hundred English acres being equal to 158½ Prussian acres.

† Compare Rogers' ' History of Agriculture and Prices in England,' vol. i.
p. 31.

hand-labour for a team-peasant, and ten days man's work and ten days woman's work for a hand-peasant.

Several paragraphs of the edict are taken up with provisions for so apportioning the burdens on the holdings that nothing shall prevent their dismemberment and being sold or exchanged in single parcels. Among these provisions is one preventing the peasant from mortgaging his estate above one-fourth of its value.

Where corn rents are not paid punctually, the lord of the manor can exact services instead.

PART II.

The class of holdings treated of in the second part, are those held at will, or for a term of years or for life. In these cases the landlord gets an indemnity of one-half of the holding under much the same conditions as in the case of the hereditary holdings. When the conditions differ, they do so in favour of the lord of the manor.

By the edict, of which the above are the main provisions, entirely new conditions of land occupation were inaugurated, and corresponding changes became necessary in the other branches of the agricultural system.

The "Edict for the better Cultivation of the Land," published on the same day, had these changes in view.

Fully to understand what these changes were, and what was the nature of the agricultural reforms to be introduced into Prussia, the picture of the peasant community as a microcosmic reproduction of the old community of the mark must be kept in mind. The peasant occupier's tenement is situated, apart from his land, in a village or township ; his estate is made up of a number of single lots or parcels (Grundstücke) distributed over the three main divisions or *Fields* (Fluren, Campi) into which the arable mark is divided. Often intermixed with these peasant parcels, and subject to the same obligatory cultivation, are parcels of demesne lands. In addition to his individual rights of possession in the arable mark, controlled by the common rights of pasturage on the stubbles, he has common rights in the common pasture, which common rights he shares with the lord of the manor. Besides these rights he has rights of pasture, &c., in the forest lands of the demesne proper. The sum total of these individual and common rights make up the peasant holding, correlative to which are the services to be rendered to the manor. As long as these services were calculated on the sum total of the rights enjoyed by the tenant, it was of paramount importance that no dismemberment should take place. Consequently, even in the case of free-holders, none but exceptional dismemberments were allowed.

Apart then from the relations between landlord and tenant, or rather inseparably implicated in those re-lations, and therefore requiring simultaneous regulation, are the *common rights* of the peasants themselves, and the impediments which these common rights throw in the way of individual cultivation, and the free use of the rights of property about to be granted.

The ruling idea of the " Edict for the better Cultivation of the Land," as of its predecessor, and indeed of the whole legislation connected with the names of Stein and Hardenberg, is to enfranchise not the owner of land merely, but likewise the land owned by him, and to remove every impediment in the way of the soil finding its way out of hands less able to cultivate it into those better able to cultivate it. Conformably to these principles, the edict in question, in the first place, removes all restrictions still existing in the way of free exchange in land, in so far as private rights (viz., rights arising from entails, servitudes, &c.) are not affected. By this proviso the restrictions contained in paragraphs 6 and 7 of the edict of 1807 were removed, the dif-ference between tenant's land and demesne land ceased, and the lord of the manor could freely acquire the former without the previous sanction of the State. On the other hand, by the perfect liberty granted for dis-memberment (the maxim being laid down that it was better both for the cultivator and for the land cultivated

that the former should administer a small unencumbered
estate rather than a large encumbered one), the advocates
of the "petite culture" were conciliated. The passage in
the Edict is worth quoting *in extenso,* as it contains very
explicitly what we have described as the ruling idea of
the legislation we are discussing : an idea, it is true,
which only attained its full development forty years
later, but which, nevertheless, in spite of the obstacles
thrown in its way by the successors of Stein and
Hardenberg, took sufficient root even at this early
period to enable us to judge of its fruits. It is the idea
of *ownership* versus *tenancy,* and of absolute freedom of
exchange and disposal ; and special importance attaches
to it as representing principles opposed both to the
French system of compulsory division, and to the
English system of tenancy, primogeniture, and strict
settlement. The passage we refer to runs on as follows :

"The proprietor shall henceforth (excepting always
where the rights of third parties are concerned) be at
liberty to increase his estate, or diminish it by buying
or selling, as may seem good to him. He can leave the
appurtenances thereof (the 'Grundstücke,' or parcels
distributed in the three *Fields*) to one heir or to many,
as he pleases. He may exchange them or give them
away, or dispose of them in any and every legal way,
without requiring any authorisation for such changes.

" This unlimited right of disposal has great and manifold advantages. It affords the safest and best means
for preserving the proprietor from debt, and for keeping
alive in him a lasting and lively interest in the improvement of his estate, and it raises the general
standard of cultivation.

"The first of these results is obtained by the power it
gives to the actual proprietor, or to an heir upon
entering on his estate, to sell such portions as will
enable him to provide for his heirs or co-heirs, as the
case may be, or for any other extraordinary emergency,
leaving what remains of the property unencumbered
with mortgages or settlements.

" The interest in the estate is kept alive by the freedom

left to parents to divide their estate amongst their children as they think fit, knowing that the benefit of every improvement will be reaped by them.

"Lastly, the higher standard of cultivation will be secured by land—which in the hands of a proprietor without means would necessarily deteriorate—getting into the hands of a proprietor with means, and therefore able to make the best of it. Without this power of selling portions of his property, the proprietor is apt to sink deeper and deeper into debt, and in proportion as he does so the soil is deprived of its strength. By selling, on the other hand, he becomes free of debt and free of care, and obtains the means of properly cultivating what remains to him. By this unhindered movement in the possession of land, the whole of the soil remains in a good state of cultivation; and this point once attained, increased industry and exertion will make it possible to attain a yet higher point, whereas a backward movement, except as the result of extraordinary mischances from without, is not to be apprehended.

"But there is yet another advantage springing from this power of piecemeal alienation which is well worthy of attention, and which fills our paternal heart with especial gladness. It gives, namely, an opportunity to the so-called small folk (Kleine Leute), cottiers, gardeners, boothmen, and day labourers, to acquire landed property, and little by little to increase it. The prospect of such acquisition will render this numerous and useful class of our subjects industrious, orderly, and saving, inasmuch as thus only will they be enabled to obtain the means necessary to the purchase of land. Many of them will be able to work their way upwards, and to acquire property, and to make themselves remarkable for their industry. The State will acquire a new and valuable class of industrious proprietors; by the endeavour to become such agriculture will obtain new hands, and by increased voluntary exertion more work out of the old ones."

The edict next enacts, as a supplementary measure to the "Edict for the Regulation of the Relations between

Lords of the Manor," that in the case of hereditary leaseholds (Erbpächte) the services and fines may be commuted into rent-charges, and these rent-charges redeemed
by a capital payment, calculated at four per cent.

It next proceeds to deal with the *common rights* of the
peasants and of the lords ; and here it fairly owns its
inability to carry out the principle of the free owner on
the free soil. The great mass of the peasant holdings
are dispersed in small open "commonable" intermixed
fields over the area of the arable mark ; and the common
rights of pasturage over the arable mark necessarily
chain down the individual cultivator to the modes of
cultivation compatible with these common rights. To
disentangle this complicated web must be the work of
time and of special legislation. The edict therefore
announces a future law on the subject, and for the
present confines itself to making provisions by which one
third part of such "commonable" fields can be freed from
the common rights of pasturage and placed at the
absolute disposal of individual proprietors. The rights of
pasturage in the forest lands of the manor are more
easily disposed of ; the advantageous terms on which full
rights of property are obtainable by the peasants render
it possible to make stringent regulations in regard to the
exercise of those rights, in the interest of the landlord
and for the preservation of the forests.

To guard against the possibility of a return to the
double ownership system, the edict lays down the rule
that though a landed proprietor may settle labourers
on his estate, and pay for their services in land, such
contracts are never to be made for more than twelve
years.

The edict concludes by expressing it to be his
Majesty's wish and will that agricultural societies should
be formed in every part of the country, for the purpose
of collecting and diffusing knowledge. The expenses
of these societies, and the salaries of their secretaries,
will be paid out of the Exchequer, and the societies themselves will be placed in communication with a central
office in the capital, whose business it will also be to

Y

establish and maintain model farms in various parts of
the country for the diffusion of agricultural knowledge.
Besides this more or less unofficial machinery, provision
is made for official agricultural boards to be established
in each district; but these arrangements, having been
superseded by subsequent legislation, need not be referred to.

The two edicts of the 14th September, 1811, may be
considered as the culminating point of the legislation
which goes by the name of Stein and Hardenberg.

Two important laws, it is true, immediately connected
with the foregoing, were published in 1821, the one
having reference to the regulation of common rights, the
other to the commutation of servitudes into rent-charges,
and to the redemption of the latter. Our space does
not admit of our describing the former of these two laws,
all-important as is the question of these common rights,
and of the way they were dealt with, to a correct appre-
ciation of the agricultural system of Prussia. The
latter law was superseded by the much more drastic and
complete measure passed in 1850, and need not therefore be more particularly dwelt upon here.

That which it is of importance to bear in mind is that
these laws were the necessary complements of the foregoing legislation, and that unless this legislation had
been itself cancelled, it was impossible for these laws
not to have been passed. They were carried, as it were,
by the momentum of the Stein and Hardenberg legislation; but the impelling force which had imparted its
momentum to that legislation had died out long before,
and other forces had taken its place.

" Le nommé " Stein * had already, previously to the
edicts of 1811, been driven out of the service of the
Prussian crown by the mandate of Napoleon. Belonging to the class of statesmen to whom recourse is instinctively had in times of trouble, and from whom men

* " Le nommé Stein cherchant à exciter des troubles en Allemagne est
déclaré ennemi de la France. . . . . . . Il sera saisi de sa personne partout
où il pourra être atteint de nos troupes ou celles de nos alliés.
" En notre camp impérial de Madrid le 16 Décembre, 1808.—Napoleon."

who desire a quiet life, and who consider that sufficient
unto the day is the evil thereof, instinctively shrink
when the storm has passed by, he did not return to
office when the French were driven from the soil of
Germany.

We are not here concerned with his general schemes
of political reform, intimately as they are connected
with his agrarian legislation. It is sufficient to note
that what may be termed his structural reforms, with
the exception of the reform of the municipalities, remained in their draft form. The representative and
self-governing institutions, which were to replace the
jurisdiction of the manor and the " status pupillaris " in
which the peasant community stood towards the manor,
were never called into life, and are at this very moment
occupying the attention of the Prussian legislature.

What he did succeed in carrying through was the
reform of the Prussian administration, and the creation
of the ablest and the most patriotic bureaucracy which
ever weakened the plea for self-government by the plea
of good government. It was against the serried ranks
of this bureaucracy that the manorial reaction tried the
edge of its sword. At first on the prosaic ground of
vested interests, later on with the picturesque accom-
paniments of a mediæval revival. The completion of the
great work of agrarian reform was prevented and kept
in abeyance for upwards of a generation. Some of its
features even were grievously disfigured, but the massive
torso itself could not be moved from its place. Königsberg and Stein had engraved their mark indelibly on
the history of Prussia.

The most directly retrogressive step was the declaration of the 29th of May, 1816, which limited the action
of the " Edict for the Regulation of the Relations between
Lords of the Manor and their Peasants" to farms of a comparatively large size, without abrogating the provisions
of the " Edict for the better Cultivation of the Land "
which did away with the constitutional difference between
peasant's land and demesne land, and established the
principle of free trade in land. By the combined effect

Y 2

of these two principles the " so-called small folk," whom
the latter edict so ostentatiously took under its protection—*i. e.*, the great mass of small holders, who did not
cultivate with teams—were placed at a huge disadvantage, for where their tenures were hereditary, they
continued burdened with feudal services and dues ; where
they were not hereditary, they were evicted wholesale.

By a later declaration, in 1836, twenty-five Prussian
acres is fixed as the minimum of a holding having the
right to be enfranchised.

THE LEGISLATION OF 1850.

The legislation of 1850 was in the highest degree
prolific ; but we need only concern ourselves with the
two great laws of the 2nd of March.

1. The Law for the Redemption of Services and Dues
and the Regulation of the Relations between the Lords
of the Manor and their Peasants.

2. The Law for the Establishment of Rent Banks.

The former of these laws abrogated the "dominium
directum," or overlordship of the lords of the manor,
without compensation; so that from the day of its
publication all hereditary holders throughout the Prussian monarchy, irrespectively of the size of their
holdings, became proprietors, subject, however, to the
customary services and dues, which by the further provisions of the law were commuted into fixed money
rents, calculated on the average money value of the
services and dues rendered and paid during a certain
number of years preceding. By a further provision
these rent-charges were made compulsorily redeemable,
either by the immediate payment of a capital equivalent
to an 18 years' purchase of the rent-charge, or by a
payment of $4\frac{1}{2}$ or 5 per cent. for $56\frac{1}{12}$ or $41\frac{1}{12}$ years, on a
capital equivalent to 20 years' purchase of the rent-charge.

The law for the establishment of rent banks provided
the machinery for this wholesale redemption. By it the
State, through the instrumentality of the rent banks,
constituted itself the broker between the peasants by

whom the rents had to be paid, and the landlords who had to receive them.

The bank established in each district advanced to the latter in rent debentures, paying 4 per cent. interest, a capital sum equal to 20 years' purchase of the rent. The peasant, along with his ordinary rates and taxes, paid into the hands of the district tax collector each month one twelfth part of a rent calculated at 5 or $4\frac{1}{2}$ per cent. on this capital sum, according as he elected to free his property from encumbrance in $41\frac{1}{12}$ or $56\frac{1}{12}$ years, the respective terms within which at compound interest the 1 or the $\frac{1}{2}$ per cent., paid in addition to the 4 per cent. interest on the debenture, would extinguish the capital.

The account given of these rent banks in Mr. Hutton's pamphlet, p. 18, is so clear and exhaustive, that it would be lost labour to attempt to improve on it here.

The legislation of 1850 was no more than the efficacious application of the principles contained in the edict of 1811. At first sight, two new principles appear to have been introduced, viz., the absence of compensation for the " dominium directum," and the elimination of the principle of payments in land. But if we look at the matter more closely, these differences amount to little. The " dominium directum," as before observed, deprived of its material contents, i. e., of the services and dues, was absolutely valueless to the overlord, whilst, on the other hand, the immediate and simultaneous entrance into full proprietary rights on the part of the many thousands of holders who were affected by the law of the 2nd of March, was calculated to exercise a moral effect of the greatest magnitude.

As regards the non-commutation in land, it will be remembered that the edict of 1811 laid down the rule that the services of holdings less than fifty Prussian acres in size should be commuted in rent-charges only. Now it is probable that most of the holdings over this size had been redeemed prior to 1850, so that practically the law of the 2nd March had only to deal with the smaller kinds of holding, for which the commutation of services

by a rent-charge had been provided by the edict of 1811.
It was not by the newness of the principles, therefore,
but by the incomparably superior machinery for applying
the principles, that the legislation of 1850 established its
superiority over that of 1811, and obtained such much
larger results in comparatively so short a time.

Such in very rough outline is a sketch of the agrarian
legislation of Prussia during the present century. Neither
the space nor the time at our disposal have allowed us
to do more than attempt to point out its chief incidents,
and connect these with the general agricultural history
of the Teutonic race. The identity of this history in the
earlier stage of the several Teutonic communities, has
already been dwelt upon. Given this identity, it necessarily followed that at some time or other in the
development of each Teutonic community, the same problems presented themselves for solution. According
as they have been solved in one way or the other, the
entire social and political condition of the several communities has been modified. The organic change common
to all, and which constitutes, as it were, the turning-
point in their several histories, is that from cultivation
in common to cultivation by *individuals*, or, to use two
old English terms, from "champion country" to "severall." To the student of English history, the word
which corresponds to this change is "enclosure," the
true significance of which has, however, not always been
seized by either English or foreign writers on the subject.*
The great "enclosing" movement in the sixteenth century
is usually described as if it had merely had for its object
to turn arable land into pasture. Its importance as a
joint effort on the part of the lords of the manor to
withdraw their demesne lands from the "communion"
of the township has been overlooked. That this object
was in itself highly desirable, and the "conditio sine quâ
non" of any improvements in agriculture is undeniable;

---

* An invaluable contribution to the history of this complicated subject has
been made this year by Professor Nasse of Bonn, in a paper entitled 'Ueber
die Mittel alterliche Feldgemeinschaft und die Einhegungen des Sechszehnten
Jahr hundurts in England,' to which we refer any of our readers who may
doubt the conclusions we have come to in the following pages.

it was an organic change through which every Teutonic community had necessarily to pass. The evils which attended the process in England at the time referred to arose from the fact that instead of being effected by impartial legislation, as has been the case in Prussia during the present century, the change was forcibly brought about by the one-sided action of the landlords. Any one acquainted with the practical difficulties experienced in Germany in making analogous separations, will readily comprehend all the injustice which one-sided action in such a process on the part of the stronger must have implied. In the most favourable case, the withdrawal of, say, one-third,* or one-half of the land from the "commonable" arable land of a township, such half or third portion, be it remembered, consisting, in many cases, of small parcels intermixed with those of the commoners, must have rendered the further common cultivation impossible, and thereby compelled the freeholders and copyholders to part with their land and their common rights on any terms. That in less favourable cases the lords of the manor did not look very closely into the rights of their tenants, but interpreted the customs of their respective manors in the sense that suited them best, and that instead of an equitable repartition of land between the two classes, the result was a general consolidation of tenants' land with demesne land, and the creation of large enclosed farms, with the consequent wholesale destruction of agricultural communities or townships,† is well known to every reader of history.

* In a majority of cases the tenants' land in a manor was much in excess of the demesne land.

† Cf. Hen. VII. 4, cap. 19, "an acte against the pulling down of tounes." "Toune" is here used in its original sense, viz., as the equivalent not of a *walled* city, but of a *fenced*-in village—"villa," "villata." "Tun," which is the same word as the German "Zaun," means *fence*. The "tunskip" or township was therefore the enclosure within which the tenements of the community, with their garden lots, &c., were permanently fenced off from the unenclosed commonable mark. For the arable mark, as such, was unenclosed—the "Fields," "fluren," "campi," being only temporarily fenced in whilst the grain crops were growing and until they were harvested. Hence it was the *permanent* enclosing of the several lots held in the open unenclosed arable mark which constituted withdrawal from the community, and which, where it was done on a large scale, necessarily led to the break up of the "communion" of the township.

That the result of the newly-acquired liberty of agricultural operations was to increase sheep farming is equally well known ; but the two facts are usually brought into immediate connexion with each other, without reference being made to the primary fact which governs the two, viz., not the enclosure of arable land as such, but of " commonable " arable land.   The immense increase in stock, apparently without any diminution in the amount of corn grown (for during the period when the clamour against the enclosures was hottest, the price of corn remained uniformly low), was the result of the natural improvement in agriculture, caused by the change from " champion " to " severall," which enabled more produce of all kinds to be got out of the land with less labour.

We have called attention to this great crisis in English agriculture during the sixteenth century—1st. Because we believe that it affords the correct analogy to the Prussian agricultural crisis in the nineteenth century ; And, 2nd. Because the matter not only possesses great historical interest, but is still of practical importance ; for the change we have been describing was by no means completed in the sixteenth century.   Down to the present century, very large portions of England were still cultivated in common, on the old Three Field System,* and the work of enclosure is not done yet.

Now, speaking with all diffidence, we cannot but believe that legislators called upon to frame Enclosure Acts might find their task made easier to them by a knowledge of the principles and practice which during the last sixty years have been applied to similar legislation, not in Prussia only, but in every State of Germany.   England is the only Teutonic community (we believe we might say, the only civilized community now existing) in which the bulk of the land under cultivation *is not in the hands of small proprietors.* Clearly, therefore, England represents the exception, and not the rule ; and no exception can be understood without a knowledge of the rule.

* Cf. A Review of the Reports to the Board of Agriculture from the Midland department of England, by Mr. Marshall, York, 1815.

Three great countries—England, France,* and Germany—began their political life from a similar agricultural basis. In each of them the great conflict between *immunity* and *community*, between *demesne land* and *tenant* land, between the *manor* and the *peasant*, has had to be fought out.

In England the manor won; the peasant lost. In France the peasant won; the manor lost. In Germany the game has been drawn, and the stakes have been divided. Each system can be defended and passionately pleaded for. Each has much to be said for and against it.

We have not been able to do more than call attention to the general analogies of the question, hoping that some abler pen than ours may be tempted to take up the subject, and examine the land history of the United Kingdom in connexion with the land history of kindred nations.

Should our hope be realized, we shall feel that in an infinitesimal degree we shall have fulfilled our duty as members of the Cobden Club, and at least trimmed the lamp of international knowledge.

    *   *   *   *   *   *

Considering the object for which this volume of essays has been written, it may seem incumbent upon us before we come to a close to estimate how far the precedent afforded by Prussia is available for the purposes of Irish legislation.

We confess ourselves, however, unequal to a task which would presuppose a far different acquaintance with the agricultural relations of Ireland than any we possess.

All we can do is to hazard a review of the Irish land question from the standing ground which we can conceive a man, penetrated with the wisdom of the principles upon which the legislation of Prussia is founded, might occupy.

* Of course we do not class France as a Teutonic country, though its land institutions were of distinct Teutonic origin. It is probable that the Celto-Romanic elements which so soon overpowered the Teutonic elements of French society contributed to the solution of the conflict in the way peculiar to France.

1. The first thing which such a man would do would be to point out the impossibility of directly applying that legislation to the present state of Ireland. Turning as it does upon what the Germans call the "constitutional" difference between "demesne" land and "tenants'" land, in the mediæval acceptation of those terms, it could be applied directly only where that difference existed.

2. He would express in no measured terms his condemnation of a system of tenancy-at-will. Here we can speak *ex cathedrâ*, there being a remarkable paper extant in which Stein expresses his opinion on uncertain tenures.

3. He would probably set aside primogeniture, entails, and strict settlements. On large estates held by corporations he would look with no friendly eye. The "dead hand" fills him with peculiar horror. He everywhere wishes to see the living hand grasping the living soil.

4. He would insist on every rood of Irish land having a parliamentary title, and being transferable by a cheap and simple system of registration. His land and mortgage register deposited in each township with its accurate map of the district, would play an important part in his system.

5. When he came to examine the popular cry for *fixity* of tenure, he would, we are inclined to think, reject it absolutely. He would declare that it must lead to one of two things, either to the stereotyping of the system of *double ownership*, against which the whole legislation of Prussia is an emphatic protest, or to the eventual undivided ownership of the present tenants, *i.e.*, to the dispossession "en bloc" of the present proprietors. In the first case all the evils of double ownership would be aggravated by the peculiar tendencies of Irish agriculture. The tenant not having the passion for his land or the pride in it which ownership alone can give, would sublet and subdivide. The landlord, knowing that the rent due to him being a first charge on the estate, his interests, limited as they were, were safe, would look on with indifference and not interfere. In a word, the landlord would be divorced from the soil without the

tenant being married to it, and the evils of an illicit
union would be the natural result.   But the experience
of Prussia would have taught our imaginary critic that
where a variable rent is changed into a fixed rent charge,
even where the possibility exists of a periodical revision,
and of an increase at some future period in the amount
of the rent charge, the almost certain consequence is the
redemption of the rent charge by a payment of capital,
and he believes that this result would inevitably follow
in Ireland.   For supposing the periodical revision were
to take place every twenty or thirty years, what landlord
would hesitate to sell this reversionary right, and what
tenant would hesitate to buy it by any sacrifice in order
thus to enter into full proprietary rights ?   But the dispossession of the present proprietors and the substitution
of the actual tenants as the sole proprietary class, would
mean economically the withdrawal from the soil of the
class having the largest capital and enjoying the largest
credit ; and the reproduction in another shape of the
present evil of a class monopoly in the ownership of land.
One object of Prussian legislation was that *every* class
should participate in the rights and duties which flow
from property in land, and this object would be equally
defeated whichever was the monopolizing class.

6. Having rejected fixity of tenure and tenancy-at-
will, he would look to leases as the " tertium quid."   He
would require written contracts, in a form established
by law, but varying according to the modes of cultivation
in the various districts.   In the absence of such written
contract, the presumption of the law would be in favour of
the lease enjoined by the legal contract of the district,
the landlord having a right of eviction if he could prove
that the tenant had refused the legal contract.

7. He would next examine the question of improvements effected by tenants, and would establish Boards of
Arbitration, on the model of the Prussian General Commissions, but with juries composed equally of landowners
and tenants to decide questions of fact.   These boards
should determine what the value of such improvements
amounted to in each case.   This amount would con-

stitute a first charge upon the estate, and be registered
as such in the Land and Mortgage Register. It would be
left to the landlord and tenant to determine in what way
the debt should be extinguished; but a limit of time
within which the charge should be liquidated might be
fixed. Where the value of the improvements approached
or exceeded that of the fee-simple of the land, it would
be a question left to the parties, assisted by the Board of
Arbitration, to decide whether the landlord should buy
up the tenant's right, or the tenant the landlord's.

8. He would not be inclined to look with favour on
Ulster tenant right, at least where that right implied a
payment for the " good-will," in excess of the value of the
improvements made by the tenant or his predecessors, as
he would consider this another form of *double ownership.*
The Board of Arbitration would carefully discriminate
between the value of improvements and the value of the
good-will " per se ;" and would treat the former in the
way already suggested, whilst it would consider the
latter as a servitude on the estate, to be redeemed in
the manner most favourable to the landlord.

9. Having done his utmost to place the relations of
landlords and tenants on a satisfactory footing, and
having removed all difficulties in the way of free alienation, he would next occupy himself with the creation of
farmer proprietors, *i.e.,* of a middle-class proprietary.
Remembering the colonisation of waste lands by Frederick
the Great, he would see what was to be done in the way
of diminishing competition for land already under cultivation, by organized settlements on uncultivated lands,
keeping in view the fact that land, which it does not
pay to reclaim for the object of *rent*, will yield sufficient
returns when tilled as property. He would, in the next
place, by means of rent-banks, and on the Prussian
system of amortisation, facilitate every transaction by
which a landlord might desire to sell his property to his
tenants ; the rent-bank advancing the capital sum to the
landlord, and recouping itself out of a percentage added
to the rent. By means of the same machinery the
State, acting through the bank, would buy up all the

land that came into the market, and sell it to *occupiers*. The object of the State not being to make money, but to create proprietors without loss to itself, the principle of competition would not be allowed to act in these sales. Two conditions would have to be laid down : 1st, that the farm should be of sufficient size fully to maintain the proprietor and his family, according to the highest scale of comfort known in the district ; 2nd, that the intended proprietor should possess the necessary capital to work it. Where these conditions were fulfilled, the actual occupier would have the right of pre-emption. Where they were not fulfilled, he would have to be bought out, and the farm would be given to the candidate who fulfilled the conditions. Where several such candidates presented themselves with equal claims, the choice of the candidate would be decided by lot. On entering into possession, the future proprietor would have to sign a bond, by which he engaged, until he had paid up in full, neither to let nor sublet, to keep the farm-buildings in repair, &c. On his failure to fulfil these engagements, the bank would have a right to evict him on repayment of the rates already paid by him.

10. All these objects, he believes, would be attainable by use of the credit of the State, and without any cost to the taxpayers. Any spare sums of money derived from church property, or other sources, he would employ in establishing agricultural schools and model-farms in every part of the island, and in imparting an elementary knowledge of agricultural science to the national schoolmasters.

Such, we believe, is the kind of programme which our imaginary legislator, arguing from a general kind of Prussian analogy, and with only a general knowledge of the Irish Land Question, might recommend.

It must not be forgotten, however, that being, under the hypothesis of the case, a foreigner, he is, on the one hand, unacquainted with the political difficulties of the question, and, on the other hand, possessed of that belief in the omnipotent and beneficent action of the *State*, which it would not be easy to impart to an Englishman.

VI.

THE LAND SYSTEM OF FRANCE.

T. E. Cliffe Leslie.

The object of this essay is to describe the Land System of France in respect of the distribution of landed property in that country, with the rural organization in which it results, and to examine its causes and effects. In considering its causes, laws and customs relating to property (including succession and transfer), and to tenure, of necessity form prominent objects of inquiry ; but their operation is so bound up with that of economical causes and conditions, that we should miss in place of obtaining clearness by separating what may be termed the legal from the economical class of subjects of discussion. It ought, too, to be premised that although political causes, in that narrow sense of the word which relates merely to the constitution and action of the State, do not fall within the scope of the present essay, yet the fact of their existence ought not to be altogether ignored. There are such causes, and their disturbing influence is powerful. A striking illustration of the potency of this class of causes is afforded in the fact that M. Léonce de Lavergne, in his celebrated work on the 'Rural Economy of Great Britain,' refers the progress of English agriculture during the last two hundred years, in the main, directly or indirectly, to political institutions, political liberty, and political tranquillity. The influences and effects of the French land system cannot then be fairly estimated without taking into consideration matters excluded by the non-political character of these pages. On the other hand, it will be pertinent and material to their purpose to show that much which is commonly ascribed in this country to political causes (in that wider sense which comprehends all the institutions of a country, especially those relating to property in land), as the chief agencies regulating the division of the soil in France, and the modes of its cultivation, are in reality traceable to the natural play of economic forces, aided, indeed, by the law of France, but not the part of it supposed.

The contrast between the land systems of France and England, two neighbouring countries at the head of civilization, may, without exaggeration, be called the most extraordinary spectacle which European society offers for study to political and social philosophy. The English census of 1861 returned 30,766 landowners and 249,461 farmers.* The latest official statistics in France,† on the other hand (following an enumeration of 1851, now in arrear of the actual numbers), reckon no less than 7,845,724 "proprietors," including the owners of house property in towns—a number which may be assumed to denote the existence of eight million such proprietors now. Of these, according to the computation of M. de Lavergne, about five millions are "rural proprietors," of whom nearly four millions are actual cultivators of the soil. The official tables themselves return no fewer than 3,799,759 landowners as cultivators, of whom 57,639 are represented as cultivating by means of head-labourers or stewards, as against 3,740,793 cultivating their land *de leur mains.* This last figure is again subdivided into 1,754,934 landowners cultivating only their own land; 852,934 who, in addition to their own, farm land belonging to others as tenants, and 1,134,190 who work also as labourers for hire. But these figures, as already remarked, are now in arrear; and we may accept as a close approximation to the actual situation the following estimate by M. de Lavergne:—" Of our five millions of small rural proprietors, three millions possess on the average but a hectare‡ a-piece. Two millions possess

* Farmers:—Men, 224,066; Women, 22,916. Graziers, 2,449.
† 'Statistique de la France. Agriculture, 1868' (Résultats Généraux de l'Enquête Décennale de 1862).
‡ Not quite two acres and a half.

on the average six hectares. . . . . Two million independent rural proprietors, a million tenant farmers or métayers, and two million farmers and servants themselves, as well as the million farmers, for the most part proprietors of land ; such is approximately the composition of our rural population."*

It would hardly diminish the contrast of such statistics to our own, were we, in place of less than thirty-one thousand landowners, returned in our own census, to adopt the figure which M. de Lavergne has introduced into his 'Rural Economy of Great Britain,' on the authority of a statement made by an unofficial member of the House of Commons during a debate—a figure which has often since been reproduced in England on the authority of M. de Lavergne himself—namely, that there are 250,000 owners of land in the country ; although it ought to be noticed that there is reason to believe an error respecting the meaning of the technical term "freeholders" was involved in this calculation, and, moreover, that it includes a number of suburban freeholds, and by consequence an urban, not a rural class of proprietors, far less actual cultivators of land of their own.

Four millions of landowners cultivating the soil of a territory only one-third larger than Great Britain, may probably appear to minds familiar only with the idea of great estates and large farms almost a *reductio ad absurdum* of the land system of the French. Those, on the other hand, who have studied the condition of the French cultivators not merely in books, but in their own country, and who have witnessed the improvements which have taken place in it and in their cultivation year after year, will probably regard the number with a feeling of satisfaction. One thing, at least, is established by it, that property in land is in France a national possession ; that the territory of the nation belongs to the nation, and that no national revolution can take place for the destruction of private property.

But the inquiry proper to the present pages leads us to examine, in the first place, the causes of so wide a

* 'Economic Rurale de la France,' last edition.

Z

distribution of landed property in France, and, secondly, its economic rather than its political effects. Its economic effects will prove on examination to be in fact its principal cause. The notion commonly entertained in England appears, however, to be, that, originating in the confiscations of the French Revolution, the subdivision of the soil has been not only perpetuated but increased in a geometrical progression by the law of succession established by the Code Napoléon. That it did not originate with the Revolution, and that an immense number of peasant properties existed in France long prior to 1789, is indeed well known to all students of French social history; and those who have not concerned themselves with that side of history will find the fact fully substantiated in the introduction to M. de Lavergne's 'Economie Rurale de la France.' The point which calls for notice here is that, centuries before the Revolution of 1789, one of the causes of the subdivision of land in France (one which we shall find to be the chief cause in our own time) was its acquisition by purchase in small parcels by the French peasantry.

"I have in my hands." says M. Monny de Mornay, in his general report on the results of the recent Enquête Agricole, "contracts of purchase by peasants of parcels of land of less than twenty *ares* (that is to say, less than half an acre) commencing prior to the close of the sixteenth century." It was not the lack of landed property that left the peasantry of France in destitution, and drove them to furious vengeance two hundred years later; it was the deprivation of its use by atrocious misgovernment, and the confiscation of its fruits by merciless taxation and feudal oppression. But in England, also, the number of small landholders at the close of the sixteenth century was still very large, though it had once been much larger; even at the date of the French Revolution it was considerable; and in 1815 (at which date it is calculated that there were 3,805,000 landowners in France), it was, although it had steadily declined, a more significant figure than it is now. In France, on the contrary, the number has increased to about four millions engaged in the actual cultivation of the soil, in addition to nearly a million other small rural proprietors, who are the owners, at least, of a cottage. We are not here engaged to inquire into the causes of the diminution, the disappearance, one may say, of small landowners in England; but the contrast between the movement which has been steadily adding to the number in France, and that which has extirpated them in England adds interest to an investigation of the nature and causes of the French agrarian economy. The results of such an investigation can hardly fail, moreover, to throw an indirect light upon the agrarian economy of England.

As already observed, the French law of succession, which limits the parental power of testamentary disposition over property to a part equal to one child's share, and divides the remainder among the children equally, is the cause commonly assigned in England for the continuous subdivision of land in France. And of an incontestable mischief in the operation of the French law, as regards the subdivision of separate parcels, there will be occasion to take notice hereafter. But a point of much greater importance is, that the real effects of the French law of succession cannot be understood without taking into account a process of subdivision taking place in France from a different cause, one really indeed traceable in part to the structure of French law, but not the law of succession; namely, continual purchases on the part of the peasantry of small estates or parcels of land. On this subject notaries in many different parts of France have given the writer surprising information in recent years; and it has indeed for many years been a subject of such common remark in the country, that even mere railway passengers through it can hardly have failed to have come upon evidence of it. M. Monny de Mornay states with respect to it, in the chapter of his report on the division of land: "The fact which manifests itself most forcibly is the profound and continuous alterations in the distribution of the soil among the different classes of the population. In the greater number of departments the estates of 100 hectares might now be easily counted;

z 2

and taken altogether they form but an insignificant part
of the national territory. The proportion cannot be
stated in figures, because it varies from one department
to another ; one must confine oneself to saying that the
west and south have preserved more large estates than
the north and east." The north and east, he might have
added, are the wealthiest and best-cultivated zones,
though the south is now rapidly improving in cultivation and wealth, and, as will presently be shown, the
process of subdivision keeps step with this improvement.
After referring to the disappearance of estates of even
moderate size, M. de Mornay proceeds :—" All that has
been lost to the domain of large estates, all that is lost
day by day to that of estates of middle size, small
property swallows up. Not only does the small proprietor round his little property year by year, but at
his side the class of agricultural labourers has been
enriched by the rise of wages, and accedes to landed
property in its turn. In the greater number of departments 75 per cent. at least of them are now become
owners of land. Peasant property thus embraces a
great part of the soil, and that part increases incessantly.
The price of parcels of land, accordingly, which are
within reach of the industry and thrift of the peasant,
increases at a remarkable rate. The competition of
buyers is active, and sales in small lots take place on
excellent terms for the seller, when the interval has
been sufficient to allow fresh savings to reaccumulate."
This is in some degree an official statement, and official
statements in France are sometimes suspected of
exaggerating the prosperity of the nation at large ; but
it is confirmed by a superabundance of unofficial and
unquestionable authority not on the side of Imperial
Government. In one of several passages to the same
effect, in his ' Economie Rurale de la France' and other
works, M. Léonce de Lavergne, for instance, says : " The
small proprietors of land, who, according to M. Rubichon,
were about three millions and a half in 1815, are at
this day much more numerous ; they have gained
ground, and one cannot but rejoice at it, for they have

won it by their industry." And in a very recent communication* to the present writer, M. de Lavergne
observes : " The best cultivation in France on the whole
is that of the peasant proprietors, and the subdivision of
the soil makes perpetual progress. Progress in both
respects was indeed retarded for a succession of years
after 1848 by political causes, but it has brilliantly
resumed its course of late years. All round the town in
which I write to you (Toulouse) it is again a profitable
operation to buy land in order to resell it in small lots.
. . . . I have just spent a fortnight near Beziers. You
could not believe what wealth the cultivation of the
vine has spread through that country, and the peasantry
have gotten no small share of it. The market price of
land has quadrupled in ten years. But for the duty on
property changing hands (*l'impôt des mutations*), and the
still heavier burden of the conscription, the prosperity of
the rural population of France would be great. It advances in spite of everything, in consequence of the high
prices of agricultural produce."

Along with the subdivision of landed property thus
taking place, there is also, as we shall see, a movement
in the land market towards the enlargement of peasant
properties, the consolidation of small parcels, and even in
some places towards the acquisition of what in France are
considered as large estates ; as, in like manner, contem-
poraneously with the subdivision of farms, and the more
minute cultivation of the soil, there is also a counter-
process of enlargement of little farms, and in some places
even a development of *la grande culture* on a splendid
scale. But it demands our inquiry first, what are the
causes, economic and legal, of the continual subdivision
by purchase of the soil in France ? The reader will
bear in mind with respect to it, that it is by no means a
mere subdivision of existing peasant properties ; that
small properties are gaining ground in the literal sense,
and increasing the breadth of their total territory as well
as their total number. And the continuous acquisitions
of land by purchase on the part of the French peasantry

* November 6, 1869.

and labouring classes can be palpably shown to be a perfectly natural and beneficial movement ; one proceeding, in the first place, from the natural tendencies of rural economy, from the mutual interest of buyers and sellers, from the growing prosperity and development of France, as its agriculture improves, as it is opened up by railways, roads, internal and foreign trade, manufactures, and mines, and as both country and town become wealthier ; proceeding again, in the second place, from, or at least promoted by, a sound and natural legal system ; facilitating dealings with land as the interests, inclinations, happiness, in a word, the good of the community direct.

One obvious consideration presents itself foremost, though too much stress must not be laid on it, that France has aptitudes of soil and climate for several kinds of agricultural produce—the vine, for example—for which *la petite culture*, in the form of manual cultivation (a form to which we shall see hereafter that *la petite culture* is by no means confined), is almost exclusively appropriate. Too much stress must not be laid on this fact, as just said ; for the amount of cultivated territory under such kinds of produce does not amount to one-fifteenth of the whole ; but it is a fact worth mentioning, on one hand as an indication, so far as it goes, of the chimerical nature of notions prevalent in England, even among excellent farmers, of the ruinous consequences to agriculture of the subdivision of the French soil, and on another hand as presenting a particular example of a general fact of immense importance in the inquiry ; namely, that the class of productions for which *la petite culture* is eminently adapted (whether exclusively, or in common with the large system of farming) is one for which the demand steadily increases with the growth of wealth, trade, and agriculture, and the prosperity of the inhabitants of both town and country, including the small cultivators themselves.

M. Léonce de Lavergne, in his ‘ Rural Economy of Great Britain,’ after remarking—and the remark is in itself one of no small importance and instructive sugges-

tion—that, " Capital being more distributed in France
than it is in England, it is expedient that the farms
should be smaller, to correspond with the working
capital," proceeds : " The extent of farms, besides, is
determined by other causes, such as the nature of the
soil, the climate, and the kinds of crops prevailing.
Almost everywhere the soil of France may be made to
respond to the labour of man, and almost everywhere
it is for the advantage of the community that manual
labour should be actively bestowed upon it. Let us
suppose ourselves in the rich plains of Flanders, or on
the banks of the Rhine, the Garonne, the Charente, or
the Rhone ; we there meet with *la petite culture*, but it is
rich and productive. Every method for increasing the
fruitfulness of the soil, and making the most of labour,
is there known and practised, even among the smallest
farmers. Notwithstanding the active properties of the
soil, the people are constantly renewing and adding to
its fertility by means of quantities of manure, collected
at great cost ; the breed of animals is superior, and the
harvests magnificent. In one district we find maize and
wheat; in another, tobacco, flax, rape, and madder ; then
again, the vine, olive, plum, and mulberry, which, to
yield their abundant treasures, require a people of laborious
habits. Is it not also to small farming that we owe
most of the market-garden produce raised at such great
expenditure around Paris ?" And further on (notwithstanding the favour which, in his love for political
liberty and order, M. de Lavergne regards everything in
the economy of England) he observes : " Our agriculture
may find in England useful examples ; but I am far from
giving them as models for imitation. The south of
France, for example, has scarcely anything to borrow
from English methods ; its agricultural future is nevertheless magnificent." This passage was written sixteen
years ago ; and a communication to the writer cited
above shows how the predictions it contains respecting
the south of France, and the great future before *la petite
culture*, are now being realized under the eyes of its
author. But it is not in the southern half alone of

France that the peasant cultivator finds a perpetually growing demand for all the most remunerative kinds of his produce. The 'Enquête Agricole,' for instance, shows a great increase in the cultivation of the vine in the east, the west, and the centre, as well as the south; while in the north—where the vine is, on the contrary, giving way before the competition of the plant of more favoured skies—the demand for the produce of the market-gardens, the dairy, and the orchard, afford more than a compensation. It deserves, moreover, passing remark that the little gardens and orchards round the cottages of the peasantry form, by reason of their careful and generous cultivation, the greater portion of the class of land which in French agricultural statistics obtains the denomination of *Terrains de qualité supérieure.* For dairy-husbandry, *la petite culture,* with its minute and assiduous attention, has such eminent aptitude, that even with respect to England, M. de Lavergne remarks: "Althoug hevery thing tends to proscribe small farming— though it has no support, as in France, from a small proprietary and a great distribution of capital—though the prevailing agricultural theories and systems of farming are opposed to it, yet it persists in some places, and everything leads to the belief that it will maintain its ground. The manufacture of cheese, for example, which is quite a domestic industry, is well adapted to it." He adds, what is not to be left out of account, for it is not an account merely of pounds, shillings, and pence: "There is nothing so delightful as the interior of these humble cottages; so clean and orderly, the very air about them breathes peace, industry, and happiness; and it is pleasing to think that they are not likely to be done away with."*

The raising and fattening of cattle for the market is another great department of husbandry which *la petite culture* has almost to itself in France; yet it must be confessed that it is—though a marked improvement is visible—not as yet generally carried on with the same skill as in Flanders; and the art of house feeding, which

* 'Rural Economy of Great Britain.'

is the basis of the Flemish system of small farming, is still in its infancy in many French districts : a fact, however, which only opens a brighter future for *la petite culture* within them.   And we may *à fortiori*—by reason on the one hand of the hold small farming has already established over both the territory and the mind of France, and, on the other hand, of the more recent development of manufactures, means of communication, and commerce—apply the language which Mr. Caird has used with respect to England: "The production of vegetables and fresh meat, forage, and pasture for dairy cattle, will necessarily extend as the towns become more numerous and more populous.   The facilities of communication must increase this tendency.   An increasingly dense manufacturing population is yearly extending the circle within which the production of fresh food, animal, vegetable, and forage, will be needed for the daily and weekly supply of the inhabitants and their cattle ; and which, both on account of its bulk and the necessity of having it fresh, cannot be brought from distant countries. Fresh meat, milk, butter, vegetables, &c., are articles of this description ; and there is a good prospect of flax becoming an article in excessive demand, and therefore worthy of the farmer's attention.   Now all these products require the employment of considerable labour, very minute care, skill, and attention, and a larger acreable application of capital than is requisite for the production of corn.   This will inevitably lead to the gradual diminution of the largest farms, and the gradual concentration of the capital and attention of the farmer on a smaller space."*   Thus the very productions for which *la petite culture* is specially adapted are the things getting new markets with every new railway, road, manufacture, mine, and increase of national wealth ; and that ascent of rural prices in France which M. Victor Bonnet has shown to be the result of its economic development is in effect an ascent in the economic scale of peasant property and the little farm.   It follows that the subdivision of the French soil, which has been the subject of sincere regret

* Caird's ' English Agriculture.'

and pity on the part of many eminent English writers
and speakers, as well as of much ignorant contempt on
the part of prejudiced politicians, is really both a cause
and an effect of the increased wealth of every class of
the population, the seller and the buyer of land, the
landowner, the farmer, and the labourer, the country
and the town.   Instead of being, as has been supposed, a
cause of low wages, it has been a consequence of high
wages, which have enabled the labourer to become a
land-buyer—and even a cause of high wages by diminishing the competition in the labour market, and placing
the labourer in a position of some independence in making
his bargains with employers.   Instead of diminishing
agricultural capital, as many English agriculturists urge,
it is, in the language of Adam Smith, both cause and
effect of "the frugality and good conduct, the uniform,
constant, and uninterrupted effort of every man to better
his own condition, from which public as well as private
opulence is derived, and which is frequently powerful
enough to maintain the natural tendency of things
towards improvement, in spite both of the extravagance
of Government and the greatest errors of administration."

But, assuming it to be demonstrable that the subdivision of land in France is in the main the result of
natural and beneficial economic causes, it is certain,
nevertheless, that it could not take place without the
co-operation of legal causes, that is to say, of a legal
system which renders dealings in land simple and safe,
and, by comparison with the English system, inexpensive.   In the absence of natural economic tendencies
towards the subdivision of land by its purchase in small
lots, the best-constructed legal system of transfer would
only tend to its accumulation in few hands; but, on the
other hand, under such a legal system as our own, whatever
the natural tendencies of the market, the expense, difficulty, and risk of buying very small estates would make
them an altogether unsuitable and impracticable investment for the savings of the peasant and the labourer.   Even
under a law of succession like the French, there could be

no such poor man's land market in England ; the properties partitioned by inheritance would be rapidly added to the domain of the great landowner and the millionaire, able to run the risk of litigation and to procure the best legal assistance.　In France, every sale and every mortgage of land is immediately inscribed in a public registry in the *chef-lieu* of the *arrondissement ;* and any one has a right to enter and inspect the register, to satisfy himself respecting the title to any estate or parcel of land, and the charges, if any, upon it.　The director of the registry is, moreover, bound to deliver for a trifling charge a statement of the title to every estate or parcel to any one demanding it.　The private charges for the assistance of the notary in effecting a purchase vary indeed considerably, and are very much heavier in proportion on very small parcels than on large estates.　Every sale of land is moreover burdened with the much-complained-of duty of above 6 per cent.*　But the transaction is simple, expeditious, and secure ; and the fact that, in spite of heavier relative cost, high taxation, and the competition of public loans and other investments, the peasant is the great buyer of land in France, only strengthens the conclusion that the subdivision of land by the purchase of small estates is a natural and healthy tendency of the market, springing from the high profits of *la petite culture,* and at the same time from the happiness and independence which the possession of land is found by the experience of the people at large to confer.　It shows, too, the error of a common impression in England, that it is much better for a cultivator to rent a larger farm than to farm a small estate of his own.　If there be any truth in English political economy, the buyers of land in France are the best judges of their own interests ; and we have the practical testimony of the whole nation that the small estate is the better investment of the two for capital and labour.　But, moreover, under a sound system of title, and of registration of mortgages, the peasant proprietor is not debarred from increasing the size of his farm ; he can raise money expeditiously and safely on

---

* 6f. 0·5c. per 100f., inclusive of the *decime de guerre.*

his own little property, and farm adjoining land as a tenant, should he find it to his advantage. The French land system gives the small buyer of land the benefit of being able to raise capital on unexceptionable security, and that by a process which creates no impediment to its subsequent sale. And such a system, so far from tending to increase the encumbrances on land, tends necessarily, in the first place, to bring land into the hands of those who can make most of it, and secondly, to enable them to develop its resources by additional capital, and thereby to liberate it from any charges upon it.

The amount of debt on the peasant properties of France has been enormously exaggerated. M. de Lavergne estimates it at 5 per cent. on an average on their total value ; and the marked improvement in the food, clothing, lodging, and appearance of the whole rural population is of itself unmistakable evidence that they are not an impoverished class, but, on the contrary, one rapidly rising in the economic and social scale. M. de Lavergne himself arrived at the conclusion that the great estates of England were more heavily encumbered acre for acre than the peasant properties of France ; and Mr. Caird concludes his description of English agriculture thus : "There is one great barrier to improvement which the present state of agriculture must force on the attention of the legislature—the great extent to which landed property is encumbered. In every county where we found an estate more than usually neglected, the reason assigned was the inability of the proprietor to make improvements on account of his encumbrances. We have not data by which to estimate with accuracy the proportion of land in each county in this position, but our information satisfies us that it is much greater than is generally supposed. Even where estates are not hopelessly embarrassed, landlords are often pinched by debt, which they could clear off if they were enabled to sell a portion, or if that portion could be sold without the difficulties and expense which must now be submitted to. If it were possible to render the transfer of land nearly as cheap and easy as that of stock in the funds, the value of English property would be greatly increased. It would simplify every transaction both with landlord and tenant. Those only who could afford to perform the duties of landlords would then find it prudent to hold that position. Capitalists would be induced to purchase unimproved properties for the purpose of improving them and selling them at a profit. A measure which would not only permit the sale of encumbered estates, but facilitate and simplify the transfer of land, would be more beneficial to the owners and occupiers of land, and to the labourers in this country, than any connected with agriculture that has yet engaged the attention of the legislature." Such a measure the owners, occupiers, and labourers of France have long had the benefit of; and the fact that in spite of new opportunities of migration and of steadily rising wages, even the labourer in France is a great land buyer, proves the profitableness of *la petite culture*, as well as the wealth of the very humblest and poorest class of the French peasantry. Imagine the English agricultural labourers great buyers of land, and at the same time lending no small sums to the State! One ought, too, to bear in mind, at the same time, the different histories of the two countries, and the condition in which the tyranny, misgovernment, and wars of preceding centuries had left the rural population of France half a century ago, not to speak of later political disasters. Far from objecting to the subdivision of land which has resulted from the legal facilities for its transfer and mortgage, the highest French authorities are urgent for the removal of the obstacles created by the high duties on both sales and successions. " Instead of placing obstacles in the way of changes of ownership (*mutations**), the true policy would be to encourage them. In addition to the direct taxation on land (*l'impôt foncier*), landed property is subject to the much heavier burden on changes of ownership. The value of immovable property annually sold may be estimated at 80,000,000*l.*; that which changes hands by succession at 60,000,000*l.*;

---

* The term *mutations* is applied to all changes of ownership, whether by purchase or inheritance.

the duties charged upon both amounting to 8,000,000*l.* Such taxation is contrary to every principle, falling as it does on capital and not on revenue."* We are not here concerned with the policy of duties on succession; but there is one incontrovertible injustice in their incidence in France which deserves notice: namely, that the successor pays duty on the entire value of the property, without any deduction for encumbrances, so that it sometimes happens that he actually pays more than the full value of his inheritance. This monstrous system of valuation offers, of course, a great obstacle to raising capital for the improvement of land; while it adds not a little to the encumbrances already upon it; the sort of encumbrances added (sums borrowed to liquidate the duties) being moreover entirely unproductive to the owners.

There are, then, two causes of the subdivision of land in the structure of French law—the law of transfer and the law of succession. But the fact that the subdivision promoted by one of these—the law of transfer—is in perfect accordance with the interests of all parties concerned, and the natural tendencies of agriculture in a country of growing wealth suggests a very important conclusion respecting the other, namely, the law of succession. It enables us to perceive why this latter does not produce the practical mischiefs many English writers, not unnaturally, have assumed. The fact is, that (except as regards its operation upon separate parcels, where the property consists of such—a mischief easily cured in the opinion of the highest French authorities) the French law of succession tends in the main to the same result as the natural course of agriculture and free trade in land, namely, the subdivision of land. Secondly, the operation of a good law of transfer tends to cure whatever mischiefs really arise from the partitions effected by the law of succession; there being a steady flow of small lots through the land market towards those who can turn them to the best account. Lastly, it is established

* ' Economie Rurale de la France,' par M. de Lavergne.

beyond dispute that peasant property arrests an excessive partition of land among children by imposing
a check upon population. "The law of succession,"
observes M. de Lavergne, " is still the object of some
attacks, which do not succeed in shaking it. It cannot
be said of a country which contains 50,000 properties of
more than 200 hectares that the soil is subdivided to
excess. It is enough to read the advertisement columns of
the daily papers to see that lands of several hundred,
and even several thousand, hectares are still numerous.
There are even too many of them, in the sense that the
majority of the owners would be gainers by dividing
them."* Of smaller properties, again, of only six hectares
on the average (of which he reckons two millions), the
same authority adds : " The owners of these live in real
comfort. Their properties are divided by inheritance ;
but many of them are continually purchasing, and on
the whole they tend more to rise than to fall in the scale
of wealth." In place of suggesting a radical change in
the law of inheritance, he, like most French economists,
suggests only a modification of it in the case of a
number of separate parcels, together with a great
reduction of the duty on their exchange, which at
present is the same as on a sale. Rational opponents in
England of the French law of partition (that is to say,
those who are in favour of a greater liberty of bequest,
as distinguished from those who defend our own barbarous system of primogeniture and entail) ought to
take into account that the French law of succession
really effects, in the main, the very results which the
testamentary powers they advocate would produce ; as
is evident from the fact that the vast majority of French
parents do not exercise the limited power they already
possess over a part equal to one child's share. But the
main point is that already adverted to—that a good law
of transfer corrects a defective law of inheritance. Not
only is there a continual enlargement of little peasant
properties by the purchase of adjoining plots, as well as
a continual accession to the number of small plots

* ' Economic Rurale de la France.'

through the natural play of the market; but there is
even a natural flow of large capitals toward the land.
Hence M. Monny de Mornay remarks that, notwithstanding the great diminution of the total domain of
large property, and the perpetual increase in the number
of little estates through the purchases of the peasantry
and the labouring class, there has been for some years a
current of ideas and tastes on the part of unemployed
men of fortune, and of capitalists enriched by the trade
of towns, towards investment in landed property.* The
truth is that large and small property compete on much
fairer and more natural terms in France than in England,
and large buyers of land as well as small, in the former
country, are free from burdens on the pursuit of their
interests and happiness with which both are loaded in
the latter.

It follows in natural sequence that large and small
farms—*la grande* and *la petite culture*—like *la grande* and
la petite propriété, really compete on fairer terms in
France than in England; and the former and not the
latter is the place to see them on their trial, and to judge
of the natural tendencies of rural economy in respect
of each. The fact is that, while *la petite culture* is
gaining ground and growing more prosperous as well as
more perfect and more minute, large farming too has
made great progress in France. Not only is there a
great domain, within which *la petite culture* has exclusive
or special advantages, but there is a common domain,
for example, in the production of cattle, cereals, and roots,
where both may co-exist and prosper; and there is,
again, a domain within which *la grande culture* has its
own superior advantages. There were no less than
154,167 farms in France of 100 acres—a number not far
short of the total number of farms in England—at the
date to which the latest agricultural statistics go back.
There were, again, 2,849 steam threshing machines in
1862, as against 1,537 in 1852; and it is natural to
infer that the chief employment of these was on the
larger farms. In the production of sheep, again, *la*

* 'Enquête Agricole.'

petite culture has not shown itself successful in France; though it is proper to remark that the decline of sheep between 1852 and 1862 is attributed by the highest authorities, in the main, not to the subdivision of the soil (the decline in their number being a new phenomenon and subdivision an old one), but to a number of wet seasons followed by disease, to a contraction of the area of sheep-walks by the reclamation of waste land and the division of commons; to an extension of the surface under wheat; and to an improvement in quality as distinguished from quantity. Nevertheless, it appears certain that minute farming under French methods does not give sheep an adequate range, and tends to other productions. Again, both in Belgium and in France the cultivation of the sugar beet, in combination with sugar factories, is found to tend to *la grande culture*, and no finer larger farms are to be seen in Scotland than many in France, of which beet is the principal produce.

In the departments immediately surrounding Paris large farming is to be seen in the highest perfection, of which the reader who has not visited them will find a description in M. de Lavergne's 'Economie Rurale de la France.' Yet, after noticing several magnificent examples, he adds; " While *la grande culture* marches here in the steps of English cultivation, *la petite* develops itself by its side, and surpasses it in results." The truth is, as we have said, that the large and the small farming compete on fair terms in France, which they are not allowed to do in England; and the latter has, to begin with, a large and ever-increasing domain within which it can defy the competition of the former. The large farmer's steam-engine cannot enter the vineyard, the orchard, or the garden. The steep mountain is inaccessible to him, when the small farmer can clothe it with vineyards, and the deep glen is too circumscribed for him. In the fertile alluvial valley, like that of the Loire, *the Garden of France*, his cultivation is not sufficiently minute to make the most of such precious ground, and the little cultivator outbids him and drives him from the garden; while, on the other hand, he is ruined by attempts to reclaim

2 A

intractable wastes which his small rival converts into
terrains de qualité supérieure. Even where mechanical
art seems to summon the most potent forces of nature to
the large farmer's assistance, the peasant contrives in
the end to procure the same allies by association, or
individual enterprise finds it profitable to come to his
aid. It is a striking instance of the tendency of *la petite
culture* to avail itself of mechanical power, that the latest
agricultural statistics show a larger number of reaping
and mowing machines in the Bas Rhin, where *la petite
culture* is carried to the utmost, than in any other department. Explorers of the rural districts of France cannot
fail to have remarked that *la petite culture* has created
in recent years two new subsidiary industries, in the
machine maker on the one hand, and the *entrepreneur* on
the other, who hires out the machine ; and one is now
constantly met even in small towns and villages, old-
fashioned and stagnant-looking in other respects, with
the apparition and noise of machines of which the large
farmer himself has not long been possessed. Admitting,
therefore, fully an important truth in Mr. Wren Hoskyns'
remark, that " The machinery doctrine of ' most produce
by least labour' is, as applied to the soil, the doctrine of
starvation to the labourer and dispossession to the small
proprietor ; and instead of belonging to the advance of
knowledge, is a retrogression towards the time when a
knight's fee included a whole wapentake, or hundred,
and a count was territorial lord over a county :"—* regarding, with Mr. Wren Hoskyns, machinery as made
for man, not man for machinery, and the happiness and
prosperity of a large rural population as the true object
of agriculture and land systems, we see no reason to
believe that the progress of machinery is incompatible
with the persistence of *la petite culture,* still less with
that of *la petite propriété* in France.

But if large and small farming compete on fairer
terms in France, as elsewhere on the Continent, than in

----

* ' Land in England, Land in Ireland, and Land in Other Lands.' By
Chandos Wren Hoskyns, M.P.

England, and their relative position is accordingly very
different, it ought to be added that it is only in the
hands of proprietors that either *la grande* or *la petite
culture* is fairly tried in France.   It is not in the part
of the French land system against which English
criticism has been directed—the part which differs from
the English, namely, the subdivision of landed property
and peasant proprietorship—that its weak point really
lies ; it is, on the contrary, in the part which resembles
the English—the system of tenure.   The British Islands
are far from being the only country in which the
question of tenure demands and indeed engages the
earnest attention of statesmen and economists ; though
on the Continent the problem of tenure finds more than
half its solution in the system of proprietorship.   In
France there are two kinds of tenure, namely (1), by
lease, usually for three, six, or nine years (a lease for
even eighteen years being quite the exception) ; and (2)
métayage, according to which the proprietor and the
métayer divide the produce, the capital being furnished
by the one or the other in proportions varying in
different localities.   It seems to be supposed by many
writers that the métayer, if he has only half the motive
to exertion which may be supposed to influence a tenant
who has the whole of the produce subject to a fixed rent,
enjoys at least the advantage of permanence of tenure.
But such is far from being the case in France ; very
commonly the contract of métayage is but for one, two, or
three years.   The truth is, the system of short tenures
common throughout most of Western Europe has a
common barbarous origin.   It belongs to a state of agriculture which took no thought of a distant future, and
involved no lengthened outlay, and which gave the land
frequent rest in fallow ; and it belongs to a state of
commerce in which sales of land were rare, changes
of proprietorship equally so, and ideas of making the
most of landed property commercially non-existent.
It is right to observe, however, that in many parts
of France, although the stated period of tenure is
commonly short, the farm really remains commonly in

2 A 2

the same family from father to son from generation to generation, provided only the rent is paid. Now, indeed, with greatly rising prices of agricultural produce, there is a steady and general augmentation of rents; and complaint is much oftener made by tenants of the rise of rents than of the shortness of leases; first, because the tenant is seldom turned out if he farms at all decently and lives in moderation, as he usually does; and secondly, because the tenant has very often already some land of his own, has almost always, if no land, some money saved to buy it. He is not, therefore, in apprehension of being turned out naked on the world; on the contrary, he would sometimes hesitate to accept a long lease, having in view setting up altogether for himself as a proprietor. Again, although no legal customs of tenure for unexhausted improvements remain in France, where the Code has swept away all customary laws, yet compensation for some unexhausted improvements exists under the Code. In the case of manure, for example, laid on by the outgoing tenant, he gets compensation, calculated in proportion to the time during which its unexhausted forces ought to yield profit. Again, where the farming is a joint concern between proprietor and tenant, under the form of cattle-lease called *cheptel*, if the value of the joint property has been increased by the tenant, he is entitled, at the expiration of the lease, to half the additional value. For improvements, however, in the nature of drainage and irrigation no right of compensation of any kind exists; and the absence of it furnishes in part the explanation of destructive droughts even in the best-cultivated parts of France. Under peasant proprietorship, in parts both of Germany and France itself, the most perfect system of irrigation may be found. Peasant proprietorship, coupled with and in a great measure caused by, a good system of land transfer, is in truth the great redeeming feature of continental land systems, which in point of tenure are as defective as our own. A good law of transfer corrects, as we have seen, a defective law of succession, and it also goes far to remedy defective laws and customs of tenure. It is, moreover, peasant proprietorship alone that prevents the questions of both tenure and landed property from assuming the formidable shape on the Continent which they do already in Ireland, and will do ere long in England. The 'Report of the Enquête Agricole' suggests additional powers of lease in the case of husbands owning in right of their wives, and of guardians, and again a reduction of the duty on leases, with, moreover, a legal presumption of a lease for twelve years in the absence of a written one. But such measures would give about as much satisfaction, and go as far towards allaying agrarian discontent in France as they would in Ireland, were there not a large diffusion of landed proprietorship, and a facility for both tenants and labourers of passing from that status to the status of proprietor, or of combining both.

It is fortunate for France not only that peasant proprietorship already exists on a great scale, but that the tendency of the economic progress of the country, as already shown, is to substitute more and more cultivation by peasant proprietors for cultivation by tenants; and to give more and more to those who remain tenants or labourers the position and sentiments also of proprietors. The increasing demand for, and rising prices of the produce of *la petite culture* make it more and more a profitable investment of the peasant's savings and labour; and those very rising prices, and the rising wages, which also follow the development of the resources of the country, put both the small tenant and the labourer in a condition to become buyers in the land market. All improvements in the law of property, and in fiscal legislation respecting it, will tend in the same direction, since the costs attending changes of ownership and exchanges of land fall heavier on small than on large properties. All the highest agronomic authorities in France, instead of objecting to the increasing subdivision of landed property, are urgent for the removal of all legal impediments to its division, as well as those which lay disproportionate cost on its acquisition in small portions, as in those which retain it in common ownership.

The question of common ownership is one which ought not be entirely ignored in a sketch of the French land system, however brief, although but a very few words can be devoted to it here. Upwards of four million and a half hectares of land in France belong in common to various bodies, corporations, communes, and villages. Of this area, it is true that a considerable part is in forest, managed by the State, much of which it would be inexpedient to divide and deforest. But the remainder is in great part simply so much land almost lost to the country. In a review of the 'Reports of the Enquête Agricole,' at the end of last year, M. de Lavergne pronounced that an effective law for the division and sale of the common lands would do more for the increase of the agricultural wealth of France than all other administrative measures taken together; for in addition to the cultivation of land, now almost waste, that would follow, the communes themselves would obtain funds by the sale for the making of country roads, in which the southern half of France, especially, is for the most part lamentably deficient. An act was actually passed in 1860, to facilitate the division of the common lands, but it has produced but little effect. An impediment to the division of the village commons in France, which has come under the writer's observation, arises from a kind of departure of the beneficial from the legal ownership. An entire commune, made up of several villages having each its common land, is the body whose authority is requisite for a division. It may be the interest of the villagers, and their wish, to divide their own common among themselves, but the rest of the commune would often prefer to see the villager driven or induced to bring his own land, with the communal rights attached, into the land market, where they themselves might become buyers. They are not desirous of giving the villagers an additional inducement to stay where they are. If land existed in such ample abundance that every peasant could have a sufficiency of land of his own to make a comfortable subsistence, or could at least have the advantage and comfort of a cottage and garden, the joint possession by each village of an additional common domain might be regarded as a great benefit ; but such is not the situation of matters in Western Europe. Nevertheless the French communal lands, even as they are, give the French peasantry an advantage which the British peasant has been deprived of ; and they also provide a fund for the future augmentation of the possessions of the French peasantry, to which there is nothing now corresponding in England.

It is not, however, the object of the present writer to compare the land system of France to that of Great Britain. Those who institute such a comparison will remember that it would be in a great measure imperfect and even delusive if confined to a survey of the present state of agriculture and of the peasantry of France,— forward already as is the former, happy as is the latter, in many parts of that country. The history of the two countries, the comparative state of their agriculture and peasantry a hundred years ago, as well as now, must be taken into account. France has had only three quarters of a century of anything like liberty, and less than half a century of tranquillity and industrial life. Nor in any such comparison should the respective effects of the land systems of the two countries on the town as well as on the country be overlooked. Whoever reflects what the French rural population would be, on the one hand, under a land system like that of Ireland, or even England ; and what its town population would be, on the other, if instead of being a third it were more than a half of the whole nation, and if instead of having a political counterpoise in the country, it found there only greater political ferment and discontent than its own, must surely pronounce that the land system of France is not only the salvation of that country itself, but one of the principal securities for the tranquillity and economic progress of Europe.

VII.

THE RUSSIAN AGRARIAN LEGISLATION OF 1861.

By Julius Faucher, of Berlin.

Member of the House of Deputies of the Prussian Landtag.

The bondage of agricultural labour, taken off from the Russian people by the legislation of 1861, was of comparatively recent origin. It is true that, already at the dawn of recorded Russian history, we meet with the existence of slaves of the czar as well as of the nobles of his court, but these slaves were prisoners of war and their offspring, the personal property of their masters, and quite different from the peasantry, which formed the bulk of the Russian people. The noblemen who owned those slaves were themselves *no* landed proprietors in their own right, nor even vassals owing allegiance for the tenure of land, but servants of the crown, whom the crown had to feed. This, not as a rule, but often, was managed in the form of an allotment to them of crown-land, to be tilled by their slaves, either for a number of years or for life; or, but rarely, with revocable permission to leave the fruit of it to their descendants. Such nobles as did *not* own slaves were sometimes paid by the czar's abandoning to them the yield of the taxes, due to the czar by the peasantry of one or more villages. But such an arrangement did not legally impair in the slightest degree the personal liberty of these peasants. They remained the free children of the czar, entitled legally to break off their household, and to separate from their village community whenever they liked, and to join another. The yield of the taxes of the place, not that of so many distinct persons, was given in lieu of a salary.

The Russian peasants of those times were nobody's servants, but the czar's, like everybody else in the empire. Nor is it for tracing the origin of the bondage, now destroyed, that it is necessary to refer to the more remote parts of Russian history. There are other things to be understood concerning Russian village life before a judgment on the probable practical bearing of the Act of 1861 can be formed. The free village of old has to furnish the key to the future of the free village of to-day.

The division of the Russian people into Great Russians and Little Russians, signifies far more than a mere split of the language into two dialects, which, by the way, differ but little from each other. Let us state at once the salient point. Little Russia, with Kiew for its centre, is the mother-country; and Great Russia, with Moscow for its centre, is the *colony*, the one great colony whose limits are not yet fixed. Little Russia is Sclavonic, pure; the Great Russians are a mixed race, a majority being Sclavonians, undoubtedly, and who, more by dint of high culture than by the sword, were the conquerors, with a minority of the former inhabitants of the country, the Finnic tribes or Tchudes. And now the consequence of it, on which we intend to lay stress. The colony, which afterwards became the dominant part of the empire (*colonization never being completed*, that is to say, never yet having occupied the whole disposable soil), did not yet find time to undergo such changes in the form of the tenure and the tillage of land as have occurred in other places, where originally the same form prevailed as that which the Great Russians continued to preserve while constantly applying it anew, as colonists, on virgin soil.

It may be stated at once, that this form was that of the joint husbandry of a whole village. The village, not the family, was the social unit. Supplanting the family for purposes of colonization, the village, by necessity, partook to a certain extent of the character of a family. It stood under patriarchal rule. Movable property alone was individual, immovable, the land at least, was common. With the alien not belonging to the village,

not the individual, the village only, had to do. The
village always had a mother-village, and the mother-
village again had a mother-village, and so on. The
name of mother-village in general, or of mother-village to
another district village, is still attached to many Russian
towns and villages; but even where the tradition of it is
now lost, it may be taken for granted that such a
relation once existed. Nor are the most recent times
void of examples of the foundation of a daughter-village
by a mother-village, though the interference of the
masters, which the Russian villagers in the meantime had
got, had given to the colonizing movement a somewhat
different shape. The colonizing masters sometimes made
up the new villages of selected families from a whole
number of older villages in the same master's possession.
But whenever this has taken place, it was done in
disregard of the traditional feelings of the people. Though
the Russian peasants by no means cling to the soil
which has given birth to them, they cling to their fellow-
villagers. They would not have aggregated voluntarily
from different villages to form a new village. And they
like to have even the mere traditional remembrance of a
common mother-village, as children, who are still
children, like to have still a mother. I have been
witness (in the Government of Moscow, in the summer of
1867) to the fact that a whole village, which had been
destroyed by one of the numerous conflagrations of
that year, and which had lost everything; whose
inhabitants, besides, not feeling at ease where they
were, resolved to return to the mother-village of their
village, situated two hundred and fifty miles off, and
which they, or rather their ancestors, had left nearly
fifty years ago. They collected money for this purpose
from the neighbouring gentry, and even the neighbouring
villages, which fully appreciated the resolution, contributed their share.

This colonization by whole villages giving birth to
other villages, and sending them off and planting them
often at a very great distance, was necessitated by the
difficulties colonization had to encounter in those tracts

and in those times. When the Sclavonian colonization in
a north-easterly direction (which was the work of a
people already settled, not nomads, as is sometimes
conjectured) commenced, the Russians as yet had no
government worth the name which could protect the
advanced posts. It is well known that later, feeling the
want of such a government, and not understanding at all
how to manage to get a *national* government, the heads
of the villages all over the vast places already colonized
(chiefly due north of the Dnieper, where Nowgorod and
Tskoff had become trading emporiums with the north,
in the same way as Kiew was the trading emporium with
the south) were agreed upon inviting the Waraegers,
whose attacks they had just repelled by a general
popular rising, to return in peace and to govern them.
But when this took place, we find the Russians already
widely spread among the Finnic tribes of the north-
east. It seems that they had already lined the
whole net of rivers with their villages, being eager
fishermen, as the Russians are to the present day, like
all Sclavonians, and preferring, as passionate gardeners,
which they still also are, the black alluvial soil of the
river-banks. The interstices of this network of settlements, however, was still peopled with Tchude huntsmen,
among whom an isolated household of alien-born colonists,
probably, would not have been safe. Nor would the
Russians themselves, being no hunters, have been safe
from the bears and wolves which the Finnic hunters, up
to the present day, are never afraid to encounter in single
combat, even without fire-arms.

Thus the closely-packed village, in which block-house
borders on block-house along the two sides of the broad
village street, shut up at the two ends by stockades or
block-houses placed across, was the only possible, end-
lessly repeated, form of settlement.* A clearing of the
forest by common labour of the colonists had furnished
the acreage and the building material for the block-

---

* The Sclavonic and Teutonic names for a village (Russian,—derewnia;
Scandinavian,—trup; German,—dorf; Anglo-Saxon,—thorpe) have the root
in common with troops, troupe, troupeau, and signify aggregation for protection's sake.

houses. The enclosed space of the village street was the common workshop in summer, for carpentry, for making the hemp and flax ready for spinning and weaving, and for bleaching the cloth, &c. The cattle stands, threshing-floors and barns were attached to the single block-houses, showing the stage at which village-labour and village property ceased and individual labour and individual property began.

As a further consequence of colonial isolation, the village, as a rule and as far as possible, was self-sustaining. In order to be able to form an idea of the past, present, and future of the Russian people, it is of high importance to bear this original character of the Russian village settlements, easily traceable from the present state, strictly and continually in mind. The most prominent feature of a settlement, which, in the beginning and perhaps for a long time was unable to enter into commercial relations with other settlements, will be, that just the amount of acreage necessary to furnish the food and the clothing material for the villages will be tilled, *and not more.* For to till more would be far from correct management. It would merely be taking away time and labour-power from other work, just as necessary where everything that is wanted is to be done on the spot. This also indicates the corollary to be expected. Where the husbandman is not more of a husbandman than is just wanted to produce what a single family consumes, and yet is not a savage, but already accustomed to a certain degree of comfort, we must expect to see him a handicraftsman, too, of very variegated skill—a kind of jack-of-all-trades.

As said before, the possibility of constantly throwing off the surplus of the increasing population of the village by founding a daughter-village on virgin soil, was calculated to take away every stimulus to change the system, which, at the same time, was so extremely fitted to the exigencies of that primitive colonization. While all the other Sclavonian nations, the Little Russians not excepted, followed, to a certain extent, the ways of central and western Europe (a process which partly was

quickened by conquest, those farther west being almost
invariably the conquerors of those farther east), the Great
Russians alone kept the original form of settled life of
the Sclavonian race intact. Their place on the utmost
north-eastern wing of the race, putting them at the same
time out of reach of western conquest, with nothing but
huntsmen, and nomads, and virgin soil all round them,
made *expansion, not change,* their law of progress, just as
it seems to have been the case with the Chinese whom
they now are facing.

The village, at once the smallest and the largest
compass of the social thought of the bulk of the people,
now became the prototype of the empire, which beginning
with Rurik's election to the czardom, became destined
(after passing through vicissitudes of all kinds,—self-
created confusion as well as foreign invasion) to inherit the
fruits which the unassisted and unguided, modest and
silent, but continuous colonizing labour of the ancient
free Russian villagers has borne. The villagers—who
in their village governed themselves by patriarchal rule
—after they had become conscious, by means of sad
experiences, inroads of eastern nomads, and plundering
excursions of northern and western adventurers, that
the merely sentimental link between mother-village and
daughter-village was not that national solidarity of
which the hostile foreigner has to beware, considered,
after the constitution of czardom, all Russia, as far as it
already went, simply as one great village, likewise under
patriarchal rule, likewise on a soil the common property
of all, likewise sufficing to itself, and likewise having to
do with aliens only in common : and this is still the
conception which the Russian people entertain of their
state. The savage drama of the political history of the
country, the extirpation of resisting tribes chiefly in the
west, the sanguinary feuds between the princes of the
Imperial House, the partitions and repartitions of the
empire, even the struggles which accompanied the introduction and spread of the Greek Church—all this had
no bearing on what will always remain the most
interesting phenomenon connected with the rise of

Russia, namely, the growth of a very numerous *new people*, spreading over a very extensive area in a comparatively very short time, in Europe itself, without the remainder of Europe even becoming aware of it! What is recorded by Nestor shows merely that, a military government and taxation having been introduced, and a professional priesthood established (likewise borrowed from abroad, after a vain attempt to turn the native heroism to account for the same purpose), the same fights about the legalized prey had begun in Russia which constitute the political part of every other nation's history. Protection from plunder by the foreigner had everywhere to be bought from legalized plunderers at home,— and everywhere has the extent to which it was to be legal been fought for,—and everywhere did the plunderers contest the prey amongst themselves. What is *not* recorded in written records, but is shown by the results to which it has led, is the cementing process which now took place, and which marks the *second* stage in the mighty colonizing movement, going on imperceptibly in the north-east, without even the colonists themselves being conscious of its extent and significance.

While Little Russia, the true mother-country on the Dnieper, and the tracts of land on the north-west of it, bordering on Poland, and inhabited by minor Sclavonian tribes of mongrel character, now comprised under the name of Ruthenes, Russians, or Rusniaks, remained the theatre of civil as well as of foreign wars, the colony in the north and north-east, as whose starting-point the country round Nowgorod has to be considered, enjoyed a comparative repose, and had all the advantages of national and ecclesiastical unification. The foundation of village by village must have gone on unabated as well as the pushing forward of the north-eastern frontier of the settlements ; for the geographical horizon rapidly widens in the records of the historian. As a distinct race the race of the Great Russians had first been formed at Nowgorod, on originally Finnic soil, by mixture with the Finnic tribe of the locality. Along the Newa, and the large

lakes and water-courses of which it forms the mouth,
the Finns had resisted farther encroachment. Their
most warlike and proud tribes were settled there; but
farther east, where the same race occupied the whole
country north of the Oka, and even farther south, and
as far in an easterly direction as the river Ob, in Siberia,
they were too thinly spread, and too little civilized, to
form an obstruction to the constant advance of the great
Russian village colonies. They continued for some time
to fill the interstices of the network of river villages,
living the life of huntsmen or lonely settlers, as before;
but with the national unification and Christianization of
the Great Russian invaders, the time of the total absorption of the aboriginal people had arrived. They were
turned into subjects of the grand prince or czar, and
the prince, his relative and vassal who presided over the
district, and they gradually disappeared, and are still
so disappearing, among the villagers. For these latter
henceforward refused altogether to respect the hunting-
grounds left free between their villages. Simultaneously
now with the extension went on the densification of the
network of settlements. The erroneous notion is often
met with in Western Europe, that the whole of Russia
without exception is but thinly peopled. It is true that
very large parts of Russia are *very* thinly peopled, of
which more anon, but the centre of the empire, on the
Upper Wolga, on the Oka, and between these two rivers,
a lump of land by no means despicable, shows the
villages as close to each other as anywhere in Western
Europe; and if the same figure of density of population is
not found in the tables, it is not a lesser village population, but a lesser population of the towns, which are few
and far between, and sometimes very small, that accounts
for it.

The Church assisted the colonizing movement in
another way. Pilgrimage had been introduced. One
has to think of a people living in close confinement
during a long winter, followed by a short and hot
summer with protracted daylight, whose allurements produce a feeling of restlessness; of a people, moreover,

living in villages, every one of these villages looking
back upon another, often very distant, village as a mother
that claimed a visit; of a people, finally, living in community of household interests, among whom the pilgrim,
who sets out on his journey with the consent of his
fellow-villagers, need not fear of seeing his interests
neglected.   Besides, migrations of long files of emigrants
on their way to the new settlement having been of
yearly occurrence from times immemorial, and these
having been able to appeal on their way at every
village on the roadside to the remembrance of a similar
migration of the more aged and influential villages, hos-
pitality to pilgrims could not but become at once a
cogent rule.   It is so still.   Bread and the summer
drink of the country, kwass, a kind of very thin, unfer-
mented beer, are never—not by the poorest peasant—
refused to the traveller; and if payment for it be offered,
its acceptance is invariably refused with indignation.
The short nights, and the clothing—adapted even to
severe colds—permit a night's rest in the open air, if no
other is to be had.   Thus the institution of religious
pilgrimage—convenient pretext for the migratory propensities of mankind—could find nowhere a more con-
genial soil than in Russia.   It was but natural that
the place of worship to which the religious pilgrimages
were directed, and the mother-settlement, which a long-
preserved attachment, transmitted in fireside tales from
generation to generation, longed to see, in very many
instances coincided.   For the spread of convents, usually
the ostensible places of destination of pilgrimage,
followed the spread of settlements.   The neighbourhood
of a mother-village which had already many daughter-
villages, was just the place to erect a convent.

It will now be easy to imagine how colonization must
have been pushed by the increased restlessness which
the united church with its pilgrimages had brought over
the whole nation, and by their becoming conscious,
partly through the medium of their own feet and eyes,
partly through the recitals of travellers passing their
houses, of the immensity of the territory already under

their grasp, and the boundless extension of unoccupied
land in an easterly direction. The pilgrims were to
them what American emigration agents now are to
English, Irish, and German villagers. The pilgrims'
refectory in the convent, where the pilgrims from far and
near met, was their newspaper.

The seats of the princes, whose number sometimes
was very great, and the seats of the convents could not
but gradually assume the character of larger or smaller
emporiums of commerce. The swarms of peasants,
which they periodically attracted, provided for it. The
creation of a number of centres of commerce was the *real*
and *palpable* result of the establishment of Church and
State among the villagers of the great plains of Eastern
Europe. But it would be a mistake to liken the Russian
cities, even at the present day, to the cities of Western
Europe. They never became, to a similar extent, the
exclusive seats of industry. They remained pre-
eminently marts of exchange whose lot it was to introduce division of labour between village and village, not
division of labour between agriculturist and artisan,
but between the peasants of one village, who continued
to till the soil for their own sustenance, and who now
began to apply the remainder of their time, instead
of to all work, to some distinct occupation, and the
peasants of other villages, who did just the same.
Village industry is still *the* great industry of Russia.
It would be very rash to condemn this as misguided
activity. It must not be overlooked that in Russia the
time for work in the open air is shorter, and the time for
work in the house is longer, than in Central and Western
Europe. It will then easily be understood that the
settlement, which first was compelled by colonial isolation
to sustain itself, and had the disposal of a long winter
to provide by house-industry for *all* the wants of the
settlers, was not easily induced to give up the advantage
derived from house-industry in winter, when the gradual
introduction of division of labour between village and
village, through the medium of marts and exchange,
rendered house-industry more profitable.

We arrive now at institutions of still stranger appearance, when measured by the standard of Central and Western Europe, and yet easily intelligible, if it be but kept in mind that one thing binds the other in the web of civilization. Immovable property being the common property of the village, and even the title-deed of movable property being derived at some previous time from repartitions by common consent, it was but natural to the villagers to consider the whole of the trade which had sprung up between them and others *likewise as common property*. Was the son of the village, who had been permitted to set out, first on a pilgrimage, or a journey to court, then—the occasion having brought about the discovery of gain to be made by selling and buying, as a commercial traveller—alone to reap the benefit of his journey, which he could not have made had not his village been a common household? Thus the habit sprung up and became a law in the eyes of the villagers, that whoever of them, being abroad, got orders for articles to be produced by the house-industry of his village, did not get these orders for himself as speculator and employer of labour, but for the village as a whole, and that the orders were to be distributed among the villagers by common consent. And thus things are still managed to a large extent.

Thus the second—in recorded history the first—stage of Russian peasant life shows us the peasant as an *artisan*, at least where division of labour had changed him into an artisan, and a member of a society of "adventurers," who at the same time continued to produce the food necessary to feed them and their families, and partly the raw material for their branch of industry by the common husbandry of the village, which still formed the social unity of the country.

The Mongol invasion, though it lasted two hundred and twenty-five years, appears to have had no influence whatever on the life led by the villagers nor even on the spread of their settlements. The business of the Mongols was with the grand prince, the other princes, and with the clergy. They humiliated the princes and made them pay tribute, that is to say, give up part of the taxes they received from the villagers; but as for the clergy, they even took off taxation from them. The state in which the country emerged from the dominion of the nomads shows that it cannot have suffered much; perhaps it had even benefited. For it would seem as if, in the time immediately before the conquest, there had already been attempts on the part of the single princes to prevent the people from leaving their state or province for the purpose of erecting new settlements elsewhere. With the nomads the old liberty returned. It is very probable that colonization continued unabated even under Mongol rule. The immunities and favours bestowed by these shrewd Asiatics upon the priestly order cannot but have assisted colonization. For the church was not merely indirectly, through pilgrimage, but directly, through hermits and gardening convents, a colonizing agency. The priestly order, recruited from the peasantry, remained faithful to their habits and propensities.

With the withdrawal of the Mongols into Asia began the disenfranchisement of the great bulk of the peasantry, but it progressed very gradually. Records are insufficient, but the state of things met with at' a later and better-known period admits of pretty safe conclusions. The main lesson drawn from the experience of a foreign dominion was, that the bond of unity of the empire had to be drawn tighter. The rule of numerous princes, vassals of the grand prince, who now officially adopted the oriental name of Czar, or rather Zar, had to be done away with, at all events. Iwan III. commenced the struggle, Iwan IV., the Terible, brought it to a successful issue. This struggle favoured the growth of a petty nobility, formed partly of the courtiers of the late princes, whom czars left in possession of the yield of the taxes of such villages as had been allotted to them by their former masters, without insisting upon regular service on their part, merely reserving the right to summon them when wanted. Such is still the relation of the whole Russian nobility to their czar. It consisted, further, of the czar's own servants, which were partly taken from among the villagers themselves, likewise endowed with the yield of the taxes of one or more villages,—and lastly, of the proprietors of such villages, mainly situated in the western parts of Russia, which had been formed of slaves, and had always been the property of their masters.

Villages not being disposed of in such a way seem to have remained free villages or crown villages till the later years of the reign of Iwan IV., who seems to have commenced the practice, largely resorted to in later times, of turning crown villages into villages belonging to the czar, not as sovereign of the country, but as landed proprietor. Such villages, peopled by prisoners of war and their offspring, the slaves of the czar, must have existed always, just as similar villages, mentioned above, were in possession of single noblemen. But there can be little doubt that Iwan IV. in designating by a legislative act which villages were henceforward to be considered as state property (Siemschina), and which as property of the czar (Opritchina), did so for purposes of appropriating what was not his own. He appropriated in this way even cities. The lawlessness of his proceedings is proved by the amends which were made for them in later times, when at least all the cities and other property were again excluded from the Opritchina or apanage of the imperial house.

The changes effected amounted to this, that a very great number of villages, having been formerly free communities, merely paying taxes to the State, had been turned into estates of the czar and the nobility, on which the peasantry had to pay *rent*.

The amount payable remaining unaltered, and the person to whom it was to be paid remaining the same, the peasantry, perhaps, did not even become aware of the change. They may still have considered their village as a little socialistic and patriarchal republic, just as the bees in the hive are not aware that they have other masters besides their queen.

But the time was now fast approaching when every

doubt that their old liberty was gone should be removed
from them.

Popular poetry in Russia has kept alive, in
rhymed wails, the memory of St. George's day, as the
day when Boris Godsmow, the usurper, published his
ukase, by which the Russian peasant was forbidden to
quit his village without permission and passport, either
from the proprietor of the estate, into which the village
had been turned, or, where it was still a free village,
from the authority to which it was submitted. The
ukase, besides, ordained that every peasant, not being
provided with such a passport, and being found wandering
about the country, should be taken into custody, his
personal identity and his whereabouts should be ascertained, and that he should be sent back in irons to his
village, where punishment might be inflicted upon him for
having left it without permission.

Boris Godsmow is represented to have acted thus,
in compliance with the wishes of the petty landed
nobility—his main supporters. They had represented to
the Government that the fiefs they held in exchange for
service done, or service they were bound to do, were
valueless if the peasants were permitted to emigrate.
Modern writers, even Russians themselves, and still more
French and Germans, have not shrunk from justifying
Boris Godsmow and his nobles, by asserting that this was
the only means of putting an end to the nomadic propensities of the Russian people, which the Mongol invasion had fostered anew. But where is the slightest
evidence of nomadic propensities among the peasantry of
Northern Russia, *before* that time, *at* that time, and *after*
that time ? Not even the Cossacks—fugitives, as they
were, from oppression in the southern steppe—bore even
the slightest resemblance to real nomads. To colonize
and to nomadize are two very different things. Just
as well one may talk of nomadic propensities among the
English, or the Spaniards, or the Dutch, or the Germans.
The truth is, that just towards the end of the long
reign of Iwan the Terrible the colonizing movement in an
easterly and southerly direction had assumed new propor-

tions. The Khanats of Kasan and Astrachan had been conquered ; Siberia had been discovered by the Cossacks, and a large part of it conquered ; the steppe and the black country in Southern Russia had acquired a safety unknown before. The commerce of the West, the fur-trade of Nowgorod with Germany, which was more a trade of the Finnic hunters, than of the Russian village-artisans, and of Kiew with the Byzantine Empire, had almost ceased, Iwan III. having crushed the former by imprisoning German merchants, and the conquest of Constantinople by the Turks having crushed the latter. Instead of it, commerce with the East, with Central Asia, had commenced on a large scale, first introduced by the Mongols, then favoured by the conquest of the two Khanates and of Siberia. Here it was the produce of the industry of the Russian villagers that was sold ; and the further eastward they went with their settlements the more they benefited by it. The whole nation was astir with colonizing projects ; and the records of the dates of foundation of the older settlements in the East show how many of them were carried out.

But then the proprietors of the villages, now private estates, and the czar himself, as proprietor of the apanage estates, lost the advantage of *increasing* population on their estates and of an *increasing* rent from them. They, besides, lost the power of *raising* the rent. What I am about to add is mere probability, but it is probability ; a certain approach had taken place between the Russian *Government,* isolated after the fall of Constantinople from all other Governments, and one at least of the Governments of Western Europe. The *English* had found the way to the White Sea, and already Iwan IV. had exchanged embassies with Queen Elizabeth ; and Boris Godsmow continued amicable relations with the Queen, and even attempted to bring about a marriage of his son with one of her relatives. His ambassador, Mikulin, took even an active part in the streets of London in the quelling of Essex's insurrection. Mikulin had to report to the czar on English legislative institutions. In the year 1601 (Stat. 43,

Queen Eliz.), the great poor law, crowning the
efforts of the Tudor age in dealing with the difficulty of
pilgrims and vagabonds—the bane of the country, down
from the time when Henry VII. abolished vassalage—had
become the law of the land in England. It had been
preceded by Stat. 14, Queen Eliz., which ordained
that the abode of persons who could not or would not
do work was to be fixed to the parish in which they
were born, or in which they had resided during three
years, and, in case of vagabonds, during one year.
Might not Boris Godsmow, whose legislative acts in the
matter date from 1592, 1597, 1601, and 1606, belea-
guered by his nobility, and getting the convenient pretext of a famine (which broke out, engendering swarms
of beggars and a typhus-epidemic, which these beggars
carried all over the country), and informed by his
ambassador of the wise counsel, under similar circumstances of the advisers of the English queen, have
tried a Muscovite version of contemporaneous English
legislation ?   Indeed, it looks very much like it.
Proneness to imitation, and reckless boldness in trying it,
is a Russian characteristic to this day, of which more
anon.

The decisive blow had fallen. It did not at once
bring about its final results—compulsory labour of
whatever kind the master demands from his slave—but
it contained it in germ, and the development was rapid.
The first and most important consequence was, that
colonization was checked for a long time, and only re-
commenced when the masters, having become masters
in full, themselves found it profitable. The whole
seventeenth century shows the heart in the prostrated
body of the Russian peasantry still palpitating. The
enshrined spirit of liberty asserts itself in religious
sectarian movements, in agrarian risings, in bold
brigandage, under the seductive form of free Cossack life.
It was reserved for the eighteenth century to con-
summate the worst. The harmless and gentle villagers,
who for the love of wife, child, brother, sister, and
neighbour, had conquered the uncongenial eastern plain

of Europe for civilisation, now disappear, as working
agents, from the historical records of their country;
they have become mere tools to work with, mere matter
to be worked upon. They are now " mujiks "—bodies—
" tchornoi narod "—black people : something like niggers,
as it would seem. A large part of them are bought and
sold with the land; without the land, they are merely
let out, and feel themselves most favoured when they
are let out to themselves.* And yet it would be wrong
to liken their fate, even when it was worst, which is
during the time from Peter I., the Great (!), to
about the accession of Alexander I., to that of the black
slaves in the colonies of Western Europe. Patriarchal
feelings and patriarchal habits never became extinct,
either with the Russian serf or with the Russian master.
The harmless and gentle character of the villagers is the
harmless and gentle character of the nation, which
has but the fault of bearing good luck not so well
as bad luck, and of becoming drunk with transitory pride,
with still more transitory anger, and with zeal, more
transitory with them than anything else.

The attempts to relieve the fate of the peasantry
began with the government of the Emperor Nicholas.
The state of things with which he had to deal had received
a finishing stroke by a set of imperial decrees of the
Emperor Paul in the year 1797. These decrees, which
at least had restored to the peasantry the right of
electing their village heads, were left intact by Nicholas,
except as far as the " private peasants," that is to say,
the *serfs* of private proprietors, or of the czar as private
proprietor, of estates were concerned. The most important change of the Emperor Nicholas was introduced by a ukase issued in 1842, which permitted to
the proprietors of private estates to transform, by
treaties, their serfs into farmers, the Government vouch-
ing for the former serfs fulfilling the conditions undertaken by them in the treaties. The idea was to see

* The household serfs, being considered as the offspring of the slaves of
the middle ages, *were* sold without land, and, as it appears, in spite
of the law, numbers of peasants, too, under pretext that they were household
serfs.

what forms of treaties would prove the most popular
and acceptable to both sides, and then, if still need
be, to frame a general compulsory measure, in which
the contents of the popular form or forms of treaties
were to be embodied.   But very little use was
made of the expedient, as has been asserted, from the
difficulty of settling things with the mortgage holders.
The Emperor Nicholas, besides, by ukase issued in
1848, abolished the interdict to private peasants of
buying immovable property.   He further reinforced
the law interdicting the sale of peasants without land,
by forbidding its evasion by transforming peasants first
into household slaves, and also the sale of land without
peasants, if, by such sale, the village-acre was curtailed
in such a way as to amount to less than four and a half
djessatines (twelve acres) for every male villager.
Finally, he issued regulations defining more distinctly
than the law did before, how much labour, or how much
payment in lieu of labour, in a variety of cases and
places, the peasant-serfs owed to their masters.

But all this did not amount to much, when compared
with what the position of the peasantry once was, and
with what it since has become.   When the Emperor
Alexander II. announced his resolve to do justice to
the peasantry, he found still nearly one half of them—
forming with their families more than one third of the
population of the empire—to all practical purposes
slaves, tilling a soil which did not belong to them,
without being paid for their labour, during about three
days in the week, while they had to sustain themselves
and their families by their labour during the other three
days, likewise by tilling a soil which did not belong to
them, and not in the way they chose to do it, but as
they were permitted, or rather ordered to do it.

The serfs, though their number had *comparatively*
declined, formed still the largest group among the
Russian peasantry.   Next in numbers stood the *crown
peasants*, the remnant of the old free peasantry, turned
into copyholders from the crown, and governed by
servants of the crown.   Their position has not been

touched by the act of 1861, but by a recent special act, which has been framed to bring the position of this part of the peasantry into better accordance with that of the enfranchised private peasants. It must not be passed over that, at least to the eye of the foreign travelling observer, there is no marked difference of well-being visible between the villages of crown peasantry and those of private peasantry. There are Russian authors—but such as belonged and still belong to the political opposition in the empire, like Golowin and Dolgorukow—who pretend that the crown peasants had and have far more to suffer than the private peasants. Dolgorukow, in particular, whose work, ' The Truth about Russia,' was published but shortly before the act of 1861, gives a revolting description of the abuse which the functionaries of the crown, entrusted with the administration of the crown villages, make of their power. The crown peasants had then and have still to pay copyhold-fee to the crown, part of them by each head of the male population, part of them in shape of a real land-tax, and were then still burdened with a certain amount of compulsory labour, which, road-making excepted, now has been superseded by fees. The fees levied by the head yield ten millions of roubles, the land-tax thirty millions of roubles. The highest fee on the head is 2r. 86k., the lowest 2r. 15k. The copyhold-right is always a right of the village as a whole. The sale of it by the villagers was not permitted, yet they might so far dispose of it, as to barter their position with other crown peasants, or even with private peasants, on certain conditions. And they might let out the land for fifty years to other persons; an arrangement evidently designed to facilitate the erection of industrial establishments in the country.

The minor groups consisted, before 1861, firstly, of *freeholders* living in farm-yards separated from every village. They are to be met with in Great Russia, in the southern governments, in the so-called country of the black soil. They are supposed to be the Russianized remnants of the original inhabitants of the country, the Tchudes, who in the south, on the fertile soil, were not

merely or pre-eminently huntsmen, but agriculturists too.
This is very probable.   It is said that a far greater
number of them would still exist, had not Peter I.
recklessly deprived them of their freehold right, and
compelled them to become crown peasants.   They are
further to be met with in the Western Ruthene provinces;
and there they are the offspring of the lower Polish
nobility (shlachta), who invaded these provinces and
settled down in them, and afterwards were unable to
prove their noble descent.   Another group was formed
by the *serfs* who had bought immovable property since
1848.   There were further Russian bojars, whose nobility
was not proved, or was lost, and who therefore were considered as glebæ adscripti, though on their own property;
and Cossacks, whose freedom and right to their property
had been recognised.   All these groups, together with
a very small amount of Russian peasantry tilling the
property of other persons, without being serfs, namely,
of persons not entitled to *have* serfs, because not being
noblemen, and yet landowners, were evidently exceptions,
and not the rule.   The remainder was not of Russian
nationality.

The measures adopted by the Emperor Nicholas for
initiating and stimulating a voluntary abandonment of
serfdom on the part of the masters, as a rule, having
proved abortive, and yet great numbers of the masters
themselves having become fully conscious of the increasing personal danger to which they were exposed, so
long as they had to deal with the peasantry as with
their serfs, this much was considered as a settled thing,
when the Emperor Alexander II. ascended to the throne,
by himself as well as by his people, that at all events
serfdom was now to be entirely and forcibly eradicated
from agrarian legislation in Russia.   In this primary
and unconditional postulate all the world agreed.   But
nobody, not even the most strenuous advocate of unlimited
rights of property in land, conferred by superannuation
on the proprietor in legally acknowledged possession,
could hide from himself, that merely to sever the link
between master and serf, and to make this measure at

the same time sever the link between the serf and the *land*, would be, besides an historical injustice, a political blunder involving the most direful consequences. For what was to become of the enfranchised serf? An agricultural labourer? Would this be the use he would make of his freedom, that he remained what he had been, with this difference, that his master, now called his employer, could—in his idea, far worse than to whip him—turn him out of doors with wife and child, at the slightest symptom of even a justifiable disobedience? A farmer? And, if a farmer, a farmer of what? Merely of the land necessary to provide the food and clothing for the family? But, being unable to pay any rent out of the produce of this land, he would have to do other work to enable him to pay the rent. What work? Village industry? Field labour on the proprietor's land? Would not he thus legally be the same labourer as above, only with notice to quit by the year, instead of by the week, for practically it would be by the year in both cases; and in both cases the security of his sustenance, which with serfdom was perfect, would be superseded by a constant apprehension of losing his sustenance, and render him as resistless as farmer against rack-rent, as he would be resistless as labourer against depression of wages and maltreatment. Practically, in both cases his position would be exactly the same; for the rack-rent in the one case would be but another form of the depression of wages in the other. Everybody—economist as well as socialist—understood that the economical, or social law, as the reader likes, which regulates the relations between employer and labourer, and between proprietor and farmer—a law which the economist trusts, and which the socialist curses, at all events was not applicable, where the threat of the loss of a homestead and of a sustenance hitherto enjoyed by the future labourer or farmer under very different arrangements was thrown into the balance to the employer's or proprietor's advantage, and to the labourer's or farmer's disadvantage. It could not but have rapidly brought about a probably fearful state of the country. It would have soon filled the country with swarms of peasantry, wandering to and fro, now begging, now endangering the safety of the roads, and finally of the country-seats. The pretext of Boris Godsmow would have been turned into a reality.

The resolve of doing away altogether with serfdom involved, therefore, in everybody's eyes in Russia, at once a *second* resolve, namely, that of settling the *land question* between the late *master* and his late *serfs* in such a way as to prevent the bulk of the peasantry from becoming suddenly and simultaneously unsettled and homeless, and as to make the new relations between employer and labourer, or between proprietor and farmer, take their issue from positions duly balanced between them.

But this being agreed upon by almost unanimous consent, a *third* still more precarious problem at once emerged, so to speak, from the deep sea of agrarian history in Russia, and forced itself on the anxious attention of the native statesmen and writers on public affairs.

If the land was to be divided between the master and his serfs, was the single former serf to be invested with freehold property, in accordance with what had taken place under similar circumstances further west in Europe, or was regard to be had to the old national custom of common village property and joint village husbandry— the " Mir," as the language has it, in an expression not to be translated into a language of Western Europe? This custom was still alive and paramount in the horizon of peasant thought, though now in the disguise of a common household, not by common consent, and free to act as the members of the household liked, but of a common household placed under the supreme will, in the last instance, of a resident or absentee-master, belonging to another sphere of society than the members of the household themselves, and being either the czar himself or somebody else, who lorded it over the Mir, in the eyes of the peasantry at least, always in the name of the czar? The *land question between peasant and peasant* was therefore a third question embodied in the primary one of the total abolition of the bondage of agricultural labour.

It finally appeared that local administration and local jurisdiction, yes, even that amount of local legislation which can never totally be dispensed with, could not remain, with an enfranchised peasantry, what they had been before, when a good deal of the duties of administration, jurisdiction, and legislation, as far as the serfs were concerned, simply devolved on their master, whose supreme will was the Alexander's sword for cutting many a Gordian knot. The necessity to *supersede individual* will in affairs which from *private* affairs had become *public* affairs by *collective* will, was the *fourth* of the problems by which the Russian reformers had to be prepared to see their legislative abilities tried, after the removal of the stain of slavery from their national escutcheon had once become their firm resolve.

The moment has now arrived to mention the most prominent features of party division in Russia, with regard to the reform of agrarian legislation. They may be described as the economist and imperial party, on the one side, and the socialist and national, on the other, the former, at the same time, being reproached with aristocratic leanings, the latter very ostensibly professing democratic ones. It would be very erroneous to compare them in any way to Conservatives and Liberals in the sense of Western Europe. They would, both of them, repudiate it themselves with rather contemptuous laughter. The faith, the very sincere faith, of the socialist and national — which, with them, does not merely mean Russian, but Pansclavonian — party is, that it is all over with the particular form of civilization which is dominant in Western Europe. According to them, the future belongs altogether to the Russian " Mir " and to the Sclavonian race. Communism in land is designated by them as the particular Sclavonian substratum of civilization. According to them, the nations of Western Europe, who, all of them, in times dating back very far, knew of institutions similar to the Russian Mir, committed a fatal blunder already at the beginning of their career, and condemned themselves to unavoidable decay setting in sooner or later, by allowing land to become

the object of individual right of property, which, among
the Western nations, was established by the formation of
a feudal aristocracy first, and the revival of Roman law
afterwards.   Land, they argue, having never been produced, but found, derives the value which we now find
adhering to the bare acre exclusively from social, not
from individual efforts.   Rent paid to individuals has
therefore no foundation in justice, but only such rent as
is paid to meet the public expenditure of the smaller or
larger community, the parish, the county, the state.
The position of this party in regard to the land question,
as a question between noble proprietor and peasant, was
therefore to make light of the inherited or purchased
rights of the proprietor, to insist upon as much land
being taken from him as possible, and of his being
treated in future simply as one of the peasants of the
village.   Of course they were aware that they could not
entertain the hope of seeing such a scheme carried out
in our times;   and those of them who were called
upon   to take   an   active part   in   framing the new
legislation   did   not even   attempt it, strong as their
influence was.   But notice is to be taken of the existence
and collaboration of a political party and of statesmen
who, as far as they consented to leave to the noble
proprietor rights of property, singled out from the
common ones of the village, did so from reasons of
expediency, and not from inclination or conviction.   It
had its very sensible influence on the *quantitative* side of
the arrangement effected.

The confiscation of rent, on which the Sclavonian
socialists put the construction of a restoration of the
original and inalienable right of property of the community in the soil, rests evidently on a theory on which
they must be prepared to act, if it be shown to them
that its sincere adoption involves the necessity of not
merely applying it to the settlement of the affairs of the
living generation, but of a constantly repeated application.   They are, however, fully aware of this, and
do not shrink from asserting that they are not merely
prepared, but really engaged in so acting.   And they

point, for proving this, to their arduous and unconditional defence and recommendation of the Mir, which
is *their* solution of the *second* problem of the land question,
namely, of the question between peasant and peasant.

Property in the soil being considered the property of
all, it becomes evidently necessary to decide on what
title to rest the claim of the individual to work a
certain parcel of this soil. The reply of the Sclavonian
socialists is very plain; they say, let the title be
composed of his free will and of *his evident ability.*
What? the stronger or more intelligent man, or the
man with more working capital, is to get more than the
others? The reply is, this is not what, in the first place,
we are meaning. Before all other considerations, we
have in view *the man with a larger family.* In Western
Europe the difference in the number of children between
one family and the other is a more frequent cause,
particularly with the class of small landed proprietors
and of small farmers, of the increasing difference between
wealth and poverty, than laboriousness and parsimony
here, idleness and spendthriftiness there. The great
bulk of every people, under the influence of custom and
neighbours' gossip, are pretty nearly alike as to
economical habits. Yet poverty, as well as wealth, is
on the increase in the West, with the peasant population
in France and Germany, and with what is left of that
class in England. We ascribe it to the blessing not
being known there of our "Mir." In a Western village
with divided soil a family gets poorer by being blessed
with numerous children in rapid succession. For during
the first fourteen years of his life the child is a mere
burden, and while the family which the soil has to
feed grows, the soil they possess and are able to till
does not grow; and even when, fourteen years or more
later, they are enabled to till more soil, by the growing
maturity of their progeny, in numbers of cases it has
become too late, and they are not any longer in the
position to buy or farm more soil. In our "Mir" the
family is not impoverished by the birth of a child, but, on
the contrary, *enriched.* For with the number of children

2 c

increases the share of the family in the village household. Of all that is held in common and produced in common they partake a head's share more. *The birth of a male child thus is our new title to the right of husbandry on a unit-share of the soil of the empire;* and here you have the constantly-repeated application of the theory in which we believe. The "Mir" is merely a commodious instrument for effecting it. As far as the surplus of progeny in one family is counterbalanced by the sterility of other families in the Mir, the title acquired in the Mir by the birth of a child involves no curtail ment of the titles of the other members of the "Mir." Voluntary emigration into the cities is further calculated to prevent any rapid decrease of the size of the unit-share. It is true that with the birth of the child the increase of the family's ability for working the soil is but yet prospective. But what else takes place, save that a debt is incurred, which the child grown up will have to repay in similar manner? Those who have fewer mouths of children to feed have to do work for those who have more such mouths to feed. We are levying a kind of rate, not appearing in public accounts, for counteracting the effects of such inequalities between family and family for which nobody is responsible. For we do not consider anybody responsible for the number of his children. We do not believe in the doctrine of the necessity of self-imposed restraint as means to and result of a higher stage of civilization. It is against nature; it cannot be right. Our village rate for assisting numerous families, to prevent inequality of wealth to creep into our villages, invented not by theorist, but by our people themselves in times beyond the dawn of history, is the result of an instinctive forethought, for the absence of which you in the West are punished by your poor-rates. What our people pay at once, when it can be both given as well as received with a good grace, yours have to pay afterwards, when it is burdensome to give and degrading to receive—when it, besides, is unable to cure an already hereditary evil. The "Mir" of the village, of course, is only a stage in the application of the theory of communism in land. Should the increase of the population of the village have increased in such a way as to reduce the unit-share too much, we mean to resort to the old expedient of our people, colonization. We have still uncultivated land enough, and very good land too. And if we had not, we would know how to procure it. Of the new village, the nation, the empire, has to take care, as the village does of its child.

I have let the Pansclavonian socialists speak on this particular land question between peasant and peasant so extensively, selecting from what I have read and *heard* what appeared to me their most *plausible*—by no means convincing—arguments, because it is the question they have most at heart. In fact, it is the national pride which one has here to deal with. I have the impression —I cannot help it—that the Sclavonian nations, being so very late and backward with their reformatory era, must absolutely have something for themselves. Their young men, and, in Russia itself, perhaps still more the young ladies—who are very busy and enthusiastic, and undoubtedly of a general education more resembling man's highest education than is the case in any other country, England, America, and Sweden not excepted— rushed in swarms into the political arena, as soon as the death of the Emperor Nicholas, the humiliation of the Empire in the Crimean war, and the declared willingness of the Emperor Alexander II. to unfetter the forces slumbering in this great nation, had sounded the death-knell of the German tutelage under which the nation stood before. In their youthful national enthusiasm, they looked round to what was either truly Sclavonian or altogether new. The German youth did just the same after the war of liberation from the French; and the time from 1815 to 1820 in Germany bears a striking resemblance to what took place in Russia during the first five years of Alexander's reign. The Russian youth now discovered the very old Russian Mir and the very new French socialism, and had what they wanted. Now Russia need no longer lower her head before anybody. She was

as far advanced as the boldest French radicals, and yet
could proudly tell them that, what with the French had
ended as a dream, with the Russians had begun with a
reality—a reality which they had always possessed,
although in a mutilated form, despised and maltreated;
and that they possessed it still. There was no arguing
with them, for they would not argue. They *would*
believe what they liked to believe, were sharp-witted
enough—for they *are* sharp-witted—to find out the most
plausible arguments in favour of their belief, and not
sober enough—for they *are* not sober—really to busy
themselves with examining the arguments against it.

It was not the fault of the Russian socialists, when
the occasion has not been made use of to introduce the
great Russian Mir all over the empire, to make it compulsory on the enfranchised peasantry, and to make
it perpetual. However, as they profess the firm conviction that at least all the Sclavonian people still
prefer common, to individual, husbandry, they could not
but admit that to leave it *optional* with the enfranchised
peasants, if they would continue the arrangement which
they had established when free, and, as serfs, were
compelled to uphold, was all they reasonably could
insist upon.

As to the new organization of local administration,
jurisdiction, and legislation, which was concomitant with
the measure, it is manifest that the socialist democratic
party I am speaking of repudiates any other machinery
but that of election by the people to all the representative as well as executive charges and appointments of
local self-government, *with salaries*, as far as pretexts and
money for them can be got, and without any but the
most obvious disabilities. Here the necessity to secure
as many interested advocates among the people themselves of peaceful co-operation with the Government and
the aristocracy for steering the dangerous measure into
port clear of the rocks, which mark the passage of every
serious social reform, has greatly assisted the views and
the wishes of the Russian social democrats; and Russia
is perhaps at present that country in Europe which, in

the inferior parts of its political organization, comes up nearest to the ideal of democracy. The stratagem to have the part of the business more odious to the peasants done by elected but paid—very well paid—peasants, and the part more odious to the proprietors likewise by elected, but paid—very well paid—members of the class of proprietors, has been considered as a particularly lucky stroke of policy on the part of the late minister Milintine, the statesman who enjoyed the confidence of the Russian social democrats, though he did not quite belong to their number. Time only can show if it really will prove lucky.

The Pansclavonian socialists were the movement party in the affair; the more aristocratic Russian patriots, who still are looking to Western Europe as a teacher, who have begun to make political economy a favourite study, and who meditate, before all other things, the transition of their state, cautiously and by degrees, to parliamentary government—not much in favour with the Russian socialist democracy—were willing enough to do everything that was needed to re-establish the personal liberty of the great bulk of their people, but disinclined to sacrifice the interest of the class of noble landowners to any such extent as to impair their fitness for constituting a native and independent political gentry. For, without this being accomplished, parliamentary government and local self-government in Russia, according to them, would be but a dream or a sham. I must confess that from what I, as a foreigner, know and saw of the country and people, I very strongly share this conviction. The abolition of serfdom must undoubtedly, as a secondary advantage, largely contribute to the growth of such an independent gentry among the class of landowners; for he who owns serfs, be he ever so well educated, is neither independent nor a gentleman; but then neither his authority with the people of his neighbourhood, nor the weight and freedom of movement his wealth imparts to him, must be curtailed. Thus the movement party, for whom these considerations had no meaning, was faced by a resisting party, as far as the noble proprietors' interests and the

European stamp of agrarian arrangements were concerned, among the Russians themselves.

The nightmare of an essentially German rule—severe,
as is always the rule of a minority, and of a minority
of foreign nationality too—having been taken from the
country, and the reform of agrarian legislation having,
by common consent and the imperial will, been declared
to be the first and foremost business of the awakened
nation, the older, more sober, and wealthier of the
educated Russians cast their looks, in the first instance, in the same way on England as the younger
ones did on France. They saw the soil of England
divided into huge lumps of landed property, as huge as
their own, but very much better cultivated, and yielding
splendid rent. This rent they saw paid by farmers
living on farms sometimes of considerable size, in most
cases at least of a respectable size—which, however, with
the fertility of the soil, the propitious climate, permitting the greatest number of working days in the
open air in the whole world, with the dense net of magnificent roads of all kinds, and, above all things, with a
town population standing in the relation of two and
more to one to the rural population—are equal in agricultural importance to very considerable Russian
estates. They saw these farmers bringing the whole
movable capital with them, to an amount per acre quite
beyond Russian conceptions, and sometimes even risk-
ing a part of their own capital. Thus far a most
enviable prospect arose before their view. But then
they saw a great number of agricultural labourers, not
exactly badly paid, in a great number of counties pretty
well paid, in some places, in the south-west, indeed,
insufficiently paid, but, there could be no doubt, even
where pretty well paid, *not well off*. They could not help
seeing the figures of the poor-rate in rural parishes, and
then the dwellings and the clothing! The English agricultural labourer's cottage decidedly did not come up, in
the majority of cases, to the standard of the blockhouse
of the Russian serf, either in size or in the furniture
filling the house. The clothing, cotton and cotton again,

or the smockfrock and rude shoes; and in Russia, stout
linen, woollen cloth, the sheepskin coat, and always excellent boots, almost up to the knee; the food about on a level
with that in England, perhaps a little more meat, but
less milk, butter, eggs, and river-fish; in Russia, good,
though coarse, bread in profusion; in England, better
and finer bread, but in limited quantity. In England,
peas and potatoes; in Russia, little except potatoes for
making fat cakes, but, besides peas, grits of buckwheat,
a very wholesome food, in great quantities, and lentils
and beans. The drink in both cases tea, in Russia
always of a superior quality (Congo teas); a great
difference only in the beer, which cannot be better than
in England, or worse than in Russia. But then to the
Russian kwass everybody is as welcome as to water.
It is not to be wondered at, when, after all, even many
of those Russians, who constructed the new era of their
state and their social institutions into an approach to the
forms of Western Europe, yet did not quite shut their
ear to the insinuations of their countrymen of the
doctrine of Sclavonian socialism, and from the commencement were ready to let the Mir at least have its
trial by the side of other experiments, all the more as it
was the existing form in so large a part of the empire,
apart from the serfdom, which had merely been super-
posed on the Mir.

This resolve was naturally strengthened by their eye
now falling on the farmers of *small* farms, particularly
in Ireland. For the transformation of the serfs into
labourers at one stroke had at an early period become
out of the question. The original project in this quarter
had been to transfer to the enfranchised serfs the full property of the blockhouses in which they lived, with but a
small patch of garden attached to each, without any payment on the part of the peasants, and to leave the proprietor in possession of the whole acreage. Such a settlement, at all events, would have been clear and easy
enough, and it was fancied that the gift of personal liberty
and a house, without debts, at the same time, would
be enough to content the peasants. But the strenuous

opposition of the democratic party to such a solution of the problem, the bad grace with which it was received by the Imperial Government, who looked upon the creation of an order of peasant-proprietors, or, at least, of peasant-farmers, as essentially contributing to the stability of the throne, as necessary for the business of recruiting the army, and as a guarantee of an uninterrupted increase of the population, and lastly and principally, the undeniable disinclination of the serfs themselves to part with what they had still considered as a kind, at least, of right of property, in spite of serfdom, and of ever so many personal experiences, which ought to have taught them that they had no such right, had early rendered it impossible. Thus, at least, the transitional transformation of the serfs into small farmers had already become inevitable in the immediate future. But what had been the experience where small individual farms are the rule? Why, abject misery, semi-barbarism, and, before all things, agrarian riots and agrarian crime! Thus even with *this* party the revival of the independent "Mir," as *first* form of the new peasant life, from which, as from an embryonic state, higher forms of agrarian organization were gradually to issue, soon became a settled affair. Their afterthought was, and is, of course, to get rid of it as soon as possible. An attempt to secure this possibility by a provision which made it optional with the proprietor after the lapse of a certain number of years, to turn the copy-hold—which was henceforward to form the legal and original link between the proprietor and the villagers, continuing, as free men, to work in common—into tenure at will, was likewise frustrated by the opposition of the Government. For the reasons indicated above, they had to be content with the provision, as a final compromise between the two opposed parties, that it should be made optional *with the peasants*, either to acquire the freehold of the land allotted to them, by paying a legally settled price for it in instalments, and with the assistance of Government, or to dissolve the Mir.

Thus the whole plan, under the contending influence of opposed ideas as to the future agrarian organization to be desired, assumed this general shape. The retention of the system of common husbandry by the enfranchised serfs of a village, as the cradle of an estate of peasant proprietors, created by their own free efforts, by the side of large noble proprietors of land, so that both classes of proprietors will have to show of what stuff they are made.

Events will prove whether the result of this competition between the two systems will be a constantly increasing peasant proprietary, owing to further purchases of land effected by the peasantry, or the absorption of property in the hands of the nobles, who will then have to turn it to account by free labour, instead of by the labour of serfs, or by letting their land probably in farms of larger size to the most intelligent and enterprising of the peasant class. The " Mir " or copyhold, which evidently will retain the weakest part of the peasantry, would serve all the while as a safeguard against the spread of pauperism of the West European character, as a kind of agricultural workhouse under the management of the inmates themselves, but not, as will be seen, without control ; a workhouse endowed with a not inconsiderable amount of soil, for which rent is to be paid.

Now as to the main provisions in which this general idea has been embodied.

It is unnecessary to dwell upon that part of the legislation which had for its object to restore personal liberty. The Russian people have thus acquired rights which in Europe are general rights, so far, at least, as they are valid against any private person.

The provisions concerning the partition of the land between the proprietor and the peasants are the first point of interest. The proprietor of a village is bound to hand over to the villagers, in hereditary copyhold against payment of rent, an amount of land, the exact size of which depends on local circumstances, and on friendly agreement between the proprietor and the peasants ; but there is a minimum fixed on the male head of the village population. To understand that this was possible, the law revived or rather reinforced by the Emperor Nicholas has to be kept in mind, that no proprietor was to be allowed to sell land without peasants, unless enough was left to the village to amount to $4\frac{1}{2}$ djessatines (about 12 acres) per male head of the population.

But in the same way as a minimum is fixed, a maximum also is fixed. For this purpose, European Russia (Finnland, the German Baltic provinces, and the kingdom of Poland were not affected by the measure) was divided into three zones : the steppe, the country of the black soil, and the provinces belonging to neither. These three zones were again subdivided into respectively 12, 8, and 9 districts. In the steppe districts, the minimum and maximum were made to coincide ; the legal share on the male head was fixed at 3 djessatines in the most densely-peopled district, and at 8 djessatines in the most thinly-peopled. In the two other zones, the minimum was made to form a third part of the maximum. The maximum, in some cases amounting to 7 djessatines, shows the lowest figure in the district in Moscow, where 3 djessatines were fixed as maximum, and consequently one djessatine, amounting to not quite three acres, was deemed sufficient to form the minimum. The ground built upon or enclosed as yard or garden entered into the calculation. The real extent of the grant will have been, in most cases, that of the "Nadel," that is to say, of the land which the peasants had under cultivation for sustaining themselves and their families while serfs.

It was settled that where the Nadel exceeded the new legal maximum, and the proprietor preferred to insist upon the maximum being respected, the land to be transferred from the Nadel to the proprietor's own share was, in the first instance, to be selected from among such land as was not manured, such pasture-land as had not the advantage of being inundated in spring, if possible from wooded land, if such (which, however, was rare) had formed part of the Nadel ; and especially it was to be

taken from the parts of the acreage forming the Nadel most
distant from the village, or separated from it by the
proprietor's own land.   Manured land was to be cut off
from the Nadel only as far as no land not manured could
be found for making up the proprietor's legal share.
Pasture-land improved by inundation in spring was not
to be cut off at all, except with the consent of the peasants, and even then the proportion of such land to the
whole acreage must not be altered. If such pasture land,
for instance, had formed the tenth part of the Nadel,
and 100 djessatines were to be taken from the Nadel,
not more than 10 djessatines of such pasture-land
must form part of the land to be cut off.   Kitchen gardens, and hop and hemp fields, were likewise not to be
transferred from the Nadel to the proprietor's share
without the consent of the peasants.

Where the Nadel was *less* than the new legal minimum,
the land by which the minimum was to be completed
was to be adjacent to the Nadel, and consisting of soil
really worth tilling.   Only where such soil adjacent to
the Nadel was not to be found, or where the proprietor's
dwelling was erected and his garden laid out upon it, or
where all the adjacent land was manured or inundated,
retained before by the proprietor, land *not* adjacent
to the Nadel might be taken to make up the minimum.
But then, at all events, the land nearest to the village
was to be taken for the purpose, and a cattle-path to
the village was to be let free, without entering into the
account as landed property.

It will be seen from this what precautions were taken
to prevent the proprietor from mutilating the self-sustaining completeness of peasant husbandry from the
beginning.   The animus of those who had the paramount
influence in framing the details of the measure is clear ;
they wanted a stable " Mir," or, if the peasants should
prefer to dissolve it, a stable peasantry founded on
individual property.

For the first two years a provisional agreement (by
way of experiment) was admissible. During the next
six years the proprietor, but not the peasants, had the

right of insisting upon a definitive settlement, the expenses being borne by the proprietor.   Minor details, all strictly in keeping with the general spirit of the measure, and whose number and variety is very great, cannot be mentioned here.   Great part of them has reference to the different forms of husbandry in use in the different parts of Russia.   Others refer to the erection of new and the pulling down of old houses.   Part of them had merely a transitory character.

For the space of nine years after the new regulations had become the law of the land, it was rendered *obligatory* on the peasantry to keep the land in copyhold against payment of rent.   Only this much was allowed, that by free agreement between the proprietor and the peasants, on the proposition of the latter, a reduction of the peasant's share to one-half of the maximum, where this at first had been exceeded, could be effected.   But this was then to be the definitive size of the peasant's share.   It was further allowed, that if the peasants in common should have purchased, in the way which will be described beneath, a part of the land, transferred to them first as copyhold, before the nine years were elapsed, such part not being less than one-third of the maximum, the peasants should have the *right* to renounce retaining the copyhold of the remainder.   If, finally, the proprietors should resolve to make a present to the peasants of so much land as formed one-fourth of the maximum, and the peasants should agree to accept it, then, too, the peasants might renounce the remainder in copyhold, even before the obligatory nine years were elapsed.

This, in the interest of arriving as quickly as possible at the establishment of a proprietary peasantry holding common *or* individual property, was rather an ingenious provision, but in form very Russian !   First, the peasants are compelled to remain as copyholders, *peasants*, for the space of nine years after they had ceased to be serfs.   Thus, it was hoped to get them accustomed to peasant life under freedom, by means of a little coercion, as the only pardonable and transitory remnant of serfdom,

namely, the coercion of continuing to till the soil as
copyholders instead of as serfs.   If they should feel the
burden of the compulsory payment of the copyhold-fee
too extensive, an escape is left them by their becoming
proprietors of a smaller amount of land.   And the proprietor of the estate, too, is stimulated to secure to himself a less curtailed estate, by assisting the peasants in
becoming freeholders.

Should a decrease of the (male) population of the
village take place during the first nine years amounting
to at least one-fifth of the whole, and *not* proceeding from
peasants emigrating from the village and disconnecting
themselves, with the consent of the other villagers—liable
each for all and all for each—from their joint liability,
but arriving from *other* causes, then, the peasants should
likewise be entitled to renounce a corresponding part
of the copyhold enforced upon them.

Here the disconnection of single peasants from the
joint liability, with the consent of the others, in spite of
the compulsory nature of the copyhold, demands explain-
ing.   The explanation, which consists simply in the condition that the peasant thus liberated must already
have become a *peasant proprietor*, is furnished by another
provision of the law, which follows here.

Should, namely, a peasant be the proprietor of at least
double of the maximum per head of land, not forming
part of the common copyhold, and being situated at no
greater distance from the village than 15 versts (10
miles), then he was to be free to renounce to his share in
the copyhold the land which was allotted to him of the
common copyhold continuing to form part of it, and he
himself continuing a member of the political commune.
In such villages where the institution of the Mir was
unknown, and the Nadel divided into hereditary lots (in
the West, with the Little Russians and Ruthenes), every
peasant who should have become the proprietor of land
amounting to double the maximum per head, should
be entitled to renounce to his hereditary lot in the
copyhold in the same way, the lot becoming copyhold
of the others *in common;* and also if he had purchased

such an amount of land from the proprietor of the estate himself out of the common copyhold land.   But in both cases it would be necessary that either the other villagers remaining liable for the whole amount of copyhold rent, and the proprietor of the estate too, should consent to let him free, or that the proprietor of the estate should renounce to so much copyhold rent as corresponds to the contribution to it of the peasant desirous to quit, or that the peasant pays down the capitalized value of the rent, calculated at 6 per cent., due by him.   It is the *law*, only destined to compel the peasants to remain peasants at least for the space of nine years, which has let him off because he has given other security for his remaining true to his order; as far as *private* interests are affected, an agreement *or* payment is still necessary.

The anxious efforts of the Government to make a freehold peasantry proceed from the measure of emancipation of the serfs become here again visible.

After the lapse of nine years—a time now fast approaching—the copyholders with joint liability still left may renounce to such part of the copyhold land as any one of its members has renounced before.   It will only then become more clearly discernible to what extent henceforward landed property of large size, landed property of small size, and copyhold will enter into the agrarian state of the country.

There was one way left for the proprietor of the estate and the peasantry on it agreeing to avail themselves of it, viz., a partition of the land, leaving the whole acreage in the hands of the proprietor, and the houses, kitchen gardens, and some pasture land only as copyhold, with option to purchase it, in the hands of the peasants, namely, on an application from both parties to Government to confer upon the village the character of a market town. It appears that there has been little resort to it, or, perhaps, Government has been tardy in lending assistance.

In attempting to prevent as much peasant husbandry as possible from being discontinued, the legislature did not forget the emergency of the peasants' temporarily

failing to meet their liabilities. It was, of course, necessary, in the case of arrears of rent, to place a corresponding
amount of land again at the disposal of the proprietor of
the estate. But it was provided that during the first
nine years, either the joint copyholders, or, where hereditary lots are the custom, any single member of the community, not being himself in arrears with rent, might
step into the dormant copyhold right, after every third
year's harvest had taken place. After the lapse of the
nine years, the right of the peasants to step into quies-
cent copyhold titles can be exercised but once, three
years after the seizure. If it then be not exercised,
the land will return definitively to the proprietor of the
estate.

The money paid down by peasants resolved to give
up their share in the joint copyhold, as capitalization of
their running liability, was ordered to be reserved as
guarantee-fund for the combined copyholders discharging
their liabilities. But it was made optional with the
proprietor of the estate to have the money paid out to
himself on his renouncing to the amount of rent thus
capitalized.

Now as to the way of fixing *the form* and amount of
the compulsory copyhold-fee—by far the most difficult
part of the whole proceeding.

It was assumed—with what right a foreign observer is
unable to say—that a sudden and absolute transition in
the form of a compulsory rent from the form of labour
to the form of money was inadmissible, if it was everywhere to be rendered possible for the villagers to discharge their liabilities. It was deemed to the interest
of the preservation of an order of peasants as numerous
as possible, to acquiesce not merely in a remnant of coercion in general, but even in a remnant of compulsory
labour, the law prescribing in lieu of what amount of
money it should stand.

In both cases as well where labour was chosen as
the form of the rent, as where money was chosen,
the maximum of peasants' land on the male head of the
village population was made the legal starting-point

of the calculation. The rent due for a share coming up to the maximum was laid down, in the form of labour, as amounting to forty days of man's labour and thirty days of woman's labour. Where the actual share did not come up to the maximum, the amount was to be reduced in proportion. Three-fifths of the days were to be summer days, and two-fifths winter days. For each half summer day in addition to the three-fifths, a winter day falls out. The number of working days due by the whole community of copyholders, during either of the two half-yearly periods is to be divided by the number of weeks ; and the proprietor of the estate cannot claim more working days in the course of a week than fall within a week. The number of working days falling within a single week is to be divided by three, and on no day of the week can he claim more than a third part. He is, however, entitled to add the odd days of both divisions, but never more than one working day per week, and one working day per day. Two working days of a horse are to be considered equal to one working day of a man. The men discharging the labour incumbent upon the community are to be taken from among the men between 18 and 55 years, and the woman from among the women between 17 and 50 years. It is permitted to the peasants to fill their place with a hired labourer.

It will be seen that care has been taken to keep as close as possible, in framing the law, to the custom which prevailed in the times of serfdom, of the proprietor leaving three days of the week to his serfs, and claiming the other three for himself. He has still his three days per week, only he has far less labourers to dispose of. For instead of having to claim about one hundred and thirty days, he has to claim but forty, and respectively thirty. This, especially, is what has reduced the value of Russian estates after the abolition of serfdom.

For the rent in money, too, where this form is adopted, does not make up for the working days of the serfs lost by the proprietor, being merely the equivalent of the number of working days now forming the rent of a share.   The transition from labour-rent to money-rent was made optional with the peasants, with the whole community, or with every single family—in the sense of the repartition for tilling purposes of the land by the members of the community among themselves, tjaglo—only two years after the law had become valid, and they being not in arrear with working days.   Four-fifths of the peasants having effected the transition from labour-rent to money-rent, it was made optional with the proprietor of the estate to compel the remaining fifth.   The money-rent, to which the traditional name of every tax on the peasantry, signifying very different things in different times, "obrok," was preserved, was fixed on the male head of the population, to which the number of shares corresponds, but without exact proportion to the size of the land-share.   The situation of the land in the empire was considered of higher importance, as soon as its value was to be expressed in *money*, than either the exact size or the quality of the soil, which, moreover, had been made to compensate each other as much as possible, by the legal maximum of the shares varying with the zones and their districts, and having generally, cæteris paribus, been made smaller on more fertile soil.   And it was certainly correct political economy, as soon as the money value—the value of *exchange*—of rent was in question, to pay attention to that element in the formation of land-rent which the German Von Thünen, fifty years ago, has discovered and traced with ability, in the distance of land from the market, the place of *exchange*.   Consequently it was laid down as law that the "obrok" was to amount for the maximum-share at a distance from St. Petersburgh of not more than 25 versts (15 miles) to 12 rubles (1lst. 18 sh.) on the male head, in the districts of Petersburgh, Moscov, Zaroslaw, Wladimir, Nijar-Nowgorod, and close to the banks of the Wolga, to 10 rubles (1lst. 12 sh.); in a series of other districts to 9 rubles (1lst. 8 sh.); and, where the lowest figure was applied, to 8 rubles (1lst. 5 sh.).   However, to a certain extent, the size of the share for which the "obrok" is to be paid was made to

2 D

enter the calculation, namely, by the following arrangement. In the first zone, one half of the maximum "obrok" has to be paid for the first djessatine of the real share, including the space of house and garden; for the second djessatine one fourth of the maximum "obrok" is to be paid; and the remaining fourth is to be considered as the equivalent of so much djessatines as the maximum consists of besides the two first djessatines. This leaves but a small part of the "obrok" as representing the rent of such djessatines as the real share may contain less than the maximum, and so much only is taken off from the "obrok." The regulation of the way of calculating the reduction varies a little for the two other zones.

The average maximum share being about 12 acres in size, its rent in the form of labour being set down at seventy working days, made up of male and female, of summer and winter labour, and the average rent in the form of money being 11st. 8s., it follows that the legislator has estimated the rent of an acre in Russia at 2s. 4d., and the wages of agricultural labour at 5d. a day.

Both estimates are far from coinciding with the prices actually obtainable in the open market. Wages almost everywhere are much higher, so that it is advantageous to the peasantry to pay "obrok," instead of working for the proprietor. Land is both much dearer *and* much cheaper. Land under actual tillage by peasants as a rule is dearer; so that such peasants as pay "obrok" have been gainers of wealth by the measure, beside the amount of freedom they have acquired.

There is another "obrok" to be paid by the peasantry for the houses, stables, barns, gardens, improvements on pasture land, &c., in one word, for the fixed capital, which forms part of the copyhold-grant. For this purpose four classes of villages were formed. Such as are exclusively devoted to agriculture, and which offer no peculiar advantage to their inhabitants, have to pay $1\frac{1}{2}$ rubles on the male head; such as are carrying on branches of industry, particularly market-gardening, culture of hemp and beet-root for sale, &c., have to pay $2\frac{1}{2}$ rubles; such as enjoy evident local advantages,

being situated in the neighbourhood of Petersburgh or
Moscow, &c., have to pay 3½ rubles; and the fourth
class consists of villages whose local advantages are so
great—for instance, villages in suburban relation to towns
of 20,000 inhabitants and more—that not merely a
higher house-obrok but also a higher land-obrok is
founded on justice. Here the provincial committee is
entrusted with settling the amount of liabilities, a limit
being, however, drawn by law.

The " obrok " is to be paid six months in advance, if
the proprietor insists upon it. Otherwise an agreement
may be come to, which is then binding upon both
parties, like the amount of the obrok itself, for the space
of twenty years, after the lapse of which a new arrangement may take place. The obrok is collected in the same
way as the public taxes, by the elected functionaries of
the local self-government. The promise of the Government was to enforce it with all possible rigour.

The most important, however, of the main provisions
of the Act of 1861 is that which refers to the *right* of
the peasants to purchase the copyhold on which they
are living. They were *compelled* to accept the copyhold ;
but, in compensation, the proprietor of the estate is *compelled* to accept their money, if they are able and willing to
buy either each his own share, dissolving the community,
or together the whole of the grant, continuing the community. The legal price is 16⅔ fold the amount of the
" obrok." They are entitled to purchase the farm-yard
alone or together with the land, the " obrok " for the one, as
has been seen, being separated from the " obrok " for the
other. This option, left to them, has been the subject
of much controversy. The proprietors would have preferred to see the whole village do either the one or the
other. Where the community is not dissolved, and not
inclined to purchase the land in common, each single
peasant may yet assert his right of purchasing his own
share, but on condition that he pays one-fifth more than
the purchase-money otherwise would amount to.

Government has undertaken to assist the peasantry in
purchasing the land, by advancing, on the security of the

" obrok " collected by their agents, part of the necessary
sum, amounting to four-fifths where the whole grant is purchased, and to three-quarters where a part of it of certain
size is purchased, in form of bonds of the Imperial Bank,
bearing five per cent. interest, or titles to rent, guaranteed
by Government, which afterwards are to be taken in exchange for such bonds of the bank.   They are to be paid
over at once to the proprietor of the estate or to his
creditors.   Only such peasants, of course, can receive the
benefit of governmental assistance who have already
turned the labour-rent into " obrok."   But Government,
always in the interest of securing the existence of a
numerous order of peasants, has placed another condition on their assistance.   The purchase-money is only
advanced in behalf of such peasants as consent to purchase the dwelling-houses and farm-yards *with* the land.
This also will tend to lessen the number of cases—apprehended by the proprietors—of a part of the peasants in a
village purchasing the houses and farm-yards *with* the
land, and a part *without* it.

As yet it is impossible to judge of the full practical
bearing of this great agrarian reform among one of the
most numerous and influential nations of the earth,
holding in possession such an immense territory.   A
considerable number of peasant proprietors, partly individuals, partly communities, have already sprung up.
In my opinion, the difference between single and common
property is greater, and of greater importance, than that
between freehold and copyhold.   Should the " Mir " prevail, colonization undoubtedly will be favoured by it, as it
was in olden times, and as seems to have been the
case thousands of years ago in China, where the most
populous nation of the earth has derived its strength in
colonization from similar agrarian institutions.   But interior social progress will be weak, as it always has been in
Russia, and as it has been in China.   And the country
will continue to be in danger of despotic political and
social institutions.   For nations who are in the habit of
sacrificing so much of their individuality as to become,
in their daily life, the slaves of a majority, are always at

but one step's distance from becoming the slaves of a master.　Had the ancient Russian villages not been communists, they would not have become slaves ; not the law, but their individual weakness, which knew not how to resist the abuse of the law, has cost them their liberty.

From the little I have seen of the Russian peasants, I do *not* think that the Mir will continue for any length of time to be popular with them.　I have a presentiment that they will shortly and strongly disavow by their acts that they are what the philosophers who pretend to speak in their name represent them to be.　I fancy that I have discovered very great resemblances between them and the peasantry, of mixed German and Sclavonic blood, in the Eastern provinces of my own country—Prussia.　If I am right in this, then anything rather than communistic habits and leanings are to be expected from them as free men ; and I hope it will be so, in the general interest of civilized humanity.

VIII.

FARM LAND AND LAND-LAWS OF THE UNITED STATES.

By C. M. Fisher.

Counsellor-at-Law, United States.

INTRODUCTION.

This Essay is intended to convey some general idea of the actual distribution of land in the United States; the proportion of landowners to population; the laws which relate to land as to facilities of transfer, descent, &c. ; as well as some information as to the fitness of the Irish emigrant for becoming the owner and cultivator of land.

In a country so vast as the United States, there must necessarily be few individuals whose opportunities for observation can be sufficiently extensive to enable them to speak positively upon all the foregoing points, as relating to the country at large. It will also be seen that in America the enormous amount of lands eminently suited for agriculture, must necessarily influence the operation and working of the laws affecting land; and to the former fact, perhaps, more than to the laws, must be attributed the great prosperity of the country, which, to the man of observation, must be apparent in the driving of the ploughshare over wide fields between the two great oceans of this half-continent, and from the inland seas of the north to the tropics; in establishing, according to the census of 1860, above 2,440,000 farms, and in creating cities rivalling some of the proud capitals of Europe which had been founded a thousand years ago. These, with towns and villages, numbered at the above date 28,000, and contained at that time a fraction less than 5,000,000 of houses; pointing, in a significant way, to the industry of our population.

THE LANDS OF THE UNITED STATES.

The agricultural area of the United States, by the last census, in 1860, embraced 163,110,720 acres of improved land, and 244,101,818 acres of land unimproved. In other words, for every two acres of improved land there were, at the period in question, three acres of land connected therewith not under cultivation; while the gross aggregate of uncultivated territory, fertile and waste, swells to 1,466,969,862 acres.

This fact determines the agriculture of the country. Land is abundant and cheap, while labour is scarce and dear. Even in the older-settled States there is much land that can be purchased at extremely low rates; and, by a recent Act of Congress known as the Free Homestead Law, every citizen of the United States, or any foreigner who shall declare his intention of becoming a citizen, can have a farm of 160 acres without charge. As good land as any in the world is offered to actual settlers on these easy terms.

Under such circumstances it is evident that the high-farming system of agriculture which is practised in some older and more densely-populated countries, where labour is abundant and the land mostly under cultivation, cannot, as a general rule, be profitably adopted at present in this new country. It has been said that American agriculture is half a century behind that of Great Britain. In one sense this is perhaps true. Our land is not as thoroughly under-drained, manured, and cultivated as that of England, Scotland, or Belgium; but we can, and do now, produce a bushel of wheat at much less cost than the most scientific farmer of England can by the best approved method of cultivation, *even if he paid nothing for the use of his land.*

The following Table exhibits the amount of improved, unimproved, and cash value of farm lands, the aggregate population, and the number of farmers and farm-labourers in each State, as collected from all the official records of most recent date procurable.

The total population is, I believe, now estimated to

be upwards of 40,000,000, and at the period when the next census will be taken, 1870, next year, the expectation is that the population will be found to number even 42,500,000.

TABLE.

Name of State.	Amount of improved lands in 1860.	Lands unimproved.	Cash value.	Aggregate population.	Number of Farmers.	Number of Farm Labourers
	Acres.	Acres.	$			
Alabama . .	6,385,724	12,718,821	175,824,622	964,201	. .	14,282
Arkansas . .	1,983,313	7,590,393	91,649,773	435,450	48,475	8,350
California . .	2,468,034	6,262,000	48,726,804	379,994	20,836	10,421
Connecticut	1,830,807	673,457	90,830,005	460,147	30,612	11,489
Delaware . .	637,065	367,230	31,426,357	112,216	7,284	4,122
Florida . .	654,213	2,266,015	16,435,727	140,424	7,534	1,329
Georgia . .	8,062,758	18,587,732	157,072,803	1,057,286	67,718	19,567
Illinois . .	13,096,374	7,815,615	408,944,033	1,711,951	153,646	47,216
Indiana . .	8,242,183	8,146,109	356,712,175	1,350,428	158,714	40,827
Iowa . . .	3,792,792	6,277,115	119,899,547	674,913	88,628	27,196
Kansas. . .	405,468	1,372,932	12,258,239	107,206	15,572	3,660
Kentucky . .	7,644,208	11,519,053	291,496,955	1,155,684	110,937	36,627
Louisiana . .	2,707,108	6,591,468	204,789,662	708,002	14,996	5,483
Maine . . .	2,704,133	3,023,538	78,688,525	628,279	64,843	15,865
Maryland . .	3,002,267	1,833,304	145,973,677	687,049	27,696	12,920
Massachusetts.	2,155,512	1,183,212	123,255,948	1,231,066	45,204	17,430
Michigan . .	3,476,296	3,554,538	160,836,495	749,113	88,657	35,884
Minnesota. .	556,250	2,155,718	27,505,922	172,023	27,921	. .
Mississippi	5,065,755	10,773,929	190,760,367	791,305	46,308	7,972
Missouri . .	6,246,871	13,737,939	230,632,126	1,182,012	124,989	39,396
New Hampshire	2,367,034	1,377,591	69,689,761	326,073	35,392	10,152
New Jersey .	1,944,441	1,039,084	180,250,338	672,035	30,325	18,429
New York. .	14,358,403	6,616,555	803,343,593	3,880,735	254,786	115,728
North Carolina	6,517,284	17,245,685	143,301,065	992,622	85,198	19,119
Ohio . . .	12,625,394	7,846,747	678,132,991	2,339,511	223,485	76,484
Oregon . .	896,414	1,164,125	15,200,593	52,465	7,861	1,260
Pennsylvania .	10,463,296	6,548,844	662,050,707	2,906,215	180,613	69,104
Rhode Island .	335,128	186,096	19,550,553	174,620	6,875	3,510
South Carolina	4,572,060	11,623,859	139,652,508	703,708	35,137	6,312
Tennessee . .	6,795,337	13,873,828	271,358,985	1,109,801	103,835	25,990
Texas . . .	2,650,781	22,693,247	88,101,320	604,215	51,569	6,537
Vermont . .	2,823,157	1,451,257	94,289,045	315,098	38,967	14,022
Virginia . .	11,437,822	19,679,215	371,761,661	1,596,318	108,958	30,518
Wisconsin . .	3,746,167	4,147,420	131,117,164	775,881	93,859	31,472
Colorado Territory }	. .	. .	. .	34,277	195	. .
Dakota Territory }	2,115	24,333	96,445	4,837	495	. .
Nebraska Territory }	118,789	512,425	3,878,326	28,841	3,982	455
Nevada Territory }	14,132	41,986	302,340	6,857	140	74
New Mexico Territory }	149,274	1,265,635	2,707,386	93,516	5,922	5,461
Utah Territory	77,219	12,692	1,333,355	40,273	3,832	670
Washington Territory }	81,869	284,287	2,217,842	11,594	1,653	257
District of Columbia }	17,474	16,789	2,989,267	75,080	246	89

The laws of the United States and the various States of the United States do not differ very materially as to the method of conveying real estate.

Many of the States have by special legislation defined certain words, so as to simplify the mode or form of making deeds of conveyance, and perhaps it will not be out of place to recite at length the usual form of such a deed.

" This Deed, made the_____day of_____, in the year _____, Between (here insert the names of the parties) Witnesseth : that in consideration of (here state the consideration) the said _____doth (or do) grant unto the said_____All &c. (here describe the property, and insert covenants or any other provisions).

" Witness the following signature and seal (or signatures and seals)."

By the same legislation it is provided as follows :

Every such deed, conveying lands, shall, unless an exception be made therein, be construed to include all the estate, right, title or interest whatever, both at law and in equity, of the grantor in or to such lands.

Whenever, in any deed, there shall be used the words, " The said grantor (or the said_____) releases to the said grantee (or the said _____) All his claims upon the said lands," such deed shall be construed as if it set forth that the grantor hath remised, released and for ever quit claimed, and by these presents doth remise, release and for ever quit claim unto the grantee, his heirs and assigns, all right, title, and interest whatsoever, both at law and in equity, in or to the lands and premises granted, or intended so to be, so that neither he nor his personal representative, his heirs or assigns, shall at any time hereafter have, claim, challenge or demand the said lands and premises, or any part thereof, in any manner whatever.

A Deed of Lease may be made in the following form, or to the same effect : —

" This Deed, made the ____ day of _____in the ____year _____Between (here insert the names of parties) Witnesseth : that the said_____ doth demise unto the said _____his personal representatives and assigns, All &c. (here describe the property) from the ____day of____for the term of____ thence ensuing, yielding therefor during the said term the rent of (here state the rent and mode of payment).

" Witness the following signature and seal."

When a deed uses the words, " the said covenants," such covenant shall have the same effect as if it was expressed to be by the covenantor, for himself, his heirs, personal representatives and assigns, and shall be deemed to be with the covenantee, his heirs, personal representatives and assigns.

A covenant by the grantor in a deed, " that he will warrant generally the property hereby conveyed," shall have the same effect as if the grantor had covenanted that he, his heirs and personal representatives will for ever warrant and defend the said property unto the grantee, his heirs, personal representatives and assigns, against the claims and demands of all persons whomsoever.

A covenant by any such grantor, " that he will warrant specially the property hereby conveyed," shall have the same effect as if the grantor had covenanted that he, his heirs and personal representatives will for ever warrant and defend the said property unto the grantee, his heirs, personal representatives and assigns, against the claims and demands of the grantor, and all persons claiming or to claim by, through, or under him.

The words " with general warranty," in the granting part of any deed, shall be deemed to be a covenant by the grantor " that he will warrant generally the property hereby conveyed." The words " with special warranty," in the granting part of any deed, shall be deemed to be a covenant by the grantor " that he will warrant specially the property hereby conveyed."

A covenant by the grantor in a deed for land " that he has the right to convey the said land to the grantee," shall have the same effect as if the grantor had covenanted that he had good right, full power and absolute authority to convey the said land, with all the buildings thereon and the privileges and appurtenances thereto belonging,

unto the grantee, in the manner in which the same is
conveyed, or intended so to be by the deed, and according
to its true intent.

A covenant by any such grantor " that the grantee
shall have quiet possession of the said land," shall
have as much effect as if he covenanted that the
grantee, his heirs and assigns, might, at any and all times
thereafter, peaceably and quietly enter upon and have,
hold and enjoy the land conveyed by the deed, or intended so to be, with all the buildings thereon, and the
privileges and appurtenances thereto belonging, and
receive and take the rents and profits thereof, to and for
his and their use and benefit, without any eviction, interruption, suit, claim or demand whatever. If to such
covenant there be added " free from all incumbrances,"
these words shall have as much effect as the words,
" and that freely and absolutely acquitted, exonerated,
and for ever discharged, or otherwise by the said grantor
or his heirs, saved harmless and indemnified, of, from, and
against any and every charge and incumbrance whatever."

A covenant by any such grantor, " that he will
execute such further assurances of the said lands as may
be requisite," shall have the same effect as if he covenanted that he, the said grantor, his heirs or personal
representatives, will at any time, upon any reasonable
request, at the charge of the grantee, his heirs or assigns,
do, execute, or cause to be done or executed, all such
further acts, deeds, and things for the better, more
perfectly and absolutely conveying and assuring the
said lands and premises hereby conveyed, or intended
so to be, unto the grantee, his heirs and assigns as his or
their counsel, shall be reasonably devised, advised or
required.

A covenant by any such grantor, " that he has done
no act to incumber the said lands," shall have the same
effect as if he covenanted that he had not done or
executed, or knowingly suffered any act, deed, or thing,
whereby the lands and premises conveyed, or intended
so to be, or any part thereof, are, or will be charged,
affected, or incumbered in title, estate, or otherwise.

In a Deed of Lease, a covenant by the lessee " to pay the rent," shall have the effect of a covenant that the rent reserved by the deed shall be paid to the lessor, or those entitled under him, in the manner therein mentioned: and a covenant by him "to pay the taxes," shall have the effect of a covenant that all taxes, levies, and assessments upon the demised premises, or upon the lessor on account thereof, shall be paid by the lessee, or those claiming under him.

In a Deed of Lease, a covenant by the lessee that " he will not assign without leave," shall have the same effect as a covenant that the lessee will not, during the term, assign, transfer, or set over the premises, or any part thereof, to any person, without the consent in writing of the lessor, his representatives or assigns : and a covenant by him that " he will leave the premises in good repair," shall have the same effect as a covenant that the demised premises will, at the expiration, or other sooner determination of the term, be peaceably surrendered and yielded up unto the lessor, his representatives or assigns, in good and substantial repair and condition, reasonable wear and tear excepted.

No covenant or promise by a lessee that he will leave the premises in good repair, shall have the effect if the buildings are destroyed by fire, or otherwise, without fault or negligence on his part, or of binding him to erect such buildings again, unless there be other words, showing it to be the intent of the parties that he should be so bound.

A covenant by a lessor " for the lessee's quiet enjoyment of his term," shall have the same effect as a covenant that the lessee, his personal representatives and lawful assigns paying the rent reserved, and performing his or their covenants, shall peaceably possess and enjoy the demised premises for the term granted, without any interruption or disturbance from any person whatever.

And if in a Deed of Lease it be provided that " the lessor may re-enter for default of   days in the payment of rent, or for the breach of covenants," it

shall have the effect of an agreement that if the rent
reserved, or any part thereof, be unpaid for such number
of days after the day on which it ought to have been
paid, or if any of the other covenants on the part of the
lessee, his personal representative or assigns, be broken,
then, in either of such cases, the lessor or those entitled
in his place at any time afterwards, into and upon the
demised premises, or any part thereof, in the name of
the whole, may re-enter, and the same again have,
repossess, and enjoy, as of his or their former estate.

All deeds are valid between the parties, whether recorded or not, but void as to creditors and other purchasers, unless recorded in the town, county, or district
in which the land intended to be conveyed may be
situated.

The records touching a lot or parcel of land, exhibited
by the books of the registry office where situated, and
of which authenticated certificates are readily procurable
for a small fee, are always held to be good evidence of
ownership, even in the absence of the Deeds of Conveyance themselves.

The ordinary fee charged for preparing simple leases
or deeds is from one to two dollars (say from 4*s.* to 8*s.*),
and fifty cents (or 2*s.*) for recording a deed.

The laws governing the distribution of land belonging
to the estates of intestates are not exactly the same in
each State, yet, upon examination of the laws of the
various States, it will be found that there is but slight
difference, and the distribution or division of such estates
is made between and among the children, both male and
female, in equal proportions, and the representatives of
a deceased child—such representatives of a deceased
child taking only such portion as the parent would have
taken if living. And when the estate is inconsiderable,
or when it cannot be divided without great injury, that
is to say, when partition would materially lessen its
value, the Court having jurisdiction may decree the
whole or any part of the land to one of the heirs, who
would be called upon to pay such sum of money to the
others as Commissioners appointed by the Court should

deem to be just and fair. When it is considered advisable that the land be so decreed to any one of the heirs, the eldest male is to be preferred to the others, and the males to the females. I believe this to be a wise discretion, which is possessed by the various Probate Courts; and it is generally a matter of agreement among all interested in the estate—which of the heirs shall take the land, and how much money the heir so taking shall pay to the others for their shares.

The widow, if any, is entitled to the use of one-third of all the real estate during her lifetime, which may be set out or apportioned to her by Commissioners whom the Court appoint for that purpose. She is also entitled to such proportion of the personal estate as the Court may assign to her, for her own absolute use; and this assignment is not to be less than one-third of the value of all that may remain, after the payment of the debts of the intestate.

This method of distributing estates tends to prevent large holdings, as at the death of any large holder his estate would, in almost all instances, be divided amongst those who might come after him; and, in cases of small farms, by the provisions of the law already referred to, injurious subdivisions are avoided. Again, although all the children of a landholder would share in the division of the estate, yet if the old homestead were insufficient to provide each with a farm, those who might receive their share in money would have the wherewithal to assist them to acquire new lands in the great West, or in other ways to make homes for themselves.

In Virginia, and in other parts of the South, very large grants of land were made before the organization of the United States, and at a time when lands were of inconsiderable value, which grants have been farmed as plantations, and with slave labour. Before the late war, although the children of an intestate shared equally in the distribution of such an estate, yet it was customary for some of them, by purchase, to become the owner of the whole estate, or else it was sold in block to any purchaser who might be found, and the proceeds equally divided.

With slave labour, such products as cotton, tobacco, rice, &c., could only be grown with advantage upon large plantations; and the Southern States, with these large holdings, and only slave labour for their cultivation, although more favoured by nature, have, it appears to my mind, not made the rapid progress of the Western and Middle States, with their smaller holdings of land. Since the abolition of slavery and the substitution of free and skilled white labour, I incline to the opinion that smaller holdings will hereafter be found the rule in the South, and in fact I am aware that many large plantations have recently been parcelled into several farms, with a view to their being worked in accordance with the altered circumstances of the South.

Foreigners may buy and hold land in the United States, upon being naturalized (or upon filing in the office of the clerk of the proper Court, a declaration of intention of becoming naturalized), the same as a native-born citizen; and in some few States, such as Georgia, Wisconsin, &c., aliens may hold land.

Of the emigrant settlers, those from Ireland, in many instances, make good and thrifty farmers, and acquire considerable property; but still a large proportion of the Irish are always to be found among the labouring population. Their qualifications for making good settlers are not so rare as might be generally supposed by an eye-witness of the agricultural performances of many small Irish tenant-farmers in their native land.

In America, industry and hard work, when directed to the cultivation of land, offer greater rewards than in Ireland, and this fact appears to have a marked effect upon many an Irish emigrant. Again, a description of husbandry which an English well-to-do farmer might consider slovenly, is, perhaps, as well calculated to make profit out of a newly-cleared farm as a more careful system would be; and so even a comparatively ignorant man may, by turning his attention to farming, surely reap a good return and ultimate independence, provided he devote himself with diligence to the work. And with such examples before him the newly-arrived emigrant is constantly stimulated to exertion in a similar direction. I could point to many instances in the State of Vermont, and in others, where a comparatively ignorant and penniless Irish emigrant had, almost immediately after arrival, arranged for the purchase, on time, of a lot of land; then worked as a labourer until he had got together a few dollars to purchase implements, seed, and a little food, the latter in the shape of a barrel of flour, some salt pork, tea, &c., forming sufficient for one season, and who had, without any other aid, managed to struggle on until a succession of harvests found him a rich man in comparison with his former condition. The feeling of " becoming one's own landlord," of " owning the fee-simple of land," is one that has been spoken of, in my hearing, by this class of persons, and appears to me to be calculated to afford, and does afford, great individual gratification, and must at the same time act as a strong incentive to exertion in the right direction ; and I would say further, that I believe it to be the first great ambition of every Irish emigrant to become the owner of real estate. Even many who continue to work as labourers for years after their arrival in the country, will constantly speak of a time when they hope to have a farm of their own, a hope which, it may be, from the cultivation of habits which debar the accumulation of capital sufficient, or from other causes, they are delayed or prevented from realising ; and then, after time elapses, perhaps, influenced by a feeling of contentment with the present, they may, and, I regret to say, occasionally do, augment that no inconsiderable class called " loafers," who live a hand-to-mouth sort of existence.

In the Eastern and Middle States the farms are not large. The average I believe to consist of from fifty to two hundred acres of land, and many of even less extent.

Land in most States is valued by properly-appointed assessors once in five years, for the purposes of taxation ; and before the late war the tax upon land was light, being raised for local and school purposes only. Even now, I believe it is not more than one per cent. upon the appraised value of land.

2 E

The following extracts from the statutes of some of the various States, in regard to descent and distribution of land, may be taken as a sample of the statutes of the others upon the same subjects.

EXTRACT FROM GENERAL LAWS, UNITED STATES.

Ordinance of Congress (sitting under the Articles of Confederation) for the Government of the Territory of the United States north-west of the River Ohio, passed 13 *July,* 1787.

1. Be it ordained by the United States in Congress assembled, That, &c.

2. Be it ordained by the authority aforesaid, That the estates both of resident and non-resident proprietors in the said territory, dying intestate, shall descend to, and be distributed among their children, and the descendants of a deceased child in equal parts, the descendants of a deceased child or grandchild to take the share of their deceased parent in equal parts among them; and where there shall be no children or descendants, then in equal parts to the next of kin, in equal degree; and among collaterals, the children of a deceased brother or sister of the intestate shall have, in equal parts among them, their deceased parent's share; and there shall in no case be a distinction between kindred of the whole and half blood; saving in all cases to the widow of the intestate her third part of the real estate for life.

STATE OF MASSACHUSETTS.

Extract from Laws relating to Descent and Distribution of Real Estate. Chap. 91.

Section 1.—When a person dies seised of land, tenements, or hereditaments, or of any right thereto, or entitled to any interest therein, in fee simple or for the life of another, not having lawfully devised the same, they shall descend, subject to his debts (except as provided in chapter one hundred and four), in manner following:

First.—In equal shares to his children and the issue of any deceased child by right of representation; and if there is no child of the intestate living at his death, then to all his other lineal descendants; if all the descendants are in the same degree of kindred to the intestate, they shall share the estate equally; otherwise they shall take according to the right of representation.

Second.—If he leaves no issue, then to his father.

Third.—If he leaves no issue nor father, then in equal shares to his mother, brothers, and sisters, and to the children of any deceased brother or sister by right of representation.

Fourth.—If he leaves no issue, nor father, and no brother nor sister, living at his death, then to his mother to the exclusion of the issue, if any, of deceased brothers or sisters.

Fifth.—If he leaves no issue, and no father, mother, brother, nor sister, then to his next of kin in equal degree; except that when there are two or more collateral kindred in equal degree, but claiming through different ancestors, those who claim through the nearest ancestors shall be preferred to those claiming through an ancestor who is more remote.

Provided,

Sixth.— If a person dies leaving several children, or leaving one child and the issue of one or more others, and any such surviving child dies under age and not having been married, all the estate that came to the deceased child by inheritance from such deceased parent shall descend in equal shares to the other children of the same parent, and to the issue of any such other children who have died, by right of representation.

Seventh.—If at the death of such child who shall have died under age and not having been married, all the other children of his said parent are also dead, and any of them have left issue, the estate that came to such child by inheritance from his said parent shall descend to all the issue of the other children of the same parent; and if all the issue are in the same degree of kindred to the child, they shall share the estate equally; otherwise they shall take according to the right of representation.

Eighth.—If the intestate leaves a widow and no kindred, his estate shall descend to his widow; and if the intestate is a married woman and leaves no kindred, her estate shall descend to her husband.

Ninth.—If the intestate leaves no kindred, and no widow or husband, his or her estate shall escheat to the Commonwealth.

Section 2.—An illegitimate child shall be heir of his mother and any maternal ancestor, and the lawful issue of an illegitimate person shall represent such person and take by descent any estate which the parent would have taken if living.

Section 3.—If an illegitimate child dies intestate, without lawful issue, his estate shall descend to his mother.

Section 4.—An illegitimate child whose parents have intermarried and whose father has acknowledged him as his child, shall be considered legitimate.

Section 5.—The degrees of kindred shall be computed according to the rules of the civil law; and the kindred of the half blood shall inherit equally with those of the whole blood in the same degree.

Section 6.—Any estate, real or personal, given by the intestate in his lifetime as an advancement to any child or other lineal descendant, shall be considered as part of the intestate's estate, so far as it regards the division and distribution thereof among his issue, and shall be taken by such child or other descendant towards his share of the intestate's estate ; but he shall not be required to refund any part thereof, although it exceeds his share.

Section 7.—If such advancement is made in real estate, the value thereof shall be considered as part of the real estate to be divided ; if it is in personal estate it shall be considered as part of the personal estate ; and if in either case it exceeds the share of real or personal estate respectively that would have come to the heir so advanced. he shall not refund any part of it, but shall receive so much less out of the other part of the estate as will make his whole share equal to those of the other heirs who are in the same degree with him.

Section 8.—All gifts and grants shall be deemed to have been made in advancement, if they are expressed in the gift or grant to be so made, or if charged in writing - by the intestate as an advancement, or acknowledged in writing as such by the child or other descendant.

Section 9.—If the value of the estate so advanced is expressed in the conveyance, or in the charge thereof made by the intestate, or in the acknowledgment by the party receiving it, it shall be considered as of that value in the division and distribution of the estate ; otherwise it shall be estimated according to its value when given.

Section 10.—If a child or other lineal descendant so advanced dies before the intestate, leaving issue, the advancement shall be taken into consideration in the division and distribution of the estate ; and the amount thereof shall be allowed accordingly by the representatives of the heir so advanced, as so much received towards their share of the estate, in like manner as if the advancement had been made directly to them.

Section 11.—Nothing contained in this Chapter shall affect the title of a husband as tenant by the courtesy, nor that of a widow as tenant in dower, nor her right to any part of the real estate of her husband given to her by law in lieu of dower.

Section 12.—Inheritance or succession, " by right of representation," takes place when the descendants of a deceased heir take the same share or right in the estate of another person that their parent would have taken if living.   Posthumous children are considered as living at the death of their parent.

MASSACHUSETTS.

Homestead Law.—Chap. 104.

Section 1.—Every householder having a family shall be entitled to an estate of homestead, to the extent in value of eight hundred dollars, in the farm or lot of land and buildings thereon owned, or rightly possessed by lease, or otherwise, and occupied by him as a residence; and such homestead and all right and title therein shall be exempt from attachment, levy or execution, sale for the payment of his debts, or other purposes, and from the law of conveyance, descent, and devise, except as hereinafter provided.

Section 2.—To constitute such estate of homestead and to entitle property to such exemption, it shall be set forth in the deed of conveyance by which the property is acquired, that it is designed to be held as a homestead; or after the title has been acquired, such design shall be declared by writing, duly signed, sealed, acknowledged, and recorded, in the registry of deeds for the county or district where the property is situated. But the acquisition of a new estate of homestead in either of said modes, shall operate to defeat and discharge any estate or right of homestead previously existing.

PENNSYLVANIA.

Law regulating Descent and Distribution of Real Estate.

The real and personal estate of a decedent, whether male or female, remaining after payment of all just debts and legal charges, which shall not have been sold or disposed of, by will, or otherwise limited by marriage settlement, shall be divided and enjoyed as follows, viz. :—

Where such intestate shall leave a widow and issue, the widow shall be entitled to one-third of the real estate for the term of her life, and to one-third of the personal estate absolutely.

Where such intestate shall leave a widow and collateral heirs, or other kindred, but no issue, the widow shall be entitled to one-half part of the real estate, including the mansion-house and buildings appurtenant thereto, for the term of her life, and to one-half part of the personal estate absolutely.

Where such intestate shall leave a husband, he shall take the whole personal estate, and the real estate shall descend and pass as hereinafter provided, saving to the husband his right as tenant by the courtesy which shall take place, although there be no issue of the marriage, in all cases where the issue, if any, would have inherited.

The real estate of such married woman, upon her decease, shall be distributed as provided for by the intestate laws of this commonwealth now in force. * * * Subject to the estates and interests hereinbefore given to the widow or surviving husband, if any, the real estate of such intestate shall descend to and be distributed among his issue, according to the following rules and order of succession, viz. :—

If such intestate shall leave children, but no other descendant, being the issue of a deceased child, the estate shall descend to, and be distributed among, such children.

If such intestate shall leave grandchildren, but no child or other descendant being the issue of a deceased grandchild, the estate shall descend to, and be distributed among, such grandchildren.

If such intestate shall leave descendants in any other degree of consanguinity to him, the estate shall descend to, and be distributed among such descendants.

If such intestate shall leave descendants in different degrees of consanguinity to him, the more remote of them being the issue of a deceased child, grandchild, or other descendants, the estate shall descend to and be distributed among them as follows, viz. :—

Each of the children of such intestate shall receive such share as such child would have received, if all the children of the intestate who shall then be dead, leaving issue, had been living at the death of the intestate.

Each of the grandchildren, if there shall be no children, in like manner shall receive such share as he or she would have received if all the other grandchildren who shall then be dead, leaving issue, had been living at the death of the intestate, and so on in like manner to the remotest degree.

In every such case, the issue of such deceased child, grandchild, or other descendant, shall take, by representation of their parents, respectively, such share only as would have descended to such parent, if they had been living at the death of the intestate.

It is the true intent and meaning of this Act, that the heir at common law shall not take in any case, to the exclusion of other heirs and kindred standing in the same degree of consanguinity with him to the intestate; and it is hereby declared, that in every case which may arise, not expressly provided for by this Act, the real, as well as the personal estate, of an intestate shall pass to and be enjoyed by the next of kin of such intestate, without regard to his ancestor, or other relation, from whom such estate may have come.

WISCONSIN.

Law relating to Descent of Real Estate.—Chap. 92.

Section 1.—When any person shall die, seised of any lands, tenements, or hereditaments, or of any right thereto, or entitled to any interest therein, in fee-simple or for the life of another, not having lawfully devised the same, they shall descend, subject to his debts, in manner following : —

1. In equal shares to his children, and to the lawful issue of any deceased child by right of representation ; and if there be no child of the intestate living at his death, his estate shall descend to all his other lineal descendants ; and if all the said descendants are in the same degree of kindred to the intestate, they shall share the estate equally, otherwise they shall take according to the right of representation.

2. If he shall leave no issue, his estate shall descend to his widow during her natural lifetime, and after her decease to his father ; and if he shall leave no issue or widow, his estate shall descend to his father.

3. If he shall leave no issue nor father, his estate shall descend to his widow during her natural life, and after her decease in equal shares to his brothers and sisters, and to the children of any deceased brother or sister, by right of representation : provided, that if he shall leave a mother, she shall take an equal share with his brothers and sisters.

4. If he shall leave no issue, nor widow, nor father, his estate shall descend in equal shares to his brothers and sisters, and to the children of any deceased brother or sister, by right of representation : provided, that if he shall leave a mother also, she shall take an equal share with his brothers and sisters.

5. If the intestate shall leave no issue, nor widow, nor father, and no brother nor sister, living at his death, his estate shall descend to his mother, to the exclusion of the issue, if any, of deceased brothers or sisters.

6. If the intestate shall leave no issue, nor widow, and no father, mother, brother, nor sister, his estate shall descend to his next of kin in equal degree, excepting when there are two or more collateral kindred in equal degree, but claiming through different ancestors, those who claim through the nearest ancestor shall be preferred to those claiming through an ancestor more remote : provided, however : —

7. If any person shall die, leaving several children, or leaving one child, and the issue of one or more other children, and any such surviving child shall die under age, and not having been married, all the estate that came to the deceased child by inheritance from such deceased parent shall descend in equal shares to the other children of the same parent, and to the issue of any such other children who shall have died, by right of representation.

8. If, at the death of such child who shall die under age, and not having been married, all the other children of his said parent shall also be dead, and any of them shall have left issue, the estate

that came to said child by inheritance, from his said parent, shall descend to all the issue of other children of the same parent, and if all the said issue are in the same degree of kindred to said child, they shall share the said estate equally ; otherwise, they shall take according to the right of representation.

9. If the intestate shall leave a widow, and no kindred, his estate shall descend to such widow.

STATE OF ILLINOIS.
Extract of Law relating to Descent of Estates.

Section 46.—Estates, both real and personal, of resident or non-resident proprietors in this State, dying intestate, or whose estates, or any part thereof, shall be deemed and taken as intestate estate, and after all just debts and claims against such estates shall be paid as aforesaid, shall descend to, and be distributed to his or her children, and their descendants in equal parts ; the descendants of a deceased child or grandchild taking the share of their deceased parent in equal parts among them ; and when there shall be no children of the intestate, nor descendants of such children, and no widow, then to the parents, brothers, and sisters of the deceased person and their descendants in equal parts among them ; allowing to each of the parents, if living, a child's part, or to the survivor of them, if one be dead, a double portion ; and if there be no parent living, then to the brothers and sisters of the intestate and their descendants.   When there shall be a widow and no child or children or descendants of a child or children of the intestate, then, the one-half of the real estate, and the whole of the personal estate shall go to such widow, as her exclusive estate for ever ; subject *to her absolute disposition and control to be governed in all respects by the same rules and regulations as are or may be provided in cases of estates of femes sole ; if there be no children of the intestate or descendants of such children, and no parents, brothers, or sisters, or descendants of brothers and sisters, and no widow, then such estate shall descend in equal parts to the next of kin to the intestate, in equal degree, computing by the rules of the civil law ; and there shall be no representation among collaterals, except with the descendants of the brothers and sisters of the intestate ; and in no case shall there be a distinction between the kindred of the whole and the half blood, saving to the widow, in all cases, her dower, as provided by law.

Section 47.—When any feme covert shall die intestate, leaving no child or children, or descendants of a child or children, then the one-half of the real estate of the decedent shall descend and go to her husband, as his exclusive estate for ever.

Section 51.—Where any of the children of a person dying

intestate, or their issue, shall have received from such intestate in his or her lifetime, any real or personal estate, by way of advancement, and shall desire to come into the partition or distribution of such estate with the other parceners or distributees, such advancement, both of real and personal estate, shall be brought into hotchpot with the whole estate, real and personal, of such intestate ; and every person so returning such advancement as aforesaid, shall, thereupon, be entitled to his or her just proportion of said estate.

Section 52.—If any man shall have one or more children by any woman whom he shall afterward marry, such child or children, if acknowledged by the man, shall, in virtue of such marriage and acknowledgment, be thereby legitimated, and capable in law to inherit and transmit inheritance, as if born in wedlock.

Section 53.—If any single or unmarried woman, having estate either real or personal, in her own right, shall hereinafter die leaving one or more children, deemed in law illegitimate, such child or children shall not on that account be disinherited ; but they and each of them, and their descendants, shall be deemed able and capable in law to take and inherit the estate of their deceased mother, in equal parts among them, to the exclusion of all other persons : provided, that if there shall be no such child or children, or their descendants, then and in such case the estate of the intestate shall be governed by the rules of descent, as in other cases where illegitimates are excluded.

Section 54.—In all cases where any person shall die intestate, leaving real or personal estate in this State, and a child or children, commonly called posthumous children, shall be born unto him after his decease, within the usual time prescribed by law, such child or children shall come in for their just proportion of said estate, in all respects as though he, she, or they had been born in the lifetime of the intestate.

Section 128.—Where any heir of an intestate has received money, goods, chattels, or real estate from such intestate, if the amount so received shall be charged to such heir by said intestate, the same shall be taken into computation in making distribution of the estate upon being brought into hotchpot as aforesaid : provided, that an heir who has received from the intestate more than his share shall in no case be required to refund.

State of Kansas.—Chapter 80.

Extract of Law relating to Descents and Distribution.

Section 5.—One-half in value of all the real estate in which the husband at any time during the marriage had a legal or equitable interest, which has not been sold on execution or other judicial sale, or to which the wife has made no relinquishment of her rights, or which may not be necessary for the payment of the debts of the deceased husband, shall, under the direction of the Court, be set apart by the executor as her property in fee-simple, upon the death of the husband, if she survives him.   Continuous cohabitation as husband and wife, is presumptive evidence of marriage for the purpose of giving the right aforesaid.

Section 6.—Such share shall be so set off as to include the ordinary dwelling-house, and the land given by law to the husband as a homestead, or so much thereof as will be equal to the share allotted to her by the last section, unless she prefers a different arrangement.   But no different arrangement shall be permitted where it would have the effect of prejudicing the rights of creditors.

Section 7.—The share thus allotted to her may be set off by the mutual consent of all the parties interested, when such consent can be obtained, or it may be set off by referees appointed by the Court.

Section 8.—The application for such admeasurement by referees may be made at any time after twenty days and within ten years after the death of the husband, and must specify the particular tracts of land in which she claims her portion, and ask the appointment of referees.

Section 9.—The Court shall fix the time for making the appointment and direct such notice thereof to be given to all the parties interested therein as it deems proper.

Section 10.—The referees may employ a surveyor, if necessary, and they must cause the widow's share to be marked off by metes and bounds, and make a full report of their proceedings to the Court as early as practicable.

Section 11.—The Court may require a report by such a time as it deems reasonable ; and if the referees fail to obey this or any other order of the court, it may discharge them, and appoint others in their stead, and may impose on them the payment of all costs previously made, unless they show good cause to the contrary.

Section 12.—The Court may confirm the report of the referees, or it may set it aside, and refer the matter to the same or other referees, at its discretion.

Section 13.—Such confirmation after the lapse of thirty days, unless appealed from according to law, shall be binding and conclusive as to the admeasurement, and she may bring suit to obtain possession of the land thus set apart for her.

Section 14.—Nothing in the last section shall prevent any person interested from controverting the general rights of the widow to the portion thus admeasured.

Section 15.—The widow's portion cannot be affected by any will of her husband if she objects thereto, and relinquishes all rights conferred upon her by the Will.

Section 16.—Subject to the rights and charges hereinbefore contemplated, the remaining estate of which the decedent died seised, shall, in the absence of other arrangements by Will, descend in equal shares to his children.

Section 17.—If any one of his children be dead, the heirs of such child shall inherit his share, in accordance with the rules herein prescribed, in the same manner as though such child had outlived his parent.

Section 18.—If the intestate leaves no issue, the whole of his estate shall go to his wife; and if he leaves no wife nor issue, the whole shall go to his father.

Section 19.—If his father be previously dead, the portion which would have fallen to his share by the above rules shall be disposed of in the same manner as though he had outlived the intestate, and died in the possession and ownership of the portion thus falling to his share, and so on through each ascending ancestor and his issue, unless heirs are sooner found.

Section 20.—If heirs are not found in the male line, the portion thus inherited shall go to the mother of the intestate, and to her heirs, following the same rules as above prescribed.

Section 21.—If heirs are not thus found, the portion uninherited shall go to the wife of the intestate, or to her heirs, if dead, according to like rules ; and if he has had more than one wife, who either died or survived in lawful wedlock, it shall be equally divided between the one who is living and the heirs of those who are dead, or between the heirs of all, if all are dead, such heirs taking by right of representation.

Section 22.—If, still, there be property remaining uninherited, it shall escheat to the territory.

Section 23.—Illegitimate children inherit from the mother, and the mother from the children.

Section 24.—They also inherit from the father whenever they have been recognised by him as his children; but such recognition must have been general and notorious, or else in writing.

Section 25.—Under such circumstances, if the recognition of relationship has been mutual, the father may inherit from his illegitimate child.

Section 26.—But in thus inheriting from an illegitimate child, the rule above established must be inverted so that the mother and her heirs take preference of the father and his heirs, the father having the same right of inheritance in regard to an illegitimate child that the mother has in regard to one that is legitimate.

Section 27.—Property given by an intestate, by way of advancement to an heir, shall be considered part of the estate, so far as regards the division and distribution thereof, and shall be taken by such heir towards his share of the estate, at what it would now be worth if in the condition in which it was so given to him.

Section 28.—But if such advancement exceeds the amount to which he would be entitled, he cannot be required to refund any portion thereof.

Section 29.—All the provisions hereinbefore made, in relation to the widow of a deceased husband, shall be applicable to the husband of a deceased wife. Each is entitled to the same rights or portion in the estate of the other, and like interests shall in the same manner descend to their respective heirs. The estate of dower and by courtesy are hereby abolished.

Section 30.—Children of the half blood shall inherit equally with children of the whole blood. Children of a deceased parent inherit in equal proportions the portion their father or mother would have inherited, if living.

STATE OF GEORGIA.—Chap. 3.   Article 1.

Extract of Laws relating to Inheritable Property and the relative rights of the Heirs and Administrator.

2451. Upon the death of the owner of any estate, in realty or negroes, which estate survives him, the title vests immediately in his heirs-at-law. The title to all other property owned by him vests in the administrator of his estate for the benefit of the heirs and creditors.

2452. The following rules shall determine who are the heirs-at-law of a deceased person :—

1. The husband is sole heir of his intestate wife.

2. If the intestate dies without children, or the descendants of children, leaving a wife, the wife is his sole heir.

3. If there are children, or those representing deceased children, the wife shall have a third part, unless the shares exceed five in number, in which case the wife shall have one-fifth part of the estate. If the wife elects to take her dower, she has no farther interest in the realty.

4. Children stand in the first degree from the intestate, and inherit equally all property of every description, accounting for advancements, as hereinafter explained. Posthumous children stand upon the same footing with children in being upon all questions of inheritance. The lineal descendants of children stand in the place of their deceased parents ; and in all cases of inheritance from a lineal ancestor, the distribution is per stirpes and not per capita.

5. Brothers and sisters of the intestate stand in the second

degree, and inherit, if there is no widow, or child, or representative of child. The half-blood on the paternal side inherit equally with the whole blood. If there is no brother or sister of the whole or half-blood on the paternal side, then those of the half-blood on the maternal side shall inherit. The children or grandchildren of brothers and sisters deceased shall represent and stand in the place of their deceased parents, but there shall be no representation farther than this among collaterals.

6. The father, if living, inherits equally with brothers and sisters, and stands in the same degree. If there be no father, and the mother is alive, and a widow, she shall inherit in the same manner as the father would. If the mother is not a widow, she shall not be entitled to any portion of such estate, unless it shall be that of the only or last surviving child of the mother, in which event she shall take as if married.

7. In all degrees more remote than the foregoing, the paternal and maternal next of kin shall stand on an equal footing.

8. First cousins stand next in degree; uncles and aunts inherit equally with cousins.

9. The more remote degrees shall be determined by the rules of the canon law, as adopted and enforced in the English courts prior to the fourth day of July, A.D. 1776.

2453. Whenever any feme covert, having a child or children by a former marriage, is, or becomes, entitled to property, by inheritance, at any time, or devise, antecedent in date to her last marriage, and not in trust, the possession of which is not obtained prior to such marriage, such property shall not belong to the husband of such feme covert, but shall be equally divided between all the children of such feme covert, living at the time when possession is obtained, and such feme covert. The portions of such feme covert, and her children by her last husband, shall alone be subject to be reduced to possession by, and the title vest in, such husband.

[TABLE

The following Table is republished, by permission, from the

LAND SYSTEM OF IRELAND AND GREAT BRITAIN COMPAR

We give a tabular statement of the tenures, rents, leases, wages, and produce p
erroneous views of the condition of the agriculturists and peasant proprietors, as bein
to the Earl of Clarendon for our ministers at Paris, Brussels, Berlin, &c., who can
acreable produce where subdivision of lands and small holdings, whether in the hand

	IRELAND.	GREAT BRITAIN.	
Rents per English acre .	15s. to 20s.	35s. England, 46s. Scotland .	2
„ Irish acre .	24s. 6d. to 32s. 6d.	56s. England, 71s. Scotland	4
„ „ . .	Grass farms let lower than tillage .	East of Scotland 50s. to 70s. per Imperial acre.	A
Leases and tenure	All tenures, 21, 31, 61, 99, 999, and perpetuity with lives. There are middle landlords with sub-tenants. Over half of Ireland has no leases from head landlord or lessee.	Few in England . . . . 19 to 21 years of tillage in Scotland, and 7 to 9 of grass farms.	3, G
Peasant owners . . .	Few; some holding perpetuity leases at 6d. to 5s. per acre. Scarcely any of the original lessees' families hold at present.	Few in Great Britain, the rich buying out the yeomen and small owners. The Statesmen of Westmoreland and Cumberland, of 30 acres, disappearing.	2:
Small proprietors . . .	On old leases, and by purchase under Landed Estates Court.		0
Small farmers and holders .	142,000 of 13 acres, at £8 rent, and 175,000 of 4½ acres, at £4 rent, as stated by the Right Hon. Robert Lowe.	Few, except in west and south-west of England, and highlands of Scotland.	V
Medium and large farmers and graziers	Ten millions of acres in grass, giving very little employment.	Large tillage farms . .	L
Wages	Numbers in the middle rank of life. 10d., 1s. to 1s. 6d. per day, formerly 5d., 8d., 10d., and 1s.	2s. 6d. to 3s., Scotland . 2s. to 2s. 6d., England.	
Interest on mortgages . .	4 to 5 per cent	4 to 5 per cent. 1	
And by banks . . .	5 to 7 per cent.	4 and 6 per cent.	10
Value of land per acre	£30 to £45 .	£50 to £100	
„ Tenant right . .	£10 to £15 in Ulster . .	None.	
Produce per acre of wheat in bushels.	26 average . . . . 38 to 40 in high farming.	29 44 in high farming	

One average acre cultivated in England and Scotland produces treble the meat, grain, and green cr
A farm of 670 English, or 430 Irish acres, under a proper rotation of crops, gives £1,200 to £1,300
labour; hence the Irish have to emigrate, or remove to England or Scotland. If the grass farms were turn
We are indebted to the "Scotsman" of 12th February, 1869, for the Belgian statistics; also to M
pamphlets on Ireland, we recommend to our readers for a solution of the land question coming from pract
half those of Belgium and England, and not one-third those of Scotland.

December 24th, 1869.

ARED WITH THE CONTINENT AS TO TENURE, RENTS, PRODUCE, WAGES, ETC., ON AVERAGE SOILS.

e per acre of Ireland, Great Britain, Belgium, France, Prussia, and other countries of Europe, from which it will be seen that very eing superior to ours and our neighbours in Great Britain, have been entertained. Wishing the statement to be tested, we sent copies an report to the government as to the facts. We wish also to call the attention of our readers to the figures, and especially the small auds of proprietors or cultivators, exist.

	BELGIUM.	FRANCE.	PRUSSIA.	AUSTRIA.	ITALY, SPAIN, PORTUGAL.
	27s. to 40s.	25s. to 30s.	25s. to 32s.	20s. to 26s.	20s. to 28s.
	44s. to 65s.	40s. to 49s.	40s. to 51s.	32s. 6d. to 42s.	32s. 6d. to 42s.
	Average rise since 1830, 2 per cent. per annum.				
	3, 6, and in a few cases, of 9 years. Great demand for land.	6, 9, and in a few cases of large farms, 18 years.	6, 9, to 18 years. State lands 18 years.	9 to 18 years.	Rents one-half to one-third the produce in kind or cash. 3, 5, and 7 years, except for large farms of 18 years.
	The short tenure with the small holdings on the Continent is against improvement in agriculture.				
	250,000, about half tenants under 2 acres, 20,000 of 30 acres, 10,000 of 100 acres, 1,000 of 250 acres; average of all, 11 acres. Average number of small holders from 1 to 5 acres, 400,514 out of the total of 572,550 in 1856; most of them in Hainault and Luxembourgh.	Millions of small owners, under Code Napoléon, holding over half the area.	900,000 under 4 acres	Numerous, from 15 acres lowest to 60 acres largest of the peasant estates. Some large farms worked by owners and tenants.	Chiefly small owners or tenants of 15 to 20 acres.
	Over ⅔ of Belgium worked by large farmers and owners.	10 acres considered necessary for a family.			
	Very large beet farms	Large beet farms in the north.	Some large farms held by owners and tenants. Much beet grown.		
	Few middle class tenants like the British farmers, chiefly peasant owners or small tenants eking out a poor life, worse off than labourers in the east of England and Scotland.				
	8d. to 1s. 8d.; average 1s. 1d.	1s. 2d. to 1s. 8d.; average 1s. 4d. Working 16 hours and Sundays.	1s. to 1s. 3d.; in Silesia, 6d. to 10d.	9d. to 10d.	9d. to 10d.
			Labourers harder worked and worse off than in England.		
	10 per cent.	10 per cent.	10 per cent., unless in state bank land loans.	10 per cent.	10 to 14 per cent.
	10 per cent.	10 per cent.	Few banking facilities on the Continent.		
	£50 to £85	£40 to £60 Some small estates bringing more.	£40 to £60.		
	None.	None.	None.	None.	None.
	21	14	17 Silesia, 10.	15 to 16.	12 to 14.

een crops of one acre on the Continent, owing to the subdivision and the small holdings there.
£1,300 in wages in the east of England and Scotland, while the same extent in Ireland under grass gives only £50 to £60, making a difference of £1,150 to £1,250 paid in
re turned into tillage, double the meat would be fed, besides the raising large crops of grain, and employing the people.
o to Mr. Howard's report on "Continental Farming," which, with Mr. Read's, Mr. M'Lagan's, Mr. Caird's, Mr. M'Combie's, and Mr. Samuelson's statements, letters, an
practical men, most of them tenant farmers. Mr. M'Lagan, M.P., estimates the average rents of Ireland at 15s. per imperial, or 24s. 6d. per Irish acre, which are oc

MACMILLAN & CO.'S PUBLICATIONS.

THE LAND WAR IN IRELAND:

A History for the Times. By JAMES GODKIN, Author of "Ireland and her Churches." 8vo. 12s.

THE RIGHT HON. JOHN BRIGHT'S

SPEECHES on Questions of Public Policy. Edited by J. E. THOROLD ROGERS.

AUTHOR'S POPULAR EDITION. Extra fcap. 8vo., 3s. 6d.

LIBRARY EDITION. With Portrait. 2 vols., 8vo., 25s.

ON LABOUR : its Wrongful Claims and

Rightful Dues ; Actual Present, and Possible Future. By W. T. THORNTON, Author of "A Plea for Peasant Proprietors." 8vo., 14s. SECOND EDITION.

"A really valuable contribution. The number of facts accumulated, both historical and statistical, make an especially valuable portion of the book ; and all Mr. Thornton's writing displays a degree of thoughtful impartiality and subdued earnestness, which sets a good example to all future speculators in a field only too favourable for the exercise of strong passions or ignorant prejudices."— *Westminster Review.*

By PROFESSOR FAWCETT, M.P.

A MANUAL OF POLITICAL ECONOMY. Third and Cheaper Edition, thoroughly revised, with TWO NEW CHAPTERS on "National Education," and "The Poor Laws and their Influence on Pauperism." Crown 8vo., 10s. 6d.

THE ECONOMIC POSITION OF THE BRITISH LABOURER. The Land Tenure of England — Causes which regulate Wages — Trades Unions, Strikes, &c. Extra fcap. 8vo., 5s.

A GENERAL VIEW of THE CRIMINAL

LAW OF ENGLAND. By J. FITZJAMES STEPHEN. 8vo., 18s.

MACMILLAN & CO., LONDON.

MACMILLAN & CO.'S PUBLICATIONS.

SEVENTH ANNUAL PUBLICATION, revised and corrected on the basis of official reports received direct from the heads of the leading Governments of the World.

THE STATESMAN'S YEAR BOOK FOR

1870. By FREDERICK MARTIN. A Statistical, Mercantile, and Historical Account of the Civilized World, for the Year 1870. Forming a Manual for Politicians and Merchants. Crown 8vo., 10s. 6d.

"As indispensable as Bradshaw."—*Times.*

"A book more thoroughly useful than this we do not know. It has already made itself a positive necessity to politicians, journalists, and commercial men."— *Star.*

ANNALS OF OUR TIME.

A Diurnal of Events, Social and Political, which have happened in or had relation to the Kingdom of Great Britain, from the Accession of Queen Victoria to the opening of the Present Parliament. By JOSEPH IRVING. 8vo., half-bound, 18s. SECOND EDITION.

"A trusty and ready guide to the events of the past thirty years, available equally for the statesman, the politician, the public writer, and the general reader." — *Times.*

BY R. DUDLEY BAXTER, M.A.

NATIONAL INCOME. With Coloured Diagram. 8vo., 3s. 6d.

THE TAXATION OF THE UNITED KINGDOM: its Amount, its Distribution, and Pressure. 8vo., 4s. 6d.

THE COAL QUESTION.

By Professor JEVONS. Second Edition, revised. 8vo., 10s. 6d.

THE ADMINISTRATION OF INDIA

FROM 1859 TO 1868. The First Ten Years of Administration under the Crown. By I. T. PRICHARD (Gray's Inn), Barrister-at-Law. 2 vols. 8vo. With Map, 21s.

MACMILLAN & CO., LONDON.

16, BEDFORD STREET, COVENT GARDEN, LONDON.

January, 1870.

MACMILLAN & CO.'S GENERAL CATALOGUE of Works in the Departments of History, Biography, Travels, Poetry, and Belles Lettres. With some short Account or Critical Notice concerning each Book.

SECTION I.

HISTORY, BIOGRAPHY, and TRAVELS.

Baker (Sir Samuel W.).—THE NILE TRIBUTARIES OF ABYSSINIA, and the Sword Hunters of the Hamran Arabs. By SIR SAMUEL W. BAKER, M.A., F.R.G.S. With Portraits, Maps, and Illustrations. Third Edition, 8vo. 21*s*.

Sir Samuel Baker here describes twelve months' exploration, during which he examined the rivers that are tributary to the Nile from Abyssinia, including the Atbara, Settite, Royan, Salaam, Angrab, Rahad, Dinder, and the Blue Nile. The interest attached to these portions of Africa differs entirely from that of the White Nile regions, as the whole of Upper Egypt and Abyssinia is capable of development, and is inhabited by races having some degree of civilization; while Central Africa is peopled by a race of savages, whose future is more problematical.

THE ALBERT N'YANZA Great Basin of the Nile, and Exploration of the Nile Sources. New and cheaper Edition, with Portraits, Maps, and Illustrations. Two vols. crown 8vo. 16*s*.

"Bruce won the source of the Blue Nile; Speke and Grant won the Victoria source of the great White Nile; and I have been permitted to succeed in completing the Nile Sources by the discovery of the great reservoir of the equatorial waters, the Albert N'yanza, from which the river issues as the entire White Nile."—PREFACE.

NEW AND CHEAP EDITION OF THE ALBERT N'YANZA. 1 vol. crown 8vo. With Maps and Illustrations. 7*s*. 6*d*.

A

Baker (Sir Samuel W.) (*continued*)—

CAST UP BY THE SEA ; or, The Adventures of NED GREY.
By SIR SAMUEL W. BAKER, M.A., F.R.G.S. Second Edition.
Crown 8vo. cloth gilt, 7*s.* 6*d.*

"*A story of adventure by sea and land in the good old style. It appears
to us to be the best book of the kind since 'Masterman Ready,' and it runs
that established favourite very close.*"—PALL MALL GAZETTE.

"*No book written for boys has for a long time created so much interest,
or been so successful. Every parent ought to provide his boy with a copy.*"
DAILY TELEGRAPH.

Barker (Lady).—STATION LIFE IN NEW ZEALAND.
By LADY BARKER. Crown 8vo. 7*s.* 6*d.*

"*These letters are the exact account of a lady's experience of the brighter
and less practical side of colonization. They record the expeditions, adventures, and emergencies diversifying the daily life of the wife of a New
Zealand sheep-farmer ; and, as each was written while the novelty and
excitement of the scenes it describes were fresh upon her, they may succeed
in giving here in England an adequate impression of the delight and freedom of an existence so far removed from our own highly-wrought civilization.*"—PREFACE.

Baxter (R. Dudley, M.A.).—THE TAXATION OF THE
UNITED KINGDOM. By R. DUDLEY BAXTER, M.A. 8vo.
cloth, 4*s.* 6*d.*

*The First Part of this work, originally read before the Statistical
Society of London, deals with the Amount of Taxation ; the Second Part,
which now constitutes the main portion of the work, is almost entirely new,
and embraces the important questions of Rating, of the relative Taxation
of Land, Personalty, and Industry, and of the direct effect of Taxes upon
Prices. The author trusts that the body of facts here collected may be of
permanent value as a record of the past progress and present condition of
the population of the United Kingdom, independently of the transitory
circumstances of its present Taxation.*

Baxter (R. Dudley, M.A.) *(continued)*—
NATIONAL INCOME. With Coloured Diagrams. 8vo. 3s. 6d.

    PART I.—*Classification of the Population, Upper, Middle, and Labour Classes.* II.—*Income of the United Kingdom.*

    " *A painstaking and certainly most interesting inquiry.*"—PALL MALL GAZETTE.

Bernard.—FOUR LECTURES ON SUBJECTS CONNECTED WITH DIPLOMACY. By MOUNTAGUE BERNARD, M.A., Chichele Professor of International Law and Diplomacy, Oxford. 8vo. 9s.

    Four Lectures, dealing with (1) *The Congress of Westphalia;* (2) *Systems of Policy;* (3) *Diplomacy, Past and Present;* (4) *The Obligations of Treaties.*

Blake.—THE LIFE OF WILLIAM BLAKE, THE ARTIST. By ALEXANDER GILCHRIST. With numerous Illustrations from Blake's designs, and Fac-similes of his studies of the "Book of Job." Two vols. medium 8vo. 32s.

    These volumes contain a Life of Blake; Selections from his Writings, including Poems; Letters; Annotated Catalogue of Pictures and Drawings; List, with occasional notes, of Blake's Engravings and Writings. There are appended Engraved Designs by Blake: (1) *The Book of Job, twenty-one photo-lithographs from the originals;* (2) *Songs of Innocence and Experience, sixteen of the original Plates.*

Bright (John, M.P.).—SPEECHES ON QUESTIONS OF PUBLIC POLICY. By JOHN BRIGHT, M.P. Edited by Professor THOROLD ROGERS. Two Vols. 8vo. 25s. Second Edition, with Portrait.

    " *I have divided the Speeches contained in these volumes into groups. The materials for selection are so abundant, that I have been constrained to omit many a speech which is worthy of careful perusal. I have naturally given prominence to those subjects with which Mr. Bright has been especially identified, as, for example, India, America, Ireland, and Parliamentary Reform. But nearly every topic of great public interest on which Mr. Bright has spoken is represented in these volumes."*

EDITOR'S PREFACE.

AUTHOR'S POPULAR EDITION. Extra fcap. 8vo. cloth. Second Edition. 3s. 6d.

Bryce.—THE HOLY ROMAN EMPIRE. By JAMES BRYCE, B.C.L., Fellow of Oriel College, Oxford. [*Reprinting.*

CAMBRIDGE CHARACTERISTICS. *See* MULLINGER.

CHATTERTON : A Biographical Study. BY DANIEL WILSON, LL.D., Professor of History and English in University College, Toronto. Crown 8vo. 6s. 6d.

The Author here regards Chatterton as a Poet, not as a mere " resetter and defacer of stolen literary treasures." Reviewed in this light, he has found much in the old materials capable of being turned to new account ; and to these materials research in various directions has enabled him to make some additions.

Clay.—THE PRISON CHAPLAIN. A Memoir of the Rev. JOHN CLAY, B.D., late Chaplain of the Preston Gaol. With Selections from his Reports and Correspondence, and a Sketch of Prison Discipline in England. By his Son, the Rev. W. L. CLAY, M.A. 8vo. 15s.

" Few books have appeared of late years better entitled to an attentive perusal. . . It presents a complete narrative of all that has been done and attempted by various philanthropists for the amelioration of the condition and the improvement of the morals of the criminal classes in the British dominions."—LONDON REVIEW.

Cooper.—ATHEN.E CANTABRIGIENSES. By CHARLES HENRY COOPER, F.S.A., and THOMPSON COOPER, F.S.A. Vol. I. 8vo., 1500—85, 18s. Vol. II., 1586—1609, 18s.

This elaborate work, which is dedicated by permission to Lord Macaulay, contains lives of the eminent men sent forth by Cambridge, after the fashion of Anthony à Wood, in his famous " Athenæ Oxonienses."

Dilke.—GREATER BRITAIN. A Record of Travel in English-speaking Countries during 1866-7. (America, Australia, India.) By Sir CHARLES WENTWORTH DILKE, M.P. Fourth and Cheap Edition. Crown 8vo. 6s.

" Mr. Dilke has written a book which is probably as well worth reading as any book of the same aims and character that ever was written. Its merits are that it is written in a lively and agreeable style, that it implies a great deal of physical pluck, that no page of it fails to show an acute and highly intelligent observer, that it stimulates the imagination as well as the judgment of the reader, and that it is on perhaps the most interesting subject that can attract an Englishman who cares about his country."

SATURDAY REVIEW.

Dürer (Albrecht).—HISTORY OF THE LIFE OF AL-BRECHT DÜRER, of Nürnberg. With a Translation of his Letters and Journal, and some account of his works. By Mrs. CHARLES HEATON. Royal 8vo. bevelled boards, extra gilt. 31s. 6d.

This work contains about Thirty Illustrations, ten of which are productions by the Autotype (carbon) process, and are printed in permanent tints by Messrs. Cundall and Fleming, under license from the Autotype Company, Limited; the rest are Photographs and Woodcuts.

EARLY EGYPTIAN HISTORY FOR THE YOUNG. *See* "JUVENILE SECTION."

Elliott.—LIFE OF HENRY VENN ELLIOTT, of Brighton. By Josiah Bateman, M.A., Author of " Life of Daniel Wilson, Bishop of Calcutta," &c. With Portrait, engraved by Jeens. Crown 8vo. 8s. 6d. Second Edition, with Appendix.

" A very charming piece of religious biography; no one can read it without both pleasure and profit."—British Quarterly Review.

Forbes.—LIFE OF PROFESSOR EDWARD FORBES, F.R.S. By George Wilson, M.D., F.R.S.E., and Archibald Geikie, F.R.S. 8vo. with Portrait, 14s.

" From the first page to the last the book claims careful reading, as being a full but not overcrowded rehearsal of a most instructive life, and the true picture of a mind that was rare in strength and beauty."—Examiner.

Freeman.—HISTORY OF FEDERAL GOVERNMENT, from the Foundation of the Achaian League to the Disruption of the United States. By Edward A. Freeman, M.A. Vol. I. General Introduction. History of the Greek Federations. 8vo. 21s.

" The task Mr. Freeman has undertaken is one of great magnitude and importance. It is also a task of an almost entirely novel character. No other work professing to give the history of a political principle occurs to us, except the slight contributions to the history of representative government that is contained in a course of M. Guizot's lectures . . . The history of the development of a principle is at least as important as the history of a dynasty, or of a race.'—Saturday Review.

OLD ENGLISH HISTORY FOR CHILDREN. By Edward A. Freeman, M.A., late Fellow of Trinity College, Oxford. With *Five Coloured Maps.* Extra fcap. 8vo., half-bound. 6s.

" Its object is to show that clear, accurate, and scientific views of history, or indeed of any subject, may be easily given to children from the very first. . . I have, I hope, shown that it is perfectly easy to teach children, from

the very first, to distinguish true history alike from legend and from wilful invention, and also to understand the nature of historical authorities, and to weigh one statement against another. . . . . I have throughout striven to connect the history of England with the general history of civilized Europe, and I have especially tried to make the book serve as an incentive to a more accurate study of historical geography."—PREFACE.

French (George Russell). — SHAKSPEAREANA
GENEALOGICA. 8vo. cloth extra, 15*s*. Uniform with the " Cambridge Shakespeare."

Part I.—Identification of the dramatis personæ in the historical plays, from King John to King Henry VIII.; Notes on Characters in Macbeth and Hamlet; Persons and Places belonging to Warwickshire alluded to. Part II.—The Shakspeare and Arden families and their connexions, with Tables of descent. The present is the first attempt to give a detailed description, in consecutive order, of each of the dramatis personæ in Shakspeare's immortal chronicle-histories, and some of the characters have been, it is believed, herein identified for the first time. A clue is furnished which, followed up with ordinary diligence, may enable any one, with a taste for the pursuit, to trace a distinguished Shakspearean worthy to his lineal representative in the present day.

Galileo.—THE PRIVATE LIFE OF GALILEO. Compiled
principally from his Correspondence and that of his eldest daughter, Sister Maria Celeste, Nun in the Franciscan Convent of S. Matthew, in Arcetri. With Portrait. Crown 8vo. 7*s*. 6*d*.

It has been the endeavour of the compiler to place before the reader a plain, ungarbled statement of facts ; and as a means to this end, to allow Galileo, his friends, and his judges to speak for themselves as far as possible.

Gladstone (Right. Hon. W. E., M.P.).—JUVENTUS
MUNDI. The Gods and Men of the Heroic Age. Crown 8vo. cloth extra. With Map. 10*s*. 6*d*. Second Edition.

This new work of Mr. Gladstone deals especially with the historic element in Homer, expounding that element, and furnishing by its aid a full account of the Homeric men and the Homeric religion. It starts, after the introductory chapter, with a discussion of the several races then existing in Hellas, including the influence of the Phœnicians and Egyptians. It contains chapters on the Olympian system, with its several deities ; on the Ethics and the Polity of the Heroic age ; on the geography of Homer ; on the characters of the Poems ; presenting, in fine, a view of primitive life and primitive society as found in the poems of Homer.

"GLOBE" ATLAS OF EUROPE.   Uniform in size with Macmillan's Globe Series, containing 45 Coloured Maps, on a uniform scale and projection ; with Plans of London and Paris, and a copious Index.   Strongly bound in half-morocco, with flexible back, 9s.

This Atlas includes all the countries of Europe in a series of 48 Maps, drawn on the same scale, with an Alphabetical Index to the situation of more than ten thousand places, and the relation of the various maps and countries to each other is defined in a general Key-map. All the maps being on a uniform scale facilitates the comparison of extent and distance, and conveys a just impression of the relative magnitude of different countries. The size suffices to show the provincial divisions, the railways and main roads, the principal rivers and mountain ranges. "This atlas," writes the British Quarterly, *"will be an invaluable boon for the school, the desk, or the traveller's portmanteau."*

Guizot.—(Author of "JOHN HALIFAX, GENTLEMAN.")—M. DE BARANTE, A Memoir, Biographical and Autobiographical.   By M. GUIZOT.   Translated by the Author of "JOHN HALIFAX, GENTLEMAN."   Crown 8vo. 6s. 6d.

" The highest purposes of both history and biography are answered by a memoir so lifelike, so faithful, and so philosophical."
BRITISH QUARTERLY REVIEW.

HISTORICAL SELECTIONS. Readings from the best Authorities on English and European History. Selected and arranged by E. M. SEWELL and C. M. YONGE. Crown 8vo. 6s.

When young children have acquired the outlines of history from abridgements and catechisms, and it becomes desirable to give a more enlarged view of the subject, in order to render it really useful and interesting, a difficulty often arises as to the choice of books. Two courses are open, either to take a general and consequently dry history of facts, such as Russell's Modern Europe, or to choose some work treating of a particular period or subject, such as the works of Macaulay and Froude. The former course usually renders history uninteresting; the latter is unsatisfactory, because it is not sufficiently comprehensive. To remedy this difficulty, selections, continuous and chronological, have in the present volume been taken from the larger works of Freeman, Milman, Palgrave, and others, which may serve as distinct landmarks of historical reading. "We know of scarcely anything," says the Guardian, *of this volume, "which is so likely to raise to a higher level the average standard of English education."*

Hole.—A GENEALOGICAL STEMMA OF THE KINGS OF ENGLAND AND FRANCE. By the Rev. C. HOLE, M.A., Trinity College, Cambridge. On Sheet, 1s.

The different families are printed in distinguishing colours, thus facilitating reference.

A BRIEF BIOGRAPHICAL DICTIONARY. Compiled and Arranged by the Rev. CHARLES HOLE, M.A. Second Edition. 18mo. neatly and strongly bound in cloth, 4s. 6d.

One of the most comprehensive and accurate Biographical Dictionaries in the world, containing more than 18,000 persons of all countries, with dates of birth and death, and what they were distinguished for. Extreme care has been bestowed on the verification of the dates; and thus numerous errors, current in previous works, have been corrected. Its size adapts it for the desk, portmanteau, or pocket.

"An invaluable addition to our manuals of reference, and, from its moderate price, cannot fail to become as popular as it is useful."—TIMES.

Hozier.—THE SEVEN WEEKS' WAR ; Its Antecedents and its Incidents. By. H. M. HOZIER. With Maps and Plans. Two vols. 8vo. 28s.

This work is based upon letters reprinted by permission from " The Times." For the most part it is a product of a personal eye-witness of some of the most interesting incidents of a war which, for rapidity and decisive results, may claim an almost unrivalled position in history.

THE BRITISH EXPEDITION TO ABYSSINIA. Compiled from Authentic Documents. By CAPTAIN HENRY M. HOZIER, late Assistant Military Secretary to Lord Napier of Magdala. 8vo. 9s.

" Several accounts of the British Expedition have been published. . . . . They have, however, been written by those who have not had access to those authentic documents, which cannot be collected directly after the termination of a campaign. . . . . The endeavour of the author of this sketch has been to present to readers a succinct and impartial account of an enterprise which has rarely been equalled in the annals of war."—PREFACE.

Irving.—THE ANNALS OF OUR TIME. A Diurnal of Events, Social and Political, which have happened in or had relation to the Kingdom of Great Britain, from the Accession of Queen Victoria to the Opening of the present Parliament. By JOSEPH IRVING. 8vo. half-bound. 18s.

" We have before us a trusty and ready guide to the events of the past thirty years, available equally for the statesman, the politician, the public writer, and the general reader. If Mr. Irving's object has been to bring before the reader all the most noteworthy occurrences which have happened since the beginning of Her Majesty's reign, he may justly claim the credit of having done so most briefly, succinctly, and simply, and in such a manner, too, as to furnish him with the details necessary in each case to comprehend the event of which he is in search in an intelligent manner. Reflection will serve to show the great value of such a work as this to the journalist and statesman, and indeed to every one who feels an interest in the progress of the age ; and we may add that its value is considerably increased by the addition of that most important of all appendices, an accurate and instructive index."—TIMES.

Kingsley (Canon).—ON THE ANCIEN REGIME as it Existed on the Continent before the FRENCH REVOLUTION. Three Lectures delivered at the Royal Institution. By the Rev. C. KINGSLEY, M.A., formerly Professor of Modern History in the University of Cambridge. Crown 8vo. 6s.

These three lectures discuss severally (1) *Caste*, (2) *Centralization*, (3) *The Explosive Forces by which the Revolution was superinduced. The Preface deals at some length with certain political questions of the present day.*

THE ROMAN AND THE TEUTON. A Series of Lectures delivered before the University of Cambridge. By Rev. C KINGSLEY, M.A. 8vo. 12s.

CONTENTS :—*Inaugural Lecture ; The Forest Children ; The Dying Empire ; The Human Deluge ; The Gothic Civilizer; Dietrich's End; The Nemesis of the Goths ; Paulus Diaconus ; The Clergy and the Heathen : The Monk a Civilizer ; The Lombard Laws ; The Popes and the Lombards ; The Strategy of Providence.*

Kingsley (Henry, F.R.G.S.).—TALES OF OLD TRAVEL. Re-narrated by HENRY KINGSLEY, F.R.G.S. With *Eight Illustrations* by HUARD. Crown 8vo. 6s.

CONTENTS :—*Marco Polo ; The Shipwreck of Pelsart ; The Wonderful Adventures of Andrew Battel ; The Wanderings of a Capuchin ; Peter Carder ; The Preservation of the "Terra Nova;" Spitzbergen ; D'Ermenonville's Acclimatization Adventure ; The Old Slave Trade; Miles Philips ; The Sufferings of Robert Everard ; John Fox ; Alvaro Nunez ; The Foundation of an Empire.*

Latham.—BLACK AND WHITE: A Journal of a Three Months' Tour in the United States. By HENRY LATHAM, M.A., Barrister-at-Law. 8vo. 10s. 6d.

" The spirit in which Mr. Latham has written about our brethren in America is commendable in high degree."—ATHENÆUM.

Law.—THE ALPS OF HANNIBAL. By WILLIAM JOHN LAW, M.A., formerly Student of Christ Church, Oxford. Two vols. 8vo. 21*s.*

"*No one can read the work and not acquire a conviction that, in addition to a thorough grasp of a particular topic, its writer has at command a large store of reading and thought upon many cognate points of ancient history and geography.*"—QUARTERLY REVIEW.

Liverpool.—THE LIFE AND ADMINISTRATION OF ROBERT BANKS, SECOND EARL OF LIVERPOOL, K.G. Compiled from Original Family Documents by CHARLES DUKE YONGE, Regius Professor of History and English Literature in Queen's College, Belfast; and Author of "The History of the British Navy," "The History of France under the Bourbons," etc. Three vols. 8vo. 42*s.*

Since the time of Lord Burleigh no one, except the second Pitt, ever enjoyed so long a tenure of power; with the same exception, no one ever held office at so critical a time . . Lord Liverpool is the very last minister who has been able fully to carry out his own political views; who has been so strong that in matters of general policy the Opposition could extort no concessions from him which were not sanctioned by his own deliberate judgment. The present work is founded almost entirely on the correspondence left behind him by Lord Liverpool, and now in the possession of Colonel and Lady Catherine Harcourt.

"*Full of information and instruction.*"—FORTNIGHTLY REVIEW.

Maclear.—*See Section,* "ECCLESIASTICAL HISTORY."

Macmillan (Rev. Hugh).—HOLIDAYS ON HIGH LANDS; or, Rambles and Incidents in search of Alpine Plants. By the Rev. HUGH MACMILLAN, Author of "Bible Teachings in Nature," etc. Crown 8vo. cloth. 6*s.*

"*Botanical knowledge is blended with a love of nature, a pious enthusiasm, and a rich felicity of diction not to be met with in any works of kindred character, if we except those of Hugh Miller.*"—DAILY TELEGRAPH.

Macmillan (Rev. Hugh), (*continued*)—

FOOT-NOTES FROM THE PAGE OF NATURE. With numerous Illustrations. Fcap. 8vo. 5s.

"*Those who have derived pleasure and profit from the study of flowers and ferns—subjects, it is pleasing to find, now everywhere popular—by descending lower into the arcana of the vegetable kingdom, will find a still more interesting and delightful field of research in the objects brought under review in the following pages.*"—PREFACE.

BIBLE TEACHINGS IN NATURE. Fourth Edition. Fcap 8vo. 6s.—*See also* "SCIENTIFIC SECTION."

Martin (Frederick).—THE STATESMAN'S YEAR-BOOK : A Statistical and Historical Account of the States of the Civilised World. Manual for Politician and Merchants for the year 1870. BY FREDERICK MARTIN. *Seventh Annual Publication.* Crown 8vo. 10s. 6d.

The new issue has been entirely re-written, revised, and corrected, on the basis of official reports received direct from the heads of the leading Governments of the World, in reply to letters sent to them by the Editor.

"*Everybody who knows this work is aware that it is a book that is indispensable to writers, financiers, politicians, statesmen, and all who are directly or indirectly interested in the political, social, industrial, commercial, and financial condition of their fellow-creatures at home and abroad. Mr. Martin deserves warm commendation for the care he takes in making ' The Statesman's Year Book' complete and correct.*"

STANDARD.

Martineau.—BIOGRAPHICAL SKETCHES, 1852—1868. By HARRIET MARTINEAU. Third Edition, with New Preface. Crown 8vo. 8s. 6d.

A Collection of Memoirs under these several sections :—(1) Royal, (2) Politicians, (3) Professional, (4) Scientific, (5) Social, (6) Literary. These Memoirs appeared originally in the columns of the "Daily News."

Masson (Professor).—ESSAYS, BIOGRAPHICAL AND CRITICAL. *See Section headed* "POETRY AND BELLES LETTRES."

LIFE OF JOHN MILTON. Narrated in connexion with the Political, Ecclesiastical, and Literary History of his Time. By DAVID MASSON, M.A., LL.D., Professor of Rhetoric at Edinburgh. Vol. I. with Portraits. 8vo. 18s. Vol. II. in the Press.

It is intended to exhibit Milton's life in its connexions with all the more notable phenomena of the period of British history in which it was cast— its state politics, its ecclesiastical variations, its literature and speculative thought. Commencing in 1608, the Life of Milton proceeds through the last sixteen years of the reign of James I., includes the whole of the reign of Charles I. and the subsequent years of the Commonwealth and the Protectorate, and then, passing the Restoration, extends itself to 1674, or through fourteen years of the new state of things under Charles II. The first volume deals with the life of Milton as extending from 1608 to 1640, which was the period of his education and of his minor poems.

Morison.—THE LIFE AND TIMES OF SAINT BERNARD, Abbot of Clairvaux. By JAMES COTTER MORISON, M.A. New Edition, revised. Crown 8vo. 7s. 6d.

"One of the best contributions in our literature towards a vivid, intelligent, and worthy knowledge of European interests and thoughts and feelings during the twelfth century. A delightful and instructive volume, and one of the best products of the modern historic spirit."
PALL MALL GAZETTE.

Morley (John).—EDMUND BURKE, a Historical Study. By JOHN MORLEY, B.A. Oxon. Crown 8vo. 7s. 6d.

" The style is terse and incisive, and brilliant with epigram and point. It contains pithy aphoristic sentences which Burke himself would not have disowned. But these are not its best features: its sustained power of reasoning, its wide sweep of observation and reflection, its elevated ethical and social tone, stamp it as a work of high excellence, and as such we cordially recommend it to our readers."—SATURDAY REVIEW.

Mullinger.—CAMBRIDGE CHARACTERISTICS IN THE SEVENTEENTH CENTURY. By J. B. MULLINGER, B.A. Crown 8vo. 4s. 6d.

" *It is a very entertaining and readable book.*"—SATURDAY REVIEW.

" *The chapters on the Cartesian Philosophy and the Cambridge Platonists are admirable.*"—ATHENÆUM.

Palgrave.—HISTORY OF NORMANDY AND OF ENG-LAND. By Sir FRANCIS PALGRAVE, Deputy Keeper of Her Majesty's Public Records. Completing the History to the Death of William Rufus. Four vols. 8vo. £4 4s.

Volume I. General Relations of Mediæval Europe—The Carlovingian Empire—The Danish Expeditions in the Gauls—And the Establishment of Rollo. Volume II. The Three First Dukes of Normandy; Rollo, Guillaume Longue-Épée, and Richard Sans-Peur—The Carlovingian line supplanted by the Capets. Volume III. Richard Sans-Peur—Richard Le-Bon—Richard III.—Robert Le Diable—William the Conqueror. Volume IV. William Rufus—Accession of Henry Beauclerc.

Palgrave (W. G.).—A NARRATIVE OF A YEAR'S JOURNEY THROUGH CENTRAL AND EASTERN ARABIA, 1862-3. By WILLIAM GIFFORD PALGRAVE, late of the Eighth Regiment Bombay N.I. Fifth and cheaper Edition. With Maps, Plans, and Portrait of Author, engraved on steel by Jeens. Crown 8vo. 6s.

" *Considering the extent of our previous ignorance, the amount of his achievements, and the importance of his contributions to our knowledge, we cannot say less of him than was once said of a far greater discoverer. Mr. Palgrave has indeed given a new world to Europe.*"—PALL MALL GAZETTE.

Parkes (Henry).—AUSTRALIAN VIEWS OF ENGLAND.
By HENRY PARKES.   Crown 8vo. cloth.   3*s.* 6*d.*

*" The following letters were written during a residence in England, in
the years* 1861 *and* 1862, *and were published in the* Sydney Morning
Herald *on the arrival of the monthly mails . . . On re-perusal, these
letters appear to contain views of English life and impressions of English
notabilities which, as the views and impressions of an Englishman on his
return to his native country after an absence of twenty years, may not be
without interest to the English reader.   The writer had opportunities of
mixing with different classes of the British people, and of hearing opinions
on passing events from opposite standpoints of observation."*—AUTHOR'S
PREFACE.

Prichard.—THE ADMINISTRATION OF INDIA.   From
1859 to 1868.   The First Ten Years of Administration under the
Crown.   By ILTUDUS THOMAS PRICHARD, Barrister-at-Law.
Two vols.   Demy 8vo.   With Map.   21*s.*

*In these volumes the author has aimed to supply a full, impartial, and
independent account of British India between* 1859 *and* 1868—*which is
in many respects the most important epoch in the history of that country
which the present century has seen.*

Ralegh.—THE LIFE OF SIR WALTER RALEGH, based
upon Contemporary Documents.   By EDWARD EDWARDS.   Together with Ralegh's Letters, now first collected.   With Portrait.
Two vols. 8vo.   32*s.*

*" Mr. Edwards has certainly written the Life of Ralegh from fuller
information than any previous biographer.   He is intelligent, industrious,
sympathetic : and the world has in his two volumes larger means afforded
it of knowing Ralegh than it ever possessed before.   The new letters and
the newly-edited old letters are in themselves a boon."*—PALL MALL
GAZETTE.

Robinson (Crabb).—DIARY, REMINISCENCES, AND CORRESPONDENCE OF CRABB ROBINSON. Selected and Edited by Dr. SADLER. With Portrait. Second Edition. Three vols. 8vo. cloth. 36*s*.

Mr. Crabb Robinson's Diary extends over the greater part of three-quarters of a century. It contains personal reminiscences of some of the most distinguished characters of that period, including Goethe, Wieland, De Quincey, Wordsworth (with whom Mr. Crabb Robinson was on terms of great intimacy), Madame de Staël, Lafayette, Coleridge, Lamb, Milman, &c. &c.: and includes a vast variety of subjects, political, literary, ecclesiastical, and miscellaneous.

Rogers (James E. Thorold).—HISTORICAL GLEANINGS : A Series of Sketches. Montague, Walpole, Adam Smith, Cobbett. By Rev. J. E. T. ROGERS. Crown 8vo. 4*s*. 6*d*.

Professor Rogers's object in the following sketches is to present a set of historical facts, grouped round a principal figure. The essays are in the form of lectures.

Smith (Professor Goldwin).— THREE ENGLISH STATESMEN · PYM, CROMWELL, PITT. A Course of Lectures on the Political History of England. By GOLDWIN SMITH, M.A. Extra fcap. 8vo. New and Cheaper Edition. 5*s*.

"A work which neither historian nor politician can safely afford to neglect."—SATURDAY REVIEW.

Tacitus.—THE HISTORY OF TACITUS, translated into English. By A. J. CHURCH, M.A. and W. J. BRODRIBB, M.A. With a Map and Notes. 8vo. 10*s*. 6*d*.

The translators have endeavoured to adhere as closely to the original as was thought consistent with a proper observance of English idiom. At the same time it has been their aim to reproduce the precise expressions of the author. This work is characterised by the Spectator *as " a scholarly and faithful translation."*

B

THE AGRICOLA AND GERMANIA. Translated into English by
A. J. CHURCH, M.A. and W. J. BRODRIBB, M.A. With Maps
and Notes. Extra fcap. 8vo. 2s. 6d.

*The translators have sought to produce such a version as may satisfy
scholars who demand a faithful rendering of the original, and English
readers who are offended by the baldness and frigidity which commonly
disfigure translations. The treatises are accompanied by introductions,
notes, maps, and a chronological summary. The* Athenæum *says of
this work that it is "a version at once readable and exact, which may be
perused with pleasure by all, and consulted with advantage by the classical
student."*

Taylor (Rev. Isaac).—WORDS AND PLACES; or
Etymological Illustrations of History, Etymology, and Geography.
By the Rev. ISAAC TAYLOR. Second Edition. Crown 8vo.
12s. 6d.

*"Mr. Taylor has produced a really useful book, and one which stands
alone in our language."*—SATURDAY REVIEW.

Trench (Archbishop).—GUSTAVUS ADOLPHUS: Social
Aspects of the Thirty Years' War. By R. CHENEVIX TRENCH,
D.D., Archbishop of Dublin. Fcap. 8vo. 2s. 6d.

*"Clear and lucid in style, these lectures will be a treasure to many to
whom the subject is unfamiliar."*—DUBLIN EVENING MAIL.

Trench (Mrs. R.).—Edited by ARCHBISHOP TRENCH. Remains
of the late MRS. RICHARD TRENCH. Being Selections from
her Journals, Letters, and other Papers. New and Cheaper Issue,
with Portrait, 8vo. 6s.

*Contains notices and anecdotes illustrating the social life of the period
—extending over a quarter of a century (1799—1827). It includes also
poems and other miscellaneous pieces by Mrs. Trench.*

Trench (Capt. F., F.R.G.S.).—THE RUSSO-INDIAN QUESTION, Historically, Strategically, and Politically considered. By Capt. TRENCH, F.R.G.S. With a Sketch of Central Asiatic Politics and Map of Central Asia. Crown 8vo. 7s. 6d.

"*The Russo-Indian, or Central Asian question has for several obvious reasons been attracting much public attention in England, in Russia, and also on the Continent, within the last year or two. . . . I have thought that the present volume, giving a short sketch of the history of this question from its earliest origin, and condensing much of the most recent and interesting information on the subject, and on its collateral phases, might perhaps be acceptable to those who take an interest in it.*"—AUTHOR'S PREFACE.

Trevelyan (G.O., M.P.).—CAWNPORE. Illustrated with Plan. By G. O. TREVELYAN, M.P., Author of "The Competition Wallah." Second Edition. Crown 8vo. 6s.

"*In this book we are not spared one fact of the sad story; but our feelings are not harrowed by the recital of imaginary outrages. It is good for us at home that we have one who tells his tale so well as does Mr. Trevelyan.*"—PALL MALL GAZETTE.

THE COMPETITION WALLAH. New Edition. Crown 8vo. 6s.

"*The earlier letters are especially interesting for their racy descriptions of European life in India. . . . Those that follow are of more serious import, seeking to tell the truth about the Hindoo character and English influences, good and bad, upon it, as well as to suggest some better course of treatment than that hitherto adopted.*"—EXAMINER.

Vaughan (late Rev. Dr. Robert, of the British Quarterly).—MEMOIR OF ROBERT A. VAUGHAN. Author of "Hours with the Mystics." By ROBERT VAUGHAN, D.D. Second Edition, revised and enlarged. Extra fcap. 8vo. 5s.

"*It deserves a place on the same shelf with Stanley's 'Life of Arnold,' and Carlyle's 'Stirling.' Dr. Vaughan has performed his painful but not all unpleasing task with exquisite good taste and feeling.*"—NONCONFORMIST.

Wagner.—MEMOIR OF THE REV. GEORGE WAGNER, M.A., late Incumbent of St. Stephen's Church, Brighton. By the Rev. J. N. SIMPKINSON, M.A. Third and cheaper Edition, corrected and abridged. 5s.

" *A more edifying biography we have rarely met with.*"
LITERARY CHURCHMAN.

Wallace.—THE MALAY ARCHIPELAGO : the Land of the Orang Utan and the Bird of Paradise. A Narrative of Travels with Studies of Man and Nature. By ALFRED RUSSEL WALLACE. With Maps and Illustrations. Second Edition. Two vols. crown 8vo. 24s.

" *A carefully and deliberately composed narrative. . . . We advise our readers to do as we have done, read his book through.*"—TIMES.

Ward (Professor).—THE HOUSE OF AUSTRIA IN THE THIRTY YEARS' WAR. Two Lectures, with Notes and Illustrations. By ADOLPHUS W. WARD, M.A., Professor of History in Owens College, Manchester. Extra fcap. 8vo. 2s. 6d.

" *Very compact and instructive.*"—FORTNIGHTLY REVIEW.

Warren.—AN ESSAY ON GREEK FEDERAL COINAGE. By the Hon. J. LEICESTER WARREN, M.A. 8vo. 2s. 6d.

" *The present essay is an attempt to illustrate Mr. Freeman's Federal Government by evidence deduced from the coinage of the times and countries therein treated of.*"—PREFACE.

Wilson.—A MEMOIR OF GEORGE WILSON, M.D., F.R.S.E., Regius Professor of Technology in the University of Edinburgh. By his SISTER. New Edition. Crown 8vo. 6s.
" *An exquisite and touching portrait of a rare and beautiful spirit.*"
GUARDIAN.

Wilson (Daniel, LL.D.).—PREHISTORIC ANNALS
OF SCOTLAND. By DANIEL WILSON, LL.D., Professor of
History and English Literature in University College, Toronto.
New Edition, with numerous Illustrations.   Two vols. demy
8vo.   36s.

*This elaborate and learned work is divided into four Parts. Part I.
deals with* The Primeval or Stone Period : *Aboriginal Traces, Sepulchral
Memorials, Dwellings, and Catacombs, Temples, Weapons, &c. &c. ;
Part II.,* The Bronze Period : *The Metallurgic Transition, Primitive
Bronze, Personal Ornaments, Religion, Arts, and Domestic Habits, with
other topics ; Part III.,* The Iron Period : *The Introduction of Iron, The
Roman Invasion, Strongholds, &c. &c.; Part IV.,* The Christian Period :
*Historical Data, the Norrie's Law Relics, Primitive and Mediæval
Ecclesiology, Ecclesiastical and Miscellaneous Antiquities.   The work is
furnished with an elaborate Index.*

PREHISTORIC MAN.   New Edition, revised and partly re-written,
with numerous Illustrations.   One vol. 8vo.   21s.

*This work, which carries out the principle of the preceding one, but with
a wider scope, aims to "view Man, as far as possible, unaffected by those
modifying influences which accompany the development of nations and the
maturity of a true historic period, in order thereby to ascertain the sources
from whence such development and maturity proceed." It contains, for
example, chapters on the Primeval Transition ; Speech ; Metals ; the
Mound-Builders ; Primitive Architecture; the American Type ; the Red
Blood of the West, &c. &c.*

SECTION II.

POETRY AND BELLES LETTRES.

Allingham.—LAURENCE BLOOMFIELD IN IRELAND; or, the New Landlord. By WILLIAM ALLINGHAM. New and cheaper issue, with a Preface. Fcap. 8vo. cloth, 4s. 6d.

In the new Preface, the state of Ireland, with special reference to the Church measure, is discussed.

"It is vital with the national character. . . . It has something of Pope's point and Goldsmith's simplicity, touched to a more modern issue."— ATHENÆUM.

Arnold (Matthew).—POEMS. By MATTHEW ARNOLD. Two vols. Extra fcap. 8vo. cloth. 12s. Also sold separately at 6s. each.

Volume I. contains Narrative and Elegiac Poems; Volume II. Dramatic and Lyric Poems. The two volumes comprehend the First and Second Series of the Poems, and the New Poems.

NEW POEMS. Extra fcap. 8vo. 6s. 6a.

In this volume will be found "Empedocles on Etna:" "Thyrsis" (written in commemoration of the late Professor Clough); "Epilogue to Lessing's Laocoön;" "Heine's Grave;" "Obermann once more." All these poems are also included in the Edition (two vols.) above-mentioned.

Arnold (Matthew), *(continued)*—

ESSAYS IN CRITICISM. New Edition, with Additions. Extra fcap. 8vo. 6s.

CONTENTS :—*Preface ; The Function of Criticism at the present time ; The Literary Influence of Academies ; Maurice de Guerin ; Eugenie de Guerin ; Heinrich Heine ; Pagan and Mediaeval Religious Sentiment ; Joubert ; Spinoza and the Bible ; Marcus Aurelius.*

ASPROMONTE, AND OTHER POEMS. Fcap. 8vo. cloth extra. 4s. 6d.

CONTENTS :—*Poems for Italy ; Dramatic Lyrics ; Miscellaneous.*

Barnes (Rev. W.).—POEMS OF RURAL LIFE IN COMMON ENGLISH. By the REV. W. BARNES, Author of " Poems of Rural Life in the Dorset Dialect." Fcap. 8vo. 6s.

" *In a high degree pleasant and novel. The book is by no means one which the lovers of descriptive poetry can afford to lose.*"—ATHENÆUM.

Bell.—ROMANCES AND MINOR POEMS. By HENRY GLASSFORD BELL. Fcap. 8vo. 6s.

" *Full of life and genius.*"—COURT CIRCULAR.

Besant.—STUDIES IN EARLY FRENCH POETRY. By WALTER BESANT, M.A. Crown. 8vo. 8s. 6d.

A sort of impression rests on most minds that French literature begins with the " siècle de Louis Quatorze ;" any previous literature being for the most part unknown or ignored. Few know anything of the enormous literary activity that began in the thirteenth century, was carried on by Rulebeuf, Marie de France, Gaston de Foix, Thibault de Champagne, and Lorris ; was fostered by Charles of Orleans, by Margaret of Valois, by Francis the First ; that gave a crowd of versifiers to France, enriched, strengthened, developed, and fixed the French language, and prepared the way for Corneille and for Racine. The present work aims to afford information and direction touching the early efforts of France in poetical literature.

"*In one moderately sized volume he has contrived to introduce us to the very best, if not to all of the early French poets.*"—ATHENÆUM.

Bradshaw.—AN ATTEMPT TO ASCERTAIN THE STATE OF CHAUCER'S WORKS, AS THEY WERE LEFT AT HIS DEATH. With some Notes of their Subsequent History. By HENRY BRADSHAW, of King's College, and the University Library, Cambridge. [*In the Press.*

Brimley.—ESSAYS BY THE LATE GEORGE BRIMLEY. M.A. Edited by the Rev. W. G. CLARK, M.A. With Portrait. Cheaper Edition. Fcap. 8vo. 3s. 6d.

Essays on literary topics, such as Tennyson's "Poems," Carlyle's "Life of Stirling," "Bleak House," &c., reprinted from Fraser, the Spectator, and like periodicals.

Broome.—THE STRANGER OF SERIPHOS. A Dramatic Poem. By FREDERICK NAPIER BROOME. Fcap. 8vo. 5s.

Founded on the Greek legend of Danae and Perseus.

Clough (Arthur Hugh).—THE POEMS AND PROSE REMAINS OF ARTHUR HUGH CLOUGH. With a Selection from his Letters and a Memoir. Edited by his Wife. With Portrait. Two vols. crown 8vo. 21s. Or Poems separately, as below.

The late Professor Clough is well known as a graceful, tender poet, and as the scholarly translator of Plutarch. The letters possess high interest, not biographical only, but literary—discussing, as they do, the most important questions of the time, always in a genial spirit. The "Remains" include papers on "Retrenchment at Oxford;" on Professor F. W. Newman's book "The Soul;" on Wordsworth; on the Formation of Classical English; on some Modern Poems (Matthew Arnold and the late Alexander Smith), &c. &c.

Clough (Arthur Hugh), *(continued)* —

THE POEMS OF ARTHUR HUGH CLOUGH, sometime Fellow
of Oriel College, Oxford. With a Memoir by F. T. PALGRAVE.
Second Edition. Fcap. 8vo. 6s.

"*From the higher mind of cultivated, all-questioning, but still conservative England, in this our puzzled generation, we do not know of any utterance in literature so characteristic as the poems of Arthur Hugh Clough.*"—FRASER'S MAGAZINE.

Dante.—DANTE'S COMEDY, THE HELL. Translated by
W. M. ROSSETTI. Fcap. 8vo. cloth. 5s.

"*The aim of this translation of Dante may be summed up in one word —Literality. . . To follow Dante sentence for sentence, line for line, word for word—neither more nor less—has been my strenuous endeavour.*"
—AUTHOR'S PREFACE.

De Vere.—THE INFANT BRIDAL, and other Poems. By
AUBREY DE VERE. Fcap. 8vo. 7s. 6d.

"*Mr. De Vere has taken his place among the poets of the day. Pure and tender feeling, and that polished restraint of style which is called classical, are the charms of the volume.*"—SPECTATOR.

Doyle (Sir F. H.).—Works by Sir FRANCIS HASTINGS DOYLE,
Professor of Poetry in the University of Oxford :—

THE RETURN OF THE GUARDS, AND OTHER POEMS.
Fcap. 8vo. 7s.

"*Good wine needs no bush, nor good verse a preface; and Sir Francis Doyle's verses run bright and clear, and smack of a classic vintage. . . . His chief characteristic, as it is his greatest charm, is the simple manliness which gives force to all he writes. It is a characteristic in these days rare enough.*"—EXAMINER.

Doyle (Sir F. H.), *(continued)*—

LECTURES ON POETRY, delivered before the University of Oxford in 1868. Extra crown 8vo. 3s. 6d.

THREE LECTURES :—(1) *Inaugural ;* (2) *Provincial Poetry ;* (3) *Dr. Newman's " Dream of Gerontius."*

" Full of thoughtful discrimination and fine insight : the lecture on ' Provincial Poetry' seems to us singularly true, eloquent, and instructive." SPECTATOR.

Evans.—BROTHER FABIAN'S MANUSCRIPT, AND OTHER POEMS. By SEBASTIAN EVANS. Fcap. 8vo. cloth. 6s.

" In this volume we have full assurance that he has ' the vision and the faculty divine.' . . . Clever and full of kindly humour."—GLOBE.

Furnivall.—LE MORTE D'ARTHUR. Edited from the *Harleian* M.S. 2252, in the British Museum. By F. J. FURNIVALL, M.A. With Essay by the late HERBERT COLERIDGE. Fcap. 8vo. 7s. 6d.

Looking to the interest shown by so many thousands in Mr. Tennyson's Arthurian poems, the editor and publishers have thought that the old version would possess considerable interest. It is a reprint of the celebrated Harleian copy ; and is accompanied by index and glossary.

Garnett.—IDYLLS AND EPIGRAMS. Chiefly from the Greek Anthology. By RICHARD GARNETT. Fcap. 8vo. 2s. 6d.

" A charming little book. For English readers, Mr. Garnett's translations will open a new world of thought."—WESTMINSTER REVIEW.

GUESSES AT TRUTH. By TWO BROTHERS. With Vignette, Title, and Frontispiece. New Edition, with Memoir. Fcap. 8vo. 6s.

" The following year was memorable for the commencement of the ' Guesses at Truth.' He and his Oxford brother, living as they did in constant and free interchange of thought on questions of philosophy and

literature and art; delighting, each of them, in the epigrammatic terseness which is the charm of the 'Pensées' of Pascal, and the 'Caractères' of La Bruyère—agreed to utter themselves in this form, and the book appeared, anonymously, in two volumes, in 1827."—MEMOIR.

Hamerton.—A PAINTER'S CAMP. By PHILIP GILBERT HAMERTON. Second Edition, revised. Extra fcap. 8vo. 6s.

BOOK I. *In England;* BOOK II. *In Scotland;* BOOK III. *In France. This is the story of an Artist's encampments and adventures. The headings of a few chapters may serve to convey a notion of the character of the book: A Walk on the Lancashire Moors; the Author his own Housekeeper and Cook; Tents and Boats for the Highlands; The Author encamps on an uninhabited Island; A Lake Voyage; A Gipsy Journey to Glen Coe; Concerning Moonlight and Old Castles; A little French City; A Farm in the Autunois, &c. &c.*

"*His pages sparkle with happy turns of expression, not a few well-told anecdotes, and many observations which are the fruit of attentive study and wise reflection on the complicated phenomena of human life, as well as of unconscious nature.*"—WESTMINSTER REVIEW.

ETCHING AND ETCHERS. A Treatise Critical and Practical. By P. G. HAMERTON. With Original Plates by REMBRANDT, CALLOT, DUJARDIN, PAUL POTTER, &c. Royal 8vo. Half morocco. 31s. 6d.

"*It is a work of which author, printer, and publisher may alike feel proud. It is a work, too, of which none but a genuine artist could by possibility have been the author.*"—SATURDAY REVIEW.

Helps.—REALMAH. By ARTHUR HELPS. Cheap Edition. Crown 8vo. 6s.

Of this work, by the Author of "Friends in Council," the Saturday Review *says:* "*Underneath the form (that of dialogue) is so much shrewdness, fancy, and above all, so much wise kindliness, that we should think all the better of a man or woman who likes the book.*"

Herschel.—THE ILIAD OF HOMER. Translated into English
Hexameters. By Sir JOHN HERSCHEL, Bart. 8vo. 18s.

*A version of the Iliad in English Hexameters. The question of Homeric
translation is fully discussed in the Preface.*
*" It is admirable, not only for many intrinsic merits, but as a great
man's tribute to Genius."*—ILLUSTRATED LONDON NEWS.

HIATUS : the Void in Modern Education. Its Cause and Antidote.
By OUTIS. 8vo. 8s. 6d.

*The main object of this Essay is to point out how the emotional element
which underlies the Fine Arts is disregarded and undeveloped at this time
so far as (despite a pretence at filling it up) to constitute an Educational
Hiatus.*

HYMNI ECCLESIÆ. *See* "THEOLOGICAL SECTION."

Kennedy.— LEGENDARY FICTIONS OF THE IRISH
CELTS. Collected and Narrated by PATRICK KENNEDY. Crown
8vo. 7s. 6d.

*"A very admirable popular selection of the Irish fairy stories and legends,
in which those who are familiar with Mr. Croker's, and other selections
of the same kind, will find much that is fresh, and full of the peculiar
vivacity and humour, and sometimes even of the ideal beauty, of the true
Celtic Legend."*—SPECTATOR.

Kingsley (Canon).—*See also* "HISTORIC SECTION," "WORKS
OF FICTION," *and* "PHILOSOPHY ;" *also* "JUVENILE BOOKS,"
and "THEOLOGY."

THE SAINTS' TRAGEDY · or, The True Story of Elizabeth of
Hungary. By the Rev. CHARLES KINGSLEY. With a Preface by
the Rev. F. D. MAURICE. Third Edition. Fcap. 8vo. 5s.

ANDROMEDA, AND OTHER POEMS. Third Edition. Fcap.
8vo. 5s.

Kingsley (Canon), *(continued)*—

PHAETHON ; or, Loose Thoughts for Loose Thinkers. Third Edition. Crown 8vo. 2s.

Kingsley (Henry).—*See* "WORKS OF FICTION."

Lowell.—UNDER THE WILLOWS, AND OTHER POEMS
By JAMES RUSSELL LOWELL. Fcap. 8vo. 6s.

"Under the Willows *is one of the most admirable bits of idyllic work, short as it is, or perhaps because it is short, that have been done in our generation.*"—SATURDAY REVIEW.

Masson (Professor).—ESSAYS, BIOGRAPHICAL AND CRITICAL. Chiefly on the British Poets. By DAVID MASSON, LL.D., Professor of Rhetoric in the University of Edinburgh. 8vo. 12s. 6d.

"*Distinguished by a remarkable power of analysis, a clear statement of the actual facts on which speculation is based, and an appropriate beauty of Language. These essays should be popular with serious men.*"
ATHENÆUM.

BRITISH NOVELISTS AND THEIR STYLES. Being a Critical Sketch of the History of British Prose Fiction. Crown 8vo. 7s. 6d.

"*Valuable for its lucid analysis of fundamental principles, its breadth of view, and sustained animation of style.*"—SPECTATOR.

MRS. JERNINGHAM'S JOURNAL. Extra fcap. 8vo. 3s. 6d. A Poem of the boudoir or domestic class, purporting to be the journal of a newly-married lady.

"*One quality in the piece, sufficient of itself to claim a moment's attention, is that it is unique—original, indeed, is not too strong a word—in the manner of its conception and execution.*"—PALL MALL GAZETTE.

Mistral. (F.).—MIRELLE: a Pastoral Epic of Provence. Translated by H. CRICHTON. Extra fcap. 8vo. 6s.

" *This is a capital translation of the elegant ana richly-coloured pastoral epic poem of M. Mistral which, in* 1859, *he dedicated in enthusiastic terms to Lamartine.. . . . . It would be hard to overpraise the sweetness and pleasing freshness of this charming epic.*"—ATHENÆUM.

Myers (Ernest).—THE PURITANS. By ERNEST MYERS. Extra fcap. 8vo. cloth. 2s. 6d.

" *It is not too much to call it a really grand poem, stately and dignified, and showing not only a high poetic mind, but also great power over poetic expression.*"—LITERARY CHURCHMAN.

Myers (F. W. H.)—ST. PAUL. A Poem. By F. W. H. MYERS. Second Edition. Extra fcap. 8vo. 2s. 6d.

" *It breathes throughout the spirit of St. Paul, and with a singular stately melody of verse.*"—FORTNIGHTLY REVIEW.

Nettleship. — ESSAYS ON ROBERT BROWNING'S POETRY. By JOHN T. NETTLESHIP. Extra fcap. 8vo. 6s. 6d.

Noel.—BEATRICE, AND OTHER POEMS. By the Hon. RODEN NOEL. Fcap. 8vo. 6s.

" *Beatrice is in many respects a noble poem; it displays a splendour of landscape painting, a strong definite precision of highly-coloured description, which has not often been surpassed.*"—PALL MALL GAZETTE.

Norton.—THE LADY OF LA GARAYE. By the HON. MRS NORTON. With Vignette and Frontispiece. Sixth Edition Fcap. 8vo. 4s. 6d.

" *There is no lack of vigour, no faltering of power, plenty of passion, much bright description, much musical verse. . . Full of thoughts well-expressed, and may be classed among her best works.*"—TIMES.

Orwell.—THE BISHOP'S WALK AND THE BISHOP'S TIMES. Poems on the days of Archbishop Leighton and the Scottish Covenant. By ORWELL. Fcap. 8vo. 5*s.*

"*Pure taste and faultless precision of language, the fruits of deep thought, insight into human nature, and lively sympathy.*"—NONCONFORMIST.

Palgrave (Francis T.).—ESSAYS ON ART. By FRANCIS TURNER PALGRAVE, M.A., late Fellow of Exeter College, Oxford. Extra fcap. 8vo. 6*s.*

Mulready—Dyce—Holman Hunt—Herbert—Poetry, Prose, ana Sensationalism in Art—Sculpture in England—The Albert Cross, &c.

SHAKESPEARE'S SONNETS AND SONGS. Edited by F. T. PALGRAVE. Gem Edition. With Vignette Title by JEENS. 3*s.* 6*d.*

"*For minute elegance no volume could possibly excel the 'Gem Edition.'*"—SCOTSMAN.

Patmore.—Works by COVENTRY PATMORE :—

THE ANGEL IN THE HOUSE.

BOOK I. *The Betrothal ;* BOOK II. *The Espousals ;* BOOK III. *Faithful for Ever. With Tamerton Church Tower. Two vols. fcap.* 8*vo.* 12*s.*

** *A New and Cheap Edition in one vol.* 18*mo., beautifully printed on toned paper, price* 2*s.* 6*d.*

THE VICTORIES OF LOVE. Fcap. 8vo. 4*s.* 6*d.*

The intrinsic merit of his poem will secure it a permanent place in literature. . . . Mr. Patmore has fully earned a place in the catalogue of poets by the finished idealization of domestic life."—SATURDAY REVIEW.

Rossetti.—Works by CHRISTINA ROSSETTI :—

GOBLIN MARKET, AND OTHER POEMS. With two Designs by D. G. ROSSETTI. Second Edition. Fcap. 8vo. 5*s.*

"*She handles her little marvel with that rare poetic discrimination which neither exhausts it of its simple wonders by pushing symbolism too far, nor keeps those wonders in the merely fabulous and capricious stage. In fact she has produced a true children's poem, which is far more delightful to the mature than to children, though it would be delightful to all.*"— SPECTATOR.

THE PRINCE'S PROGRESS, AND OTHER POEMS. With two Designs by D. G. ROSSETTI. Fcap. 8vo. 6*s.*

"*Miss Rossetti's poems are of the kind which recalls Shelley's definition of Poetry as the record of the best and happiest moments of the best and happiest minds. . . . They are like the piping of a bird on the spray in the sunshine, or the quaint singing with which a child amuses itself when it forgets that anybody is listening.*"—SATURDAY REVIEW.

Rossetti (W. M.).—DANTE'S HELL. *See* "DANTE."

FINE ART, chiefly Contemporary. By WILLIAM M. ROSSETTI. Crown 8vo. 10*s.* 6*d.*

This volume consists of Criticism on Contemporary Art, reprinted from Fraser, The Saturday Review, The Pall Mall Gazette, *and other publications.*

Roby.—STORY OF A HOUSEHOLD, AND OTHER POEMS. By MARY K. ROBY. Fcap. 8vo. 5*s.*

Shairp (Principal).—KILMAHOE, a Highland Pastoral, with other Poems. By JOHN CAMPBELL SHAIRP. Fcap. 8vo. 5*s.*

"*Kilmahoe is a Highland Pastoral, redolent of the warm soft air of the Western Lochs and Moors, sketched out with remarkable grace and picturesqueness.*"—SATURDAY REVIEW.

Smith.—Works by ALEXANDER SMITH :—

A LIFE DRAMA, AND OTHER POEMS. Fcap. 8vo. 2s. 6d.

CITY POEMS. Fcap. 8vo. 5s.

EDWIN OF DEIRA. Second Edition. Fcap. 8vo. 5s.

"*A poem which is marked by the strength, sustained sweetness, and compact texture of real life.*"—NORTH BRITISH REVIEW.

Smith.—POEMS. By CATHERINE BARNARD SMITH. Fcap. 8vo. 5s.

"*Wealthy in feeling, meaning, finish, and grace; not without passion, which is suppressed, but the keener for that.*"—ATHENÆUM.

Smith (Rev. Walter).—HYMNS OF CHRIST AND THE CHRISTIAN LIFE. By the Rev. WALTER C. SMITH, M.A. Fcap. 8vo. 6s.

"*These are among the sweetest sacred poems we have read for a long time. With no profuse imagery, expressing a range of feeling and expression by no means uncommon, they are true and devoted, and their pathos is profound and simple.*"—NONCONFORMIST.

Stratford de Redcliffe (Viscount).—SHADOWS OF THE PAST, in Verse. By VISCOUNT STRATFORD DE REDCLIFFE. Crown 8vo. 10s. 6d.

"*The vigorous words of one who has acted vigorously. They combine the fervour of politician and poet.*"—GUARDIAN.

Trench.—Works by R. CHENEVIX TRENCH, D.D., Archbishop of Dublin. See also Sections "PHILOSOPHY," "THEOLOGY," &c.

POEMS. Collected and arranged anew. Fcap. 8vo. 7s. 6d.

ELEGIAC POEMS. Third Edition. Fcap. 8vo. 2s. 6d.

C

Trench (Archbishop), *(continued)—*

CALDERON'S LIFE'S A DREAM : The Great Theatre of the
   World.   With an Essay on his Life and Genius.   Fcap. 8vo.
   4*s*. 6*d*.

HOUSEHOLD BOOK OF ENGLISH POETRY.   Selected and
   arranged, with Notes, by R. C. TRENCH, D.D., Archbishop of
   Dublin.   Extra fcap. 8vo.   5*s*. 6*d*.

*This volume is called a "Household Book," by this name implying that
it is a book for all—that there is nothing in it to prevent it from being
confidently placed in the hands of every member of the household.   Specimens of all classes of poetry are given, including selections from living
authors.   The Editor has aimed to produce a book "which the emigrant,
finding room for little not absolutely necessary, might yet find room for
in his trunk, and the traveller in his knapsack, and that on some narrow
shelves where there are few books this might be one."*

   *"The Archbishop has conferred in this delightful volume an important
gift on the whole English-speaking population of the world."*—PALL
MALL GAZETTE.

SACRED LATIN POETRY, Chiefly Lyrical.   Selected and arranged
   for Use.   Second Edition, Corrected and Improved.   Fcap. 8vo.
   7*s*.

   *"The aim of the present volume is to offer to members of our English
Church a collection of the best sacred Latin poetry, such as they shall be
able entirely and heartily to accept and approve—a collection, that is, in which
they shall not be evermore liable to be offended, and to have the current of
their sympathies checked, by coming upon that which, however beautiful as
poetry, out of higher respects they must reject and condemn—in which, too,
they shall not fear that snares are being laid for them, to entangle them
unawares in admiration for ought which is inconsistent with their faith
and fealty to their own spiritual mother."*—PREFACE.

Turner.—SONNETS. By the Rev. CHARLES TENNYSON TURNER. Dedicated to his brother, the Poet Laureate. Fcap. 8vo. 4s. 6d.

"*The Sonnets are dedicated to Mr. Tennyson by his brother, and have, independently of their merits, an interest of association. They both love to write in simple expressive Saxon ; both love to touch their imagery in epithets rather than in formal similes ; both have a delicate perception of rythmical movement, and thus Mr. Turner has occasional lines which, for phrase and music, might be ascribed to his brother. . He knows the haunts of the wild rose, the shady nooks where light quivers through the leaves, the ruralities, in short, of the land of imagination.*"—ATHENÆUM.

SMALL TABLEAUX. Fcap. 8vo. 4s. 6d.

"*These brief poems have not only a peculiar kind of interest for the student of English poetry, but are intrinsically delightful, and will reward a careful and frequent perusal. Full of naïveté, piety, love, and knowledge of natural objects, and each expressing a single and generally a simple subject by means of minute and original pictorial touches, these sonnets have a place of their own.*"—PALL MALL GAZETTE.

Vittoria Colonna.—LIFE AND POEMS. By Mrs. HENRY ROSCOE. Crown 8vo. 9s.

The life of Vittoria Colonna, the celebrated Marchesa di Pescara, has received but cursory notice from any English writer, though in every history of Italy her name is mentioned with great honour among the poets of the sixteenth century. "In three hundred and fifty years," says her biographer Visconti, "there has been no other Italian lady who can be compared to her."

"*It is written with good taste, with quick and intelligent sympathy, occasionally with a real freshness and charm of style.*"—PALL MALL GAZETTE.

Webster.—Works by AUGUSTA WEBSTER :—

DRAMATIC STUDIES. Extra fcap. 8vo. 5*s*.

"*.1 volume as strongly marked by perfect taste as by poetic power.*"
NONCONFORMIST.

PROMETHEUS BOUND OF ÆSCHYLUS. Literally translated into English Verse. Extra fcap. 8vo. 3*s*. 6*d*.

"*Closeness and simplicity combined with literary skill.*"—ATHEN.EUM.

MEDEA OF EURIPIDES. Literally translated into English Verse. Extra fcap. 8vo. 3*s*. 6*d*.

"*Mrs. Webster's translation surpasses our utmost expectations. It is a photograph of the original without any of that harshness which so often accompanies a photograph.*"—WESTMINSTER REVIEW.

A WOMAN SOLD, AND OTHER POEMS. Crown 8vo. 7*s*. 6*d*.

"*Mrs. Webster has shown us that she is able to draw admirably from the life; that she can observe with subtlety, and render her observations with delicacy; that she can impersonate complex conceptions, and venture into which few living writers can follow her.*"—GUARDIAN.

Woolner.—MY BEAUTIFUL LADY. By THOMAS WOOLNER. With a Vignette by ARTHUR HUGHES. *Third Edition.* Fcap. 8vo. 5*s*.

"*It is clearly the product of no idle hour, but a highly-conceived and faithfully-executed task, self-imposed, and prompted by that inward yearning to utter great thoughts, and a wealth of passionate feeling which is poetic genius. No man can read this poem without being struck by the fitness and finish of the workmanship, so to speak, as well as by the chastened and unpretending loftiness of thought which pervades the whole.*"
GLOBE.

WORDS FROM THE POETS. Selected by the Editor of "Rays of Sunlight." With a Vignette and Frontispiece. 18mo. Extra cloth gilt. 2*s*. 6*d*. *Cheaper Edition*, 18mo. limp., 1*s*.

GLOBE EDITIONS.

UNDER the title GLOBE EDITIONS, the Publishers are issuing a uniform Series of Standard English Authors, carefully edited, clearly and elegantly printed on toned paper, strongly bound, and at a small cost. The names of the Editors whom they have been fortunate enough to secure constitute an indisputable guarantee as to the character of the Series. The greatest care has been taken to ensure accuracy of text; adequate notes, elucidating historical, literary, and philological points, have been supplied; and, to the older Authors, glossaries are appended. The series is especially adapted to Students of our national Literature; while the small price places good editions of certain books, hitherto popularly inaccessible, within the reach of all.

Shakespeare.—THE COMPLETE WORKS OF WILLIAM SHAKESPEARE. Edited by W. G. CLARK and W. ALDIS WRIGHT. Ninety-first Thousand. Globe 8vo. 3s. 6d.

"A marvel of beauty, cheapness, and compactness. The whole works— plays, poems, and sonnets—are contained in one small volume: yet the page is perfectly clear and readable. . . . For the busy man, above all for the working Student, the Globe Edition is the best of all existing Shakespeare books."—ATHENÆUM.

Morte D'Arthur.—SIR THOMAS MALORY'S BOOK OF KING ARTHUR AND OF HIS NOBLE KNIGHTS OF THE ROUND TABLE. The Edition of CAXTON, revised for Modern Use. With an Introduction by SIR EDWARD STRACHEY, Bart. Globe 8vo. 3s. 6d. Third Edition.

" *It is with the most perfect confidence that we recommend this edition of the old romance to every class of readers.*"—PALL MALL GAZETTE.

Scott.—THE POETICAL WORKS OF SIR WALTER SCOTT. With Biographical Essay, by F. T. PALGRAVE. Globe 8vo. 3s. 6d. New Edition.

" *As a popular edition it leaves nothing to be desired. The want of such an one has long been felt, combining real excellence with cheapness.*"
SPECTATOR.

Burns.—THE POETICAL WORKS AND ·LETTERS OF ROBERT BURNS. Edited, with Life, by ALEXANDER SMITH. Globe 8vo. 3s. 6d. Second Edition.

" *The works of the bard have never been offered in such a complete form in a single volume.*"—GLASGOW DAILY HERALD.
" *Admirable in all respects.*"—SPECTATOR.

Robinson Crusoe.—THE ADVENTURES OF ROBINSON CRUSOE. By DEFOE. Edited, from the Original Edition, by J. W. CLARK, M.A., Fellow of Trinity College, Cambridge. With Introduction by HENRY KINGSLEY. Globe 8vo. 3s. 6d.

" *The Globe Edition of Robinson Crusoe is a book to have and to keep. It is printed after the original editions, with the quaint old spelling, and is published in admirable style as regards type, paper, and binding. A well-written and genial biographical introduction, by Mr. Henry Kingsley, is likewise an attractive feature of this edition.*"—MORNING STAR.

Goldsmith.—GOLDSMITH'S MISCELLANEOUS WORKS. With Biographical Essay by Professor MASSON. Globe 8vo. 3*s.* 6*d.*

This edition includes the whole of Goldsmith's Miscellaneous Works— the Vicar of Wakefield, Plays, Poems, &c. Of the memoir the SCOTSMAN *newspaper writes: " Such an admirable compendium of the facts of Goldsmith's life, and so careful and minute a delineation of the mixed traits of his peculiar character, as to be a very model of a literary biography."*

Pope.—THE POETICAL WORKS OF ALEXANDER POPE. Edited, with Memoir and Notes, by Professor WARD. Globe 8vo. 3*s.* 6*d.*

" The book is handsome and handy. . . . The notes are many, and the matter of them is rich in interest."—ATHEN.EUM.

Spenser. — THE COMPLETE WORKS OF EDMUND SPENSER. Edited from the Original Editions and Manuscripts, by R. MORRIS, Member of the Council of the Philological Society. With a Memoir by J. W. HALES, M.A., late Fellow of Christ's College, Cambridge, Member of the Council of the Philological Society. Globe 8vo. 3*s.* 6*d.*

" A complete and clearly printed edition of the whole works of Spenser, carefully collated with the originals, with copious glossary, worthy—and higher praise it needs not—of the beautiful Globe Series. The work is edited with all the care so noble a poet deserves."—DAILY NEWS.

*** Other Standard Works are in the Press.

*** The Volumes of this Series may also be had in a variety of morocco and calf bindings at very moderate Prices.

GOLDEN TREASURY SERIES.

Uniformly printed in 18mo., with Vignette Titles by SIR NOEL PATON, T. WOOLNER, W. HOLMAN HUNT, J. E. MILLAIS, ARTHUR HUGHES, &c. Engraved on Steel by JEENS. Bound in extra cloth, 4s. 6d. each volume. Also kept in morocco.

" Messrs. Macmillan have, in their Golden Treasury Series especially, provided editions of standard works, volumes of selected poetry, and original compositions, which entitle this series to be called classical. Nothing can be better than the literary execution, nothing more elegant than the material workmanship."—BRITISH QUARTERLY REVIEW.

THE GOLDEN TREASURY OF THE BEST SONGS AND LYRICAL POEMS IN THE ENGLISH LANGUAGE. Selected and arranged, with Notes, by FRANCIS TURNER PALGRAVE.

" This delightful little volume, the Golden Treasury, which contains many of the best original lyrical pieces and songs in our language, grouped with care and skill, so as to illustrate each other like the pictures in a well-arranged gallery."—QUARTERLY REVIEW.

THE CHILDREN'S GARLAND FROM THE BEST POETS. Selected and arranged by COVENTRY PATMORE.

" It includes specimens of all the great masters in the art of poetry, selected with the matured judgment of a man concentrated on obtaining insight into the feelings and tastes of childhood, and desirous to awaken its finest impulses, to cultivate its keenest sensibilities."—MORNING POST.

THE BOOK OF PRAISE. From the Best English Hymn Writers. Selected and arranged by SIR ROUNDELL PALMER. *A New and Enlarged Edition.*

"*All previous compilations of this kind must undeniably for the present give place to the Book of Praise. . . . The selection has been made throughout with sound judgment and critical taste. The pains involved in this compilation must have been immense, embracing, as it does, every writer of note in this special province of English literature, and ranging over the most widely divergent tracts of religious thought.*"—SATURDAY REVIEW.

THE FAIRY BOOK; the Best Popular Fairy Stories. Selected and rendered anew by the Author of "JOHN HALIFAX, GENTLEMAN."

"*A delightful selection, in a delightful external form; full of the physical splendour and vast opulence of proper fairy tales.*"—SPECTATOR.

THE BALLAD BOOK. A Selection of the Choicest British Ballads. Edited by WILLIAM ALLINGHAM.

"*His taste as a judge of old poetry will be found, by all acquainted with the various readings of old English ballads, true enough to justify his undertaking so critical a task.*"—SATURDAY REVIEW.

THE JEST BOOK. The Choicest Anecdotes and Sayings. Selected and arranged by MARK LEMON.

"*The fullest and best jest book that has yet appeared.*"—SATURDAY REVIEW.

BACON'S ESSAYS AND COLOURS OF GOOD AND EVIL. With Notes and Glossarial Index. By W. ALDIS WRIGHT, M.A.

"*The beautiful little edition of Bacon's Essays, now before us, does credit to the taste and scholarship of Mr. Aldis Wright. . . . It puts the reader in possession of all the essential literary facts and chronology necessary for reading the Essays in connexion with Bacon's life and times.*"—SPECTATOR.

"*By far the most complete as well as the most elegant edition we possess.*"—WESTMINSTER REVIEW.

D

THE PILGRIM'S PROGRESS from this World to that which is to come. By JOHN BUNYAN.

"*A beautiful and scholarly reprint.*"—SPECTATOR.

THE SUNDAY BOOK OF POETRY FOR THE YOUNG. Selected and arranged by C. F. ALEXANDER.

"*A well-selected volume of sacred poetry.*"—SPECTATOR.

A BOOK OF GOLDEN DEEDS of all Times and all Countries. Gathered and narrated anew. By the Author of "THE HEIR OF REDCLYFFE."

"*. . . To the young, for whom it is especially intended, as a most interesting collection of thrilling tales well told; and to their elders, as a useful hand-book of reference, and a pleasant one to take up when their wish is to while away a weary half-hour. We have seen no prettier gift-book for a long time.*"—ATHENÆUM.

THE POETICAL WORKS OF ROBERT BURNS. Edited, with Biographical Memoir, Notes, and Glossary, by ALEXANDER SMITH. Two Vols.

"*Beyond all question this is the most beautiful edition of Burns yet out.*"—EDINBURGH DAILY REVIEW.

THE ADVENTURES OF ROBINSON CRUSOE. Edited from the Original Edition by J. W. CLARK, M.A., Fellow of Trinity College, Cambridge.

"*Mutilated and modified editions of this English classic are so much the rule, that a cheap and pretty copy of it, rigidly exact to the original, will be a prize to many book-buyers.*"—EXAMINER.

THE REPUBLIC OF PLATO. TRANSLATED into ENGLISH, with Notes, by J. Ll. DAVIES, M.A. and D. J. VAUGHAN, M.A.

"*A dainty and cheap little edition.*"—EXAMINER.

THE SONG BOOK. Words and Tunes from the best Poets and Musicians. Selected and arranged by JOHN HULLAH, Professor of Vocal Music in King's College, London.

"*A choice collection of the sterling songs of England, Scotland, and Ireland, with the music of each prefixed to the words. How much true wholesome pleasure such a book can diffuse, and will diffuse, we trust, through many thousand families.*"—EXAMINER.

LA LYRE FRANCAISE. Selected and arranged, with Notes, by GUSTAVE MASSON, French Master in Harrow School.

A selection of the best French songs and lyrical pieces.

TOM BROWN'S SCHOOL DAYS. By an OLD BOY.

"*A perfect gem of a book. The best and most healthy book about boys for boys that ever was written.*"—ILLUSTRATED TIMES.

A BOOK OF WORTHIES. Gathered from the Old Histories and written anew by the Author of "THE HEIR OF REDCLYFFE." With Vignette.

"*An admirable edition to an admirable series.*"
WESTMINSTER REVIEW.

LONDON:

CLAY, SONS, AND TAYLOR, PRINTERS,

BREAD STREET HILL.